THE PEOPLE FROM THE HORIZON

An illustrated history of the Europeans among the South Sea Islanders

THE PEOPLE FROM THE HORIZON

An illustrated history of the Europeans among the South Sea Islanders

Philip Snow and Stefanie Waine

Phaidon · Oxford

For Anne and Peter

Phaidon Press Limited,
Littlegate House, St Ebbe's Street, Oxford
Published in the United States of America by
E. P. Dutton and Co. Inc.,
2 Park Avenue, New York. NY 10016
First published 1979
All rights reserved
© 1979 by Phaidon Press Limited

ISBN 0 7148 2006 7
Library of Congress Catalog Card Number
79-89267

Phototypeset by Tradespools Limited,
Frome, Somerset
Printed in Italy by Amilcare Pizzi SpA, Milan

Title-page illustration: Top-hatted French officers hand-in-hand with Tikopians on their outlying Polynesian island within the Solomons (Melanesia). Drawn by Louis-Auguste de Sainson on Dumont d'Urville's 1826–9 circumnavigation (see p. 80).

Contents

Preface and Acknowledgements

We have several reasons for writing this selective and personal history of the effect of Europeans on the South Seas and that of the South Seas on Europeans. First: it is forty years since one of us was appointed to a government post in the Pacific. A third of this sizeable period has been spent in the Pacific: that time, and all the rest, has hardly known a day pass without thinking about that part of the world, and reading, hearing, talking about it. Pacific friendships have great durability. Maintaining old ones and constantly making new ones helped to evoke the idea of this book. Some of that personal experience has found its way into the narrative.

Second: it has been not so much a wind of change in the Pacific as a zephyr. Leisurely, calmly, reflectively: that is the Pacific way. We felt it was time to try and catch a little of the past as fragments inevitably slip away. Third: there is so much that has been, and is still, pictorially attractive about the Pacific that illustrations of it should be better known. We have sought to include some which are hardly known at all.

In addition, we also have two wishes. One is to awaken an interest in those who do not know a great deal about that segment of the globe. The other is to try and stimulate the interest where it already exists—now on a broad scale compared with the general ignorance before the Second World War—with a few unusual aspects that have appealed to us.

But, for so vast a part of the world, we have been obliged to set two limits so as not to outstretch ourselves and the reader. For this reason, this is essentially a synoptic view, and from a personal angle. We have tried to avoid producing an unreadable catalogue but, in so doing, we have had to discard items which we had hoped to use. There have been so many analyses of special Pacific subjects, particularly since the Second World War. Although some of them touch on our theme (how little does not), we have been obliged to generalize and not make more specific comments on anthropology, material culture, languages, flora, fauna, and customs. The other limit has been on lands and peoples. Invited to consider the whole Pacific as our oyster, we soon had to trim our appetites. So the Moluccas (important, alluring, and obscure), the Philippines, and Japanese outliers in the ocean have had to be excluded. Eastern Australia and New Zealand are on the Pacific's periphery: we have had to permit ourselves only a passing reference to the Maoris qua Polynesians. That huge, complex bulk of land, New Guinea, had of course to be included; but entertaining accounts of explorers, adventurers, travellers and anthropologists, rather less relevant than others, have had to be eschewed.

Finally, a word about words. Pacific Islanders are credited with having made the first discoveries of the places which they now inhabit. So Europeans, if described as discoverers, are to be interpreted as re-discoverers. The word Europeans includes Americans and Antipodeans, as it does in Islanders' minds. The sharp terms Blacks and Whites are uncommon in the Pacific: they are generally regarded as offensive there. Islanders or indigenous people are sometimes referred to as natives because we are all natives of where we were born, and thus there can be nothing pejorative in the word. Islanders use it in the vernacular to describe themselves.

For co-operation in a work of this kind, requiring much reference and cross-reference, checking and cross-checking, consulting, searching, testing, and drafting, our gratitude radiates in many directions.

Both of us owe more than we can say to Anne Snow and Peter Waine, not only for their forbearance, which has been magnanimous over a long period, but also for their direct and very active support. Anne's typing of four drafts, each of about 250,000 words, and the final one compressed to about a third of the original length, has been, in an understatement, a formidable task. Peter's detailed suggestions, assistance in securing sources, and his contributions to the organization of the timetable have been, in another understatement, a real strength.

Charles Snow generously gave his expert advice and precious hours away from his own writing in the prodigious shaping and crystallization that only he could bring to a work of this nature.

The late Christopher Legge in Chicago, who always shared his encyclopaedic knowledge of Oceania with us, read the final draft, providing his usual valuable comments.

In addition, we are very grateful to: Mrs. Estelle Fuller for her advice and for gifts of books, files, and pictures from the collection of her remarkable late husband, Captain A. Walter F. Fuller, and herself; Professor Dr. George B. Milner of the School of Oriental and African Studies, London University, for his advice on languages; Captain Willem van Rossem of Soest, Holland, for helping on points of Dutch history and nomenclature; Mr. John Perez Ugarte for advice on Spanish names; Sir Rex de Charembac Nan Kivell of Morocco for inestimable help and counsel drawn from his lengthy experience of the Pacific and its art; Mrs. Pauline Fanning, Director, and Mrs. Margaret Murphy, Principal Librarian, Australian National Humanities Library, Canberra, for their productive research; Captain Henry Mangles Denham for kindly allowing us to see Admiral Sir Henry Mangles Denham's collection of paintings and giving permission to select from them for reproduction; His Excellency the President of the Republic of Chile, General Augusto Pinochet, for his special interest and gifts of books in Spanish; Mrs. Enid Wise for gifts of Pacific material; Père Patrick G. F. O'Reilly of Le Musée de l'Homme and La Société des Océanistes, Paris, for ever-ready practical co-operation and advice; Mr. Harry Persaud of the Ethnography Department of the British Museum, without whose courteous, ever-willing ordering of books at the British Library and the Library of the Museum of Mankind, London, we could not have made headway; Miss Brownlie J. Kirkpatrick, former Librarian, and the staff of the Royal Anthropological Institute; Mr. Daniel

Barrett and Mrs. Audrey Gregson (Librarian) of the Museum of Mankind, London; Miss Cynthia Timberlake, Librarian, and Miss Marguerite K. Ashford, Reference Librarian, Bernice P. Bishop Museum, Honolulu, Hawaii; Miss Phyllis Mander-Jones, former Librarian, and Miss Jean Dyce, Assistant Librarian, Mitchell Library, Sydney; Mr. Monroe H. Fabian, Associate Curator, National Portrait Gallery, and Mr. Silvio A. Bedini, Deputy Director, National Museum of History and Technology, both of the Smithsonian Institution, Washington, D.C.; Señor Amando Represa, Director, Archivo General de Simancas, Valladolid, Spain; Mr. J. P. Puype, Librarian, Nederlandsch Historisch Scheepvaart Museum, Amsterdam; and, in the course of many years, the staffs of the Reading Room of the British Museum, London; the Alexander Turnbull Library, Wellington; the Central Iconograph Bureau, The Hague; the Mitchell Library, Sydney; and the Library of Congress, Washington, D.C.

It is a pleasant duty to record assistance in a number of ways, especially in latest records, including population data and in some instances most recent tourist developments, from: Mr. Sitiveni Yaqona, Public Relations Officer, Suva, Fiji; Palau Tourist Commission, Koror, Palau, Western Carolines; the late Mr. Rob R. Wright, Sen., formerly Government Photographer, Suva, and Mr. R. R. Wright, jun.; Mrs. Caroline Nalo, Publications Officer, South Pacific Commission, Nouméa, New Caledonia; Mrs. Anne MacGregor, Public Relations Officer, Ministry of Labour, Commerce and Industry, Port Moresby, Papua New Guinea; The Director, U. S. Information Service, Guam, Marianas; Mr. Geoffrey W. Stevens, Senior Information Officer, British Residency, Vila, New Hebrides; Mr. S. Gillett, Chief Secretary, Nauru; Captain John E. Peters, Chief Officer of Information, Headquarters Space and Missile Test Center, California; Hon. Naboua T. Ratieta, Chief Minister, Gilbert Islands; Mr. Kalati Mose, Secretary to Government, Prime Minister's Department, Apia, Western Samoa; Mr. Brian Amini, Director, Department of Information Services, Port Moresby; Mr. P. F. Henderson, General Manager, Cook Islands Tourist Authority, Rarotonga; Mr. J. Watson, Official Secretary, Government House, Port Moresby; Lt. Col. R. B. Tiffany, Head, Support Branch, History and Museums Division, U.S. Marine Corps; Mr. Donald M. Diment, Director, Ministry of Information, Suva; M. D. Constantin, Haut-Commissariat de la République dans l'Océan Pacifique, Bureau de Presse, Nouméa, New Caledonia; The Tonga Visitors' Bureau, Nuku'alofa, Tonga; Mr. D. E. Buffet, Administrative Officer, Kingston, Norfolk Island; Mr. Esau Tuza, Information and Broadcasting Services, Honiara, Solomon Islands; The Central

Archives of Fiji and the Western Pacific High Commission, Suva; the Director, State Archives, Iolani Palace, Honolulu; Dr. A. W. Marr, Secretary to the Tuvalu Government, Funafuti; Mr. Fergus Clunie, Director of the Fiji Museum, Suva; M. Alexandre Mocavaata, Le Directeur, and M. Patrick Picard-Robson, of Le Développement du Tourisme de la Polynésie Française, Papeete, Tahiti; Mr. S. Baksh, Librarian, University of the South Pacific, Suva; and Miss Afiafi Lefotu, Office of Tourism, Government of American Samoa, Pago Pago.

Encouragement or help, or both, directly or indirectly, has also been received gratefully from: Mr. Bryan A. L. Cranstone, Curator, and Mrs. E. J. M. Edwards, Librarian, of the Pitt Rivers Museum, Oxford; La Compagnie Générale Maritime, Paris; Mr. Charles Vesely of Chicago; Dr. Peter W. Gathercole, Director, and Mrs. Jane F. V. Roth, Keeper of the Pacific Collection, Museum of Archaeology and Ethnology, Cambridge; Professor Harry E. Maude, formerly of the Australian National University, Canberra; Mr. Reginald R. C. Caten of Queensland; Rt. Hon. Lord Paget of Northampton; Mr. Steven Phelps; Professor Dr. Albert J. Schütz of the Department of Linguistics, University of Hawaii; Miss P. J. Porter, Assistant Keeper of Manuscripts, the British Library, London; Mr. Sydney A. Spence; Rev. Bernard J. Thorogood, General Secretary, Council for World Missions, London; Mr. Robert A. Langdon, Executive Officer, Pacific Manuscripts Bureau, Australian National University, Canberra; Mrs. Viti Mabbutt; the late Mrs. Katherine Belgrave; Dr. E. Macu Salato, Secretary-General of the South Pacific Commission, New Caledonia; Mr. R. Anthony J. Forster, District Agent, Vila, New Hebrides, and Mrs. Hilary Forster; Mr. Martin Daly, Publications Officer, School of Oriental and African Studies, London University; Mrs. Diane Vahoi Daly; Mr. Peter J. Croft, Librarian, King's College, Cambridge; Dr. Sione Latukefu, University of Papua New Guinea; Mrs. Bess H. Lovett, Librarian of the South Pacific Commission; Miss Joanna Gordon; Mr. N. Kerry Lyons; Mrs. Rosemary Aird; the late Lady des Voeux; the late Dr. Humphrey S. Evans of Rotuma and Suva; Señor German Dominguez Gajardo, Secretario Nacional de Cultura, Junta de Gobierno, Santiago, Chile; Mr. George R. Ariyoshi, Governor of Hawaii; the late Mr. Harold C. Gatty of Suva; Sir Geoffrey Keynes (literary executor of Rupert Brooke); Mr. Karl Erik Larsson of Stockholm, Sweden; Professor Arthur Grove Day of Honolulu; the late Professor Dr. Alfred C. Haddon of Cambridge University; His Excellency Sir Josua R. Rabukawaqa, High Commissioner for Fiji in the United Kingdom; Mr. Robert W. Robson of Sydney; His Excellency Baron Vaea of Houma, High Com-

missioner for Tonga in the United Kingdom; Dr. Terry T. Barrow of Honolulu; Mr. Kenneth R. Bain, formerly Assistant High Commissioner for Fiji in the United Kingdom; Lt. Col. G. Desmond Pease; Mrs. Rosemary Seligman; and Mr. Roger Hughes, Pacific Area Librarian, Commonwealth Institute, London.

Finally, we are most grateful to Mr. Jean-Claude Peissel, Director of the Phaidon Press, for his advice and happy co-operation in the preparation of this book, to Mrs. Rosemary Blott, for her editorial guidance, and to Mr. Simon Lawson, for collecting the illustrations. In addition, we would like to thank the following, who have kindly given permission to quote from the cited works: the Australian National University Press, Canberra: James F. O'Connell, *A Residence of Eleven Years in New Holland and the Caroline Islands*, ed. by Saul H. Riesenberg, 1972 (pp. 118, 159); Greg Dening, ed., *The Marquesan Journal of Edward Robarts 1797–1824*, 1974 (pp. 49, 51, 52–3, 76–7); and Dorothy Shineberg, ed., *The Trading Voyages of Andrew Cheyne, 1841–1844*, 1971 (pp. 51, 52, 55, 105, 114); Cassell & Co. Ltd., London: R. A. Langdon, *Island of Love*, 1959; Evans Brothers Ltd., London: Richard Aldington, *Portrait of a Rebel. The Life and Work of Robert Louis Stevenson*, 1957; Faber & Faber Ltd., London: Sir Geoffrey Keynes, ed., *The Letters of Rupert Brooke*, 1968; Librairie Hachette, Paris: Jean Randier, *Hommes et Navires au Cap Horn*, © Hachette, 1966; The Hakluyt Society, London: Major Arthur Hugh Carrington, ed., *The Discovery of Tahiti. A Journal … 1776, 1777 and 1778 … written by her master, George Robertson*, 1948; Hamish Hamilton Ltd., London: George Sanderlin, *First Around the World. A Journal of Magellan's Voyage*, 1966; J. B. Lippincott Company, New York: From the book *Vikings of the Sunrise* by Peter H. Buck. Copyright 1938 by J. B. Lippincott Company; Copyright renewed © 1966 by Hawaiian Trush Company. Reprinted by permission of J. B. Lippincott Company; Père Patrick O'Reilly, Paris: *Tahitiens. Supplément. Répertoire bio-bibliographique de la Polynésie Française*, Publications de la Société des Océanistes, No. 17, 1966; Oxford University Press, Oxford: John Dunmore, *French Explorers in the Pacific*, Vol. II, 1969; and Count Leo Tolstoy, *What Then Must We Do?*, translated by L. and A. Maude, 1935; Pacific Publications (Aust.) Pty. Ltd., Sydney: *Pacific Islands Monthly*, March 1969, and October 1975; Stanford University Press, Stanford, Calif.: A. F. Tetens, *Among the Savages in the South Seas. Memoirs of Micronesia 1862–1868*, 1958; Yale University Press, New Haven, Conn.: R. A. Skelton, trans. and ed., *Antonio Pigafetta. Magellan's Voyage. A Narrative Account of the First Circumnavigation*, 1969.

To all these, and to anyone whose name has inadvertently been omitted, we express our appreciation. P.S., S.W.

Chapter I

Ocean Outline

The Pacific Islands were not empty when the first Europeans arrived. Where did their inhabitants come from? Why? When? Stone Age megaliths exist, but no one has claimed responsibility for them. There are a script and petroglyphs which no one can read. These relics are almost as enigmatic now as when some of them were first seen by Westerners 300–400 years ago. Controversies still abound after centuries of conjecture. Since we must confine the pre-European period to an outline, these mysteries will be discussed in a Postscript, when the people and places will be better known.

The miniature Milky Way which clusters of the Islands form in the Pacific Ocean has been split into three main regions. Nearest to the Asian continent is Micronesia (from the Greek, *mikros* = small, and *nesos* = island). Just as close to Asian islands and stretching, like Micronesia, into the centre of the Pacific is Melanesia. *Melas* being Greek for black, Melanesia, in its sense of 'islands inhabited by black people', is far less aptly named than Micronesia. Very few of the people, the most diverse in the Pacific, are black but, rather, every shade of brown. It would have been truer, as well as consistent, for this region, in contrast with Micronesia, to have been called Meganesia, the Great Islands. These volcanic lumps, occupying 400,000 square miles, make a bulkier displacement in the ocean than the other two regions put together. This leaves the partition nearest to the American continent and stretching right back half-way across to meet the other two in the Central Pacific. *Polus* being Greek for many, Polynesia is not a misconferred name.

Each of the three regions is made up of multiple archipelagoes or groups dotting the map like a pianola roll. They straggle about 11,000 miles from off-shore Asia across to America, nearly half-way round the world.

The names of the Micronesian groups—the Carolines, Marianas, Marshalls, Gilberts—do not yet have the familiar ring of Hawaii or New Guinea. Indeed some of the Islands are still relatively unknown.

The world's second largest island, New Guinea (it is twice the size of the United Kingdom), contains possibly three million people and has 600 satellite islands. However, it does not dominate Melanesia, which includes the New Hebrides, New Caledonia, Solomon, and Bismarck archipelagoes. The Fiji group is on the dividing line between Melanesia and Polynesia. Melanesians are by far the most numerous of Pacific Islanders: there are nearly five million of them.

Polynesia contains a plethora of groups—those of Hawaii, Tonga, Samoa, Pitcairn, Line, Phoenix, Tuvalu (until 1975 the Ellice Islands), the Society Islands, the Cooks, Tokelaus, Australs, Marquesas, Tuamotus, and Gambiers. Easter Island is the furthest island to the east—nearest to America. New Zealand is the most western and southern representative of Polynesia. Including Maoris, there are about 800,000 Polynesians.

The inhabitants of these regions call themselves by the name of their particular group or tribe. 'Polynesians', 'Melanesians', and 'Micronesians' are oversimplifying terms scarcely recognized by them.

Pacific peoples are not at all uniform. After a few years' residence one cannot make many mistakes in identification. Sit along a main roadside of one of the

Two Trukese, from the Caroline Islands in Micronesia.

more cosmopolitan capitals of a group, such as bustling Honolulu in Hawaii, polyglot Suva in Fiji, leisurely Apia in Samoa, both *fin-de-siècle* and *commencement-de-siècle* Papeete in Tahiti, dichotomous Vila in the New Hebrides, metropolitan Nouméa in New Caledonia, or aspiring Port Moresby in Papua New Guinea, and you can pick out, without hearing spoken words, strollers-by: pure Papuans, pure New Guineans, pure New Hebrideans, pure New Caledonians, pure Fijians, pure Indians, pure Chinese, pure Tahitians, pure Tongans, pure Gilbertese, pure Tuvaluans, pure Maoris, pure Solomon Islanders, pure Rotumans, and pure Cook Islanders; alas, almost no pure Hawaiians or Marquesans. There are the Asian-Pacific mixtures too: Chinese-Tahitian, Chinese-Fijian, Japanese-Hawaiian, Tonkinese-New Caledonian, and also those of half- or quarter-European blending with the various group representatives. What you never see is what you would, on sheer grounds of numbers, expect to see—a Fijian-Indian mixture. Although living in close proximity to each other in Fiji, there is no physical affinity between the two races.

An ultra-modern tribesman from Lake Kopiago, Papua New Guinea, Melanesia.

Small, smooth-haired, squat, dark, Mongoloid, mesocephalic: these are Micronesians. There are 200,000 of them. Western Micronesians (i.e., those nearest Asia) tend to be the more Mongoloid, closer to Filipinos and Malaysians.

Taller and darker than Micronesians, Melanesians are tight-curled, often bushy-haired; their noses are sometimes flat at the bridge and broad at the nostrils. They are Oceanic Negroid and brachycephalic, except for the short Papuans who are dolichocephalic and have retreating foreheads, prominent hooked noses and elongated nostrils. Alone among indigenous Islanders, some Melanesians have pierced nostrils for adornment with pigs' tusks, human bones, feathers, and, on occasion, glass thermometer tubes.

The fusion of Melanesians and Polynesians on the Fiji-Tonga 'frontier' in the Lau archipelago is a striking type, mentally and physically. While Melanesians are the most muscular, Polynesians are the tallest (indeed, few races stand higher and larger universally) and broadest of the Pacific peoples; they are also the palest, often just off light beige. They are dolichocephalic and often termed Caucasoid. The fact that they are inclined to corpulence at an early age is recognized throughout the South Seas as a Polynesian characteristic and by Polynesians themselves as an attribute. Their hair is straighter and longer than that of Melanesians and Micronesians, and, because they have little of it on the body and their light skin is an effective background, they were until recently the world's leading exponents of tattooing. The word *tatu*, anglicized as 'tattoo', is one of only four Pacific Island words to have entered into the vocabulary of the Western world: the others are *tabu* or *tapu* (anglicized as 'taboo', which is not near enough to the true pronunciation), *mana*, and *ukelele*. A most noticeable feature of Polynesians is their very black liquid eyes, large but not protruding: here and there are traces of the drooping Mongolian eyefold.

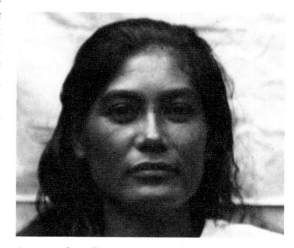

A woman from Rurutu, in the Austral Islands. Although Polynesian, her features could be of a South European or a South American.

General racial types have been mentioned briefly. Without a similarly cursory glace at geography and locations, people and places cannot be put together. For nearly all the Islands have strong physiographical differences which have dictated the way of life on them up to the present day.

In Micronesia's 2,000 islands and islets (if joined together, covering only 1,200 square miles), there is the greatest variation in style of living according to whether the islands are high or low. Rugged, steep, actively volcanic, and heavily forested land constitutes the Marianas and part of the Carolines. Coral

A Tongan girl. The hibiscus over her left ear is typical of Polynesian adornment.

The tattoo pattern on the chest and back of this Yap chief from the Carolines depicts the story of his life.

Pure Polynesians like this man are now rarely seen in Hawaii.

A Polynesian girl from Rarotonga, Cook Islands.

atolls no higher than the crown of the 80-foot-tall coconut palm compose the Marshalls, Gilberts, and other parts of the Carolines. It has been said that there is nowhere better than the Gilberts to feel unutterably remote: all is sky, horizon, and ocean. This might have been the case before the Second World War. Since then one can never forget that they were not too remote to be among the very first islands to be attacked, and captured, by the Japanese.

On the atolls, so exhilarating for brief visits, living is very circumscribed. They have practically no fresh water, and the only food is coconuts and bread-fruit, with fish and crabs. Fish caught in the spacious equatorial—and tropical—lagoons has not much taste, but Micronesians are perforce the most pisciverous of Islanders.

Material culture has been inhibited in much of Micronesia by lack of timber: the most highly developed art form has been in inlay of pearl shell.

There could hardly be a greater contrast with Micronesia than the neighbouring region, Melanesia, with its arc of 900 islands and countless but sizeable lava rocks and coral ledges stretching 3,500 miles from New Guinea to Fiji. Melanesian Islands have the largest rivers in the Pacific. In New Guinea, the Sepik and the Fly (not named after the ubiquitous pest but after H.M.S. *Fly*, which discovered the mouth of a river 500 miles long) extend far up into the interior: the next biggest in the Pacific are the Rewa River (12 miles wide at its delta) and its tributaries in Fiji. The land is mostly lush, covered with forest and liana, and is volcanic in origin. Only in the New Hebrides, Solomons, and New Guinea are the volcanoes not dormant. New Guinea in fact represents the end of the Himalayan chain from India dipping down into the largest and deepest of oceans, with the New Britain and New Ireland groups being the last remnants above the sea. With such a profusion of wood, Melanesians have reached artistic heights in the carving of it.

In Polynesia's islands, too numerous to count but adding up to a mere 10,000 square miles of land (excluding New Zealand), there is something of Micronesia's geographical extremes: spectacular mountain crags in Tahiti and the Marquesas, with active volcanoes in the Hawaii group, New Zealand, and on Niuafo'ou in Tonga; low coralline atolls in the Tuamotu, Austral, Gambier, and Tuvalu groups, where life, diet, and subsistence are much as in the flat Micronesian Islands. The South Seas have virtually the world monopoly of atolls. In the higher Polynesian Islands, activity is as varied as in the Melanesian land masses.

Conviviality is traditionally based in Polynesia around *kava* drinking. Derived from a root of the pepper family, *kava* is exclusively a Pacific property. Melanesian social intercourse, however, is centred on betel-nut chewing, and this custom is shared with East Asia.

For sheer enormity, there is nothing like the Pacific. Occupying a third of the world, it is the largest area under a single name. All the land surfaces of the earth could be contained comfortably in it.

The quintessential fact about the Pacific Islands lies in the other name by which they are known: Oceania. The volume of ocean has its effect one way or another on daily life in its islands. The Pacific's 69 million square miles are every bit as large as they sound: twenty-three times the size of the United States of America. The ocean also goes down lower than any other: its average depth is 3 miles.

This scale is simply mentioned to put what happened in half of it, Polynesia, and in the other half, Micronesia and Melanesia, in some perspective. Vaster than all oceans (or lands) put together, the Pacific's other dimension—the

90°   120°   150°   180°

CHINA

KOREA

JAPAN

TAIWAN

MIDWAY Is.   HAWA

M   I   C   R   O   N   E   S   I   A

MARIANA Is.   ·WAKE Is.

SAIPAN
TINIAN
Agaña· GUAM

PHILIPPINE Is.

Eniwetok   ·Bikini

MINDANAO   Kwajalein   MARSHALL
Is.

·YAP Is.

Koror· PALAU Is.   TRUK Is.

CAROLINE Is.   PONAPE Is.   ·MAJURO IS.
Kusaie·

PALMYRA I
WASHING

Butaritari ·GILBERT
TARAWA ·Bairiki   Is.

ADMIRALTY Is.   NAURU   Abemama
·NEW HANOVER   Betio
NEW   OCEAN   Tabiteuea·
IRIAN   NEW   IRELAND   Is.   PHOENIX
JAYA   GUINEA   BISMARCK   Is.   Is.   ·CANTON Is.
ARCH.   Rabaul BUKA   Ontong Java   ·ENDERBURY
Jayapura   NEW   Is.
INDONESIA   PAPUA   Lae BRITAIN BOUGAINVILLE
NEW GUINEA   CHOISEUL   Vaitupu
MOLUCCAS   Salamaua   SANTA   TUVALU· Funafuti
Buna   YSABEL   MALAITA   TOKELAU Is.
Kokoda·   FLORIDA   Duff Is.
TROBRIAND   Honiara· GUADALCANAL   Pukapuka Is.
Port   SAN   (Danger)
TIMOR   Moresby   SOLOMON   CHRISTOBAL SANTA   W.   AMERICAN
TORRES STRAIT   Is.   CRUZ Is.   WALLIS Is.,   SAMOA   SAMOA
LOUISIADE   Tikopia·   FUTUNA Is.   SAVAI'I ·Apia   TUTUILA
ARCHIPELAGO   BANKS Is.   UPOLU   MANUA
ESPIRITU   Pagopago
SANTO   NEW   VANUA LEVU   RABE
Santo   HEBRIDES   FIJI Is.·   TAVEUNI   TONGA Is.   NIUE Is.   PALME
MALEKULA PENTECOST   Lautoka ·Levuka   VAVA'U·   Alofi   CO
CORAL   SEA   Vila·EFATE   Nadi·· BAU   LAU Is.
VITI LEVU SUVA
ERROMANGA   KADAVU   Lomaloma
TANNA   HA'APAI·   NAMUKA·
LOYALTY   ·TONGATAPU Is.
Great Barrier Reef   QUEENSLAND   Is.   ·LIFU   Nuku'alofa· EUA
NEW   ·MARÉ
CALEDONIA
Noumea·

M   E   L   A   N   E   S   I   A

AUSTRALIA

·NORFOLK Is.   ·KERMADEC Is.

NEW SOUTH   Bay of Islands
WALES   ·Sydney   ·NORTH Is.
Auckland·
Melbourne·   NEW
Wellington·   ZEALAND
SOUTH Is.   ·CHATHAM Is.
TASMANIA

International Date Line

90°   120°   150°   180°

150°   120°   90°   60°

UNITED STATES OF AMERICA

San Francisco ●

MEXICO

Tropic of Cancer

HU
MOLOKAI
JI
HAWAII

Acapulco ●   CENTRAL
           AMERICA

PANAMA

NG Is.
CHRISTMAS Is.

Equator   GALAPAGOS Is.

ECUADOR

SOUTH

AMERICA

MARQUESAS Is.
NUKUHIVA ●
VOSTOK Is.   HIVAOA
         FATUHIVA

PERU

L Y N E S I A

Callao
SOCIETY Is. MAKATEA ● Pukapuka   Lima
AUPITI   RAROIA
BORA   MOOREA
RAIATEA TAHITI TUAMOTU
KI   Papeete
RVEY Is. FRENCH POLYNESIA ARCHIPELAGO
NGA
A   RURUTU
    TUBUAI   GAMBIER Is.
AUSTRAL Is. RA'IVAVAE MANGAREVA HENDERSON
          Adamstown ●   DUCIE
    RAPA   PITCAIRN'S Is.
        PITCAIRN GROUP

Tropic of Capricorn

EASTER Is. ○
(RAPANUI)

JUAN FERNANDEZ Is. Valparaiso ● CHILE
              Santiago ●

P A C I F I C O C E A N

150°   120°   90°   CAPE HORN ●   60°

maximum distance from Europe—was the reason why it was a long time before Europeans found their way to its horizons.

To understand the effect that the first European visitors had on natives and vice versa and to see how societies had formed themselves in the various Pacific regions, one also needs to glance at the conditions of Islanders' life before the Europeans' arrival. A special interest lies in which, if any, features of the pre-European era have survived until today.

It was not for almost 250 years after the first contacts with Europeans at the beginning of the sixteenth century that the life style of various types of Pacific Islanders began to be understood. This was because initial encounters were short and unpenetrating: Western discoverers were too often distracted by their own preoccupation with survival. The character of native society began to be clear only when later Europeans could spend more time observing it. Furthermore, at the times of first European contacts, which in themselves stretch from the beginning of the sixteenth century to the 1930s in various groups, native cultures were likely to have been as fluid as those in the Western world. It would be imprudent to think that native society did not change. An inbuilt flexibility helped to prevent European impacts from being shattering.

Differences between and within the main Pacific regions, between atolls and mountainous islands, however small, and between coastal and interior tribes could be sharp. The Polynesian social structure was not unlike that of the European visitors: its basis was high chiefs, minor chiefs, and commoners. Life was determined by who your relatives were. Rank was hereditary but there were opportunities for advancement through skills, particularly in war, although Polynesian chiefs were expected to lead in battle. Micronesian Islands were so small that society was less complex and stratified: at best, only minor chiefdoms could be built up, but status could then be passed on to relatives. In Melanesia power was not generally inherited. It could only be acquired by being the strongest or most subtle in war, in land assimilation, or in the manipulation of pigs, which represented the ultimate symbol of prestige: ageing or death often ended family supremacy and ambition.

Warfare was the spice of life, the perpetual goad keeping tribes on their toes. Playing with death—not too close to it—was the *raison d'être* of living. There was rivalry both between tribes, which made up all societies, and between islands if they were occupied by different tribes, but within settlements or villages there were rarely active quarrels.

Commoners either worked for chiefs (who could sometimes be women) or performed everyday communal requirements, such as fishing with hooks shaped from a variety of bones (it was still their Stone Age with no iron). Spears, with sharks' teeth barbs, wooden or bone points, were used by men for killing wild pigs and fish, while bows and arrows were used to kill birds. These, together with clubs, axes, and slings for hurling stones, were the modest armaments of the period. The men thatched houses, and carved canoes of a capacity, manoeuvrability, and design never subsequently excelled. They also practised arts in wood (earning European admiration). The cultivation of yams, taro, sweet potatoes, coconut palms, bananas, and fruit trees in individual garden plots is still an everyday sight (Sundays now excepted). Women's duties beyond cooking included weaving mats from pandanus and palm fronds, making decorative cloth from the bark of the paper mulberry tree (mainly in Polynesia), fishing, by wading in lagoons with nets of hibiscus bark fibre and palm fronds, and carrying firewood: still their jobs today. Hot stones in pits were the ovens for food which, as there was little other flesh than fish, fowl, pigs,

Boundaries in the Pacific Ocean between Melanesia, Polynesia, and Micronesia are not rigid, and pockets of Polynesians exist within Melanesia and Micronesia. This woman comes from Ontong Java, an outlying Polynesian atoll in Melanesia.

An Ellice Islander on Funafuti atoll in Polynesia, near its 'frontier' with Micronesia. She was photographed by Comte Rodolphe Festetics de Tolna in 1894. Funafuti's discoverer in 1819, Captain Arent de Peyster of the *Rebecca*, named the nine islands of the archipelago after the ship's owner, Edward Ellice, a British Member of Parliament.

Fish has always been an ineluctable part of the diet—and scenery—on Micronesian atolls. This village in the Kingsmill (Gilbert) Islands was drawn by George French Angas in 1865. The group was named after Captain Thomas Gilbert of the *Charlotte*, who discovered a number of atolls.

and birds, included the bodies of enemies. Cannibalism was enthusiastically practised nearly everywhere. Going further than supplying protein, it carried the belief that *mana*—supernatural power—was being transferred from the victim to the eater. Headhunting was a variation of collecting *mana*. But, in contrast, some of the first Islanders to go aboard Western ships were horrified to observe Europeans killing flies. Until recently, the deaths of close relatives were marked by mourners chopping off their own little fingers and knocking out their own teeth. Intricate ceremony surrounded—and still does—burial and the exchange between allied tribes of such products as salt, wooden artefacts, bark cloth, pandanus mats, shell ornaments, and house-building materials.

Polygamy was a part of life and sexual aberrations were virtually unknown. However, despite much interbreeding, there was little idiocy. Some infanticide existed. Children were brought up with firm gentleness, sometimes by uncles and aunts, and early inculcated in the politeness rigidly insisted upon by society. Care of the aged was a communal responsibility. Extending much wider than in Europe, the family unit could cope more effectively with social problems. No one lived on his or her own. A venerable chief could be buried before drawing a last gasp, and his many wives welcomed strangulation in preference to widowhood. The worship of spirits of ancestors and deities in wooden or stone representations was fervent. Polytheism was respectfully

15

practised: gods, often set on stone platforms, were given offerings of food. For some tribes, they were incarnated in the owl, the shark, in improbable creatures, and in the whole range of trees. Totems were prolific, and their emblems can be offended today. The economic/social/religious system of *tabu* has continued to the present day, but it was a long time before Europeans learnt to avoid infringing it. Sorcery was commonplace. The supernatural was seen in forests and in the sea; it affected communication routes, soil fertility, and the profusion of fish. Unseen powers governed those phenomena that Western science explained, if not very convincingly, to natives by the 1970s.

The drinking of *kava*, a soporific, as an element of ceremonial and a social custom, was common throughout Polynesia, probably just as much in pre-European times as at present. The chewing of betel-nut, a narcotic, in Melanesia, and the drinking of toddy, an intoxicant, in Micronesia, have survived as social indulgences to today. Feasts, consisting of quantities of turtle, dogs, crayfish, crocodile, fish, and meat in whatever available form, vegetables like the breadfruit and root crops, together with plantains, sugar-cane, and coconuts, marked occasions similar to those, for example, in France marking the first wine pressing of the year. In Oceania, the first yams of the season, offered to gods and chiefs, would be welcomed in this way. It was one custom that was to be encouraged by missionaries, who tried to acquire privileges of the chiefs for themselves: they were later to turn this festive tradition to their advantage and transfer it to Saints' Days. Dances—stylized displays by men and women—were mostly reserved too for special occasions, such as in honour of visitors. When acquaintanceships had improved, the Western explorers were invited to watch for hours on end. There were few accompanying instruments except wooden drums. The singing, habitually *en masse*, was less melodic in Melanesia than in Micronesia and Polynesia.

The general use of ceremonial to highlight or dramatize the Islanders' mode of life was to be capitalized upon by Catholic missionaries, with their inherent elaborate ritual, just as native love of singing helped to guarantee the success of the Low Churches, with their predilection for hymns, anthems, and psalms.

Primitive amusement was mostly competitive: wooden javelin throwing, wrestling, surfing, and games resembling shove-halfpenny and *pétanque*. There were riddles, guessing contests, and juggling.

Houses of fundamental design and with minimal furnishing are much as they were, even the marine dwellings on stilts in Melanesian lagoons. Sanitation was, and in the main throughout the Pacific still is, punctilious—in the bush or over the sea's edge. Before European contacts, clothing was sparse, except for high status ceremonies when paper-mulberry *tapa* (in Polynesia) and multicoloured feathers rivetted the eye. Tattooing, mainly from the thighs to the waist, caused the first European visitors to believe that the Islanders were wearing lace long johns: an impression still gained to this day.

There was, and is, little or no private ownership, except of land and intimate articles. Chiefs were expected to ornament their house exteriors and canoes. Their persons would be adorned with insignia like cowrie shells, breastplates inlaid with pearl shell, and ivory necklaces. Commoners could not aspire, without making themselves liable to ridicule, to possessions other than those required domestically. To a surprisingly wide extent, this is still the case.

The natives greeted the first Europeans with a not unnatural suspiciousness, much as they would show to intruding tribes from other islands or groups: it was heightened by the colour difference. Smiles and laughter were more readily produced in Polynesia than elsewhere. A race noticed as laughing a lot,

Maoris and Marquesans, the most enthusiastic cannibals of Polynesia, were fervent practitioners of tattooing, particularly on their faces. Marquesans even tattooed their eyelids, giving the impression, according to Herman Melville (see p.201), of peering from behind prison bars. This head of a Maori, the pattern on whom is tattooed in green, was painted by Charles Frederick Goldie at the beginning of this century. Old Maori women still have drooping lines from the edges of their mouths, which were incised in their youth.

A custom which was among the first to be abolished by European missionaries. Rev. Thomas Williams, whose ethnographic observations were vivid if biased, in 1845 on Taveuni in Fiji saw a Melanesian high chief, who was almost but not quite dead, buried alive: 'the poor old man was heard to cough after a quantity of earth had been heaped on him'. His wives had previously been strangled in preparation for what was regarded as inevitable (see p.15). The chief's successor squats mournfully, as he surveys what will be his own fate if he should become as feeble.

the Morioris of the Chatham Islands near New Zealand, was the only one to become extinct within a century of first European contact. The Chamorros of the Mariana Islands, the very first Pacific Islanders to be seen by Europeans, struggled to survive for 350 years after the experience—and then died out.

Yaws, elephantiasis, dengue fever, malaria, leprosy, and varieties of tuberculosis and venereal disease were almost certainly pre-European maladies, but data is naturally suspect so long before the first medical experts arrived.

Europeans encountering land after months and years at sea would, if they thought that they could do so without being noticed or risk of affray, help themselves to crops—wild or cultivated. This was 'thieving', quite as much as that practised by natives boarding European ships, to encounter the Iron Age for the first time, and excitedly expropriating nails as obvious replacements for their fish-bone hooks for fishing. Dinghies towed behind the great ships were also obvious temptations for Islanders. They were easily manageable craft and ready-made, unlike their own canoes, which were only produced after years of arduous hewing, with stone adzes, of tree trunks.

Once the first contacts had brought a semblance of comprehension of each other's requirements and temperaments (the reasons for anger were slow in being interpreted by either side), and once bartering could be organized with dignity, then there was hope of some friendship. This occurred more quickly among Polynesians and Micronesians, who were less reserved than Melanesians. Sometimes both Europeans and natives felt genuine regret at the ending of visits: the former at leaving the pleasures of land, the latter because the occasions had meant a break in the otherwise dominating routine of food-collecting and subsistence. For better or for worse, new breaths of air from over the horizon wafted into their society's way of life.

Time was not, and is not, of the essence in the Pacific. Perhaps the effort needed for food provision and body needs among so much fertility (and hurricane damage) occupied only two-thirds of the calendar. This left plenty of time for spiritual calls—keeping ancestors contented, observing ritual for births and deaths, carving sacrosanct objects—and for the preparation for, and practice of, war.

Briefly then, that was the background of activity and thinking in native society when Europeans first encountered it. Because of their lack of literacy until a century or so ago, there are no records of what the Islanders thought of the first Europeans. One can only imagine or surmise what influenced them from the manner in which they have absorbed European ways into their culture. It is this absence of records which makes the significance of some of the extraordinary objects seen by the first Europeans (and still to be seen in some parts of the Pacific) all the more mysterious, and which makes the correct interpretation of them probably impossible. Bafflement remains over the huge stone statues on Easter Island, and over the petroglyphs, canals, terraced pyramids, and platforms scattered around the Pacific. The peopling of such specks of land so far apart from each other and from the rest of the world is another major mystery not helped by the lack of written native records.

At the present stage of this history, these enigmas are alluded to only briefly. They are best left to the end for elaboration and conjecture, when more is known about the South Seas. It is enough to have them in mind as Pacific Islanders and Europeans move through the last four and a half centuries.

Chapter II

Earliest Discoverers from Europe

Vasco Nuñez de Balboa (1474–1517), drawn by J. Donon. The Panama Canal seaport facing the Pacific is named after him.

It is possible that the first European to see the Pacific Ocean was the Venetian, Marco Polo, from the mainland of Asia, at the end of the thirteenth century. It is known that he saw Java, Sumatra, and Indo-China. Probably he did not see the Pacific as such but only the China Sea. Marco Polo hinted that a great sea existed to the east of Chipangu, as he called Japan.

The opening up of European trade with India, the East Indies, and Japan (and China very briefly at the beginning of the sixteenth century) had brought the paramount nautical nations of the fifteenth century, Spain and Portugal, almost in touch with the Pacific. It cannot be known for certain but, until disputed, it is claimed that a Portuguese commander of otherwise little fame, Antonio d'Abreu, and the men with him were the first from Europe to see a Pacific Island, inescapably New Guinea. D'Abreu was sent in 1511 by Alfonso d'Albuquerque, Viceroy of India and creator of Portugal's power in the East, to discover the Spice Islands and to search further east. It was thus most probable that the ocean was first seen, so far as Europeans were concerned, by those sailing from Asia but not recognized by them for what it was.

At the very beginning of the sixteenth century, substantial entrepôts had been established by d'Albuquerque in the Far East at Goa in India and at Malacca (near modern Singapore), which he had captured in 1511 and found full of seamen and merchants from China, Java, Burma, and India. Portuguese zeal to discover additional sources of spice and mineral riches soon led to expeditions from the Far East to the Further East.

After their discovery of the Moluccan Islands, it would have been almost impossible for European sailors to avoid seeing the high mass of New Guinea no more than 100 miles to the east. Although they are outside the ocean, the importance of the Moluccas (Spice Islands) in Pacific history cannot be over-emphasized. So close to the Pacific as almost to belong to it, they were at one and the same time a springboard and an allurement for European penetration of the ocean. It was in venturing from them that a Portuguese ship, under Diego da Rocha, probably discovered Yap atoll in the Carolines in about 1525.

In the meantime, there had been developments from an entirely new direction. The Spanish believed that gold and other riches must surely exist beyond the Americas. Employing Indians of Central America as guides through some of the world's thickest jungle and accompanied by 190 Castilians and dogs trained to attack hostile Indians, Vasco Nuñez de Balboa, a stowaway from Jerez who had risen to be governor of Darien, decided in 1513 to cross the mountains of the isthmus joining North America with South America. He climbed a peak on the isthmus 'from whiche he myght see the other sea soo longe looked for, and never seen before of any man commynge owte of owre worlde.' He certainly saw a sea stretching to the west, but how he was sure that it was more than a vast lake is not understood, for when you observe it from that area there are myriads of islets. Yet he was certain that he was looking upon no lake or land-locked sea. Nuñez de Balboa marched down to the beach and then, fully-dressed, into the water proclaiming, half-immersed, while a notary recorded his words:

Long live the great and powerful monarchs, Don Ferdinand and Doña Juana, sovereigns of Castille, Leon and Aragon in whose name I today take real, corporal and actual possession of these seas, lands, coasts, ports and islands of the South and likewise of the kingdom and provinces which depend therefrom now and for as long as the world shall last, until the day of the final judgement of all men.

This majestic statement should have served him better. Within four years he was beheaded by his father-in-law for imaginary crimes.

The Spanish Court at once wanted Balboa's expanse of water, the Mar del Zur (South Sea) as they called it, to be investigated. They took advantage of the offer of Fernhao de Magelhães (anglicized as Ferdinand Magellan) to find a way to the Moluccas other than from the Portuguese zone of influence in the East or from the coast of America. Of semi-noble Portuguese origin, Magellan had gained much experience in navigation to India with d'Albuquerque. He was disillusioned on his return from these voyages when he was not promoted and then received only a miserable pension when he was invalided out of the navy, after being wounded in Morocco, at the age of thirty-five. He had had, however, access to the Portuguese Hydrographic Office during his service and, although there was a death penalty for divulging nautical information to non-Portuguese, Magellan offered his idea of a voyage to the Spice Islands by a route below the Americas to Emperor Charles V of Spain. Despite his reservations about allowing a Portuguese competitor to lead a Spanish expedition, Charles V agreed, but with conditions that Magellan, once at sea, steadily ignored.

Although the Portuguese and Spanish had found the way to India and the Far East by the discovery of the Cape of Good Hope, this was an altogether more demanding voyage. The caravels and equipment of the time were way behind the ambitions and bravery of the individuals. Two hundred and eighty men, comprising Dutch, French, an Englishman, Germans, Negroes, Spaniards, Portuguese, Italians, Moors, Malayans, Corfiotes, Madeirans, natives of the Azores and Canary Islands, and forty Basques, left Seville in 1519 in five ships. Nineteen were to return three years later in one ship after having made the first journey round the world. *En route*, a mutiny by three Spanish commanders misfired calamitously: they found Magellan too vigilant and utterly ruthless. One captain was stabbed to death and quartered, another was beheaded and quartered, and the ringleader was marooned to die of starvation.

On the voyage was a supernumerary, by some said to be a Venetian spying on behalf of Venice, which was cherishing maritime knowledge, by others a Lombard, and by most a Vicenzan. His name was San Antonio Francisco Pigafetta: he was twenty-seven years old and an orphan from a good family. So alive was the substance of his writings that Shakespeare used part of his travels for a scene in *The Tempest*. Pigafetta recorded as his motive for the adventure:

> I determined . . . to experience and to go . . . that it might be told that I made the voyage and saw with my eyes the things hereafter written, and that I might win a famous name . . .

Magellan was his absolute, infallible hero. 'No other', he wrote, 'had so much natural wit.'

It took forty-five days of tedious trial and error, while battling against ferocious conditions, for the small fleet to weave its way through the straits which Magellan named All Saints but which were later to be given his own

Ferdinand Magellan (1480–1521) was a ruthless commander. The battered face suggests both a cruel and a determined character.

name. Magellan was as certain as Balboa that the great South Sea entered in November 1520 was oceanic. But he had more reason for his conviction because at least no islands were in view. The new sea was tranquillity itself in comparison with the Atlantic and with the straits from which the fleet had just emerged. Magellan addressed his officers on *Trinidad*'s quarterdeck:

> Gentlemen, we are now steering into waters where no ship has sailed before. May we always find them as peaceful as they are this morning. In this hope I shall name this sea the Mar Pacifico.

The Pacific—which to many travellers seems among the great misnomers of all time—long remained so for Magellan. He underestimated the length of the voyage to the Moluccas. Early in 1521 two small uninhabited islands were seen. The first was San Pablo, as the voyaging Catholics reverentially registered it on the day of St. Paul's Conversion. It was probably Pukapuka in the Tuamotu archipelago, which may have the distinction of being the first part of Polynesia to have been seen by Europeans. The second was probably Vostok Island in the Line archipelago: it was less devoutly named Isla de Los Tiburones because of the abundance of sharks.

On 6 March 1521, the expedition finally reached a group 9,000 nautical miles from, and ninety-eight days after, emerging from the straits. Only Magellan's iron will had kept the ships going forward. Pigafetta recorded:

> We were three months and twenty days without getting any kind of fresh food. We ate biscuit, which was no longer biscuit but the powder of biscuits swarming with worms, for they had eaten the good. It stank strongly of rats. We drank yellow water that had been putrified for many days. We also ate some ox hides that covered the top of the mainyard to prevent the yard from chafing the shrouds and which had become exceedingly hard because of the sun, rain, and wind ... and often we ate sawdust from boards. Rats were sold for one-half ducat apiece, and even we could not get them ... We sailed about four thousand leagues during those three months and twenty days through an open stretch in that Pacific Sea. In truth it is very pacific, for during that time we did not suffer any storm. We saw no land except two desert islets, where we found nothing but birds and trees.

The discovery of the first inhabited group, however welcome after the ordeal, was not an auspicious opening of known European contact with Pacific Islanders. Other Pacific pieces of land were to be given congenial European names like the Friendly Islands, the Society Islands, and Pleasant Island, but the first European appellation for a Pacific group was Islas de Los Ladrones (Islands of Robbers). They are now known as the Marianas.

Magellan's fleet found that everything that was not nailed down was deemed eminently acquirable by the natives; while everything that was nailed down was subjected to attempts to extract the nails, which were high on the list of desirable objects for the non-Europeans. Magellan directed crossbowmen to shoot pilferers. Because of its significance as the very first record of European-Pacific Islander contact, Pigafetta's account is quoted in full*:

> ... the people of those islands entered the ships and robbed us so that we could not protect ourselves from them. And when we wished to strike and take in the sails so as to land, they stole very quickly the small boat called a skiff which was fastened to the poop of the captain's ship. At which he, being very angry, went ashore with forty armed men. And burning some forty or fifty houses with several boats and killing seven men of the said island, they

*There are four manuscripts of Pigafetta's journal, three in French and one in Venetian-Italian. This quotation from Pigafetta is taken (with footnotes) from R.A. Skelton's recent translation, *Magellan's Voyage: A Narrative Account of the First Circumnavigation*, Yale University Press, New Haven, Conn., 1969. It differs only slightly from the 1874 translation of Lord Stanley of Alderley (see Bibliography).

recovered their skiff. Soon after, we left, taking the same course. And before we landed several of our sick men had begged us, if we killed man or woman, to bring them their entrails. For immediately they would be healed. And know that whenever we wounded any of those people with a shaft which entered their body, they looked at it and then marvellously drew it out, and so died forthwith. Soon we left the said island going on our way. And when those people saw that we were departing they followed us for a league in one hundred boats or more and came near our ships, showing us fish and making signs that they wished to give it to us. But they threw stones, then fled away, and in their flight they passed between the boat towed astern and the ship in full sail. But this was done so nimbly and with so much skill that it was a marvel. And we saw some of those women weeping and tearing their hair, and I believe it was for love of those whom we had killed.

Those people live in freedom and as they will, for they have no lord or superior, and they go quite naked and some of them wear a beard. They have long hair down to their waist, and wear small hats after the manner of the Albanians, and these hats are made of palm. Those people are as tall as we, and well built. They worship nothing. And when they are born they are white, then they become tawny, and they have black and red teeth. The women also go naked, but that they cover their nature with a bark as thin and supple as paper, which grows between the wood and the bark of the palm tree. They are handsome and delicate, and whiter than the men, and they have dishevelled hair, very black and hanging down to the ground. They do not go to work in the fields, but do not leave their house, where they make cloth and boxes from palm leaves. Their food is certain fruit called *cochi* [and] *battate*.* They have birds, figs a palm in length, sugarcanes, and flying fish. Those women anoint their body and their hair with coconut and beneseed oil. And their houses are made of wood covered with planks or boards with fig leaves, which leaves are very large, and the houses are six fathoms wide and have only one storey. Their rooms and beds are furnished with mats made of palms and very beautiful, and they lie on palm straw, which is very soft and fine. Those people have no weapons but they use sticks with a fishbone at the tip. They are poor but ingenious, and great thieves. And on this account we called those three islands the Islands of the Thieves.

*Coconuts and sweet potatoes.

The pastime of the men and women of that country, and their sport, is to go in their boats to catch those flying fish with hooks made of fishbones. And the form of their boats is painted hereafter, and they are like *fuseleres**, but narrower. Some are black and white, and others red. And on the other side of the sail they have a large spar pointed at the top. Their sails are of palm leaves sewn together like a lateen sail to the right of the tiller. And they have for steering oars certain blades like a shovel. And there is no difference between the stern and the bow in the said boats, which are like dolphins jumping from wave to wave. Those thieves thought (by the signs which they made) that there were no other men in the world but themselves.

Fisolere, small oared vessels used on the Venetian lakes for hunting in winter.

It was an unfortunate beginning for Pacific-European relationships. As cannibalism occurs frequently in this history, it is interesting to note the reference in the account to Europeans resorting to it—for its medicinal qualities. Pigafetta mentions the bark of the palm tree being used for cloth: it would have been the bark of the paper-mulberry tree.

Guam, the largest island of the Mariana group, was the first in the Pacific known to have been visited by Europeans: its inhabitants, the pioneers in contact with Westerners, were Chamorros.

The one Englishman on board, Master Andrew of Bristol, master-gunner of the flagship and married to a Seville woman, died as the ships left the Ladrones. In the Philippines, Magellan became friendly with the Rajah of Cebu (Zzubu). The latter was a Christian, and Magellan tried to help him convert other islands to Catholicism. He reckoned that one of his men was worth 100 natives and, taking 48 men to meet 1,500, he received a poisoned arrow as well as a javelin in the leg. Pigafetta recorded:

> That caused the captain to fall face downwards when immediately they rushed upon him with iron and bamboo spears and with their cutlasses until they killed our mirror, our light, our comfort and our true guide ... He endured hunger better than all others, and more accurately than any man in the world did he understand sea charts and navigation. And that this was the truth was seen openly, for no other had such natural talent nor the boldness to learn how to circumnavigate the world, as he had almost done.

Magellan's body was never recovered. Command of what was left of the expedition for the return journey passed eventually to Juan Sebastian del Caño, probably the most underestimated name in the whole of maritime history. No contemporary painting of him has ever been found. Of humble Basque origin from Spain's smallest province, Guipuzcoa, del Caño (sometimes mis-spelt as El Caño or Elcaño), had been master, not com-

Juan Sebastian del Caño (1492?–1526) with Emperor Charles V of Spain at the end of the first circumnavigation, drawn by C. Mugica.

mander, of one of the subsidiary ships. He had survived the massacre that had crushed the mutiny off Patagonia, because, although he was Spanish and Magellan had substituted Portuguese for Spanish leaders, he was regarded as an absolutely first-class pilot.

In the last surviving ship, del Caño picked up a cargo of cloves, cinnamon, mace, nutmeg, and sandalwood in the Moluccas in December 1521 and, with forty-seven Europeans and thirteen natives, sailed via the Cape of Good Hope, bringing back the eighty-ton *Vitoria* to Seville in September 1522 after 42,000 miles and three years' absence. The vessel was in an appalling condition, as regards both structure and rations. Only nineteen of the final sixty survived that last voyage half-way round the world, including the indefatigable Pigafetta (he was eventually killed by Turks while defending Malta in 1536), who was most concerned that a day had been lost somewhere. He complained: 'I had set down every day without any interruption.' This discovery of the fact that a day is lost when travelling from east to west was disturbing: the men shuddered when they realized that for half the voyage the holy days had been observed quite inaccurately and that they had been eating meat on Fridays. Most of the nineteen, except Pigafetta, were in bad shape. Of the forty-one who did not return, Pigafetta chronicled:

> Some died of hunger, some deserted at the Island of Timor, and some were put to death for crimes. And when we cast the Christians into the sea they sank with their faces upwards towards heaven, and the Indians always with their faces down.

Vitoria was the first ship known to have circumnavigated the globe. The sphere had been proved. Sebastian del Caño was the first commander to demonstrate that the world was not flat.

Magellan's reputation has remained high in Pacific history but not especially so in Spain or Portugal. Pigafetta was totally complimentary about him throughout his narrative which, oddly, makes no reference at all to del Caño, his leader for half the voyage.

Magellan had conceived the enterprise of circumnavigation but failed to accomplish it: he discovered Magellan's Straits which were never used by the Spanish or other nations as a regular trade channel. He was the first European to cross the Pacific. He must be given credit for proving conclusively that the Americas were a continent on their own, separated by the Pacific from Asia, and for having pushed the expedition as far as he did against great odds: unfavourable weather, unseaworthy vessels, lack of navigational aids and of anything approaching proper provisioning, and the insurrectionary character of his commanders. Magellan overcame all these. Early in the voyage he had declared: 'Even if we have to eat the leather wrappings on the masts and yards, I will still go on.' That gloomy prediction was exactly what was to happen. The experience did not deter him and he did not let it deter his crew.

Del Caño's name should always be included in posterity's list of the top-class early navigators—Magellan, de Mendaña, de Quirós, Tasman, Dampier, de Bougainville, and Cook where the Pacific is concerned, although his principal feat was outside that ocean: the bringing back of a virtual wreck from it. In temporal terms he was rewarded by elevation from the status of a commoner to that of a gentleman, having arms conferred on him bearing two crossed cinnamon staves, three nutmegs, twelve cloves, and a castle with, as supporters, two Malay crowned kings each holding spice branches and a globe (which he had proved the earth to be) with the motto, *Primus circumdedesti me* (You first

Some Pacific types a century ago, painted by G. Mützel.

G. Mützel fec.

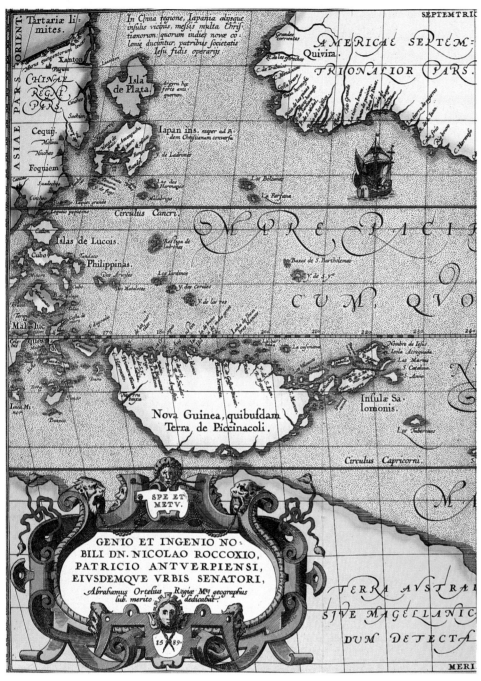

Top left: Abraham Ortelius' chart of 1592 of the *Mar del Zur. El Mar Pacifico*. It shows the only Pacific groups discovered by Europeans—the Ladrones (Marianas), atoll complexes in the Carolines and Marshalls, New Guinea, the Solomons, and the Galapagos Islands—by that date.

Bottom left: Natives of Humboldt Bay, Dutch New Guinea, ostentatiously adorn themselves in 1875. The fewer the Melanesians' clothes, the more spectacular were their embellishments. A New Hebridean seen in the 1860s sported through the nose not the customary bone or white feathers, but a glass thermometer tube. Horizontal ballpoint pens are a current fashion. This picture was painted by John James Wild on the *Challenger* expedition of 1872–6 under Captains Sir George Nares (1831–1915) and F. T. Thomson.

Below: The first known encounter between Europeans and Islanders, 1521, commemorated by Antonio Pigafetta (1492–1536) in this first sketch of a Pacific Island (Guam) and its inhabitants (Chamorros). Pictorial recording was not a serious part of exploration for another 250 years.

The expedition of Luis Váez de Torres is believed to have been the third (after those of Magellan and van Noort) on which sketches of Pacific Islanders were made. This was painted by Don Diego de Prado y Tovar in 1606, after de Torres' ship had separated from the expedition of de Quirós. It shows natives of the Bay of San Filipe y Santiago, New Hebrides, with their weapons—clubs, a spear, and a bow and arrow.

While Micronesians were depicted for the first time on the expeditions of Magellan and van Noort, de Prado y Tovar was the first to illustrate Melanesians. These are natives of the Bay of San Millán, New Guinea, 1606.

Melanesians from La Gran Baya de S. Lorenço, Pverto de Monterei, off southern New Guinea, painted by de Prado y Tovar in 1606.

Natives of southwestern New Guinea, painted by de Prado y Tovar in 1606.

28

encompassed me). That was about all he received. Yet his, by any standard, was a prodigious feat of seamanship, regarded by some as the greatest in maritime endeavour.

Charles V of Spain was very anxious for another expedition (containing no Portuguese but with Basques making up at least a third of the crew) to go through the Straits of Magellan to the Moluccas and discover what there might be on the way. Portuguese expeditions to the East from the direction of the Moluccas had encountered constantly contrary winds, and it was believed that the most profitable direction for discovery was to go from the East towards New Guinea and the Moluccas.

Seven ships left Spain three years after del Caño's struggle home. They never returned. The commander, Don Garcia Jofre de Loaysa (or Loiasa), died in the Pacific. The second-in-command and chief pilot, del Caño, suddenly became ill four days after succeeding as captain-general and died—presumably from scurvy, which had attacked him on his first voyage. The flagship alone reached the Moluccas before it was shipwrecked. Previously, it had called at Guam, where there was astonishment at finding a Spaniard: Gonzalez (or Gonzalo) de Vigo had deserted from Magellan's fleet. Taken from Guam and pardoned, he was the first European castaway of note in Pacific history.

Another expedition to the Moluccas was dispatched in 1527, this time by Hernán Cortez under the command of a cousin, Alvaro de Saavedra. They were the first Europeans to cross the Pacific from Central America to the East Indies and to see New Guinea from the opposite direction, i.e., approached from the East. Some Admiralty and Marshall Islands were discovered, as well as some of the Carolines, including Kusaie, Ponape, and Truk. The 40-mile-wide lagoon on Truk astonished de Saavedra, as well it might, being the world's largest, and female Trukese 'were so overjoyed upon seeing goats for the first time that they did not resent in the least when the goats ate their grass skirts clean to the girdle.' After one failure to sail back to Mexico from New Guinea, de Saavedra made a second effort and died in the attempt.

Mexico, as well as being the starting and ending point for further expeditions, eventful in themselves but not coming to much, became a terminus for a remarkable two-way Pacific route set up in 1565. Spanish galleons were to use it for 250 years from and to the other terminus, the newly-discovered Philippines. Acapulco-Manila was both the richest and, in theory, the most daring trade route in the world for that period. A galleon would sail at least annually from Mexico full of, in the acquisitive eyes of Dampier, the navigator pirate of whom we shall soon be hearing, 'Quicksilver, Calico and Pieces of Eight'. Peru was being transported, as it were, to the Philippines. There, the galleon would pick up gold, Chinese porcelain, and lacquerware, together with, according to Dampier, 'Spices, Silks, Callicoes and Muzlins' for the return trip to Mexico and from there to Peru, transporting the Orient to the New World. In all the 250 years only three galleons were wrecked and six vanished: a remarkable accomplishment. Despite all these crossings, however, the route was slightly north of the Island groups, and they remained undiscovered.

Callao, the main seaport of Peru, became another obvious base from which to launch expeditions into the Pacific. The Viceroy of Peru arranged with his nephew, Alvaro de Mendaña y Neyra, to search for the gold believed by Marco Polo to exist east of China. In 1567 de Mendaña took a northerly course from Callao. After a long, gruelling voyage he reached what he regarded as his destination. He named the group the Solomon Islands after King Solomon, although it appeared to him to contain none of the anticipated riches. (It has gold but all that he found was pyrites, fools' gold.) However, he had the distinction of being the first European to discover a major Pacific group. The mellifluous Spanish names which he gave to its major islands are almost unique in that they survive to this day, to the exclusion of indigenous names: Santa Ysabel de la Estrella (after his wife), San Christobal, Guadalcanal, La Florida, and Malaita. He also discovered Wake Island (named San Francisco by him), one of the most remote islands in the North Pacific.

As de Mendaña's finding of the Solomons in 1568 represents the first contact in any sort of depth between Europeans and Pacific natives, his journal and that of his chief pilot, Hernando Gallego, deserve to be noted. First, however, an account of a hurricane encountered in the North Pacific, east of Wake Island, is of particular interest as such conditions, or threats of them, were in the background of the whole stream of voyages. Hardly a voyage in the Pacific escaped some such experience, if not quite so desperate. The first known record is in the *True and Correct Account of the Voyage to the Western Isles in the Southern Ocean by Hernando Gallego, the Chief pilot, 1567*:

> ... We lay with our sails furled, because there was much wind; and we were rolling with the tempest from the north-east, for we were in a cross sea without sails; and the wind came upon us with such fury as I had never before seen from the north-east, although I had been forty-five years at sea, and thirty of them a pilot. Never have I seen such heavy weather, although I have seen storms enough. It frightened me, for being with our sails furled, as we were, there came such a sudden onset of wind and sea, that it made us heel over below the water, up to the middle hatch on the port side of the ship; and it had not been battened down and caulked as I had ordered it to be caulked, and the boat unplugged, when I saw signs of storms. We were deluged with water, and were in such a plight that the sailors and some of the soldiers were swimming about inside the ship, trying to launch the boat; and it pleased God and His Blessed Mother that it should go into the sea, full of cables and water, for the sailors and soldiers were not sufficient to launch it. I presently ordered the sailors to set the fore-stay-sail a little; and although they had not let out more than two reefs, the stay-sail was torn into two thousand pieces and there was nothing left of it but the bolt-ropes. The ship was on her beam ends for more than half an hour, till they cut away the mast ...

De Mendaña's *Narrative* is as lucid as one would expect the journal of an educated aristocrat to be: it includes these comments on the Santa Ysabel people:

> One day there came to the ship some Indians belonging to another chief, in four canoes, in which they brought three women; and when they saw that we had no women with us they thought to tempt us by asking us to buy them. I made signs to them that we refused, and that we could not bear the sight of them, and bade them take them away, which they did immediately. Some of these women are well-favoured, and fairer than those of Peru; their hair is very red, and cut short beneath the ear ... While I was hearing Mass on shore he [a Santa Ysabel man] arrived with fifteen canoes full of men, well provided with arms, and he sent me a quarter of human flesh which seemed to be that of a boy, with some roots of vinahu, saying to me in his language, 'Naleha, Naleha!' which signifies 'Eat it'. I accepted the present, and, being

Don Alvaro de Mendaña y Neyra (1541–95) made two great voyages, twenty-eight years apart. His was a treble achievement: he was the first European to find a principal Pacific archipelago and, discounting New Guinea, the first to visit a Melanesian group (the Solomons in 1568); he was then the first to discover a Polynesian archipelago (the Marquesas in 1595). This portrait of de Mendaña was drawn by C. Lepano.

greatly grieved that there should be this pernicious custom in that country, and that they should suppose that we ate it, I ordered everyone to stand aside so that the tauiqui might see what was done. Then I caused a grave to be dug at the water's edge, and had the quarter buried in his presence, and said to him in his language, 'Teo naleha arra', which signifies 'I do not eat it'. He regarded this very attentively, and seeing that we set no value on the present, they all bent down over their canoes like men vexed or offended and put off and withdrew with their heads bent down.

The hospitality declined by de Mendaña did not prohibit the ultimate in friendship, common throughout the Pacific, being afforded to him. Gomez Hernandez de Catoira, holding the assorted titles of Chief Purser, Custodian of Objects for Barter, and Comptroller for His Majesty, in his account stated that:

> a chief asked Mendaña by signs to tell him his name and when he said he was called Mendaña he took it for himself and said Mendaña should call himself Vylevanarra and that he would call himself Mendaña, for they are fond of exchanging names and that he might not forget it he kept saying over and over again 'Mendaña, Mendaña'.

It was as long as twenty-eight years later that de Mendaña, still searching for the riches that he had failed to find the first time, tried again. This time, in 1595, he took his wife, Doña Ysabel de Barreto, and, as chief pilot, Pedro Fernández de Quirós, a Portuguese working for Spain and another of the underestimated names in Pacific Oceanic history, together with nearly 400 others, including women, to set up a colony. Such was the hit-and-miss process of navigation and the imprecision of mapping that de Mendaña could not find the Solomon Islands again. This failure was also due to the great secrecy that surrounded Spanish discoveries: they were kept so secret that the discoverers themselves were frustrated.

Quite early in the voyage (after one of his four ships had disappeared, never to be seen again), de Mendaña discovered the Marquesas. It was the first Polynesian archipelago to be found by Europeans. De Mendaña's is the first account of Polynesian ethnology and culture, as his earlier record had been the first on Melanesians. But, regrettably, his narrative had to include the fact that, after a stay of just over a week, 200 Marquesans—men, women, and children—were killed. De Quirós lamented that the Islanders and the visitors could not understand each other. The Islanders thought that the pale faces of their visitors were those of their ancestors returning: there was speedy disillusionment.

De Mendaña also discovered Santa Cruz in Melanesia, and tried to found a colony there with himself as sovereign. He died, and the command passed to Doña Ysabel de Barreto, his impetuous, able, but severe wife, who allowed the crew to shoot Santa Cruz natives at will. De Quirós was not unnaturally thankful when, after sailing to the Philippines, the expedition returned to Peru.

De Quirós, aged thirty on that voyage, had been closely observant throughout. Having the chance (to the annoyance of Doña Ysabel) of leading his own expedition from Peru, he set out, at least nominally, for the Solomons. In fact, however, he followed his own instinct in search of Terra Australis Incognita. It had been firmly believed for a century or more that there must be, in addition to Europe, Asia, Africa, and America, a fifth and southerly continent; for, without it, the equilibrium of the globe would be so affected that the

Coco-nuts.   Screw-pine.   Coco-palms.   Boat, with Outriggers, being freighted with Copra.   Coral-reef.

Lighting a Fire.   Clump of Banana-trees.   Catching Sea-animals during low water.

Wooden supports for the head   Kava-bowl

whilst sleeping.   and drinking cups.

earth would capsize. After Australia had been discovered, it was still thought for quite a while longer that a larger land mass must also exist. De Quirós had by 1605 become a religious fanatic: as well as finding the Unknown Continent, his intention in the expedition was to convert as many natives as he could to Catholicism. Taking a more southerly course in 1605 than others, but being carried further north by winds than he wished, he was the first European known to have made *en route* in 1606 this miscellany of discoveries: Ducie and Henderson Islands in the Pitcairn group, the Banks group, the Duff group in the Solomons (not seen again by a European for nearly two centuries and then by Wilson of *Duff*—see p.123), and Tikopia, a Polynesian outlier in the

In the eyes of the earliest Europeans, Polynesians seemed to enjoy an enviably placid way of life but, as this picture demonstrates, they could also be very active.

Olivier van Noort (1558–1627), drawn by Crispijn de Passe, senior in 1601. Van Noort made the fifth circumnavigation of the world in 1598–1601. As the second (that of Drake), third (that of Cavendish), and fourth (that of Sebald de Weert in 1598–1600) made negligible contact with Pacific territory, van Noort's was the next most important (for the Pacific) circumnavigation after the Magellan-del Caño odyssey.

Pedro Fernandez de Quirós (1560?–1614), like de Mendaña, could not find the Solomons again, but he discovered much else. Another ship with him, under Luis Vaéz de Torres and Don Diego de Prado y Tovar, separated from his expedition in 1606 and, while observing that New Guinea was an island, came within a metaphorical inch of discovering Australia. This portrait of de Quirós was drawn by C. Mugica.

Solomons. In the Cook group, a gold ring with an emerald on an old woman, a chief's red hair, a cedar pole of Central American style, and an Iberian-looking dog were all noticed on La Conversion de San Pablo. De Quirós' Catholic passion made him call this atoll by that improbable name. He missed Santa Cruz in his aim for the Solomons, but when he reached the New Hebrides he was certain that this group was the Unknown Land, the fifth continent sought for so long. The one island in the group that he called at was large and mountainous, but only by Pacific standards. In what the venerable maritime historian, J. Holland Rose, termed 'holy exultation', de Quirós gave it the most appropriate name that his inspiration allowed: Austrialia del Espíritu Santo.

The 'Austrialia' was in honour of King Philip III of Spain, who was also Archduke of Austria.

De Quirós was the last of the eminent discoverers for Spain or Portugal. These countries had been combined under Philip II in 1580 who, very shortly afterwards and with much bearing on Pacific history, lost his kingship of the Netherlands.

The decline of imperial Spain and Portugal was beginning to start. So far as empires go, they were not long-lived but they were remarkably enterprising. It was they who first made the Pacific known, for better or for worse, to the European world.

In the closing stages of the Portuguese-Spanish hegemony, there were two voyages in the Pacific by ships of a country new to the area and commanded by buccaneers rather than by discoverers. Sir Francis Drake, after discovering California in 1579, went in *Golden Hind* to the Moluccas, taking a very northerly route across the Pacific in order to harass better the Spanish. He is known to have visited the Ladrones fifty-eight years after Magellan, and although he is presumed to have seen some of the Gilberts, Carolines, and Marshalls, the particular islands are not identifiable.

His circumnavigation in 1577–80, the first by an Englishman, was not one primarily of exploration; nor was that which followed: a circumnavigation by another Englishman, Thomas Cavendish, a Suffolk gentleman, in 1586–8. Like Drake's, his activities in the Pacific were mostly to disrupt Spanish comfort

Opposite, top left: *Eendracht*, under Willem Corneliszoon Schouten and Jacob Le Maire (see p.37), in 1616 off Cocos Island (Coconut Trees, later Boscawen, now Tafahi) in the Tongan group, with Verraders Island (Traitors, later Keppel, now Niuatoputapu), in the background. Tongans can be seen jumping off the ship with their loot.

Pigafetta, in 1521, first depicted Micronesians, but it was not until 1606 that de Prado y Tovar painted the first Melanesians. It was another decade before the first Polynesians were drawn.

Opposite, top right: There was intense excitement among the Polynesians as Schouten and Le Maire made their way in the lagoon to the Hoorn or Horne Islands (Futuna and Alofi in the Wallis and Futuna group) in 1616 (see p. 37). Some shots fired from the dinghy following the ship at the over-eager occupants of approaching canoes, however, would not seem to augur the happy landing which was in fact made.

Les Habitans de l'Isle de la Droues

Right: The fourth expedition to depict artistically the Pacific was probably the 1614–18 circumnavigation of Admiral Joris van Spilbergen (1568–1620). Here, oriental-style headwear and differing types of native boats are shown off Guam.

Opposite: Probably the second pictorial record made of the Pacific: it shows Micronesians from Guam in the Ladrones (later Marianas) in 1600, and was drawn on Olivier van Noort's expedition of 1598–1601.

Ashore, Schouten, Le Maire, and some of their men mingle with inhabitants of the Horne Islands. One of the very earliest representations of Europeans meeting Islanders, it is a scene of much animation. Of ethnographical value is the inclusion (in the centre) of the mixing of the pre-chewed *kava*—which the visitors could not bear to swallow.

rather than to find out what was in the ocean besides rich ships. In *Desire*, he too went from California via the Ladrones, bartering iron there for fruit, fish, and coconuts, to the Moluccas.

These first English incursions, although global in scale, were less important in a story of European Pacific discovery than the accomplishments of minor Iberian rivals half-way through the sixteenth century. Less celebrated, but making more contact with islands, were Inigo Ortiz de Retes (or Rotha), who took possession of Western New Guinea in 1545, and a Basque, Miguel Lopez de Legazpi, acting similarly in parts of Micronesia twenty years later.

When de Quirós died in Panama in 1615, Spain gave up the chance of being the first to discover the Unknown Continent. By surrounding the Pacific with secrecy, making it a sealed-off area in theory but not in practice, the Spanish were for a long time underrated in history for their achievements.

Chapter III

Later Discoverers from Europe

The Dutch made some splendid voyages in the Pacific, following the Portuguese and Spanish decline. It is surprising that they were able to do so, at least so quickly. Holland is a small country, with a modest amount of coast. It had been heavily ruled by Spain's quite alien culture and had pluckily achieved independence. But this was only in 1580, and within a score of years the Dutch republic was a major maritime power. It had been partly helped by the disastrous Spanish attempt to invade England with an armada. Nevertheless, from 1580 to 1640, until the Dutch Navy became so powerful, Spain's possession of the New World, Oceania, most of Africa, and the East Indies made it a more powerful empire than any since that of Rome. A very important Dutch step was to supplant the Portuguese in the Spice Islands, and to establish bases in the East Indies for entering the Pacific from Asia. In the first exuberance of freedom, after their rebellion against Spain, the Dutch sent no less than sixty-five ships between 1597 and 1602 to open up routes to the Spice Islands.

In 1605, Willem Janszoon van Amsterdam departed from Java and, while off New Guinea, became, so far as is known, the first European to discover Australia, at that time named New Holland.

Willem Corneliszoon Schouten, a master-mariner, and Jacob Le Maire, a merchant, while in search of the Great South Land, discovered in 1615 an alternative to Magellan's Straits. These, despite or because of being bounded by land on two sides, were notoriously difficult to get through under pure sail. In going further south below Tierra del Fuego into wild, open seas, Schouten and Le Maire rounded Cape Horn—named after Schouten's birthplace, Hoorn—in quicker time:

> We met big waves and a swell rolling in from the South West. The blue colour made us think that on our starboard side away to the South West lay the ocean, the great South Sea to which we had found a passage. That we had indeed discovered a channel hitherto unknown and hidden gave us great joy.

Willem Corneliszoon Schouten (1567–1625), above, and Jacob Le Maire (1585–1616), below, were the first Europeans to visit a number of islands in Polynesia and Melanesia in 1616.

They went on across the ocean and were the first Europeans to discover three of the Tongan Islands. After other discoveries, including important ones in the Bismarck archipelago, they ended their great voyage in 1616 at the Moluccas. There, they were arrested by fellow Dutchmen as interlopers, as they had arrived from the wrong direction and under the wrong company (the West India Company, as opposed to the East India Company). Le Maire died on the return journey via Africa, aged thirty-one.

Arguably in the top navigational class was another Dutchman, Abel Janszoon Tasman. There is no doubt that his pilot-major, Frans Jacobszoon Visscher, was of the highest quality. From Batavia (now Djakarta), Tasman, a minor business official of untraceable but certainly more humble origin than most of the previous discoverers, sailed in 1642 in search of the gold and silver supposed to exist east of the Sea of Japan towards Australia. He missed Australia, although he went round it, by about 100 miles, but found Van Diemen's Land (named Anthony van Diemens Landt after the Governor-General of Batavia: later it was given Tasman's own name). He seemed to go

half-way round Australia and then passed in 1642 between the two main islands of New Zealand, which he called Staten Landt. There, his men were in an unfortunate conflict with Maoris in Murderers' Bay; some Dutch were killed, and he was glad to move on to Tonga. Tasman was relieved to find that Tongans did not show any hostility. In fact they showed delight, particularly the ladies, at his sailors' performances on fiddles, flutes, and trumpets.

Abel Janszoon Tasman (1603–59). Only two portraits of him exist that are likely to be authentic. This one, attributed to Jacob Gerritsz Cuyp (c. 1594–1652) and believed to have been painted in 1637, is considered to be the most trustworthy. With Tasman are his second wife and his daughter by his first wife.

Amsterdam Island in 21. 20. S. Long. 176.56. W. a London?

A. *Our Ships at anchor in Diemens road.* B. *Small stroas belonging to the King of the Country.* C. *Vessells or stroas joined together with one Deck.* D. *A Fishing stroa* E. *Their coming on board with Coco Nuts &c.* F. *The Kings residence.* G. *The place where our Boats lay when they went to Water.* H. *The place where they came to meet Our people with Flags of Truce.* I. *The place where Our people kept Guard.* K. *The Kings Belay in an inclosure where He received Our people.* L. *The King & His Nobilitys washing place.* M. *Their Vessells at Anchor.* N. *This peoples manner of Sitting standing, & their Cloathing.* O. *The Bay where the King lives & His Galley lyes to which Tasman gave the Name of Maria's Bay from M. Van Diemens Spouse.*

Although the perspective is odd, this drawing of Amsterdam Island (Tongatabu, the main island of Tonga), made during Tasman's voyage in 1643, is among the best of the earliest pictorial records. It is generally credited to have been Tasman's own work.

From Tonga, he sailed literally across coral reefs, bumping over them, in the Fiji group. It was to be as long as about 150 years before even one of the 300 islands in the centrally placed Fiji group was to be visited by a European (Cook). After failing to do more than scrape the reefs of Fiji, which he named Prins Willem's Islands, Tasman skirted the coasts of New Britain, New Ireland, and New Hanover without recognizing that they were separate islands. However, by the time he returned to Batavia in 1643, he had covered much new valuable Pacific space. He was the first European to penetrate, from the Asian direction, the South Pacific in depth.

Tasman's place in the first rank of discoverers is marginal. He was not a circumnavigator. He covered less sea than most, as he started for the Pacific from the East Indies, and missed much but only by a little: in those times that was bad luck rather than bad management. He died in Batavia in 1659, aged fifty-six, having found no material riches. His treatment of the Island people was generally amicable.

After Drake and Cavendish, the next British buccaneer in the Pacific, nearly a century later, was William Dampier. Born on a Dorset farm in 1652, he was a man of not very distinctive appearance, with origins as lowly as Tasman's, but he became one of the most distinguished Oceanic figures. He had been on the sea for ten years (including being marooned at one stage) before, at the age of twenty-seven, he joined a group of buccaneers. This gang captured several Spanish ships in the Bay of Panama and reached Juan Fernandez Island, 340 miles off the Peru coast, in 1680. Dampier and his pirate colleagues had no sooner arrived than three Spanish ships were observed approaching. Dampier was good at looking after himself. Leaving a faithful Indian behind on Juan Fernandez, he escaped and joined:

> One Mr. Cook, an English native of St. Christopher, a Creole as we call all born of European parents in the West Indies. He was a sensible man and had been some years a Privateer.

Dampier was a born survivor. He spent two years with John Cook and then, in 1685, departed on a voyage as navigator with Charles Swan in *Cygnet* from Central America to the Ladrone Islands. There was nearly a mutiny before, to the crew's great joy, Guam was sighted. Dampier reported:

> . . . I was afterwards informed, the men had contrived first to kill Captain Swan and eat him when the victuals was gone, and after him all of us who were accessory in promoting the undertaking of this Voyage. This made Captain Swan say to me after our arrival at Guam. 'Ah, Dampier, you would have made them but a poor Meal'; for I was as lean as the captain was lusty and fleshy.

Over a century and a half after Pigafetta, Dampier gazed penetratingly at Guam:

> The Natives of this Island are strong bodied, large limb'd and well shap'd. They are Copper-coloured, like other *Indians*: their hair is black and long, their Eyes meanly proportioned; they have pretty high Noses; their lips are pretty full, and their Teeth indifferent white. They are long visaged, and stern of countenance; yet we found them to be affable and courteous. They are many of them troubled with a kind of Leprosie . . .

Buccaneer, three times circumnavigator, and a natural scientist, Captain William Dampier (1652–1715) holds his *A New Voyage Round the World* (1697), rightly acclaimed for its literary style and remarkable narrative. In this picture by Thomas Murray, his countenance is rather sad and, by experience, justifiably wary.

High technical praise was then recorded: ' . . . I do believe they sail the best of any Boats in the world.'

Refreshed by Guam, Swan and Dampier were able to extend the voyage to the Philippines, but the crew were tired and wanted to go home. After a mutiny in which Dampier was imprisoned, the vessel sailed without Swan from Mindanao for China, the Cape of Good Hope, and England. Swan, left ashore, tried to get away but was murdered by Mindanao natives.

Dampier continued to survive. Suffering much from dropsy, he was advised by a native to have himself buried up to his neck in hot sand. This cured him. Tired of freebooting, Dampier asked on one voyage to be put ashore off the Nicobar Islands in the Indian Ocean. Making his way to Madras, he managed to obtain from the East India Company a 'painted prince', Jeoly, from Mindanao. Tattooed all over, the 'prince' was taken by Dampier to England in 1691, but the latter had made no money in his dozen years' absence as a pirate and he was soon obliged to sell his exhibit, who then died.

Right from the beginning, however, Dampier had kept a journal which he had preserved from danger of shipwreck in bamboo made watertight with wax. The publication of his *A New Voyage Round the World* in 1697 brought him instant fame for his talent as a writer, the brilliance of his observations, and for his nautical enterprise. Full of high drama and sharp perception of human nature and facts, this was the forerunner of ethnographical recording by explorers. His was the first work to bring the Pacific into wide literary awareness: every gentleman's library had it. It inspired others to write on the area—a superior of his, Captain Woodes Rogers, for one. Jonathan Swift located his satire in Pacific Utopias: his voyager, Gulliver, was to discover the incredible in the South Seas.

Dampier had effectively punctured the Spanish monopoly of Pacific knowledge that had, as soon as gained, been put into secret archives. Dampier declared:

> Spaniards have more than they can well manage. I know yet, they would lie like the Dog in the Manger; although not able to eat themselves, yet they would hinder others.

He was not to be hindered. The Royal Society had been founded in 1663. This was the beginning of an enlightened era. Dampier helped in the stimulus and was in turn stimulated. He had dedicated his narrative, based on twenty-three years' experience, to the Society and expressed a desire to help his country further. King William III ordered in 1699 an expedition to investigate unknown countries, particularly New Holland (Australia) and New Guinea. Dampier was selected by the First Lord of the Admiralty, the Earl of Pembroke, to command H.M.S. *Roebuck* with fifty men for the purpose. Although his corvette was in poor condition, he sailed along the north side of New Guinea, discovering in 1700 the strait between that island and New Britain now known as Dampier's Passage. But his ship sank at anchor on the return at Ascension Island in 1701, and he returned with his men on other ships to England. Two years later, some English merchants requested him to take a couple of ships to the South Seas. The mate on one of the vessels (*Cinque Ports*, not commanded by Dampier) was Alexander Selkirk. Aged twenty-six and from Fife, Selkirk, markedly contumacious, could not tolerate his bad-tempered captain, Thomas Stradling, and, after rounding Cape Horn, he asked to be put ashore at Juan Fernandez in 1704. Put ashore he was, with his chest, bedding, mathematical instruments, books, stationery, and a gun. Immediately, he changed his mind and pleaded to be taken back again, but Stradling refused and abandoned him.

Dampier, on the other ship, *St. George*, crossed the Pacific from Juan Fernandez to Java, where he was imprisoned by the Dutch and returned to England, once again without any money. He was given a last voyage in 1708, this time as pilot, subordinate to Captain Woodes Rogers in *Duke* which, with another ship, was to raid Spanish and French ships in the Pacific in the Drake-Cavendish tradition. Once again Dampier rounded Cape Horn and called at Juan Fernandez, where there was a remarkable reunion. A man 'clothed all in goatskin who seemed' to Woodes Rogers 'wilder than the original owners of his apparel' was seen waving a white flag: it was Alexander Selkirk. He had endured complete human solitude for four years and four months, amusing himself by singing and dancing with cats and kid goats which he had tamed. His homemade calendar was wrong by two days. On an excellent recommendation from Dampier, Selkirk was made second mate of *Duke*. His astonishing story was included in Woodes Rogers' *A Cruising Voyage Round the World* and embellished by Daniel Defoe as *The Life and Strange Surprizing Adventures of Robinson Crusoe*. It made Defoe's fortune (there are accounts of Selkirk having asked Defoe to look over his narrative and of the reply that it was worthless), but did nothing to keep Selkirk from impoverishment. The melancholy Selkirk wanted to return to Juan Fernandez, but he died at sea as a naval lieutenant, aged forty-seven.

Both *Duke* and her sister ship were very successful in taking prizes off the American coast. As pilot, Dampier would this time have had a considerable share of the booty had he not died in London in 1719, four years before the prize money was divided.

Nautically, Dampier must be placed in the highest class of navigators, if not of commanders. He was both too capricious and too self-effacing to control the crews of his era. Three circumnavigations, four remarkable voyages in all, nearly 300 years ago, speak for themselves. His philosophy was admirable: 'The farther we went, the more Knowledge and Experience I should get, which was the main Thing that I regarded.' He was the first to observe natural history and meteorology with acute perception. As a person, he was regarded by all the very different people with whom he mixed as charitable, humane, scientific, and literary, a man of real, self-made talents of a wide order.

The beginning of the eighteenth century and the appearance of a natural scientific mind like Dampier's straddling it and the end of the seventeenth century is a convenient stage to make a distinction between the European discoverers and the European explorers. The Spanish, Portuguese, and Dutch discoverers had come across quite a lot in the Pacific which they did not necessarily understand very clearly. Their contact with the Islanders, who were the first discoverers, had been limited. By the time their vessels had made landfalls, the visitors were, to put it mildly, exhausted. They wanted to do nothing but restock their provisions and water and pause to gather strength for the return journey—which was only too well known to be arduous, time-consuming, and perilous.

The discoverers were less interested in the way of life of the natives than in what they might find to take back to Europe as material reward for their aleatory voyaging. In general, all they did was to sight islands for European records: they landed on some, but only briefly. They were different from the explorers in that they did little reconnoitring of islands or observing of inhabitants, and they carried with them virtually no artists. Nevertheless, the few observations that they did make were significant because they were the first to be recorded. In too many instances, the lives of natives were of little value—and yet so were those of fellow Europeans at that time, as Magellan had little hesitation in demonstrating off Patagonia. Great navigational mistakes were made and huge opportunities missed, often narrowly. It has always to be remembered, however, that it was not until half-way through the eighteenth century that maritime technology was spectacularly improved: vessels were better built, provisions were more nutritional, there was greater concentration on, and ability in, cartography, and, most important, instruments were developed for fixing positions and aiming more accurately for specific destinations.

Natives of Verkwikkings-Eyland (Refreshment, now Makatea) in the Tuamotu archipelago hurling stones at the men of Admiral Jacob Roggeveen (1659–1729), an episode in 1722 depicted in 1728 by M. Balen. Roggeveen named the island after fruit and vegetables found on it. When he had discovered Easter Island earlier in 1722, Roggeveen had also had an unhappy confrontation with the Islanders, which resulted in a dozen natives being killed, and so, when he found Borabora and Maupiti, in the Society Islands, and Samoa, he kept his distance from the inhabitants.

Roggeveen's sighting of two major Samoan islands (see p.43) rounded off the great Dutch era of discovery which had lasted for more than a century. This sketch by A. Legrand after Elié Le Guillou, the surgeon on the 1837–40 expedition of Jules Sébastien César Dumont d'Urville (see p.80), shows the 'king' of Apia, Samoa, being massaged. His queen pummels his head, which he will then lay on the nearby headrest.

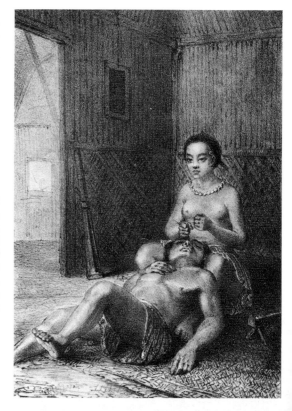

Chapter IV

Earliest Explorers from Europe

The only known portrait of Captain Samuel Wallis (1728–95).

Samuel Wallis, a Cornishman aged thirty-eight, was perhaps the first explorer within the meaning used in the previous chapters. He made the important discovery of Tahiti in 1767 (it had been seen by de Quirós but forgotten: the Spanish acknowledged Wallis' achievement). Tahiti was the largest island seen in the South Seas since Tasman had come across New Zealand and the last Dutch discoverer, Jacob Roggeveen, had found the Samoan group in 1722.

Wallis' arrival in Tahiti was not auspicious. The first Tahitians to go on board his ship, *Dolphin*, leapt overboard when one of them was butted in the rear by a goat and they saw it standing on its hind legs about to charge again. There were skirmishes too at first. It was a Pacific Island tradition (and, in some areas, still is) that anything asked for is expected to be given. The Tahitians asked for nails and iron when they saw them on the ship and could not appreciate that they held *Dolphin* together. Offended by their requests being turned down, they formed an early judgement that Europeans were mean.

Unlike previous discoverers of islands in the Pacific, Wallis elected to stay in Tahiti long enough to gain some knowledge of its hospitable people and beautiful terrain. There was much sorrow on both sides at *Dolphin's* departure after more than a month's stay. He left innovations: some turkeys, a gander, a goose, a cat, and a looking-glass.

Wallis' report on Tahiti was so glowing that other explorers, whalers and traders following in the next twenty-five years gave the dangerous Tuamotu archipelago a miss and made for Tahiti.

The observation of the transit of Venus across the sun, due to take place in 1769, was much in English scientific minds at that time. Thoughts were being given to a location in the Pacific, probably the Marquesas or Friendly Islands. Wallis' return in 1768, when Cook's South Seas expedition was being prepared for the purpose, settled uncertainty: Tahiti was decided upon. Wallis' discovery of it set off a chain of activity: by the French (de Bougainville was already in the area—see p.46), and by the Spanish.

Wallis had been ill for a major part of his outward voyage and was restored to health by the massage of Tahitian women. With him on the journey was an interesting character: master of *Dolphin*, George Robertson, a well-meaning, kindly, and physically very strong man who was both an expert navigator and, despite his idiosyncratic spelling and punctuation (he blithely ignored full stops), literary exponent. His *Journal* was perhaps the first true ethnography of the South Seas, having a breadth that exceeds Dampier's narrative of his sojourn on Guam nearly a century earlier. Vivid, imaginative, amusing, full of information, and lively, the following excerpts from Robertson's *Journal* merit reading despite the grammatical peccadilloes:

> [When natives came out on canoes in Tahiti]... we made signs to them, to bring of Hogs, Fowls and fruit and showd them coarse cloath Knives sheers Beeds Ribons etc., and made them understand that we was willing to barter with them, the method we took to make them Understand what we wanted was this, some of the men Grunted and Cryd lyke a Hogg then pointed to the shore —oythers crowd Lyke cocks to make them understand that we wanted

fowls, this the natives of the country understood and Grunted and Crowd the same as our people, and pointed to the shore and made signs that they would bring us off some . . .

. . . At Noon all the traders Wooders and Liberty men came off to Dinner and brought off two of the natives to Dinn with them, the one was the old mans Sun who assisted the Gunner but the Oyther was one of their cheefs or great men, he appeard to be a Sensable well behaved man, about thirty years of Age, and about five foot nine, well made and very good features of a dark Mustee colour we showd him the Ship, and he took very particular notice of every thing which we showd him, and seemd greatly surprized at the construction of our ship, this day the Capt and first Lieut. was both able to sit up, and we all Dinnd in the Gun roum, with the cheeff allong with us, after spreading the cloath we all set doun and made him set doun in a chair, but before he sit doun he vewed the chair all round then set doun and vewed the plates knives and forks with great attention, but the instant he saw the Dinner set doun, he laid doun his plate and toutched nothing untill he was helpt, we hade a very Excellent dinner, which consisted of Broth made with two fine fat fowls, two do. rosted, a rosted pig, rosted yams, Plantains, Bananas Soft Bread, bisquet apple pudding and apple pye—all of this he eate a part off, and took very great notice of the manner that we eate with our Spoons knives and forks, and used them in the same manner that we did and helpt him selfe with fowl pig yams etc. the same as we did.

We hade very Good claret Madeira, port, Rum and Brandy Grog and excellent good London porter, but his choice was water, he smelt and tasted the Wine and Grog but lyked neather but hobernobd with water and seemd greatly pleasd when we all toutchd Glasses with him, he observed us wipe our mouths before we drank, with our pocket handcurchiefs this made him a little uneasy he having nothing of that kind, and seemd unwilling to use his cloaths I therefor gave him the corner of the table cloath to wipe his mouth . . . but the thing which pleasd and Astonishd Jonathan the most of all, was the picture of a very handsome well drest young Lady, in Miniature, which the Docter Showd him, we made him understand that this was the picture of the women in our country and if he went with us he should have one of them always to Sleep with, this put him in such raptures of Joy thats its imposible for me to describe he hugd the picture in his breast and kist it twenty times, and made several oyther odd motions, to show us how happy he would be with so fine a woman, we all supposed Jonathan to be one of the first rank . . .

. . . They have a very particular Custom in this country which is this at the age of Sixteen they paint all the men's thighs Black, and soon after paint cureous figures on their Legs and Arms, and the Ladys seems not to exceed the age of twelve or thirteen when they go through that operation. I suppose they look upon themselves as men and Women at the age of sixteen and twelve. When I again went into the Captns cabin the Queen took it in her head that I was painted after the manner of her country therefor wanted to see my legs thighs and Arms, and rather not disoblidge her I showed her all, which greatly surprized her and she would not beleve that I showed my skinn untill she feelt it with her own hands, she then wanted to see my breast which I likeways showd her, but it surprized her most of all my breast being full of hair, she supposed I was a very strong man and Certainly of Age altho not painted, she then began to feel my thighs and legs to know if they hade the Strength that they seemd to have, I then put my legs in position that they feelt both stiff and strong which made her look very hard in my face, and

Captain Wallis and his uniformed officers made a profound impression on 'Queen' Purea of Tahiti and her ladies in 1767. In this engraving by J. Hall, dated 1773, a frond, the universal emblem of friendship in early South Sea encounters, is extended towards the visitors. More tangible favours followed.

calld out with Admiration Oh, Oh, Oh, and desired the Chief to feel my legs, which I allowed him to do and he seemd greatly Astonished as well as She, After that they hade a long talk, and the Queen laid hould of me to left me up, but I prevented her, without her being Sensable of the reason why she could not left me up, this Surprized her most of all and she calld Oh Oh and talkd again for some time to the Chief, who made a Sign for me to Left her, which I did with one Arm and carryed her round the Cabin, this seemd to pleas her greatly and She Eyed me all round and began to be very merry and cheerful and if I am not mistaken by her Majts behaviour afterwards this is the way the Ladys here trys the men, before they Admit them to be their Lovers . . . By that time dinner was near ready and the Queen insisted on our staying dinner, but as I hade posative orders from the Capt. I was oblidged to deprave my Selfe of the honour of dinning with her Majesty, when she found I was posative to go. She spock to the old Woman which I cannot help thinking was her Mother, as She sufferd non oyther to take the least Liberty with her, then the old Lady laid hould of me, and Endeavourd to detain me, and when she found nothing would preveal on me to stay dinner, She made me understand with very plain Signs, that I should have her Daughter to Sleep with, and when that hade not the desired Effect, the old Lady pointed

45

to two very handsom Young Ladys, and made us understand that the Young Gentn and I should have them to sleep with, thinking that would tempt us to stay I then Excused my Selfe in the best Manner I could, and Laid hold of the Queens hand and the Old Ladys to take my leave, at the same time made them understand that I would soon come Back from my Own Country and Sleep with her in my Arms, this pleased both and I parted with the old Lady, who seemd extreemly well pleased, but the Queen laid hould of my Arm, and Came allong with me doun to the Water side ...

... At the last House where we Calld, their was two of the handsomest Young Ladys that I ever saw upon the Island. One in particular was fully as fair and hade as Good features as the Generality of Women in England, hade she been drest after the English manner, am certain no man would [have] thought her of Another Country; I first shaked hands with two fine Jolly old people, which I supose was the Young Ladys parents: but they were both of a Mullato colour—I then shaked hands with the Young Ladys who was both fine brisk spirited women, the fairest seeing that I took more notice of her than the oyther began to be very Merry and we compaird skinns and hers was rather fairer and Whiter nor mine, in short I took so mutch notice of this fine Young Lady that I hade almost forgot her Majst who was conversing with the old people But on her looking round and Observing My Young freind deeply ingadged with the oyr young Lady and me seemingly so fond of her which was so very fair, this put the Queen a little out of humor, and she immediately brock up the conversation with the old people and Said something to the young Lady which I was talking with that made her very unhappy I was sorry to see the Young Lady unease, and took her in my Arms to Comfort her—but the instant I laid hold of her, the Queen laid hold of my arm and gave the poor Young Lady so cross a look in the face, that I realy beleve she soon after fainted, this realy made me a Little unhappy, but knowing it was my duety to pleas the Queen, I indeavourd to recover my surprize, and did all I could to pleas her Majst but After that she would enter no House, but in a manner Lead me to the boat side, where she waited untill I went off to the ship.

The redoubtable Robertson was to be given command of several British ships in the American War of Independence.

Accompanying Wallis from England was Philip Carteret in *Swallow*, which Carteret judged to be 'one of the worst, if not the very worst of her kind, in His Majesty's Navy'. He thought Wallis separated deliberately after the Magellan Straits. The disintegrating *Swallow* soldiered on, discovering Pitcairn's Island and being the first to find the Solomons since de Mendaña precisely 200 years earlier. Not being well disposed to natives, Carteret was a discoverer rather than an explorer.

The first of many great French figures in the Pacific now appears. Louis-Antoine de Bougainville was unlucky to miss by a year the distinction of being the first European known to have discovered Tahiti, but he covered much of the Pacific and was the first in parts of the Louisiades and New Hebrides. He named Choiseul and discovered Bougainville, islands in the Solomons: these names have endured until today. A plant with insignificant flowers and exotic leaves became known as bougainvillaea. He could avoid the privations no better than any of the early voyagers but he could tolerate them with the best. On his circumnavigation, food being very short, he recorded in his journal: '... at supper we ate some rats and found them very good'. Nearly 250 years earlier

Captain Philip Carteret (1733–96). He received grudging and inadequate official recognition of his contributions to discovery.

Louis-Antoine de Bougainville (1729–1811). Cheerful, brisk-looking, sharp, and pertinacious, his versatility has hardly ever been excelled. This engraving of him is by Emile Lassalle.

Pigafetta had agreed. The first distinguished French Pacific explorer, Vice-Admiral Major-General Comte Louis-Antoine de Bougainville had a distinctly unusual career. He was elected a Fellow of the Royal Society in England at the age of twenty-seven for a treatise on integral calculus. Then, as an army officer, he tried to save Montcalm in the battle of Quebec. At that time, he had an affair with an Iroquois chief's daughter and, twenty-one years later, was disconcertedly confronted by a full-blooded Iroquois relation. In 1790, the Revolutionary regime made him naval commander-in-chief with the rank of vice-admiral. Napoleon made him a senator and a count.

De Bougainville immersed himself in Tahiti: he was utterly captivated by it. For him, it was Eden, the place surpassingly beautiful, the people incomparably attractive. Calling it *La Nouvelle Cythère* (the birthplace of the Greek goddess of love), he believed that this was the ideal haven depicted in the philosophy of Jean-Jacques Rousseau. The latter advocated that the best way to opt out of a miserable world was to become a noble savage. He had elevated this ideal above reality or common sense, but de Bougainville had seen the paradise. His widely successful report in 1771, *Voyage Autour du Monde . . .*, was what France had been conditioned by Rousseau to hope for. He took a 'Greek god' back with him as a showpiece to Europe: Ahutou, Ahutoru, or Aotourou—the first Tahitian in the Western world.

La Nouvelle Cythère's remoteness from reality and its promises of the sweet life contributed to the spirals of expectation that gave rise to the revolution eighteen years later.

The late eighteenth century became inflamed by the tales of sailors who returned home from the Islands. They had been enraptured by the perfumes greeting the ships from the palm-lined coasts and lushly-forested slopes, by the seductive, deep black, liquid eyes, by the softness, and the tranquillity. There was genuine sadness on both sides at parting: the Europeans realized that they were leaving the closest to paradise that they would ever see, while the natives experienced an acute sense of anticlimax, with the novelty and excitement being replaced by their former humdrum existence.

De Bougainville made valuable, if idealized, observations on the Tahiti way of life. He had with him scientific experts. It was his surgeon-botanist, Philibert de Commerson, who publicized Tahiti in 1769:

> This is the only place on earth where people live without any vice and prejudice, without any requirements and dissensions.

Expeditions had not yet included any artists. Cook was the first to recognize the importance of their inclusion and his expeditions represented the pictorial beginning for the Pacific. He also took the greatest steps in the direction of ethnography, as well as in many other fields.

When James Cook set out on his first circumnavigation in 1768, there were large gaps unexplored in the Pacific. By 1779, when he died, these had been filled in by him. De Lapérouse told Arthur Phillip, Governor of New South Wales: 'Cook had left me nothing but to admire'. The great myth of Terra Australis was blown away, as was the belief in a practical way by sea to the north from the Pacific to the Atlantic. Cook was the first Pacific explorer *par excellence* and the first Pacific ethnographer. The chart of the Islands is much as he left it in 1779.

Andrew Kippis, who published *A Narrative of the Voyages round the World . . .* nine years after Cook's death, started off the work on his hero: 'Captain James

Cook had no claim to distinction on account of the lustre of his birth or the dignity of his ancestors.' His humble origin as one of nine sons of a Yorkshire agricultural labourer and the start of his career as an able-bodied seaman in 1755 are frequently referred to in descriptions of Cook's appearance. No contemporary historian disputed his impressive bearing.

Cook was said to enjoy the pleasures of the table but not too many others. There was in him an austere strain. Zimmerman noted:

> He would often sit at the table with his officers without saying a word and was always very reserved ... On Saturdays he was as a rule more friendly than on other days: he would then drink one more glass of punch than was his custom and this to the health of all beautiful women and maidens ...

He was certainly the epitome of the man of action. Cook was described by a number of his officers who wrote about him as indefatigable, never wanting to sit down and rest, ceaselessly at work, being quite capable of tolerating the most frugal conditions: he could also keep himself detached from the multiple joys that Tahiti and Tonga could offer. Very tall for the period in which he lived (he was over 6 feet), Cook's demeanour and movements were noted by all to be dignified to an extent thought aristocratic by his countrymen and princely by the natives. One or two writers say that he had a sense of humour to some extent, but this is hard to tell from the portraits. Most consider that he was matter-of-fact and not given to enthusiasms. But in much of his professional life, a sense of humour was probably not easy to retain or advisable to show. His whole approach was that of a professional.

Four great advances had just been made in maritime technology. Cook was given the job of trying them out on his voyages. All, with his methodical handling, were eminently successful, and the aid which they gave him cannot be overstated. They were: the sextant for the closer calculation of latitude, the *Nautical Almanack* just instituted by the Astronomer Royal, which survives to today, annually recording the movements of the moon, and improved chronometers, which solved the problem of finding longitude. Finally, Cook was exhorted to introduce the latest hygienic methods and medical materials, particularly against the scourge of long-distance voyages, scurvy, resulting directly from a deficiency of Vitamin C. Cook introduced daily rations of sauerkraut and vinegar and reduced overcrowding.

Added to these navigational and nutritional advantages were two other benefits: the backing of the Royal Society, and a rich patron, Sir Joseph Banks, then aged twenty-four, who was to dominate the Royal Society for forty years.

Cook's first expedition was primarily for the purpose of observing the transit of Venus across the sun, which happens once in 100 years, in the Southern Hemisphere. Secondly, and secretly, he was to look at whatever he might come across, particularly the continent in the south. Banks, the naturalist, who was to show a distinct faculty for friendship with Pacific natives, was hardly less exultant than de Bougainville over the paradise of Tahiti. His interest in everything was a high-class kind of inquisitiveness: this characteristic contributed to the expedition's success. This initial voyage in 1768–71, unique in being the first to have a comprehensive staff of scientists, was given, as were Cook's other two voyages, an artist, Sydney Parkinson, a botanical draughtsman and a Quaker, who died of malaria and dysentery on the return voyage. For the second voyage the artist was William Hodges who, for no very clear reason, except perhaps as an adherent of the Rousseau-de Bougainville school, painted the natives in flowing Grecian robes. To those knowing the

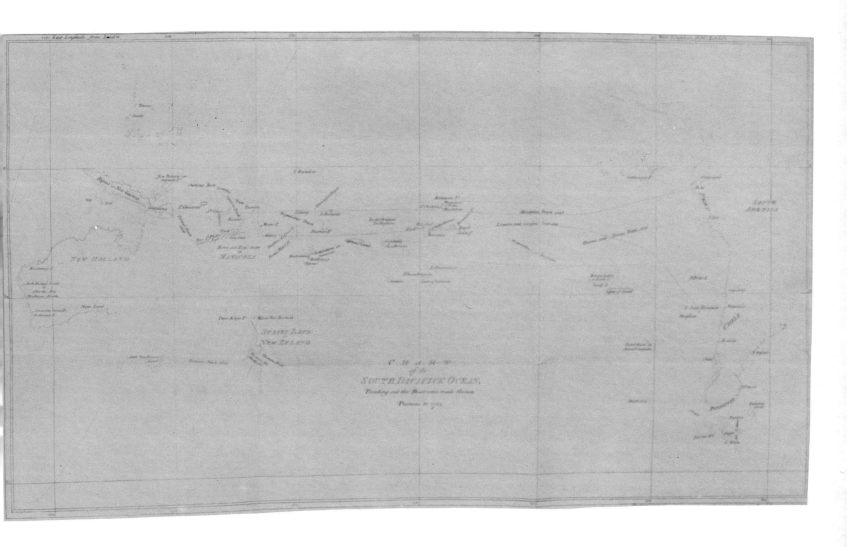

Alexander Dalrymple's 'Chart of the South Pacifick Ocean, pointing out the Discoveries made therein Previous to 1764', published in 1770. This can be regarded as the state of the discoveries before Cook began his voyages of exploration. Dalrymple (1737–1808) was passed over by the Admiralty in favour of Cook for the command of the first of these.

Pacific his Polynesians are unrecognizable and, as figures, whether Pacific or otherwise, they are bad. But early expedition artists were expected to paint everything, and their work was naturally uneven. To be fair to Hodges, his landscapes and seascapes are superb. Fortunately, he was too busy finishing off his work on the second voyage to be considered for the third. The draughtsman on that voyage, John Webber, the son of a Swiss sculptor who had settled in England, and unofficial artists such as James Cleveley, carpenter, and William Ellis, surgeon's mate, fortunately repaired much of Hodges' ethnographic and aesthetic damage.

As regards the prime object of the first voyage, the transit of Venus was covered successfully during a three months' stay in Tahiti—although, despite elaborate precautions, this was nearly sabotaged a few hours before the time of the transit by Tahitians absconding with the quadrant. A side benefit of the voyage was the discovery of four islands, named by Cook the Society Islands.

Practically the only Tahitian weakness in those early European eyes was the native belief that the objects on the ships were theirs for the taking. It was simply because they had not reached the Iron Age and did not possess nails (in great demand for fish hooks), guns (for the all-important ambitions of con-quest), and less important articles like mirrors. The very first contact with European goods was characterized by a compulsive desire to acquire them by any possible means.

Cook's patience was naturally subject to strain, but he was probably more tolerant than anyone else when faced with these occurrences of pilfering. They recur throughout almost all early contacts between Polynesians, Melanesians, and Micronesians and their Western visitors. Natives were seeing for the first time what they readily recognized as articles to simplify their daily activities: house and boat-building, fishing, hunting, and fighting. The use of nails, hooks, and spears, speedily made from the iron which they had not known to exist, was an astonishing revolution. Europeans had gone through such a revolution themselves, but sixteenth-century discoverers had forgotten the sig-nificance of the change which had occurred millennia before their time. They made few or no allowances for the impact on the natives. Cook was the first to offer a wide degree of humanity and tolerance. It was a long time, in some areas a full century, before his example was followed.

After leaving Tahiti, the ship's doctor found that a number of the crew were suffering from venereal disease, which he promptly treated with mercury. Tahitian women were responsible, but they are believed to have contracted the disease from Wallis' and de Bougainville's crews; however, this is not certain.

The sparkling achievement of this first voyage was when Cook's ship,

Maoris hoped to intimidate strangers by protruding their tongues. This drawing was made by Sydney Parkinson (1745–71) on Cook's first circumnavigation of 1768–71.

Endeavour, having turned to search for the southern continent, identified New South Wales (which Cook rather cumbersomely called it) as part of Australia. At last the fifth continent had been found—not of course Terra Australis Incognita, the existence of which he disproved. He had sailed from Cape Horn to Tahiti and then round New Zealand (Tasman's Staten Landt or Nova Zeelandia), charting it with meticulous brilliance. He delineated the shape of its two major islands, sailing between them on a strait later called after him. When he got back to England via the Cape of Good Hope, thirty-eight of the ninety-four crew had died, nearly all from dysentery and none from scurvy. The only seaman never ill was a sailmaker aged seventy-six. 'What is still more extraordinary in this man is his generally being more or less drunk every day', Cook commented.

Cook was instantly in demand for another expedition, this time with no specific scientific object but a roving brief to discover and explore what he could in the South Seas. Banks and Cook had got on well together but on their return there were differences of opinion, particularly when Banks wanted alterations made in the structure of the new vessel to accommodate more scientists. Banks had also arranged for a woman disguised as a boy to be his valet (this seemed, following a precedent set by de Bougainville's surgeon-botanist, to be a ruse common to naturalists). Further additions to his suite included an orchestra in scarlet and gold livery. In the end Banks, although he soon renewed his support for Cook, did not feel that he wanted to make another journey under his

A rare drawing by Captain Cook himself. It depicts the neat compound, surrounded by a low wall, possibly of burnt coral, of a chief in Raiatea, Society Islands. The stunted arboreal clumps on the right appear to be banana trees. The Society Islands were named by Cook not, as often supposed, to commemorate the Royal Society, but because 'they lay contiguous to one another'.

command and went to a very different destination, Iceland.

The second voyage (1772–5) in *Resolution* was from Cook's viewpoint the most satisfactory of all. Sailing via the Cape of Good Hope almost to the Antarctic zone and then returning to New Zealand, he zigzagged across vast stretches of the Pacific, filling in the map with discoveries right and left—some Tuamotu atolls, Palmerston, and major parts of the New Hebrides. He also went to Tahiti again and to New Zealand for a third time. He thought that the New Hebridean scenery was unsurpassingly beautiful, but found the natives:

> the most ugly, ill-proportioned people they ever saw ... they are a very dark-coloured and rather diminutive race, with long heads, flat faces and monkey countenance ... had we made a longer stay we might soon have been on good terms with this ape-like nation.

Cook noted that the inhabitants of one island in this group, Malekula, expressed admiration by 'hissing like geese'.

Cook then discovered New Caledonia. This name and that of the New Hebrides, which he also conferred, have endured to today. Visual similarities between the New Hebrides and the Scottish Hebrides, between New Caledonia and Scotland (Caledonia), have been hard to sustain. The Isle of Pines, which he discovered near New Caledonia, was more aptly named. Cook named Tonga the Friendly Islands, quite unaware that there was a plan among chiefs to kill him. He was not always lucky with his names, but he was capable of deep introspection. Perhaps his most significant observation was on his third voyage:

> Our occasional visits may in some respects have benefited its inhabitants but a permanent establishment amongst them, conducted as most European establishments amongst the Indian nations have unfortunately been, would, I fear, give them just cause to lament that our ships had ever found them out

On Cook's second circumnavigation (1772–5), William Hodges' excess of whimsical artistry was a waste of ethnographic record. Although he was later elected to be a Royal Academician, Hodges (1744–97) abandoned painting for banking, but this led to bankruptcy and (suspected) suicide. Cook is shown here by him landing on Middleburgh Island (Eua) in Tonga, while a native in the boat holds up a leaf as a sign of goodwill.

Basic intercourse. A Maori exchanges a crayfish for a handkerchief, given by a member of the crew of Cook's *Endeavour*. This scene was painted by an unidentified member of the crew or, perhaps, by Cook himself.

... it is my real opinion that it would have been far better for these people, never to have known our superiority in the accommodations and arts that make life comfortable, than, after once knowing it, to be left again, and abandoned to their original incapacity of improvement. Indeed, they cannot be restored to that happy mediocrity in which they lived before we discovered them, if the intercourse between us be discontinued. It seems to me, that it has become, in a measure, incumbent on the Europeans to visit them once in three or four years in order to supply them with those conveniences which we have introduced among them. The want of such occasional supplies will, probably, be felt very heavily by them, when it may be too late to go back to their own less perfect contrivances, which they now despise and have discontinued since the introduction of ours. For by the time that the iron tools of which they are now possessed, are worn out, they will have almost lost the knowledge of their own. A stone hatchet is, at present, as rare a thing amongst them, as an iron one was eight years ago: and a chisel of bone, or stone, is not to be seen.

Above: A view of Moorea, near Tahiti. The pencil sketching by James Cleveley, a carpenter on Cook's third expedition, was crisp; the colouring, however, was by his brother, John, an acknowledged marine painter but who, never having been to the tropics, failed to capture the Pacific's rich tones.

Opposite: The expedition of Schouten and Le Maire was the first to land on New Ireland in 1616. This inhabitant was painted after a drawing by Louis Auguste de Sainson more than 200 years later.

Cook was less idealistic and more analytical than de Bougainville. He saw the nobility of the Polynesians and, unlike de Bougainville, something else. Beauty and handsomeness, dignity and warmth of impulse: these he observed in the Indians, as he and his colleagues still termed the Islanders. Unreliability, quick temper resulting in treachery, calculated cunning and dishonesty: he saw these too. Seen in the round, men anywhere in the world are much the same. This knowledge was a disillusionment eventually for the de Bougainville faction but not for the followers of Cook, who expected nothing else.

Another example of his self-questioning was after landing on Erromanga in the New Hebrides. After accepting the green branch that he had offered, the Erromangans suddenly changed their mood. Several natives were killed and two of Cook's men were wounded. He wrote:

Right: Omai, the second Society Islander to visit Europe and the first in England, was painted by William Parry in 1775 with the ebullient Sir Joseph Banks (1743–1820) and the Swedish botanist on Cook's first expedition, Daniel Carl Solander (1736–82). When he was taken back to his island in 1777 after two years in England, where he fascinated all whom he met, Omai clung on to Cook and did not want to go ashore: he died about two years later, never having been able to settle down to his island life again.

Opposite: This portrait of James Cook (1728–79), painted by Sir Nathaniel Dance-Holland (1735–1811) in 1776, just before the final voyage, is a most skilful likeness. The marks of concentration and firmness could be the ambivalent signs of brief exhibitions of passion. Heinrich Zimmerman, a German on the last voyage, when Cook was worn-out, recorded: 'Cook was very strict and hot-tempered, so much so that the slightest insubordination of an officer or sailor upset Cook immediately.'

It is impossible for them to know our real design. We enter their ports and attempt to land in a peaceable manner. If this succeeds all is well, if not we land nevertheless and maintain our footing by the superiority of our firearms. In what other light can they first look upon us but as invaders of their country?

Because Banks had wanted, on the first voyage, to show off Tupaia (the real name of *Dolphin*'s Jonathan, described by Robertson—see p.44), and needed a replacement when Tupaia had died *en route*, a Tahitian was duly brought to England. Omai was no chief, but he gave himself the status of one. There was no doubt about his social impact. Banquets, chess, opera houses, grouse shooting, mansions, the House of Lords—he took all these in his casual stride during his two years' stay. On being presented by Lord Sandwich to King George III, he bowed and said: 'How do, King Tosh'. He seemed to many to represent the Rousseau concept. After he left England, Covent Garden staged *Omiah* [sic] *or, With Captain Cook around the World*, a very successful musical comedy.

Cook was the first European known to have visited one of the Fiji group, practically its most isolated island: Vatoa or Turtle Island in the Lau archipelago, as near to Tonga as to Fiji. He had been warned in Tonga that the Fijians were cannibals of the utmost ferocity: with extreme prudence he kept his distance. It was he who brought back to England the name Fiji, which is the way (almost) that Tongans then pronounced (and still do) Viti, the true native name. He also discovered uninhabited Norfolk Island.

In 1776, the third expedition was made via the Cape of Good Hope in *Resolution*, with William Bligh as master. Some of the Hervey Islands were discovered. At one, the only native to go on board promptly fell over a goat and was too overcome to provide information. Goats had a way of making their presence felt in early European-Islander contacts.

It was in 1778 that Cook discovered the Hawaii group. He himself considered it 'in many respects the most important discovery made by Europeans throughout the extent of the Pacific Ocean.' Somewhat prosaically, he called the islands after Lord Sandwich. However, the inhabitants thought he was a god, or at least semi-divine. They interpreted his coming as the return of Lono, who had gone across the sea, promising to return in a large ship. Cook was given the unique honours accorded to the event: commoners bowed down as they would to one of their chiefs when he passed, he was clothed in the sacred red *kapa*, and fed with pigs consecrated by priests.

> In the course of my several voyages I have never met with the natives of any place so much astonished as these people were. The very instant I landed the collected body of natives all fell flat upon their faces.

Cook took this in his stride, only finding it a little difficult to have to eat as part of the ceremony 'putrid hog', even when it was politely premasticated, and even though a midshipman recorded that Cook's taste was 'surely the coarsest that ever mortal was endowed with'.

Cook made three visits to the Sandwich Islands. On the first, in preparation for a polar voyage, his ships were loaded to capacity with whatever the Islanders could be persuaded to give. It is believed that the natives did not begrudge this provisioning, although it is known that it left them short. The

John Webber (1750?–93) depicts amiability at Namuka, in the archipelago which Cook named the Friendly Islands.

Right: On his third voyage (1776–9) Cook watched, and John Webber depicted in 1777, on a Tahiti *marae* (see p.94) one of the more unpleasant Pacific Island customs—human sacrifice.

Below: This Mangaian had a convenient place in which to put his choicest European acquisition. He was the only native of Mangaia, the southernmost island of the Cook group, to venture on board *Resolution* in 1777, and was drawn by John Webber.

going rate for two large hogs was one nail. Inflation had reached Hawaii: on Wallis' discovery of Tahiti twelve years earlier, the Tahitians had given one medium size hog for one nail. As this voyage continued, it was not to Cook's liking. His show of temper, which had up to then been little seen, became more evident. Ships of that time were expected to work in conditions both of the greatest tropical heat and of the severest polar cold. Probing into the ice at the very north of the Pacific, where America and Asia are nearly joined (and once were), was too trying for everyone. The ships could not deal with the impacted ice, and the men could not withstand the cold. Not reluctantly, the expedition was obliged to return to the Sandwich Islands for warmth and relaxation late in 1778, after ten months' absence. It was during the next two months that the deification occurred. When the Islanders saw the expedition leave in early 1779 they are thought to have expressed some relief, as when an over-indulgent guest leaves one's house and decanters dry. They gave their visitors an enthusiastic send-off, and there was the utmost amity on both sides. But storm damage forced the ships to return to anchor within a week. The Hawaiians seem to have been alarmed to see the fleet coming back so soon. They thought of the drain on their resources that had not yet recovered. Fruit, vegetables, hogs, ceremonial ornaments and adzes, feather capes of the grandest colours: all had been bestowed more than generously. This magnanimity could not be repeated. The ships were not welcomed on the beach by the crowds that had seen them off. Things went badly from the start of their return. As a new mast was needed, a camp had to be set up on shore so that a tree could be felled and laboriously shaped. A shore party had misunderstandings which resulted in the rough treatment of natives. There were reports of pilferage, no doubt by way of recoupment for all the gifts that had been conferred; but the most daring feat of

all was the overnight theft of the cutter, which was tied up to the stern of Cook's own ship.

At this Cook became angrier than had ever been witnessed. He decided to lead personally an armed party of ten ashore to invite the leading chief back to the ship as a semi-hostage until the cutter was returned. This was a tactic used by many explorers. On the beach there were harrowing scenes as the wives of the chief clung to him. Cook had probably not made sufficiently clear the nature of the semi-hostage arrangement: it might have been misinterpreted as the permanent capture of their leader. Meanwhile, news reached the now considerable gathering on the beach that a chief had been killed in another part of the island by a party from the ships. Tempers on both sides were frayed, a Hawaiian threatened Cook with an iron spike (a gift from *Resolution*), and it was decided not to proceed with the idea of the chief going on board. Cook fired at the threatening Hawaiian but did not hurt him. This encouraged the Hawaiians' aggression. Cook fired again, this time with real ammunition, and killed a native. He then broke his own rule by momentarily turning his back on the natives to give an order to his men. No sooner had he done so than he was clubbed and speared, dying instantly. Four marines were also killed. Shots were fired from the boats waiting near the shore (the lieutenant in charge was later criticized for not taking sufficient action). The boats had to return to the ships without the bodies of Cook and the marines, which had been dragged

In 1778, the Sandwich Islanders bestowed upon Cook, their first European discoverer, honours reserved for a god. In this painting by John Webber, he is being clothed in Hawaii's sacred red *kapa* by the pagan priests.

into the bush. Parts of Cook's body, recognized by a hand that had been heavily scarred when he was injured in the battle with the French at Quebec, were returned and consigned to the waters of Kealakekua Bay. In the meanwhile, his head had been taken to the compound where human sacrifices were made and where chiefs were buried, and his bones had been distributed amongst the highest chiefs so that they could hoard the *mana* that they contained—the highest honour that could be paid. The flesh had been previously scraped from the bones and burnt.

The ships had to leave, but not before there had been a measure of reconciliation. There were apologies from the Sandwich Islanders, the new commander, Charles Clerke, who had been on all Cook's voyages, having decided to take no reprisals. This was after there had been unauthorized desultory fighting, many natives showing bravery against the guns and being killed. Some thought that the motive for the attack had been to test Cook's divinity.

Clerke died very soon afterwards from consumption. It was left to John Gore to take *Resolution* and to James King to take *Discovery* back to England in 1780.

There were signal recognitions of Cook as an international figure. In 1779, Benjamin Franklin sent recommendations, subject to American Congress

Cook's own chart of his discoveries, dated 1784, showing the routes of his three voyages—each remarkable in its accomplishment. When looked at in conjunction with Dalrymple's chart of 1764 (see p.49), it can be seen that most of the Pacific Islands had now been discovered.

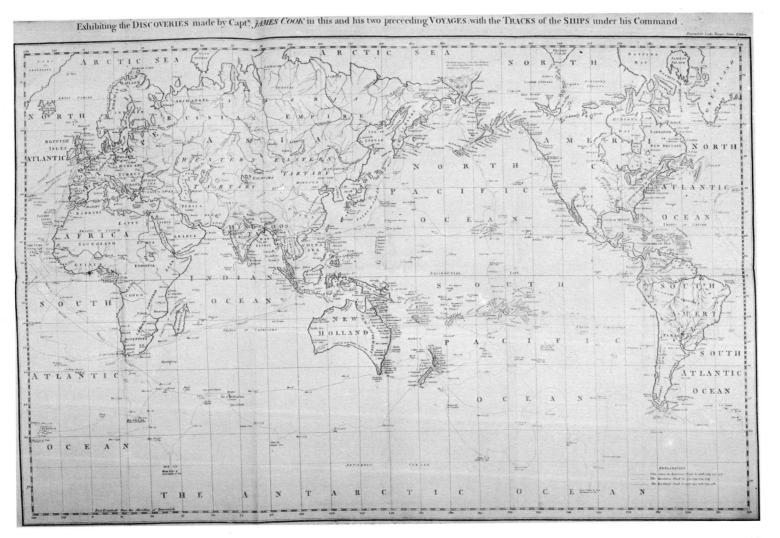

Exhibiting the DISCOVERIES made by Captⁿ. JAMES COOK in this and his two preceeding VOYAGES with the TRACKS of the SHIPS under his Command.

approval, to captains of the armed American ships, currently at war with Britain, not to obstruct the great English navigator in any way, but to afford all assistance. In the event, Congress did not support Franklin and ordered Cook's capture. The British Admiralty were so appreciative of Franklin's magnanimous act that, after the voyage, a copy of Cook's narrative was sent to Franklin and the Royal Society presented him with a gold medal struck to commemorate the voyage. Another remarkable recognition followed nine days after Franklin's exhortation. This was an order from the Secretary of the Marine Department of France to all commanders of ships at war with Britain, informing them of Cook's

> being on the point of returning to Europe and such discoveries being of general utility to all nations it is the King's pleasure that Captain Cook shall be treated as a commander of a neutral and allied power

and instructing all to refrain from hostilities despite the state of war between the countries. The King of France, like Franklin, was given the specially struck gold medal. But Cook had died two months earlier: the news had not reached Europe.

By the time he was killed, Cook had spent more time at sea and had covered greater distances than probably any other commander in international maritime history. He had secured more land and sea bases than any other navigator. His exploration of the Pacific did not start until he was forty years old. Cook's paramount bequest was cartographical accuracy for those who followed fast and furiously. None of the outlines of coasts were drawn with greater delicacy and accuracy than that of New Zealand. His map of it after the second voyage was remarkably close to the modern one, as was that of the Pacific coast of Australia. Those of the Islands proper were not quite so neat, but they were useful enough.

With the undisputed discovery of Hawaii by Europeans in 1778, the map of the Pacific was, except for small islands, practically as it is now. It had taken about 250 years to fill in the land on the ocean.

Chapter V

Later Explorers from the Western World

It was immediately after Cook's voyages, which overlapped its War of Independence, that America came into Pacific history, almost 200 years ago.

At the same time, a drama in several acts was to be a surprising, tragic, hopeful, comic, courageous, bizarre part of Pacific history. The mutiny itself in *Bounty* is so well known that only one or two facts need be mentioned: it will be more important to see how its consequences affected the Pacific.

Lieutenant William Bligh, of a good Cornish family, had been on two voyages with Cook, who never recorded any criticism of him. Bligh had the highest respect for Cook, not least for his techniques of discipline so fundamental for controlling the crews of the period. Selected by the Admiralty to collect breadfruit trees in Tahiti, Bligh was then to take them half-way round the world to St. Vincent and Jamaica, where breadfruit, a vegetable and not a fruit, would be the staple diet for slaves in the sugar plantations. The first officer on H.M.S. *Bounty*, Fletcher Christian, the brother of a Cambridge professor of law, had served under Bligh twice previously.

Bligh was intolerant of shortcomings but is judged to have punished them less severely than Cook would have done. He was certainly a nagger, but was less of a sadist than many contemporary commanders. He was considerate about the health of the crew, who were all volunteers—this was unusual, as warships often had to resort to press-gang methods. The destination of Tahiti was the attraction.

The voyage to Tahiti was, like all those of the period involving that length of time at sea, very wearing all round. But no one died. It was not surprising that the six months' sojourn on Tahiti in 1788–9 among such hospitable men and, in particular, women, should have unsettled everyone except Bligh who remained, as Cook would have done, aloof from human frailties under his eyes. Bligh was permissive during the unprecedented long stay; he thought that Tahiti was the finest island in the world. Christian formed an attachment with a Tahitian woman and many of the crew would have been happy to stay in surroundings which were so idyllic compared with the obnoxious ones on board and the unromantic ones at home. The loading of breadfruit trees complete and Bligh having given up his cabin entirely to the pots, *Bounty* sailed off towards the West Indies. It had not gone any further than the nearest group, Tonga, when no one is certain quite what happened or, more accurately, why it happened. For 28 April 1789, Bligh had this entry in his journal:

> Just before sunrise, Mr. Fletcher Christian, officer of the watch, Charles Churchill, master-at-arms, and several others came into my Cabbin while I was fast asleep.

He was given no time to dress. It was a gentlemanly mutiny except for a few oaths. Bligh, with eighteen others, was put on board *Bounty's* open launch (23 feet long, 2 feet deep, and 6 feet wide) and set adrift, with no firearms, but a mast, sails, spare canvas, saws, nails, four cases of water, bags of biscuit, twenty-six pieces of pork, two gourds of water, some bottles of wine, his spirit case, and captain's uniform. Just as the craft separated, Christian handed Bligh a book of nautical tables and his own sextant: surprising gifts from a mutineer whose future depended on his captain not outliving him. Two memorable voyages in different directions now occurred.

Bligh showed supreme navigational skill, audaciously setting course for Timor in the Portuguese East Indies, 3,618 nautical miles away. Hurrying in the overloaded boat, 7 inches above the sea, through the plethora of islands reputed to contain the most voracious cannibals, he was the real European discoverer of the Fiji archipelago. Spears from chasing canoes just fell short. Timor was miraculously reached in forty-one days. Bligh's exploit showed the practicability of very long voyages by Polynesians on generally larger, safer craft than his.

He and his crew (five of whom died beforehand) reached England on a Dutch ship to report the insurrection. At Timor, Bligh left descriptions of the mutineers, including this:

> Fletcher Christian, master's mate, aged 24 years, 5 ft. 9 inches, eyes blackish, of very dark complexion, dark brown hair, strong make; a star tattooed on his left breast; tattooed on his backside; his knees stand a little out, and he may be called rather bow legged. He is subject to violent perspirations, particularly on his hands, so that he soils anything he handles.

After seeing Bligh off, Christian immediately had the breadfruit trees thrown overboard and, to shouts of 'Huzzah for Otaheite', took *Bounty* with his twenty-four supporters off to Tubuai in the Australs. They could not decide where to settle. They stocked up in Tahiti, and the sixteen of the crew who chose to stay there were given a half-share of arms, wine, and clothing. Then *Bounty* left Tahiti, Christian and the minority admitting to themselves that it was inviting the inevitable catching-up of the law to remain. In *Bounty* were nine mutineers, six Polynesian men, nineteen women, and one child. With the exception of Christian's woman and that of Isaac Martin, the others thought they had only gone aboard for the night. When the ship was a mile out, one woman jumped overboard to swim ashore. *Bounty* went nine miles off Tahiti to Moorea and landed six women, who were described later by Martin's attachment as 'rather ancient'.

This was the second of the remarkable voyages as a consequence of the mutiny. There was in Bligh's library on board a book by Hawkesworth which contained a description of Carteret's discovery, twenty-three years earlier, of remote and presumably uninhabited Pitcairn's Island. Other islands were looked at. Pitcairn's Island took a lot of finding but, after four months and a zigzag transit of 3,000 miles, it was sighted on 12 January 1790. Christian went ashore with four others for two days. Alexander Smith related that Christian returned to the ship

> with a joyful expression as we had not seen on him for a long time past ...
> The island had exceeded his most sanguine hopes: in its fertility, its beauty, its temperate climate and, above all, in its now demonstrated inaccessibility.

There was no harbour and no lagoon: it was rugged and clandestine. Isolation was completed when Matthew Quintal burnt the ship without consulting the others.

Christian was reported by Smith to have been very morose soon after settling: he would spend whole days in a cave stocked with food in the most unapproachable part of the island. After four years, when one of the mutineers took the wife of one of the Tahitians, the servants had their own mutiny. They are believed to have shot Christian when he was in his yam plot (but Christian

Le Comte de Lapérouse (1741–88). His was the last of the Pacific expeditions to be lost with all men and ships. Two hundred and fifty years had passed since some pioneering Spanish expeditions in the Pacific had suffered a similar fate. (A recent theory by Robert Langdon has been researched to indicate that there were survivors from a caravel in de Loaysa's expedition in 1526, who circulated significant Basque culture and genetic influence throughout Eastern Polynesia.) This portrait of de Lapérouse was engraved by Delpech from a drawing by A. Maurin.

In the opening year of the French Revolution, de Lapérouse had turned down an application to travel on the expedition by a young military cadet named Napoléon Bonaparte.

may have previously escaped from the island: a former *Bounty* colleague was confident that he saw him in a Plymouth harbour alley twenty years after the mutiny). They then shot John Williams and the American, Isaac Martin; they chopped off John Mills' head and crushed that of William Brown. Smith had a musket ball through his throat but saved his life by offering money. Edward Young had been secreted away by women, while William McCoy and Matthew Quintal, said to be the roughest mutineers, had fled into the bush of the highest part of the island. McCoy made a plant for distilling spirits: inflamed with them, he threw himself off the top of the island. When Quintal tried to take another wife, Smith and Young killed him with an axe in, it was claimed, self-defence. A year later Young, the best educated of the refugees, died of asthma. This left only Smith (his face, much pitted with smallpox, identified by Bligh), the Tahitian servants, and the women. Smith and the women managed to kill the servants: now there were only himself, eight or nine women, and several small children left on the island. He became profoundly religious, presumably out of thanksgiving. He also reverted to his original name, John Adams.

It was not until 1808, eighteen years after the settlement, that an American whaling ship looking for seals found Pitcairn's Island. A canoe, with three occupants, approached the ship. One called out in rather hesitant English: 'What ship is that? Where do you come from?' The reply was given: 'It is the ship *Topaz* of the United States of America. I am Mayhew Folger, her master, an American.' The canoe spokesman asked: 'You are an American? You are from America? Where is America? Is it in Ireland?' The captain asked: 'Who are you?' From the canoe: 'We are Englishmen.' The captain: 'Where were you born?' Then followed this exchange. 'On that island which you see.' 'How then are you Englishmen if you were born on that island which the English do not own and never possessed?' 'We are English because our father was an Englishman.' 'Who is your father?' 'Aleck.' 'Who is Aleck?' 'Don't you know Aleck? Well, do you know Captain Bligh of the *Bounty*?' Then it all suddenly made sense to Folger. He told Adams of the victories of Howe, St. Vincent, Duncan (with whom Bligh, unknown to Adams, had been fighting), and Nelson. Adams listened attentively, and then rose from his seat, took off his hat, swung it three times round his head with three cheers, threw it on the ground in sailor style, and called out: 'Old England forever!'

Folger informed the British Admiralty of what he had found on his visit to Pitcairn's Island, but they were too preoccupied with the war against France to spare a ship to go after one mutineer. Adams lived on until 1829, when he died at the age of sixty-five. The population then numbered sixty. Adams's government of the island had been as stern and puritanical as would have satisfied the highest British authorities: they might almost have chosen him in London and sent him out for the job. Captain Frederick William Beechey, in H.M.S. *Blossom*, noted in 1825 that dancing was allowed only once a year—on the King of England's birthday. He found joy and frivolity, or any tendency towards it, wholly lacking. Unable to get to sleep for evening hymns, Beechey was woken early by morning hymns.

Pitcairn's map began to acquire islets, coves, points, and names heard today: Bitey-Bitey, Ed's Coc'nuts, Little George's Coc'nuts, Red Dirt, Headache, Ah Cut, Stinking Apple, Big Belly, Up ha Beans, Break im Hip, John Catch a Cow, and Oh Dear.

In the meanwhile, H.M.S. *Pandora* had been sent from England, under Captain Edward Edwards, in 1790 to search for the mutineers. He found on

Tahiti fourteen who had decided to make the island their home—two had been killed. Edwards shackled them in a cage on deck: 11 feet long, it was called Pandora's Box. The mutineers were chained to the deck. They had been wrested from the Tahitian women and children, who clung to them. One woman languished to death through grief. *Pandora* stayed six weeks in Tahiti and then was wrecked on the Great Barrier Reef. If one of the crew had not released the mutineers from the box, they would all have drowned. As it was, four did drown, together with thirty-one of *Pandora*'s crew. The surviving ten mutineers were taken to England for a court martial. Six were sentenced to death (of whom three were pardoned and three were hanged) and four were acquitted. One of the pardoned, a midshipman, was to become a senior captain.

During the court martial, Bligh was back in Tahiti uprooting 4,000 breadfruit trees. This time, no mutiny prevented his getting them to the Caribbean. Instead, it happened after delivery: the West Indian slaves flatly refused to like the new vegetable.

About a year before *Bounty*'s mutiny, another remarkable event had occurred which had historical consequences. On a number of exploring commissions, Comte Jean François Galaup de Lapérouse visited Easter Island, Hawaii, Samoa (Roggeveen and de Bougainville had sighted it, but de Lapérouse's men were the first Europeans to land), and Tonga. He then set off in 1788 from Botany Bay in Australia for the Solomons, but his two ships completely vanished.

More than three years later, Vice-Admiral Antoine Raymond-Joseph de Bruny, Chevalier d'Entrecasteaux, went in search of de Lapérouse in *La Recherche*, accompanied by *Espérance* under Huon de Kermadec. Despite their preoccupation with the effects of the revolution, the French National Assembly decided that a search had to be undertaken, as de Lapérouse's expedition was the intended counterblast to Cook's achievements. A Provençal, commemorated by the Quai d'Entrecasteaux at Papeete in Tahiti, by an eponymous group off New Caledonia, and by an obscure plaque in a broken-down wall near landing steps in the beautiful old port of Nice, d'Entrecasteaux opened up parts of darkest Melanesia.

He and de Kermadec, however, did not discover what had happened to de Lapérouse and, indeed, did not return to France themselves. D'Entrecasteaux died, aged fifty-four, of scurvy, dysentery, and exhaustion in 1793 near the Admiralty Islands. De Kermadec had died just before in New Caledonia. The expedition's command passed to Lieutenant Elizabeth-Paul-Edouard de Rossel who, on the return journey, was captured and imprisoned in England for thirteen years. He eventually became a rear-admiral and died in 1829.

The Tongans had shown their special form of humour to the naturalist on the d'Entrecasteaux expedition, Jacques-Julien de Houton de la Billardière, a pioneer in ethnology who lived to the age of ninety-nine. Having learnt their words for hundreds and thousands, he pressed them for the Tongan words for a million, 100 million, and 1,000 million. They gave him their most obscene words for these concepts. These terms were solemnly recorded in his published catalogue.

In 1791, the first American discoverer came into Pacific history. Joseph Ingraham was the first from the Western world to find three North Marquesan Islands. Immediately afterwards, in the same year, Etienne Nicolas Marchand, voyaging from Marseilles via Cape Horn, took possession of one of Ingraham's discoveries for France. The contact made by Marchand's men

Vice-Admiral Antoine de Bruny, Chevalier d'Entrecasteaux (1737–93), only narrowly missed finding the de Lapérouse wrecks. He identified, however, for the first time, the Solomon Islands over 200 years after their initial discovery by de Mendaña, and made findings of his own in Melanesia, including the individualistic Trobriands.

with the natives contrasted with earlier Spanish treatment, when Southern Marquesans had been fired upon for 'sport', as though they were dangerous beasts. Marchand recorded:

> Quite a number of women were seen in the islanders' canoes which paddled out to us from Santa Christina and Dominica, many of them young and attractive. Their glances and gestures left little doubt of their intentions, which were confirmed when the men with them acted as interpreters. The women were allowed on board, greeted by a crew upon whom six months of effort had not extinguished their natural feelings. After some hard bargaining the women did not hesitate to go below deck. The curtain must be drawn on what followed. Sufficient to say that at dusk the young Marquesan women reappeared on deck, laden with every imaginable trinket which they had obtained in exchange for the only commercial asset at their disposal.

Edmund Fanning, the first American circumnavigator, quickly followed Ingraham into the area. The first of his country to write an account of enduring value, his *Voyages Round the World* is of high quality throughout. His description of barter in the Marquesas in 1798 crystallizes what had been, and was to be, the experience of all early travellers:

> Iron, in any shape, they were most anxious to obtain: the beads and toys were held in little estimation: the small looking-glasses and bright buttons, when handed to them they would turn over and over, examining every part very carefully before they gave up their articles, then after pondering on the *pros* and *cons*, they would return the glasses, and point to the pieces of iron hoop.

A chief who had brought William Crook (a missionary left behind by another ship the year before—see p.124) out to Fanning showed an embarrassing interest in the ship's pistols. Fanning ingeniously

> told him they were *tabooed* by the superior chief in my country. The explanation was highly satisfactory, and the respect they have for anything *tabooed* appeared to close all his interest in anything about the pistols.

An interesting aspect of cross-culture was recorded when

> an old chief came on his own to the ship with a green branch and a small pig. When on deck he insisted on paying homage, but such I informed him, while raising him from this posture and handing him to a seat on the quarter-deck, was not the manner of salutation when friends meet friends in my country, and as such I hoped we had now come together, adding, that I myself was but a chief like himself; yet, said he, as I was given to understand through the interpretation of Mr. Crook, there is this difference, you came from the thunder in the clouds and are therefore more powerful than even my king.

The following sentence conveys some of the South Seas euphoria that touches all, even the most cynical of us:

> The fragrance of these green valleys, brought off to us by flaws of wind at intervals, was truly delicious, and a person that has at no time enjoyed it, can scarcely be able to conceive with what delight we received it, after having been for a length of time at sea; it actually seems to take hold upon the feelings in such a manner as to reanimate the whole system.

In the extreme loneliness of the mid-Pacific he found an island, of which he simply says: 'We gave it the name.' Discovered in 1798, Fanning's Island, no

Admiral Adam Johann von Krusenstern (1770–1846). On the pioneering Russian circumnavigation of 1803–6, he had two future celebrated explorers with him: Thaddeus von Bellingshausen, and a fifteen-year-old cadet, Otto von Kotzebue. All were Estonians, following the Basques of the early 1500s as pre-eminent Pacific seafaring leaders from small European regions.

more than 8 feet high, was to be a vital British servicing point in the Pacific cable between Canada and Australia via Fiji for nearly eighty years up to 1963.

The first nineteenth-century voyage in the Pacific was in a British ship, *Margaret*, on which John Turnbull was business manager. He reached Tahiti after being wrecked, and commented fully on this contact between European and Tahitian cultures:

He (King Otoo) remained a long time in silent admiration, gazing at everything he saw, with an air at once stupid and forbidding. The unusual stupidity of his look and manners at this his first interview was doubtless the effect of an immoderate use of the Ava, a plant which produces an intoxication similar to that of the opium amongst the Turks. In our subsequent conversations we found him lively and entertaining and fond of questioning us on such different subjects as might be supposed to interest a curious and therefore intelligent savage. Such were, in what direction lay Pretanee (their name for England), where Botany Bay, where the country of the Spaniards, where America, and Owhyee, which seemed to be the chief foreign countries of which he had any knowledge: whether in England there were many fine women; and whether muskets and gunpowder were in abundance in our country—the article of religion was not once touched upon, nor any inquiries whatever made relating to it. From the confined circle of their ideas, it was impossible to give them any conception of the arts, the manufactures, the wealth, or resources and enjoyments of Europeans: besides they are fully persuaded that their own is the finest country on the face of the globe, although they set so high a value on many of the tools, ins-

Above: Otto von Kotzebue (1788–1846) circumnavigated the world three times, twice in command of an expedition, before he was thirty-eight years old. *Rurik* and *Predpriate* were respectively the first and second ships of which he was captain.

Below: Von Kotzebue, exploring the Marshall Islands on his 1815–18 voyage, is carried ashore on natives' shoulders. His exploration of this obscure archipelago, named after Captain John Marshall of the *Scarborough*, who saw many atolls in 1788, was the most comprehensive in the first half of the last century.

Although the first European ship to find Penrhyn Island (now Tongareva, in the Cook Islands) was Captain William Sever's *Lady Penrhyn* in 1788, no other Europeans visited it until von Kotzebue's expedition in 1816. The natives were unafraid of the Europeans, but the melancholy of their song was noted. Louis Choris, the gifted painter, was aged twenty-one.

truments and other useful articles of Europeans as not infrequently to seek them at the hazard of their lives ... From their extreme desire to procure spirituous liquors, and other intoxicating substances, and the dreadful effects they produce on them, the introduction of liquors by Europeans or an acquaintance with the art of distilling, would infallibly be the destruction of the country ... Indeed there does not occur a greater difficulty for all European ships in the South Seas than that of keeping their crew together, such is the seduction of that life of indolence, and carelessness, which the several Islands hold out. The beauty of the country, particularly that of

Right: Von Kotzebue with Kamehameha I in 1816. The painter, Louis Choris, clutches his sketchbook in the foreground. The Russians were at first treated coolly by the Hawaiians, who feared abduction. Soon reassured, the latter proceeded to lavish attention on their visitors.

Opposite: James Cleveley's drawing (aquatinted by his brother) of Cook's death in 1779 at Kealakekua Bay, Hawaii, is clearer than those by others and is recognized as the most accurate version. He was present at the scene that morning.

Otaheite, and still more the facility with which the necessaries of life may be procured, are temptations too powerful to sailors exhausted with the fatigue of a long voyage. Add to this the women and the difficulty of retaining our seamen against so many attractions will excite no further surprise ...

The beginning of the nineteenth century saw a procession of explorers of four main nationalities: Russian, French, American, and British. The Dutch, Spanish, and Portuguese had by now deserted the ocean.

Right: Matavai, Tahiti, painted by Lejeune and T. A. de Chazal on Louis Isidore Duperrey's circumnavigation in *Coquille* in 1822–5. This expedition ranged far and wide, and discovered a Tuamotu island: by now there were   few islands left to find. A screw pine stands starkly on the right.

Russian interest was first shown in the Pacific in the voyage of 1803–6 of Rear-Admiral Adam Johann von Krusenstern in *Nadezhda*, with Captain Yury Fyodorovich Lisyansky in *Neva*. Von Krusenstern, an Estonian of noble origin, was accompanied by Georg Heinrich von Langsdorff, a German surgeon and naturalist, who wrote an excellent account. In the Marquesas, they had the unusual experience of being greeted by two Europeans who were tattooed and dressed as Marquesans. One was Edward Robarts, an Englishman, the other was Jean-Baptiste Cabri, from Bordeaux. They had been deadly enemies for years on the islands but von Krusenstern managed to reconcile them. Both had somewhat improbable futures. Cabri, stranded on *Nadezhda* when a gale blew up, was taken on to Siberia: he became a teacher of swimming to the corps of marine cadets at Kronstadt. Robarts ended his career as a police constable in Calcutta.

Von Langsdorff made this observation on Marquesan women:

But however prodigal of their favours and however ready to follow a sailor that held out a hand to them, the female sex were still not without a certain

De Lapérouse (1741–88) receiving orders from King Louis XVI in 1785, painted by Nicolas André Monsiau. The disappearance of ships was not uncommon in those days, but the search for, and the finding of, those of de Lapérouse had unusual consequences.

degree of modesty. They seemed to be considerably distressed when they had lost their aprons, and crept about with their hands in the position of the Medicean Venus in attitudes which presented a beautiful spectacle to the philosophic observer. Those who had not been deserted by their garments were particularly anxious to adjust them properly.

The eternal magic of the mirror drew comment:

> A looking glass was no less an object of their astonishment. It was not improbable that some of them had already seen such a thing, yet they all looked behind the glass to discover the cause of this wonderful appearance.

Von Krusenstern changed the name of the Hervey Islands, so called by Cook, to that of the Cook Islands. His expedition was to have been the first Russian circumnavigation. But on the return home, Lisyansky missed out a call at St. Helena, which had been planned with von Krusenstern: this break in the agreement enabled Lisyansky to be a fortnight ahead of von Krusenstern on his return to Kronstadt, and therefore technically to be the first Russian circumnavigator.

Four great Russian voyages followed. Two of these were by another Estonian, Otto von Kotzebue, who made circumnavigations in 1815–8 and 1825–6. He was twenty-seven years old in 1815. Striking pictorial and ethnographical work on the Islands was carried out, but von Kotzebue was disillusioned to find how far Tahiti was removed from de Bougainville's

Von Bellingshausen and his officers, in full uniform despite the tropical heat, share breakfast ashore with the King of Tahiti. Paul Mikhailov depicted the scene in 1820. On another occasion, von Bellingshausen reported: 'I invited them all to come into the cabin, and they sat down on the divans. The King repeated "Russian, Russian" several times, then pronounced the name "Alexander" and, finally having said "Napoleon", he laughed. He probably wished us to understand that he knew something of European affairs.'

paradise. Hypocrisy, puritanism, bigotry, and pettiness were too prominent.

From 1819 to 1821, yet a third Estonian, Admiral Baron Thaddeus (or, variously, Fabian Gottlieb) von Bellingshausen, combined remarkable Pacific exploration, like Cook before him and Dumont d'Urville and Wilkes after him, with significant Antarctic surveying. One of von Kotzebue's ships, *Seniavin*, also circumnavigated the world again, this time in 1826–9, under Admiral Fyodor Petrovitch Lütke, a native of St. Petersburg. Exploring the Carolines, Solomons, New Zealand, and New Hanover, a feature of Lütke's voyage was the outstanding friendliness shown to the Islanders and reciprocated by them. This was particularly evident in the Carolines, not least in the case of the women.

The great distances that their ships had to travel from their European ports to the Pacific led the Russians to conclude that they could not start any colonization—or, if they did, that they could not maintain it. This is the reason why, from then until the 1970s, Russian maritime activity in the Pacific was largely confined to whaling ships. It is why Russia gave up competing with France, Britain, and America for any settlement on Pacific Islands, for which the powerful voyages under von Krusenstern, von Kotzebue, von Bellingshausen, and Lütke had put them in a good position.

National characteristics were reflected in the names given to Pacific Islands. Spanish names, pietestic but euphonious, have endured, particularly in the

Above: Admiral Count Fyodor Petrovitch Lütke (1797–1882). Living to the age of eighty-five, he was one of the longest-surviving Pacific discoverer-explorers.

Above: Baron Friedrich de Kittlitz illustrates here the Russians and Islanders setting off together on an excursion, during the visit to the Carolines of Admiral Lütke's expedition of 1826–9.

Opposite: On Lütke's circumnavigation of 1826–9, there was much fraternization with the natives, as can be seen in this drawing by Aleksandr Postels of a Carolines' village.

Below: Admiral Baron Thaddeus von Bellingshausen (1779–1852) looked more like a suave ambassador than an intrepid explorer on *Vostok*. This portrait of von Bellingshausen was drawn by Paul Mikhailov in about 1820.

Solomons. The Dutch were laconic and blunt: Schouten and Le Maire saw dogs and flies in the Tuamotus and were attacked in Tonga, so they called the islands Dogs, Flies, and Traitors. Roggeveen named others Deceptive, Pernicious, Disastrous, and More Trouble. The English varied. Carteret fawningly honoured titles (Bishop of Osnaburgh's, Earl of Winchelsea's, Duke of Gloucester's) and institutions (Admiralty), but he did also immortalize a midshipman (Pitcairn's). Cook was uninspired (New Caledonia, New Hebrides) and misled (Friendly Islands, with chiefs plotting his assassination, and Savage Island, to the chagrin of the amicable Niue Islanders). Despite being the first to see so much, Bligh almost overlooked naming anything—merely a New Hebrides archipelago after Banks, a few islets, a shoal, a reef, and some boat passages. The French went in for a little eponomy (Bougainville, D'Entrecasteaux, Kermadec, and Marchand), as did the American, Fanning, who, the day after he discovered Fanning Island, found another, which he called Washington after his president.

If their nomenclature had survived, the Russians could have made a Pacific map read like a Tolstoy novel. Von Kotzebue started gently with Eschscholtz (later Bikini), Tschitschagoff, and Rimski-Korsakoff in the Marshalls. Von Bellingshausen believed abbreviations unseemly as he proceeded through two Tuamotu Islands a day: Count Wittgenstein, Admiral Chichagov, Graf Miloradovich, Prince Volkhonski, Lieutenant-General Yermolov, General Graf Osten-Sacken, Grand Duke Alexander Nikolaievich, Field Marshal Prince Barclay de Tolly and, triumphantly, Prince Golentischev-Kutuzov-Smolenski. When the last became Makemo and the others reverted to indigenous names, cartographers were not the only people to be relieved.

In 1817–20 there was the first circumnavigation by a man and wife, both upper-class French. Louis Claude de Saulces de Freycinet dressed his wife, Rose Marie, aged twenty-two, in sailor's clothes: out at sea she resumed her own identity and clothes, astonishing the crew, and kept a diary which she illustrated neatly. Jean René Constant Quoy, the surgeon-naturalist with them, found a visit to the various queens of Kamehameha I in Hawaii a gripping experience:

> It was truly a strange spectacle to see in a small apartment eight or ten great human bodies, semi-naked, the least of which weighed at least three hundred pounds, lying down flat on their stomachs. Not without difficulty we found a place where we too could lie down so as to conform to custom . . . Most of these female colossi which one could say seemed to exist merely to eat and sleep, stared at us in a dull-witted manner.

Americans were at this time understandably starting a permanent interest in Oceania, deeper than the whaling and sealing ventures from New England. It was an American, Benjamin Morrell, who, between 1822 and 1831, had more than the usual range of experience of Pacific explorers. His narrative contains hyperbole but also a freshness and vigour that was to be maintained in American travel writing until the present day. Parts of it were put into fiction by Edgar Allan Poe. In the course of three Pacific voyages, Morrell makes a strong refutation of the usual reason given for cannibalism, which will be discussed later (see p.124). His observation is important as coming from one so close in time to the custom:

> Maoris devour the bodies of their enemies; but not from a physical appetite or relish for human flesh, as many suppose. Such an appetite or relish was never yet experienced by any cannibal that ever existed. The horrid rite is performed merely to appease a moral appetite, far more voracious than that of hunger. It is done to express the extent of their hate, their vengeance or rather an insatiable malice that would pursue its victim beyond the confines of the grave; for it is an article of their religious creed that the soul of a man thus devoured is doomed to eternal fire. On this subject I speak from personal observation and experience; for I have had much to do with cannibals as will appear in the sequel. I have been present when the New Zealanders have celebrated their victories on the field of battle, and witnessed their disgusting banquet, at which their own stomachs revolted with every symptom of loathing, often attended with reaching, and sometimes vomiting. I have witnessed this horrible scene several times with the same irresistible inference; otherwise I should not thus hazard so bold a contradiction of popular opinion.

Near Bougainville Strait and Ontong Java atoll off the Solomons, Morrell had two strongly contrasting experiences. First, all went very well:

> Having finished our repast, I presented the Queen with a pair of scissors, a small knife, and a few beads, which her majesty most graciously deigned to accept, and appeared to be in an ecstasy of delight, especially with the scissors, of which I quickly taught her the use. The knife and the scissors excited universal admiration, which was quite natural in a group of beings who had never before seen a piece of iron or steel, and whose best tools were made of a shell or a piece of stone. The sensation which these treasures produced having somewhat subsided, their curiosity was again directed to

my goodly person. No one, however, with the exception of King Nero himself, ventured to touch me; and he performed the feat with as much tremulous caution as the novice evinces when for the first time he applies a lighted match to the priming of a cannon. Having satisfied himself that I was constructed of bones and flesh, like his own race, and that the white paint could not be rubbed off my ebony skin, he turned to his chiefs and councellors in great astonishment, and harangued them at some length, on so wonderful a phenomenon. The whole company listened to him with less reverence than amazement—remaining as motionless as statues, with straining eyes and gaping mouths. His majesty then desired me to open my vest and shirt-bosom, that he might try the same test on the colour of my body; but the result only increased his astonishment. Every one of the men, by turns, now approached, and satisfied themselves that my skin was neither a white well-fitted garment, nor its colour the effect of artificial means. But not one of the females would venture to touch my bosom, and I was inclined to attribute this shyness more to modesty and feminine delicacy than to personal fear.

Jules Sébastien César Dumont d'Urville (1790–1842), depicted by A. Maurin in 1833. So square a jaw must surely denote an infinite stubbornness. His two expeditions (in 1826–9 and 1837–40) came closer than any others to those of Cook in thoroughness and were only approached in contemporary scientific merit by that of Charles Wilkes in 1838–42.

Then, after selecting a spot for curing bêche-de-mer (sea-slugs—see p. 110) and after twenty-eight men had landed to build the necessary hut, with the agreement of the leaders and people, all again went well until—and it is a familiar story of Pacific-Western intercourse—boats were stolen. In the confrontation, as many as fifty arrows were fired into one of Morrell's men. Morrell recorded:

> I took a telescope and directed my attention to the island. Fires were kindled on the beach, in every direction, among the dead bodies of my unfortunate crew, from which those hell-hounds were cutting the flesh, and roasting it in the fire; and then, with savage ferocity, tearing it to pieces with their teeth, while from the half-cooked fragment the fresh blood was running down their ebony chins.

Morrell left with alacrity what were named the Massacre Islands—twelve officers and men had been killed. But he decided to return three months later:

> A fleet came out immediately and was fired on. It was scattered completely. A small canoe was seen later. A voice from it was heard: 'It is I—old Shaw, come back again ... ' His wasted, emaciated form was lacerated with wounds; his face, deprived of the bushy whiskers which formerly shaded his cheeks, was bedaubed with paint. In short, he was the spectre of wretchedness, with the exception of his eyes, which were burning with unspeakable joy.

Leonard Shaw had been left for dead three months earlier. He had been about to surrender when he saw his colleagues being roasted. He hid for a fortnight before he was caught and clubbed. His broken skull was filled with sand and he lived precariously, having to trap rats to survive. When Morrell's ship returned, Shaw persuaded the head man that if he went out to it he could stop the bombardment of the village. In the end the treacherous leader was killed, Shaw was saved, and the skulls of five colleagues retrieved and buried.

Abandoning the Massacre Islands, Morrell visited the Solomon Islands, New Britain, New Ireland, and New Guinea with extreme vigilance. Making one of the longest sequences of attempts at contact with deepest Melanesia, he was disillusioned to find, apart from in New Ireland, increasing inhospitality. New Guineans are described by him with great strength of feeling:

Many of them came off to the vessel in several large canoes, with the usual articles of barter, coconuts, breadfruit, plantains, and shells. They were negroes of a large stature, and some of them appeared to possess considerable acuteness. Their features are coarse and ugly, and the expression of their countenance is a mixture of ferocity, malevolence and crafty treachery. In one word, their visage is a true index of their character, and it bears the most savage, inhuman bloodthirsty appearance I have ever met with, the cannibals of the Massacre Islands when most infuriated not excepted. Their complexion is of the negro black; hair short, curled, and crisp; flat nose, thick lips, and monkey chin. But they have one redeeming feature, and that is the forehead, which is high, prominent, and smooth, indicating intellectual capacity, penetration, and decision, in a much greater degree than is ever seen in the African.

To Morrell, man was vile, the country 'beautiful beyond description'. The birds of paradise that he saw could not have represented to him a greater contrast to the human inhabitants.

Although Morrell seemed only to meet the wildest Pacific Islanders, those who represented their countries on the other side of the world were more civilized. Indeed, the King and Queen of Hawaii made such a good impression when they visited London in 1824 that they were fêted wherever they went. But they both died of measles while they were there. The British Government arranged for H.M.S. *Blonde* to take their bodies back to Honolulu. The ship went round Cape Horn, stocked up with land tortoises for provisions at the

One of Dumont d'Urville's ships, *L'Astrolabe* (formerly Duperrey's *La Coquille*—see p.190) in 1827 on the reef at Tongatabu, now Tonga's capital. Some Tongans keenly scrutinize the flotsam, while others sit with legs crossed, their backs turned to the dramatic episode, which *L'Astrolabe* survived, and which was recorded by Louis Auguste de Sainson, a former Admiralty clerk.

Galapagos Islands, and was given an unforgettable reception by the Hawaiians for what Sir Peter Buck has described as 'one of the most generous acts that one country has ever extended to another'. It cannot be seen how the British could have acted otherwise. In Hawaii, an old man was pointed out to *Blonde*'s officers as having eaten Cook's heart, which was hanging up in the temple in preparation for ritual burning, mistakenly 'supposing it that of a Pig'.

A secret instruction to the commander of *Blonde*, Lord Byron (cousin of the poet), was that he should establish sovereign rights over Hawaii if it was necessary to forestall any other nation having the same intention. Britain considered that it had special rights in Hawaii. Byron was authorized, if pressed, to set up only a protectorate. However, he judged that no British action was merited.

It was about this time, 1826, that the puzzle of the disappearance of de Lapérouse thirty-eight years earlier was solved. The search for him had cost the lives of d'Entrecasteaux and de Kermadec. The solution was fortuitous. An enormous, red-haired Irish sandalwood trader, Peter Dillon, once a beachcomber in Fiji, visited a Prussian, Martin Bushart (or Buchert), whom he had earlier taken from Fiji for safety to the Solomons. There, he noticed a French

A French officer (possibly Dumont d'Urville) is greeted with a gift by a Tongan chief and his wife and with reservations by a local dog. *Kava* awaits him in the house in this domestic scene in the Vava'u group, drawn by Louis Le Breton, the surgeon on the 1837–40 expedition of Dumont-d'Urville. Tongan appetites unfortunately could not long resist the sheep, given to them by the visitors for the purpose of breeding rather than of feasting.

silver sword-guard and other European articles ascertained to have come from the wrecks of two ships in the Santa Cruz group. Taken to Paris, these objects were proved to have come from de Lapérouse's ships: Dillon was given a high honour and an annuity by the King of France.

In the first half of the nineteenth century, exploring expeditions were reaching a new level of scientific sophistication, whether they were French, Russian, American, or British. This was pre-eminently true of those led by Dumont d'Urville and Wilkes. How fortunate it was that this crucial period, just before Western infiltration began on an appreciable scale, was captured by capable and imaginative artists. Rear-Admiral Jules Sébastien César Dumont d'Urville was first sent to the Pacific to verify de Lapérouse relics under the water in the Santa Cruz group. He made two great expeditions in 1826–9 and 1837–40: the text of his accounts and those of collaborators show how science was gaining ground. The hydrography that he supervised complemented Cook's work. The scientific material—on mineralogy, flora, languages, and ethnology—was the best collection up to the 1840s. It was the misfortune of Dumont d'Urville to be one of the first people to be killed in a railway accident in 1842: a curious end to a life that was picturesque from his twenties, when he secured the Venus de Milo for France.

Following close on Dumont d'Urville's last expedition was another in the most ambitious category. After Cook's voyages, it had been recognized in America that the Pacific was the most promising area for scientific exploration. Specified purposes of the United States Exploring Expedition of 1838–42 were:

(1) to note accurately the position of islands and harbours and rocks along the paths of United States whalers and traders (2) to release from the islands unhappy captives left there by wrecks (3) to suppress misconduct on American vessels, prevent mutiny and desertions and endeavour to end cruelty, licentiousness and extortion in the islands (4) to look for land in the South Polar Seas (5) to collect specimens and facts to subserve the advancement of science in natural history, etc.

Opposite: These Hawaiian chiefs appear rather somnolent in their conference with Rear-Admiral Abel Aubert du Petit-Thouars (see p. 170), illustrated in 1838 by Louis Jules Masselot.

Below: Charles Wilkes (1798–1877), engraved by A. H. Ritchie. Disenchanted with missionaries' sermons, some of his officers thought that chickens, if introduced early and in great quantities, would eliminate the need for cannibalism and hence for the presence of missionaries.

The account and considerable scientific reports following this voyage form perhaps the peak of American expedition reporting. It was not, however, a happy voyage. For America's first national expedition it was considered desirable to have a naval officer and naval ships. The command was finally given to Charles Wilkes, in appearance Lincolnesque but actually, as events showed, lacking in resolution as well as in seamanship. From the first day of sailing to the last berthing in America, his fellow commanders expected him to incur a collision or lose a vessel. This was both the largest fleet—six ships—sent out up to that date by America and the last totally under sail. Despite Wilkes' deficiencies, it was largely through his persistence, a quality that he possessed in abundance, that the scientists' reports were published at all or at least without prodigious delays. His narrative is full of fresh observation. It was not new to notice:

> Musquitoes are exceedingly annoying to strangers, but I did not remember that natives were troubled by them. Their bodies being well-oiled is a great preservation against the bites of these insects.

But, writing of an Erromangan met in Tonga, Wilkes found a new, if uncommon, antidote:

Opposite: As Dumont d'Urville's expedition was leaving Tongatabu in 1827, natives seized some sailors, whom they wanted to remain. De Sainson shows here that Dumont d'Urville felt obliged to oppose this whim of the Friendly Islanders.

81

Among other peculiarities of this native of Erromanga it was stated by the low whites that instead of wrapping himself up in tapa at night like the Tongese he was in the habit of burying himself in the sand to avoid the mosquitoes.

Men from H.M.S. *Rattlesnake*, under Captain Owen Stanley (1811–50), meeting natives at Redscar Bay, Papua, depicted by T. H. Huxley in 1848.

Going to Fiji from Tonga, most of the officers drew up wills: they had learnt, like Cook in Tonga, of Fiji's fierce reception of Westerners.

In Tahiti, two missionaries admitted to the expedition that their success in evangelizing had been exaggerated. Some regard for private possessions had been taught to the natives; worship of idols and human sacrifices had been suppressed; and a secret society practising infanticide had been eliminated. But the missionaries in 1840 were disappointed: the Tahitians seemed to have retained their own special sense of morals and were unaffected by Christian ethics. Wilkes persuaded Queen Pomare IV of Tahiti to have a prison and police. The Calabooza Beretanee on Broom Road had no sooner been established than it received its most celebrated inmate: Herman Melville, the writer (see p.201).

From the mid-nineteenth century on, the remaining story of exploration is of deepest Melanesia. New Guinea was the last to have its Western explorers, and they were mostly from Britain and Australia. Expedition after expedition found the inhabitants suspicious of the Europeans, and serious observation was much delayed. For no apparent reason, however, there were exceptions, and some Islanders showed no apprehension: the women of Brumer Island on the southeast coast of New Guinea were only too keen to show their tattooing. John MacGillivray on H.M.S. *Rattlesnake* (1846–50), however, wrote that:

> None of the women that came on board possessed even a moderate share of beauty (according to our notions) but many of the young men and boys were strikingly handsome. Women appeared to be treated as equals and to exercise considerable influence over the men.

In the same region, Captain John Moresby in H.M.S. *Basilisk* (1870–4) at least achieved a minor triumph of nomenclature:

> Facing each other boldly were two peaks, far above all compeers, 11,400 feet high. Their relative position and their greatness suggested irresistibly the names I gave them—Mounts Gladstone and Disraeli. In connection with this, I wrote to each of those eminent men for permission to confirm my action, and, in due course I received the following replies . . .

The assistant surgeon on H.M.S. *Rattlesnake*, Thomas Henry Huxley (1825–95), grandfather of Aldous and Julian, was also a competent artist. He drew in 1848 this picture of the slashing of a few liana creepers among tree ferns, entitled *Cutting through the 'Scrub' at Rockingham Bay, New Guinea*. Huxley became an eminent biologist and president of the Royal Society.

Gladstone wrote:

HAWARDEN CASTLE,
August 12th, 1874.

Sir, I have the honour to acknowledge the receipt of your letter of June 24, and to return my best thanks for the compliment you have paid me, little deserved as it is, in naming after me the highest peak of the Finisterre Range in New Guinea.

Allow me to subscribe myself, sir,
Your most faithful servant,
W. E. GLADSTONE.

Captain Moresby, R.N.,
H.M.S. Basilisk.

10, DOWNING STREET,
August 17, 1874

DEAR SIR,

Allow me to acknowledge the compliment you have paid me by planting my name on the north-east coast of New Guinea, and in selecting a god-father so distinguished for the peak which faces Mount Disraeli.

I am, dear sir,
Faithfully yours,
BEN: DISRAELI

Alfred T. Agate, on Wilkes' expedition of 1838–42, captured this not infrequent feature of explorer/Islander contact at Utiroa, a village on Tabiteuea in the Gilberts. A native has been noticed by him surreptitiously hooking some irresistible object away from sailors, off their guard as they enjoy the delectable view.

84

Later Disraeli remarked: 'I hope we shall agree better in New Guinea than we do in the House of Commons.'

In 1858, Alfred Russel Wallace, primarily an ornithologist, was the first European to reside in New Guinea, where he noted much besides birds: perhaps his greatest reward was to see the breathtaking profusion of male birds of paradise, of which the finest variety was known as the King of Saxony.

An intrepid Italian bird collector, Luigi Maria d'Albertis, reached the centre of New Guinea in 1876 and also scored an artistic triumph:

> To keep them in good humour and amuse them, I sang for them in the evening some airs from Italian operas, and collected the whole population in front of my marea. My success was immense. I was applauded, and compelled to repeat some of the pieces which pleased them most. The most celebrated of our artists would have envied me at that moment. There is no doubt that the natives love and appreciate music; their attention proves this. The women especially seemed enchanted! I ought to confess, however, that I should not venture to sing in any other country than New Guinea . . .

He used dynamite to defend his camp on Yule Island from all approaches and wore a light coat-of-mail under his cotton jacket, challenging natives to throw spears at him. It was hardly surprising that in native eyes he possessed supernatural powers. D'Albertis lived alone and was unharmed, but his Chinese

Luigi Maria d'Albertis (1841–1901) eagerly explores the Fly River, New Guinea, in a steam launch.

crew were mostly devoured by headhunters of the Middle and Upper Fly River. This did not dishearten him. Out of sheer verve he fired off rockets of gunpowder, phosphorus, and magnesium. He died in Rome aged sixty, after he had built a Papuan-style house in the Pontine Marshes. His fascinating work, published in 1880, was entitled *New Guinea: What I Did and What I Saw*.

In the estimation of many, the finest scientific expedition, certainly so far as the Pacific was concerned, took place in the last quarter of the nineteenth century. At the end of 1872, *Challenger*, as large as 2,300 tons, principally a sailing ship but nominally a steam corvette, left England with six scientists on board. They made a detailed survey of Tonga, Fiji, New Guinea, Hawaii, Tahiti, and Juan Fernandez, and returned in 1876. In addition to the monumental official report in fifty-six volumes—the most complete scientific record of the ocean ever made—which took thirteen years to publish, at least six other accounts were written. One of these, by Lord George Campbell, noted in the Admiralty Islands:

> Waiting by myself on the shore for the rest to come down, I was minutely examined by some women, in which I lent them my very best aid. They stooped and felt my boots, so I put my foot up on a canoe. From the boots they turned their attention to my socks, which they pulled down, and were much puzzled and delighted with my white skin. I firmly believe they thought our hands and faces painted; my arms too they thought much too nice. In short they admired me immensely and I felt much flattered.

But then again presents were given and more trouble broke out:

> This is always the way: give them nothing and they could not be more civil and pleasant; open a bag of trade-gear, and the demon of jealousy makes them savages at once.

He was not impressed by Hawaii:

> I must again say that to me there is nothing South Sea Islandish about the Sandwich Islands—nothing in the scenery, vegetation or birds, nothing in the natives, chiefly because, I fancy, they are universally dressed and uglyly dressed—the men in trousers and the women in shapeless sacks. To this dressing is ascribed in great part the rapid decrease of the population—colds and consumption following on intermittent nakedness one moment, on heavy clothing the next.

On the voyage much emphasis was placed on the measuring of oceanic depths. The deepest recorded was 26,700 feet, not quite equal to the height of Everest above sea level. When the last volume of the scientific results of this remarkable exploring voyage was published two years before the twentieth century, there was little left to be known about the Pacific, land or ocean; apart from of course New Guinea, which was still barely touched upon.

The years crept on and New Guinea imperceptibly opened up. The exploration, however, was by no means complete by the beginning of the First World War.

Chapter VI

Castaways and Beachcombers

The first Europeans actually to stay in the Islands were perhaps equally divided between those who wanted to and those who had no choice. There were also some who had not elected to stay but had changed their minds—and vice versa. Seas full of uncharted reefs and vessels extremely difficult to manoeuvre contributed to quite a large number of men being cast away on islands. Survival depended largely on whether the island concerned was in Polynesia, Micronesia, or Melanesia. Did the island have food and water? Were the inhabitants cannibals? There was also the vital question of whether it was an island with a recognized policy of killing those discovered on the shore 'with salt-water in their eyes'.

This policy was dictated mostly by cannibal urges but was possibly also a kind of quarantine regulation. It may have been to guard the people from introduced diseases or other menaces to the existing way of life, although it is unlikely that they thought as scientifically as this. Sailors knew that their only hope of survival in some groups was immediately to try and make themselves objects to be tolerated rather than destroyed. Rapidly they would, if they could, demonstrate some aspect of European culture lacking in native society but likely to appeal to the Islanders. On the beaches, they would perform diverting tricks with mirrors and matches, which the natives had never seen before. Watches also held sufficient fascination for the Islanders to make them stay execution. Above all, if the powder was dry, the discharge of a musket was the prime *coup-de-théâtre*. If they could save their lives by being of practical use, the castaways would then endure an unchosen way of life in the hope that a ship would turn up one day and rescue them. On the rare occasions that this happened, they then had the problem of how to escape from a society in which,

Europeans were greatly attracted to the Marquesas Islands. Fraternization, the tattoo fashion, and, inevitably, pigs make up this scene, recorded by Romuald Georges Ménard during du Petit-Thouars' expedition of 1836–9 (see p.170).

with their introduction of iron and primitive machines, they had made themselves indispensable. A few, however, were so enticed by the conditions in the Islands, which contrasted sharply with eighteenth-century shipboard life, that they merged themselves totally into their new part of the world.

Thoughts along these lines were the motives of the other type of pioneering residents in the South Seas. It did not always require a shipwreck to change entirely a man's way of life. After long, arduous voyaging away from homes, to which often for one reason or another they had no wish to return, the sweet smell of earth and vegetation and the visits of attractive-looking people were sufficiently heady for them to decide to exchange the sea for land. Logs of hundreds of ships show in copper-plate script numerous entries of this kind: '————Bay. September 25 1801. Stephen Marlow broke ship'. There might have been a search for the defaulter, depending on the territory that he had chosen to hide in. Seldom was he caught: the penalty was a great incentive to conceal oneself securely until the ship had sailed off. Like the castaway, the prospective beachcomber's chance of survival depended on whether he was in Melanesia, Micronesia, or Polynesia.

Almost anywhere in Polynesia seemed irresistible to the deserter. The lush greenness promised an easy life. There never seemed to be anything but paradisial qualities about the Polynesian people of whatever group. Many of their islands, other than atolls, were of such a size as to allow the beachcomber some anonymity or individuality of existence.

For many years, Samoa offered little encouragement to beachcombers, although this incident in early Samoan-European contact illustrated by Duché de Vancy in 1787, was not often repeated. At Tutuila, de Lapérouse (see p.66) initially noted that: 'The manners of the women were soft, lively and engaging, and the men were very handsome. The wood pigeons will eat only out of human hands.' Then his second-in-command, Vicomte Chevalier Fleuriot de Langle, was massacred along with eleven others. Magnanimously refraining from taking reprisals, de Lapérouse hastened to escape from 'this lair more hideous through the cruelty of its inhabitants than the dens of lions and tigers.'

Much of Micronesia, with its myriads of atolls, held some inhibitions. The islands' very minuteness, and their shortage of vegetation, put off some who had seen more promising areas. But Micronesian people were more pleasing than those whom sailors had seen in most of Melanesia. Beachcombers were understandably wary of committing themselves to existence in or near Melanesian groups, with their inhabitants' predilection for cannibalism and an aggressive lifestyle.

It was inevitable that mistakes should be made. Some were fatal, others were regretted. After their experiment, the beachcombers *manqué* would be watching as anxiously as castaways for masts to come round the bays in the hope that a captain would take them away.

What they thought and felt, what they saw and experienced, has been recorded in a rich collection of narratives by castaways and beachcombers. Some of them made instant impressions in Europe and America when they were published. Others are still coming to light slowly as research on the Pacific intensifies. Many are surprisingly well written when it is considered that in almost every case, certainly of a beachcomber, the author was not of the officer class and barely literate.

Of course there was no class discrimination in one's chances of being thrown by shipwreck on to an island: castaways' records are therefore more of a mixture of the literate and less literate than are those of beachcombers. Nevertheless, the natural material available to beachcombers in the form of remarkable customs and ceremonies observed (if not always understood), the flora and fauna noted (if not always accurately), and the prosaic matter of daily life, combines to convey the feel of the Islands in a way that very few transitory explorers could hope to achieve. Some of the journals and diaries have had to be edited by men skilled in writing and, consequently, there is a great deal of unevenness. But where one narrative might gain enormously by having been recounted to a first-class writer, as the castaway, William Mariner, did to Dr. John Martin, another, like William Lockerby's account, is just as effective in its stark simplicity. Most of the famous castaways and beachcombers are indeed known by their own edited or unedited descriptions. But there are a few who did not leave records and are known only from mentions by visitors to the Islands.

Sometimes a beachcomber would alter his status by acquiring some land on which to plant a crop and sell the produce, thereby becoming a pioneering trader. But the terms beachcomber and trader were sometimes merged by early commentators. In his introduction to F. W. Christian's *The Caroline Islands*, Admiral (later Sir) Cyprian Bridge had this to say:

> Those who believe that the 'beachcomber' or the copra trader of the South Seas is necessarily a scoundrel err grievously. There is proportionately to their numbers, as much honesty, sobriety and energy as amongst any other body of business men. They have their black sheep, no doubt: let the community which has none throw at them the first stone!

The first Europeans to settle among Samoans, who called them Papalagi (those who broke through from the horizon), were of the worst possible kind. They were criminals being transported from Botany Bay to Norfolk Island in shackles, which they broke: they murdered the captain and all but two of the crew of their prison ship. It is not clear why the cautious Samoans allowed the seven criminals and two crew to land. But land they did, and the ship was left to founder. Ashore, one of them, Young, killed two of his companions and was in

Formidable equally against interlopers, rival tribes, prospective beachcombers, and enforced castaways, the Gilbertese were more than capable of defending their vulnerable atolls. Here is an Islander dressed for battle in coconut-fibre armour, with a sharks' teeth spear and a porcupine-like helmet of fish skin. These Micronesians were belligerent and inclined to melancholy. In contrast, their Polynesian neighbours, the Ellice Islanders, were easy-going and effervescent.

turn killed by The Blacksmith, who was himself then murdered by Tom the Devil. Tom the Devil ingratiated himself with a chief but was eventually killed by other Samoans. Two of the remaining beachcombers were of slightly better quality. Tom Franklin took the line of claiming to be the brother of the King of England. Big-Legged Jimmy established a special kind of church for himself and his companions. It preached polygamy and had sea shanties for hymns. He had disappeared by the time Rev. John Williams of the London Missionary Society arrived. Although he had been an ironmonger in England, Williams would not have found Big-Legged Jimmy a compatible spirit.

One of the most thorough and entertaining descriptions of a stay (enforced in his case) relates to Tonga. It is that of William Mariner as recorded by Dr. John Martin. A captain's clerk from London with a name that could scarcely have been more apposite, Mariner left Gravesend in 1805 on an English privateer, *Port-au-Prince*, in search of adventure which, in the terms of the commission to the captain, was to molest French ships. They put in at a Tongan island for repairs in 1806. This was just the opportunity that an ambitious chief, Finau Ulukalala II, needed to strengthen his aim of making himself paramount. Capturing the ship, Finau had many of the crew clubbed to death, but he spared Mariner and arranged for one of his wives to adopt him. Eight Sandwich Islanders and twenty-five Europeans were also spared and lived in Tonga for many years. One of the most engaging parts of Mariner's narrative told to Dr. Martin runs:

> ... some of the natives brought Mr. Mariner's watch, which they had procured from his chest, and, with looks of curiosity, inquired what it was. He took it from them, wound it up, put it to the ear of one of them, and returned it. Every hand was now outstretched with eagerness to take hold of it;—it was applied in turn to their ears;—they were astonished at the noise it made;—they listened again to it, turned it on every side, and exclaimed, '*Mo-ooi*'! (It is alive!) They then pinched and hit it, as if expecting it would squeak out. They looked at each other with wonder, laughed aloud and snapped their fingers. One brought a sharp stone for Mr. Mariner to force it open with. He opened it, in the proper way, and showed them the work. Several endeavoured to seize hold of it at once, but one ran off with it, and all the rest after him. About an hour afterwards, they returned with the watch completely broken to pieces; and, giving him the fragments, made signs to him to make it do as it did before. Upon his making them understand that they had killed it, and that it was impossible to bring it to life again, the man, who considered it as his property, exclaiming *mow-mow* (spoiled!) and, making a hissing noise, expressive of disappointment, accused the rest of using violence, and they in turn accused him and each other.

Mariner was most reluctantly allowed to leave after four years' residence with the chief. He was aged twenty-one when he told his story to Dr. Martin in London. It is in many ways the supreme account of the earliest European-Pacific Islander contact. Scarcely recognizable as the same individual when he returned in 1810, Mariner's love of adventure had become sedated. Although his book was celebrated, he chose to be a merchant's accountant and then a stockbroker. However, his death in 1853 was almost as dramatic as the start of his adventures: he was drowned when a small boat overturned on the Thames. Mariner's may be the most realistic and, at the same time, the most poetic of all these accounts.

Edward Robarts' journal covers the longest period of any beachcomber put

The first woman to circumnavigate the world with her husband, Louis (1779–1842): Rose Marie de Freycinet (1795–1832) (see p.76). Their ship, *L'Uranie*, was wrecked off the Falklands. J.E.V. Arago, their superlative artist, enriched the Pacific with his pictorial records: some of his albums were lost but, undismayed, he read excerpts from *Robinson Crusoe* to the castaways, all of whom survived, Rose to die of cholera in Paris in 1832.

Thoughts of desertion were inevitably encouraged by such performances as these. This sketch by A. Legrand after Elié Le Guillou shows tattooed Marquesan women entertaining French sailors on *La Zélée*, during Dumont d'Urville's expedition of 1837–40 (see p.80).

on record in the Pacific—twelve years—and starts at an earlier date than any other. It is wholly confined to the Marquesas. A sperm-whale hunter, he decided to desert his ship, *New Euphrates*, in 1798, relating:

> But ah, how was my mind torturd! The thoughts of my native country, my friends and all that was dear to me, each was present to my view, but I found no rescource but to quit the ship.

A first impression of the Marquesas was:

> In the even before sun down, numbers was seen swiming from the shore. As they came near we was very agreeably surprized to find they was a party of Ladies come to pay us a visit ... They were dressd in pettycoats made of leaves of a tree, [so] that when they got out of the water they made no bad appearance ... [Later, a chief] led me to his house and introduced me to his royal consort who receivd me with every mark of friendship. I was greatly surprized at the figure of this lady. I did not expect to have found so handsome a woman in this remote part of the globe. Her skin was white and delicate, her countenance open and mild, commanding respect, her brows finely archd. Her tresses flowd in natural ringlets on her shoulders, which gave her an agreeable appearance. Here was beauty in its native charms, no help from paint, french chalk, or poisonous washes, which is used in Some

parts of globe much to the hurt of them that make use of this destroyer of beauty ... Great numbers of inhabitants came to see me, my being the first white man that ever came to that part. In fact some was afraid to come near me, [and] said I was a ghost. Others said I was from the sky. I endeavoured to undeceive them. Some of the fair sex would come and feel my hands, arms and feet. Others more rude would pinch me to see if I had feeling. However I bore all patiently and by degrees they was less troublesome. After a short time I began to pay my visits among the people of rank, every one makeing me a present, more or less, of cloth, Turbans, bandages, etc. I was treated with the greatest respect at every house I visited. I was seldom at my new home. In fact I had a general home at every house. I was never at a loss for a roof.

Robarts' sojourn was less eventful than the career of Rev. George Vason (or Veeson) in Tonga. Vason was one of *Duff*'s heavy load of missionaries sent out by the London Missionary Society and the Countess of Huntingdon from England in 1796 (see p.123). A twenty-four-year-old bricklayer from Nottingham, Vason adapted to Tonga in a slightly unexpected fashion. Put ashore to convert the inhabitants, his first act was to abandon the faith which had propelled him to the South Seas: he took two Tongans as wives and became a heathen chief. It seemed that he would stay forever in Tonga, until the killing of missionaries convinced him that he should take the opportunity that arose of escape on an East Indiaman. Back in England, he returned to Nottingham. He did not become a missionary again but married a native of that city and rose to the unlikely position of governor of Nottingham town gaol.

Most beachcombers were tattooed, involuntarily or for prestige. Here, a Marquesan tattooer at Nukuhiva practises his art, the fee for which was a hog's head brought by the woman's husband. The scene was sketched by W. Tilesius during von Krusenstern's voyage of 1803–6 (see p.72) and drawn by H. Alexander Orloffsky.

Of the Polynesian beachcombers, Archibald Campbell must be easily the most intrepid. Born near Glasgow in 1787, he was apprenticed to a weaver at the age of ten and to a ship at thirteen. When he was seventeen years old, he was press-ganged to serve on a naval frigate, but he escaped. At the age of nineteen he joined a ship for China. He was only twenty when, after being shipwrecked in 1807 off Kamschatka in Siberia, he had to have both feet amputated by a Russian doctor because of frostbite, which also caused the loss of a finger and a finger-joint. Calling at the Sandwich Islands on a Russian ship, his physical condition attracted the compassion of the Queen of Owhyee (Hawaii) who, after a visit to the ship with the King, attired in a blue coat and grey pantaloons, invited him to reside in the royal compound. The captain of the Russian ship told them that Campbell could make and repair sails and weave cloth. An American, William Moxely, was told by the King to eat with Campbell and to interpret for him. Campbell's main meal was a dish of taro pudding, salt fish, and consecrated pork, no other food being permitted in the King's house. He stated:

> A plate, knife and fork, with boiled potatoes were however, always set down before Moxley and me by his Majesty's orders. He [the King] concluded his meal by drinking $\frac{1}{2}$ a glass of rum, but the bottle was immediately sent away, liquor being tabbood or interdicted to his guests. Breakfast and supper consisted of fish and sweet potatoes.

Campbell also reported:

> During my stay there were nearly 60 white people on Wahoo. Although the great majority had been left by American vessels, not above $\frac{2}{3}$ of them belonged to that nation: the rest were almost all English and of these 6 or 8 were convicts escaped from New South Wales. The King had a considerable number in his service, carpenters, joiners, masons, blacksmiths and bricklayers. Some solid and industrious; many idle and dissolute, getting drunk whenever an opportunity presents itself. It is no uncommon sight to see a party of them break a small cask of spirits and sit drinking for days till they see it out. There were few exceptions. William Davis, a Welshman residing with Isaac Davis, used to rise every morning at 5 and go to his fields where he commonly remained until the same hour in the evening. This singularity puzzled the natives not a little: but they accounted for it by supposing that he had been one of their own countrymen who had gone to Otaheiti or England after his death and had now come back to his native land. There were no missionaries while I was there: I was often much surprised by this.

The King had given Campbell 60 acres of land near Pearl Harbour. After thirteen months on Wahoo (Oahu Island, where Honolulu is located), a ship came in and Campbell wanted to leave. The King asked him to convey his compliments to King George III:

> I told him I had never seen him, like thousands of others. Much surprise at this! Asked if he did not go about among his people to hear their wants, I said that men did it for him. The King shook his head: Other people, he said, could never do it as well as himself.

In 1810 Campbell left Hawaii and returned to England after six years' absence. He deserved better of life: there was nothing for him to do but to crawl along the streets of Edinburgh and Leith grinding a barrel-organ.

Jean-Baptiste Cabri (1779?–1822), a beachcomber in the Marquesas (see p. 72), drawn by H. Alexander Orloffsky from a sketch made by W. Tilesius during von Krusenstern's voyage of 1803–6. Cabri was taken by von Krusenstern to Russia, where he performed 'savage' dances on the stage. Polynesians were enthusiastic tattooers because their pale skins showed off the patterns to great advantage: Cabri's skin would have been especially reflective.

Opposite: John Young, a castaway, (see p. 169) became governor of Hawaii and advisor to Kamehameha III (1813–54). In this engraving by A. Pellion in 1818, he looks well able to take care of himself. His half-Hawaiian granddaughter married King Kamehameha IV (1834–63).

Left: Rev. George Vason (1772–1838), during his career as a heathen chief in Tonga.

Below: Captain James Wilson (1760–1814) of *Duff* died of natural causes after a markedly adventurous life. His expedition of 1796–8 was a navigational feat of a high order (see p.123). The proselytizers left by him in the Islands were not so successful: some were frail or human enough not to attempt to beat the Islanders but to join them in their ways of life.

E.H. Lamont, an Irishman trading from San Francisco, was shipwrecked off Penrhyn Island in *Chatham* under Captain George Snow in 1853, and his *Wild Life Among the Pacific Islanders* was published in 1867. Everything was plundered from the wreck, plenty of *marae* (stone platforms) were found on an unspecified stay (probably about a year) in the Penrhyn group, and several marriages were almost contracted by Lamont before a ship eventually took him to Rarotonga.

94

His account is full of the habits of the Islanders whom he was cast among. Always with an eye for attractive girls, he came across a Marquesan face treatment:

> This girl was celebrated as a beauty but at the present time her face was so disfigured by some green pigment with which it was smeared that it was difficult to distinguish a single feature of it. When this pigment which is worn for a week or two is washed off the skin appears much fairer, a circumstance which may in some measure account for the fact that the females of the Marquesas are of lighter complexion than those of the South Seas generally.

Of Tahitians he said:

> The natives are extremely indolent, and since their original games and dances, which were very licentious, have been abolished by the missionaries, they have few amusements except cards, of which they are passionately fond, spending whole days over them and gambling away not only all their money but even their clothes.

At Aitutaki in the Cook Islands, Lamont considered:

> ... we may be permitted to doubt whether the transformation of the natives to Europeans of the modern type is altogether a desirable consummation. The coal-skuttle bonnets, cropped hair, and sanctified look, are poor substitutes for the sunny locks, bright eyes, and happy countenances of these children of nature.

His efforts to communicate with Marquesans were singularly unproductive:

> One sceptic, however, shrewdly suspecting that I did not understand them, advanced towards me, and placing a hand on each shoulder while he brought his face close to mine, shouted at the top of his voice some words, each of which was slowly and distinctly uttered. Then, drawing back, apparently satisfied that I must comprehend that, he encouragingly waited my reply. In the same deliberate manner I placed a hand on each of his shoulders, which made him appear a little nervous, though he looked round with a smile, and made some remark evidently to this effect, 'You see I found the way to make him understand me!' But what was his consternation when, in his own loud and distinct manner, I shouted, 'I-don't-understand-one-word-you-say!' He looked perfectly bewildered, and, with the rest of his countrymen, seemed to think it was an utterly hopeless case.

Arguably the most entertaining of all the beachcombers can be claimed by the Carolines. James F. O'Connell maintained that his account of a residence of eleven years there and in New Holland (Australia) was true, but one ought to regard it with some scepticism. On a voyage to Japan in 1826, in the course of which a missionary was to be dropped off at Kusaie in the Carolines, O'Connell's ship was overwhelmed at Ponape and towed to the beach. There, all were deprived of their clothing, whale-irons, tubs, shaving mirrors, and muskets. Although the blue veins showing through the white skins were admired in the general South Seas manner by clicking of teeth, O'Connell was sure that the next step was for him and his colleagues to be eaten. By way of distraction, he 'determined to try the experiment of dancing on a savage audience'. His Irish jig was appreciated, and O'Connell was relieved to find that the roasting preparations he had noticed were not for the Europeans but for dogs, a main

Below: Kamehameha I of Hawaii (1753–1819) (see p.167), painted by N. Tikhanov in 1818, patronized those beachcombers and castaways able to add to his hegemony. The King left callers in no doubt of his status, even if they were taken aback by his dress. Von Kotzebue stated that it 'consisted of a white shirt, blue pantaloons, a red waistcoat, and a coloured neckcloth', and that it 'surprized me very much for I had formed very different notions of the royal attire'.

ingredient of a feast in some islands at that time. O'Connell was tattooed all over, an eight-day process, followed by some special patterning to indicate that he was now married to the daughter of a chief:

> She was only about fourteen years of age, affectionate, neat, faithful, and, barring too frequent indulgence in the flesh of baked dogs which would give her breath something of a canine odour, she was a very agreeable consort.

O'Connell's descriptions of customs, such as for mourning, of ceremonies like *kava* drinking and cannibal rites, and of the building of houses and canoes—some of which did not have much longer to survive, and so were not observed by other Europeans—illustrate the way in which beachcombers could, and did, make contributions to ethnology. Among his notes was this comment:

> I happened accidentally to feel a sick man's pulse. This was noted by the observant natives . . . I gave them the best illustration in my power . . . telling them that any thing faster or any thing slower was 'no good'. The beating of the pulse at the wrists was a remarkable discovery to them; all made . . . a dive at the wrists of every one when first suspected of ill health. Once on the scent, they followed it, and detected the throbbing of the temples . . . It was really amusing to see how like civilized people they could ride a hobby to death . . .

Beachcombers had dreams of a life like that of this Hawaiian chief, drawn relaxing in his house by Louis Choris in 1822.

These natives of Uea, Loyalty Islands, were sketched by Commander (later Admiral) Richard Aldworth Oliver in 1849 on H.M.S. *Havannah*'s voyage under Commodore John Elphinstone Erskine (1806–87), patron of the distinctive beachcomber, 'Cannibal Jack' Diaper. The male Islanders bleached their hair with lime.

In 1833, he was able to board a vessel. A year after leaving the Carolines, he published his colourful and no doubt somewhat coloured account. His early history, before Australia and the Carolines, has never been traced: it is possible that O'Connor was not his real name. What is known for certain is that his last days were spent as a tattooed dancer, advertised as 'Sailor of the South Sea', on a Mississippi steamboat, on which he died in 1852.

Melanesia's beachcombers of note were nearly all based in Fiji. An exception was Nicholas (Niklos) Minster, a beachcomber of Kiriwina in the Trobriands group, close to New Guinea. Nick the Greek had escaped from the penal establishment in New Caledonia. He was an ingenious man, like several of the more picturesque beachcombers. His most famous achievement was to

William Bligh transferring breadfruit trees in 1791, on his second voyage to Tahiti (see p. 66). In the centre is Otoo, who, although not the principal chief in Tahiti as Cook and others assumed, became recognized by Europeans as King Pomare I (1743–1803). This illustration of early trading was painted by T. Gosse.

offer himself as pilot for a French warship which was searching for him in New Caledonia. His offer to guide it through the perilous waters was gladly accepted. The warship was taken on a wild-goose chase through the Papua archipelago, where the French became impatient at not finding their man and paid Nick off with a handsome fee for the pilotage. A turtle-shell trader in the Louisiades when he was not involved in murder, he invariably used native women as crew for his vessel.

A somewhat similarly ingenious beachcomber was Charley Savage, a Swede whose name was Kalle Svenson and who had been a seal-hunter before beachcombing in Fiji. As he understood musketry and could reassemble the only gun found on *Eliza*, in which he had been shipwrecked, he was adopted by the paramount chief of Bau, who was attempting to enlarge his sphere of influence. Savage asked for, and was supplied with, a number of wives (they amounted to thirty, some of very high rank) in return for ensuring Bau supremacy in warfare. Very much the superior person, wearing Western clothes, and second only to the paramount chief in power, his tactics were to stay well behind the front line, out of range of arrows, clubs, and stones. He insured himself further by being carried only as far as the rear lines in a weapon-proof enclosure of coconut fibre. After six all-powerful years, he made the mistake of being ambushed in 1813 while trying to earn some money with which to replenish the ammunition so vital to his success. After being suspended by six men head down in a pool of water and drowned, he was eaten, his bones being made into sail-needles. A Chinese known as Luis was clubbed and cut up with Savage: they were then put in the ovens together. Luis had been the first known Chinese resident in Fiji. A witness lucky to escape was Peter Dillon, who solved the de Lapérouse expedition mystery (see p.79).

Beachcombers flourished throughout the nineteenth century. There is room for only one vivid example—the experiences of William James Diaper (sometimes spelt by him Diapea). His autobiography was made available by Rev. James Hadfield, a Methodist missionary in the New Hebrides, in a work entitled *Cannibal Jack*, one of the names by which Diaper was known—the others were 'John Jackson' (by which he was known for thirty years) and 'Silver Eyes'. This comment by Hadfield in his introduction shows that missionaries and cannibals were not necessarily antipathetic:

> Some may wonder that a missionary should assist in broadcasting Cannibal Jack's occasional disparaging and even hostile criticisms of missionaries. He serves an excellent purpose in revealing the conditions of native life before the arrival of missionaries.

Hadfield met Cannibal Jack as late as 1889 in Mare, one of the Loyalty Islands, where he found him staying with a friend, Dirty Jerry Imber. Imber combined beachcombing with being doctor and storekeeper of the area and was proud of being named Dirty. Grimy he was: he considered that washing his face would result in a bad cold. Cannibal Jack had gone to this group as he was wanted by the French for murder in New Caledonia in 1860: his autobiography covers the period 1843–7 in Fiji. Diaper, a lean Englishman from a landowning family, through his ability to mend muskets, acquired turtle shell and pigs. With these sources of wealth, he acquired six wives. It was his mastery of musketry—as with Savage and others—that enabled him to survive against the natives who, nevertheless, as he reported plaintively,

> will insist on knocking the saltwater from my eyes . . . Let me pause to relate that, notwithstanding the fact that I have been killed outright some half-a-

dozen times in these Fiji Islands—it being a matter of mere arithmetic only, inasmuch as I have been half-killed more than, or at any rate, quite a dozen times already, and as twelve halves are six wholes the world over, so that apparent misnomer is easily accounted for. There was a fascination in this kind of life, most of it in the youthful and green portions of it but lasting into and through the yellow and sere and even now I am verging on the allotted period.

From Diaper come some of the most dramatic accounts of the intricacies of cannibal rites and of the custom of chiefs' wives being strangled when their husbands died. Missionaries to him were 'good, bad and indifferent'. He acknowledged having thirty-eight children. For a century, the true authorship of the *Narrative of John Jackson*, which deals with an earlier period than his autobiography, was in doubt until the late Christopher Legge recently identified it as another work of Diaper's. This *Narrative* is full of original and startling material. As John Jackson he was employed by Commodore John Elphinstone Erskine on H.M.S. *Havannah* as an interpreter. It was Erskine who induced him to write his account. Diaper died in 1891 in the Loyalty Islands.

As administrators became established and spread their control throughout the groups, beachcombers found a 'dropout' existence increasingly hard to

The enticement that affected explorers' senses after months on the ocean. The Marquesan natives among Fatuhiva's jagged, mysterious peaks were, however, ferocious cannibals. Robert Taylor Pritchett, whose bright colours are faithful, was the artist on Charles J. Lambert's steam-yacht, *Wanderer*, in 1880–2.

The castaway, James O'Connell (1808–52), entertaining Ponapeans with a dance on the beach to divert their attention from another favourite Caroline Island amusement—roasting and eating Europeans. This is an illustration from pamphlets sold at O'Connell's later performances on American stages.

maintain. However, until recently, it remained possible to be a European beachcomber of sorts, and Philip Snow has met a number in various circumstances. In nearly every case, they were marked by a sweet gentleness, rarely to be found among Europeans of different status in the groups. It is convenient to drop into the first person here.

Only a fortnight after my posting to Lomaloma in 1940 as District Commissioner of the Lau archipelago, Howard Landseer Tripp asked if I could see him. He was the son of a former harbourmaster at Lomaloma. Its brief phase as a port had declined abruptly and after 1890 jobs were scarce. The ex-harbourmaster's son had elected to live his life on the edge of a small village of Fijians just along the beach. He had not been well for many months, and was now gravely ill.

I walked along the beach from my office towards his house, ignoring the invitation of the signpost standing at a crooked angle beside a casuarina tree: 'To the Botanical Gardens', it said. That signpost was a relic of Victorian prosperity. The path, full of holes, with land crabs somnolently in possession, was checked by a muddy creek oozing out to the lagoon. In a clearing of

feathery acacias and squat breadfruit trees, with only a line of low, tasselled barringtonia separating the coral sand of the clearing from that of the beach, was his house. It was half-thatch, one-quarter weatherboard and corrugated-iron, and one-quarter missing.

I found him lying on a heap of mats on the floor, tossing about under a mosquito net. His emaciated hand was held by his Lauan wife, who fanned him with her free hand. He looked much older than his fifty years.

There was no furnishing in his house beyond a few achromatic pictures of Old Lomaloma. I persuaded him, in between his bouts of delirium, to let himself be taken to the Lomaloma hospital. As this was against all his adopted Fijian mode of living and thinking, I had to press very hard. But taken to hospital he was. This was done very gingerly by four of his wife's relations, who took off the door of a copra shed to serve as a stretcher. Once he was there, Howard, to his credit, gave himself up as few Europeans did, wholly and with total faith, to the Fijian medical practitioner, who performed a remarkable operation on his thigh, extracting from it a massive elephantiasis ulcer.

A fortnight later Howard, his frame still gaunt, his face white-grey and shrunken, but his eyes exhilarated with the pleasure of a life found painless again, propelled himself on a crutch the few yards along the beach from the

First a beachcomber, then a sandalwood trader and pork dealer, and ultimately the discoverer of de Lapérouse's fate, Peter Dillon (1785–1847) (see p.79), together with Martin Bushart, luckily survived this Fijian attack in 1813. The powerful beachcomber, Charley Savage, and a Chinese man were devoured.

hospital to my office. Gravely, he put sixpence on my desk for any fund there might be to help England win the war. In hospital he had heard Fijian patients talking about the news that they had heard on the wireless, telling each other that the war in France was going extremely badly for England. He hoped, he said, that he was not being pessimistic, but he believed that in fact we would be pushed out of France back into England, and that the invasion and conquest of England itself might not be far off.

For him, living his food-bartering life almost completely outside the currency system, the gift of sixpence was the equivalent of a gift of a hundred pounds from me. Howard took his official receipt for the donation with care. Burying it somewhere in what passed as trousers, he put on his battered straw hat and, barefooted, shuffled off along the beach to his lunch of crabs and octopus. I noticed that he never scanned the beach as he moved along. Beachcombers seldom live up to their name.

The term 'beachcomber' has come to mean a degraded, debauched type of European in the South Sea Islands, lurching blearily through each day and lying furtively through each night. In the real sense, it simply means a European who, for some reason or another, has chosen to live the life of a South Sea Islander.

William Bligh (1754–1817) and his loyal companions in 1789, when they were put off H.M.S. *Bounty* into an uncovered, overcrowded launch (see p.64), painted by Robert Dodd in 1790. Bligh's indomitable spirit enabled them to escape the usual fate of castaways. In a soggy journal, he kept accurate details of the mutineers, as well as of the islands discovered, but modestly not named by him, during the 3,618 miles' voyage.

Very few beachcombers, however, are romantic figures. There cannot be much glamour when one is so close to the bare process of survival. Even so, a character I came to know and like in my very first days in Fiji, when I was stationed in the Rewa River district, came near to it. Milton Craig, J.P., was a very amiable and distinctly unusual beachcomber, with a variegated history. He came from a relatively wealthy English family: his father was the first Liberal M.P. for Staffordshire, and a brother became a baronet. Milton taught music at an Austrian ducal home for a while and then, with a twin brother and another brother (who soon died), broke away in 1889 and arrived in Fiji to start a new life. They established a remarkable household, at first at Levuka, and later at Lodoni on the main island of Viti Levu. Their house was noted for its unending hospitality, its air of genteel forbearance, its grubbiness, and its lack of material possessions. The twin lived until he was seventy-five, while Milton died during the Second World War, aged eighty-seven. He had married a devoted Fijian, Mathilda, who owned a little land through her clan. Milton kept one or two cattle and some poultry on it, enough to provide his milk, butter, eggs, and, now and then, meat. This basic existence was supplemented by the Government paying him a salary of £20 a year to act as postmaster of Lodoni (a collection of thatched huts: the name means London). This involved little more than five minutes' work a day, selling the occasional stamp and receiving the odd letter. Despite his impecuniosity, his integrity and status were such that, with popular approval, the Government made him a Justice of the Peace. This was an honorary position: the extent of his duties was to sign, for no fee, a very occasional court document.

Fletcher Christian and his eight European colleagues on Pitcairn's Island were the most celebrated of the first deliberate castaways (see p.64). The sole landing-place—at Bounty Bay—was sketched in 1825 by Frederick W. Beechey (1796–1856), the captain of H.M.S. *Blossom*, during his voyage of 1825–8 (see p. 65). Landing on the island has always been hazardous—a fact that met Christian's requirement and still makes the visitor hold tight to the side of the longboat.

Milton's face was softly rounded, his silver moustache drooped, his white hair was always tousled. He exuded benevolence, fair-mindedness, and gentle humanity—rare qualities in a small, heterogeneous community. He reminded me always of Campbell-Bannerman, despite his singlet riddled with holes, his long, dirty shorts, and his lack of socks and shoes.

His house, a wood and corrugated-iron cabin on small stilts, was always in bizarre confusion. A bureau in one corner, where he stood apologetically to sign the one court paper a week brought to him for the purpose by a constable, had papers, notes, gadgets, and discards scattered over every available space. The one piece of furniture to sit on, a deck-chair, was torn half across its width. Light gleamed up through gaping cracks in the unstained floorboards, and a sack acted as a mat at the ill-fitting door. His pet owl gave deliberate, appreciative blinks from among the cobwebs of the unlined tin roof. Two lean dogs and twice as many unsmooth cats ravenously watched one's every movement at meals, which were taken perched on the edge of upturned boxes. Tinned meat in large red quantities on the kitchen table was a special feast, but you had to be alert to beat the outstretched necks of the dogs as you hurried it to your mouth, shaking off a double layer of flies *en route*. The tongues of the two dogs on either flank met under your chin, but the animals remained unrebuked. That was part of Milton Craig's charm. The cultured tone of his voice, the breadth of his conversation and tolerance were the main contributions to the meal. Milton Craig would have been an attractive figure in any setting: it did not matter that it was under the popping petrol lantern of a tin hut in Lodoni.

The castaways' settlement on Pitcairn in 1825, later named Adamstown, drawn by F. W. Beechey. John Adams (see p.65) is watching the cooking. In 1800, ten years after the arrival of the castaways, he was the only man, mutineer or native, still alive—among nine women and nineteen children.

When I was posted to the Lau archipelago from Rewa, I met no more of that rare breed (except Howard Landseer Tripp), even in the remotest of the Fijian Islands, although they might have been considered the ideal setting for them. It was in other parts of the Fiji group that beachcombers seemed to thrive, near little townships with a tradition of *laissez-faire* European settlement and, more to the point, boasting hotels.

The bar of the Hot Springs Hotel in etiolated, steamy Nasavusavu used to be crowded, not from each sundown but from each midday (opening time), with beachcombers, near-beachcombers, bush personalities, and dead-beats. Each of these might have made a character for Somerset Maugham in his less tight-lipped vein. They had enough about them—it was not cash—to persuade the manager to keep their glasses filled. However, when copra began to command a higher price, a heavier dose of orthodoxy came to the Hot Springs. The beachcombers then either moved to more sympathetic corners or faded away.

Not far from Nasavusavu, on a lonely island in Natewa Bay, there lived until his death in the late 1940s a fine example of an island eccentric. He was not quite a beachcomber because he was a hair's breadth from minimum subsistence level. He not only lived in a very small and broken-down shanty of a store, he owned it. W.W. Wright was known by scarcely anyone. Apart from a predilection for lame dogs and rare ones, I regarded it as part of my duty in any district in my charge to meet as many of its assorted characters as I could. So, late one evening, in my first month in this district, I called upon Wright. He told me that I was the first European to visit him for fifteen years. In honour of my visit he groped into a dark corner of the tin hovel. I could not see, and had no urge to imagine, what had settled in the cobwebbed recesses. He brought out a mildewy bottle, but I was reassured to see that it appeared to be air-tight, dust-tight, and insect-tight. Over the madeira (which was not at all bad), he told me that, before coming to Fiji, his life had been spent in a wine vault in England. He spoke of England, and the quick journey by horse-drawn tram from his home to the vaults, as though he had left it only yesterday—he had not in fact been there this century. He had lived alone on his tiny island, just large enough for his shack, a pig-run, and a score of palm trees, for fifty-four years, having been born in Yorkshire some twenty years before that. How he came to Fiji he never told me. He was still knowledgeable about wines and, for a man who lived in such deliberate isolation, about odd things in Fiji. He knew that I had just come back from captaining the Fiji cricket team in New Zealand. As a Yorkshireman, he had been unable to resist asking Fijians, who came out from the mainland to get essential supplies from his store, how we had got on. It must have been an enormous effort for him to seek this news from them. He made no secret of the fact that he had never attempted to have any sort of contact with his closest neighbours: he was, indeed, proud of it. This completely antisocial existence puzzled the gregarious Fijians more than anything else about him. He was wildly abusive on the subject of Fijians, although he knew where my sympathies lay. I think he understood that I had promised to spend the night in the village among his hereditary enemies: at low tide he saw me half-way across the mud flats between his island and the village—half-way, and decidedly no further. My last view was of a small, dogged figure with dirty white hair and a very oily hurricane lantern trudging obstinately back into solitude. He died two years later. He left his tiny island to the Fiji Society for the Prevention of Cruelty to Animals.

Until recently, there lived on the island of Taveuni two peculiar Europeans, believed to be Germans, although they were known by the flat English name of

The first internationally known half-European, half-Islander. Thursday October Christian (1790–1831), the part-Tahitian son of the castaway, Fletcher Christian, was the first to be born on Pitcairn. Wearing a plumed hat, he was depicted by Lt. John Shillibeer in 1817 on the first British ship, H.M.S. *Briton* (accompanied by H.M.S. *Tagus*) to visit Pitcairn since *Bounty*. His physique and manner deeply impressed Captains Sir Thomas Staines and Philip Pipon, but he died when the Islanders tried to reside in Tahiti in 1831 (see p.150).

Parkins Christian, great-great-grandson of the arch-castaway, Fletcher Christian, photographed at Pitcairn in 1946. He was the chief magistrate. His Pitcairnese language, a combination of Tahitian and eighteenth-century English, was difficult to understand.

Morrisby. The younger, although not very old, had a black beard down to his knees. At least, those who saw him said so—I never met him. He had been a recluse for thirty or more years, ever since their arrival on the island after the First World War. Only the rare, unwelcome visitor to their decrepit shack ever set eyes on him. He would sit all day and all evening almost hidden by the disordered pile of dust-shrouded papers and brown-edged books round him. For the last ten years, Logan Morrisby, the senior of the two, told me that he and his brother never spoke to each other. One early morning in the late 1940s, Logan woke me up to announce, in hushed tones vibrating with anxiety—very different from his normal regimental sergeant-major bellow—that his brother was missing. And had been for three days: he had not notified me earlier because he had expected him to return. This agitation in a man normally so full of force was pitiful. I sent out search parties into the thick bush on the side of the extinct volcano, Des Voeux Peak, which lay at the back of their house as well as mine. We combed the beach. No trace of this hermitic brother was ever found.

Logan, who lived until his mid-eighties, hated all Fijians indiscriminately and vehemently: they in turn were contemptuous of him. Apart from this embarrassing attitude, I quite liked him. Candour of an utterly naked kind and the sturdiest independence of spirit were his great qualities. In his thick, dirty, blue serge suit, braces, flannel shirt, and heavy black boots, all amounting to a daily defiance of the tropics that he loathed, his impact was never less than emphatic. He conceded not an inch physically or mentally to the tropics. He had the white moustache of a senior walrus, the head of a bull-seal, and a normal speaking voice like the trumpeting of a sea-elephant. Bent over a vice, fashioning the barrel of a shotgun in his corrugated-iron workshop at the edge of a track on the Taveuni slopes, he looked, in his steel spectacles, for all the world like a studious craftsman of the previous century. He had Teutonic dexterity in making firearms. Never did a man live in more inapt surroundings: why he elected to do so I never obtained the slightest clue. He, like Wright, was not so much a beachcomber as a period eccentric. He would never be short of cash—he had a professional skill that a beachcomber by nature would be likely to lack.

The economics of beachcombing were fine-drawn. For those who once contemplated abandoning a European existence for one of leisure in the South Seas, the following material facts about beachcombing in Fiji in the first half of the twentieth century may be of interest.

Money was (and is) a necessity for a European in Fiji: (a) to enable him to meet the income tax above certain levels—this did not apply to the beachcomber; and (b) for Residential Tax—every person under sixty had to pay £2 a year. This the beachcomber had to find. Indeed, to get into the colony he had to show some funds. Modesty being a prerequisite in the South Seas, he would have needed clothes, if only a *sulu* (skirt). Toothbrushes and razors would have been an extravagance. So would furniture, in any hut which he might have gained as a grace-and-favour dwelling from the head of a village disposed to accept a tame, mild European. Beds, with life at its plainest, as Paris *clochards* testify, could have been dispensed with; so could mosquito nets (but only in extreme necessity). The beachcomber could have done without a lamp: he would not have done any reading or writing after darkness fell at about 6 p.m. all the year round, even if reading or writing materials were somehow needed for the daytime. He would have depended on the moonlight for any outside nocturnal activity. A morsel of bushland could have been acquired in which he

An outstanding High Commissioner for the Western Pacific and Governor of Fiji (1904–11): Sir Everard im Thurn (1852–1932), painted by J. H. Lorimer. Of Swiss German parentage, he was once a museum curator. He remained a considerable anthropological scholar, and made notable contributions to our knowledge of beachcombers.

could have planted, from cuttings given him by friends, his *dalo* (taro, his staple diet) in the Fijian manner, with a pointed piece of stick used as a fork. There would have been the ubiquitous breadfruit tree to pluck from, providing a second vegetable. He could have grown *yaqona*, the crushed roots of which, mixed with water, supply both a satisfying drink and something of a mild narcotic. *Yaqona* (*kava*) is also a first-class appetite depressant, which he could have taken on the days when he was hungry.

He would have needed a fishing spear, because if he wanted to vary his diet of *dalo* with mullet, king-fish, grouper, and octopus he would have had to stir himself and amble about on the outer reefs. Then he would have needed a good eye to ensure reasonable success with his spear, but he would have had to be only moderately agile to catch the multifarious crabs. He could have made his

At the beginning of this century, the length of the waterfront in Levuka, Fiji, represented a five-minute stroll: a score of hotels lined it for the beachcombers' delectation.

own *suluka*, the pungent native cigar, from crude tobacco rolled in banana leaves. He would have needed to collect firewood and keep embers perpetually glowing for his cooking-fire and *suluka*-kindling. For toilet paper he could have used layers of coconut husk, as the more remote Fijians do: for a lavatory the bush.

In this way, and for the minimum outlay of about £10, the beachcomber, once in the Islands, could have enjoyed a meatless, breadless, tealess existence, with only the worry of the annual Residential Tax to meet. If he was ill, the public hospital would have fended for him. Because he was living on a breadless diet, his teeth probably would not have deteriorated. If he tried to live at a slightly higher level, with tinned fish or fresh meat as an occasional extra item of food, or if he strove to acquire occasional luxuries, such as a mirror, a mosquito net, or a petrol lamp to help his crab collecting, he would have needed an annual income of about £100. But this would have meant a surrender of personal freedom to the extent of having to work on a plantation as a copra cutter for some months each year: this would almost certainly have been the only way that he could procure the necessary income.

Times have now changed, and inflation and independence have affected beachcombing in Fiji. It would be impossible today for anyone to enter the country for the purpose. That has gone. As for a Fiji national subject already in the Islands wishing to change his way of life and become a beachcomber, it would still be possible, but the tax and other financial requirements are more demanding and the corner hard to find.

Chapter VII

Traders and Whalers

As the purpose of many Western expeditions to the Pacific had been to note what commodities the Islands possessed which could be in demand in the rest of the world, it is not surprising that traders and whalers should follow hot on the explorers' heels. Accounts of voyages had been published and their commercial aspects scrutinized by Western merchants.

Promoters and leaders of expeditions had been disappointed to find in the South Sea Islands no obvious riches like gold, silver, and silks—or even spices with which to compete with the Spice Islands. Commercially, explorers had brought little excitement back to the Western world. So much that the Pacific possessed was not sufficiently alluring: breadfruit, yams, taro, and bitter citrus neither stimulated the palate nor were likely to swell the pocket.

Sandalwood and bêche-de-mer (trepang or sea-slug) were new and esoteric, but little reward for the long and perilous journeys necessary to reach them. They were both in great demand in China, however, and therefore became important bargaining merchandise with which to exchange the Chinese tea, silks, jewels, and exotic woods so much in demand in Europe.

At the beginning of the nineteenth century, sandalwood was found in some quantity in Polynesia (in Hawaii, Rarotonga, the Society Islands, Tonga, and Samoa) and in Melanesia (in Fiji, the New Hebrides, and New Caledonia).

These houses (after a drawing by R. Seman) over a West New Guinea lagoon are typical of the architectural style that has existed in parts of Melanesia for centuries (see p.16). They are hygienic, cool, and easy to defend. The earliest European traders to visit such native settlements would find few changes today.

Benjamin Morrell (1795–1839), a bêche-de-mer trader, and called 'The biggest liar in the Pacific' (see p.76). His accounts, however, have not been disproved.

The sandalwood tree is stunted and generally unimpressive in appearance, but the wood was intensely fragrant to the Chinese nose. Incense, tapers, and aromatic boxes for religious rites in temples were made out of it, as were joss sticks, kept burning constantly, according to Fanning, a pioneer in the trade, in honour of the Chinese god, Josh. Medicines and perfumes were made of oil distilled from it. Ships sailed mostly from Australia—surprisingly, there were no Chinese craft—in search of the trees that grew most profusely in a few parts of Fiji, New Caledonia, New Hebrides, and Hawaii. An indentation on the Bua coast of Vanua Levu in Fiji is still charted as Sandalwood Bay: it is where Oliver Slater, a castaway, began the trade in 1800, to be killed fifteen years later in Fijian intertribal warfare. It was a trade likely to lead to trouble, as Peter Dillon recorded:

> ... the sandalwood came in but very slowly. The natives in our neighbourhood begged several times of the captain to assist them in their war and promised, as a reward for such service, to load the ship with the desired article in two months after their enemy was conquered.

Natives were far from united in dealing with traders. Tribes within groups fought each other to supply the trees and to receive the axes, knives, scissors, chisels, cloth, iron, and whales' teeth that they were able to extract from their visitors. They would often plunder each other to obtain these desirable objects and, occasionally, the even more coveted muskets and ammunition. The sandalwood depredations were so thorough that in fifteen years—by about 1815—the trees had been eliminated in Fiji. In the New Hebrides, the tree-cutting started about a decade afterwards and ended correspondingly later. In Hawaii the trees were all felled by 1825: the trade had only started in 1810. As the tree grows extremely slowly, the sandalwood trade, although highly lucrative, was one of the shortest in commercial history.

The bêche-de-mer trade started before the demise of the sandalwood tree and continued for much longer. For thirty years up to 1850, it was Fiji's main export. Indeed, while nowadays one rarely sees a sandalwood tree anywhere in the Islands, it is difficult to take a walk along the inshore coral reefs at low tide without treading on bêche-de-mer. These thick black slugs lie motionless just below the water or sometimes exposed to the hot sun. There is no way in which the slugs could be made attractive to Westerners: baked, roasted, raw, covered with icing sugar, or soaked in Grand Marnier, they would stick in the Occidental gullet. These Oriental delights, lifted off the floor of the lagoon, were despatched to the port of Canton in China, together with (for Europeans) the scarcely more enticing sharks' fins. The Chinese greeted them with enthusiasm, valued them for their aphrodisiac qualities (which were mythical), and ate them as smoked slug soup.

The conduct of many traders was bound to lead to repercussions from natives. Cecil Foljambe, while on H.M.S. *Curaçoa* in the British Navy's Australasian Station, was sweepingly condemnatory in 1865:

> I find the sandalwood traders have much to answer for. They, and indeed most of the white men in the Islands, are the very scum of England and America. They are afraid to show their faces in civilized places and make the poor natives what they are. They try to cheat them, practising greater cruelties than the cannibals themselves are capable of. For instance, one captain of a sandalwood schooner the other day boasted that, having taken his cargo of sandalwood, and as he was sailing along the coast he shot down

A bêche-de-mer house in Fiji, drawn by Alfred T. Agate (1812–46). The sea-slugs are being cured on platforms in the smoke of slow-burning fires. Agate was the principal artist on Charles Wilkes' Exploring Expedition (1838–42), known as the Ex. Ex. (see p.80). His brilliant drawings, some of which were lost in a shipwreck, added to the ethnographical and geographical knowledge of the Pacific.

Sandalwood traders were often capable of extreme cruelty to natives. Here, they are confronted by the missionary, John Gibson Paton (1824–1907), at Tanna in the New Hebrides in 1861 (see p.127).

unoffensive natives as they stood on the beach for the charitable purpose of spoiling the trade for the next comers . . . can you wonder after this that they detest white men and would kill and eat them when a chance occurs?

Sometimes the sandalwood and bêche-de-mer traders kidnapped natives, who were just as profitable as their exotic cargo. Benjamin Boyd was a London stockbroker until he became a trader, planter, labour recruiter, and, finally, a sheep farmer and whaler. In 1847, he seized sixty-five natives of the New Hebrides from a sandalwood ship and took them to New South Wales, where

Left: The Islanders were vulnerable to European kidnappers and to unscrupulous dealers. This native of Honolulu, looking like a freelance trader, was drawn by Lt. Carl Skogman on the 1851–3 voyage of the Swedish frigate, *Eugenies*.

Opposite: Admiralty Islanders greeting d'Entrecasteaux with gifts in 1793 (see p.66). The latter was as skilful in his contacts with the wilder Melanesians as he was with the Polynesians. However, trade between Islanders and Europeans, although in a sometimes totally unexpected form, as in the Admiralty Islands, was seldom as rewarding as it was hoped it would be.

he lived. There, the New Hebrideans were employed as shepherds, but they soon died. Four years later Boyd, known alternately as an enterprising private empire builder or a supreme scoundrel, went to the Solomons on his yacht, *Wanderer*, with John Webster and a large amount of gold. He intended to set up a Papuan republic or confederation under his own control, but he disappeared—presumed killed and eaten on San Christobal Island. Webster survived to write an account of the last of *Wanderer* and died in New Zealand sixty-one years later.

Many of the traders simply came and went, without giving anything in return. They took it for granted that the natives had no right of possession of the material wealth of their countries. Others, in leaving iron, virtually revolutionized Island culture.

Native reaction to the European invasion was recorded by Dillon:

> I have often conversed with savages, who informed me that when first they beheld the Europeans they supposed them to have descended from the clouds; nor could they imagine what our business was in their country unless to carry off their provisions, wives, and children, as slaves—this idea being grounded on the universal practice in those islands of men carrying off the women and children of their enemies in their expeditions.

Much opportunity for European-Islander contact was afforded by the indispensable process of careening a vessel. After long voyages, hulls had to be scrubbed with boiling water but, to reach the bottoms, the weight had to be lightened by removing the upper masts and guns. This meant a long stay. *L'Artémise*, in which Cyrille Pierre Théodore Laplace (1793–1875) made his circumnavigation of 1837–40, is here the object of attention in Tahiti in 1839, watched warily by, amongst others, two hogs. Such contacts created a brisk trade in live pigs and salt pork with the Tahitians.

Sometimes, traders would find their occupation more devious than they expected: they found that they had to procure pigs, pearl, and turtle-shell from the Solomons with which to barter for sandalwood in the New Hebrides. In these transactions, both in the Solomons and the New Hebrides, there would be sharp practice on each side, with the inevitable result: battles and fatalities. Because of the traders' experiences, the Solomon Islanders came in the 1840s to be regarded as antagonistic to European visitors—not without good reason.

Pearls had been seen by the earliest explorers in nearly all parts of the Pacific, often in natives' earlobes. But even by the time of *Dolphin*'s discovery of Tahiti, the natives had learnt not to wear these jewels when they came out to barter. Too many pearls had been given away for too little. However, large pearl beds were known by traders to exist. The principal port of Mangareva Island, Rikitea, was a considerable trading centre for the gems and for nacre over a short period at the beginning of the nineteenth century. Like bêche-de-mer and sandalwood, this trade, largely from the Tuamotus and Cooks, mostly passed through the port of Canton.

Trading in coconut oil thrived longer in the Central Pacific Islands—in the Gilberts and in the Yap complex of the Carolines. It started early in the nineteenth century and continued for about seventy years, until systematic planting of coconut plantations yielded copra on a commercial scale. Turtle-shell trading had its moments but never knew the peaks of the trade in sandalwood, sea-slugs, and pearls.

Coercion and deceit were the most unpleasant sides of the Western character shown in early commerce, while *naïveté* and greed were the besetting frailties of the Islanders. At first no match for the traders, the natives soon polished their wits to ensure that barter was reasonable. In less sophisticated areas, like the Admiralty group, however, babies would be offered in exchange for trinkets dangled in front of their eyes.

It might be thought that articles of ships' food could have been bartered with natives. After all, some Islanders were literally eating off the ground. The inhabitants of New Ireland and of Jesus Maria Island in the Admiralty group would look for clay under boulders in the bush. Having washed it to remove impurities, they would knead the clay and have it smoked. Clay *fumé* was then wrapped in leaves and hung up, as Westerners hang pheasants, until it was ripe for consumption. The early New Guinea Administrator, Hugh Hastings Romilly, says tentatively:

> It must, I should think, be terribly indigestible ... It tasted not unlike very bad chocolate, but that might have been partly due to the smoking. I found that the cockroaches on board ship were very fond of it.

Nevertheless, the Islanders did not want European food. All the traffic in nourishment (not extending to smoked clay) was in the other direction—from shore to ship.

Chiefs vying for power in Tahiti—a struggle that marked most of the nineteenth century and was to make the group easy for a Western nation to acquire—traded briskly with visiting ships. With the aim of expanding power rather than increasing security, muskets were foremost in their demands and, in return for pork, traders parted with many firearms. Some of the first missionaries did not discourage this trade at all and, indeed, occasionally acted as agents for the traders.

Individual traders or small commercial companies soon became the first Europeans to have regular contact with the Pacific Islands. One distinctive individual was Andrew Cheyne, the illegitimate son of a substantial landowner in the Shetlands. He has left one of the most vivid accounts of any Pacific trader in his journals for 1841–4. From the start, he realized that the success of his trading would depend on finding out what natives actually wanted, rather than what they ought to want: he refrained from interfering in their customs. After trading on the Isle of Pines off New Caledonia, in 1842 he tried to establish a commercial empire in Ponape, with a central depot for provisioning whalers and a headquarters for his own trade in bêche-de-mer and turtle shell. Returning to the Shetlands, he married and published a classic on the Western Pacific. He took his wife out to Australia on a boat full of convicts. Their son was to become an eminent surgeon and a baronet, known as Sir Wilson Watson, as Andrew's parents-in-law forbade the use of the surname Cheyne. They never forgave the trader for taking their daughter out to the Pacific in such bad conditions: she died of consumption in England in 1855. Cheyne acquired 10,000 acres near Koror in the Palaus and planted sugar, coffee, cotton, indigo, and bananas. In 1866, he was strangled by the chief of a tribe which was hostile to one with which he had aligned himself. As a result, a warship was sent to Koror and the chief was executed.

Cheyne was a courageous, humourless man, hard in his judgement of others. In his journal, he noted more of what he saw than of what he heard. He observed cannibalism first-hand in 1841 on the Isle of Pines:

> The Natives ... are Cannibals, and always eat the bodies of their enemies slain in battle, not merely to gratify their revenge, but to satisfy their craving appetite for this sort of food ... [Natives] seemed much surprised to find that we were not cannibals. They prefer Human flesh to any other sort of food, and say it tastes much sweeter than Pork ... They prefer the flesh of women and children to men ...

At Lifu in the Loyalty Islands:

> Their fondness for it [human flesh] is such, that when a portion of it has been sent some distance to their friends as a present, the gift is eaten, even if decomposition has begun before it is received ... Natives say the flesh of the white man tastes Salt.

On the Isle of Pines, he noted that:

> they have no Idea of any other country existing but their own and the adjacent Islands—and believe the 'Papalangis' ... come from the skies—and after sailing to the edge of the visible Horizon, that we fly off into the air—!

The New Caledonians could not understand to what use the sandalwood tree was put by the Papalangis from Europe. Seeing biscuits being eaten, they concluded that they were made of sawdust from the tree. They were convinced that ships' salt beef and pork were human flesh: no larger animals than the dog existed in their world. An interesting observation by Cheyne, bearing in mind the date, 1842, and the locality, Ouvea, off New Caledonia, where European ships had not been unknown, is that the natives' only diseases were:

> Elaphantiasis ... Hydrocele ... Rheumatism appears to be the most common disease—it generally affects them in the long bones of the legs—they relieve it by making an incision in to the bone, over the part affected ...

Much of Honolulu's early importance was based on its being a whaling centre. This lithograph by Burgess shows Diamond Head and Waikiki around 1850.

Cheyne was perhaps the outstanding example of an early trader who was also a pioneering planter and ethnographer. Unfortunately, there were some whose sporadic appearances in the Islands were nothing but destructive. Foljambe observed in 1865, while at Havannah Harbour in the New Hebrides: 'I think that the savage nature of these people is in a great measure brought out by the traders trying to cheat them.' One has only to read the adventurous account of Captain William T. Wawn, a recruiter for the Queensland labour trade from a huge area of the Pacific between 1875 and 1890, to feel sympathy for natives thrust into contact with Europeans of that kind. When legislation prohibited the import of human beings for Queensland plantations; Wawn simply could not understand the spoiling of the sport. There were plenty of others like Wawn, but none perhaps as volatile as the self-styled Colonel James Toutant Proctor from the Mississippi delta. As a Confederate lieutenant, he lost a leg at the age of seventeen in the Civil War, was awarded a Royal Humane Society medal for saving three British sailors in 1873, became a trader and cotton planter in Fiji, and was active on the fringe of blackbirding (see p.157) as a recruiting agent. Proctor moved to the New Hebrides where, on Tanna, he interrupted a feast of human flesh and saw confirmation of the fact, which he had been told by ancient anthropophagi, that the palm of the hand was the *pièce-de-résistance*. Philip Snow was also told this by the only cannibal he has personally known. Alfred Cort Haddon took an expedition to the Torres Straits and Papua in 1901. Thirty-four years later Philip Snow knew him well. Then in robust old age, Haddon explained that, in the cause of inescapable anthropological study, he had proved that the ball of the thumb, only if very well cooked, was marginally preferable to the palm.

Proctor would make much capital out of his wooden leg. Commanding his boots to be pulled off, he would allow his leg to come off in the same movement and would then bully the horrified natives into procuring labour recruits for him. For added *mana* he would sometimes stick a knife into his leg or fire a shot into his foot, but he abandoned this ploy when a native tried the other leg with a knife. Called by William Diaper a 'pistolman', he has been described as 'energetically villainous'. Missionaries said that 'he had the spirit of a slavedriver and was a curse wherever he went'. The last four years of his life were quite out of character: he worked as a clerk in the Civil District Court of New Orleans.

As the Pacific opened up, so another industry began to profit from it in the first half of the last century—whaling. Explorers in the Pacific had seen whales, particularly the sperm or cachalot species, previously thought to prefer colder waters. There are few more impressive sights than whales blowing water high above the Pacific on the ocean's more placid days. One has pure admiration for the creature and concern for its safety. Whalers had neither. They were men of extreme intrepidity and complete callousness. Whales provided their livelihood and the hunters could not afford any sentiment. The slaughter of so immense and vibrant a creature is an horrific sight: the sea is coated thick with blood over a wide area. Cutting it up on board a whaler and boiling it to make blubber must be one of the most odoriferous and generally unpleasant of tasks that men have chosen to adopt.

The oil, particularly from the sperm whale, improved domestic lighting all over the Western world. Its bone went into corsets. Its nutritional use has always been limited, except for the unfortunate modern discovery that it caters for one of the most profitable of all industries, pet food. In the Second World War it was a substitute for meat. So far as the Pacific was concerned, the whaling industry was almost an American monopoly in the nineteenth century. Whaling had started from Nantucket in about 1783 and went through its most adventurous phase up to 1830. From then until 1860, American whaling was at its financial zenith.

The Bay of Islands, in the North Island of New Zealand, was the principal centre for South Pacific whaling while, from 1819, Honolulu was the main centre for the North Pacific. The majority of whaling ships using both places were from New England.

From early in the nineteenth century, whales pursued off New Zealand brought crews into contact with Maoris. In return for provisions to cater for long periods at sea (fresh water, pork, vegetables, fruit, women, and coconut oil was the order of priority), whalers exchanged much the same articles as sandalwood and bêche-de-mer traders: iron tools, muskets, tobacco, rum, calico, ammunition, and, in the Fiji group, the ivory teeth of the sperm whale. These were the same shape as traditional wood and stone symbols of power and wealth, but they were much more impressive in ivory. In Fiji today, the polished whale's tooth is still the most gracious, indeed the only appropriate, gift at births, marriages, deaths, welcomes, and farewells, and it is the only currency for many activities governed by custom.

Crossing and criss-crossing the Pacific, captains of whaling ships treated the discoveries they made as merely part of their voyages. They got to know their ports of call, and soon showed a preference for the Marquesas and Tahiti—and for Hawaii until missionaries made life more difficult for them. Whaling was such an arduous life, with long periods spent in the open sea far from the lagoons, that the highest number of deserters came from whaling ships. Herman Melville's short sojourn as a refugee in the Marquesas will be

Herman Melville (1819–91), the writer, who first accumulated his raw material as a whaler (see p.201). This portrait was painted by Joseph Oriel Eaton.

described later (see p.201): all the horrors of the whaling life stand out in his *Moby Dick*.

Away from ports longer than traders, whalers were rougher in their manners. They were the pioneering importers of rum and other strong spirits. Missionaries had supported many traders, whom in some cases they had preceded to the Islands, but they were almost solidly anti-whalers. Whalers, regarding them as kill-joys, were equally solidly anti-missionaries. Introducing alcohol was not the whalers' only wickedness: missionaries noticed that many natives had also become addicted to tobacco.

Meanwhile, in about the middle of the last century, trading became rather more than freelance. The company of an enterprising wealthy merchant and shipowner, Johann Cesar Godeffroy, from a Huguenot family exiled to Hamburg, established North Pacific headquarters in Honolulu in 1845 and South Pacific headquarters in Apia in 1856. Godeffroy und Sohn started an empire throughout Polynesia, Micronesia, and Melanesia. Profitability was based on exporting copra, the sun-dried kernel of the coconut. Copra was sent from the plantations to bases away from the Pacific for pressing and extracting the oil. In 1865, the firm sent out Alfred Friedrich Tetens to trade with Yap and Palau Islanders and also, with enlightenment, to collect Pacific artefacts for Godeffroy's private museum in Hamburg. Tetens left entertaining memoirs of itinerant trading from 1862 to 1868. The first traders had to be as resourceful as the first beachcombers in gaining the interest and patronage of Islanders. Tetens had recourse to this on Yap, where the

> king ... was about to receive from me a gift of priceless worth as proof of our special friendship. At this announcement there was a deathly silence in the hall; every eye was fastened on me ... Accordingly I opened the box, took out a match, and, since there was no other article handy, lighted the match by a quick motion, as seamen do, on my trouser leg. As soon as the flame was visible, there arose a drawn-out, deafening roar of astonishment which was far more thunderous than that which had greeted the glass beads. As soon as the king held the present in his hands, he wished to strike a match for himself ... Although the king's hand which held the match passed with wonderful strength over the royal thigh, yet, since this was quite bare of any covering, the match naturally refused to light, and left not only on the striking surface but also on the pained face of the king visible traces of an unhappy surprize. Davis now grasped the stubborn match and lighted it on the fibre skirt of the nearest chief's wife. Before the king repeated this easy method, his right hand soothingly fondled his sore spots; this time his skill was rewarded—the wooden splinter burst into flame to the delight of His Majesty! The king repeated this marvel several times, but his discovery did not afford him any practical benefits. On the contrary, he was often delayed because he was convinced that the match would light only if struck on the same skirt he had first used. For this, the wearer attained great honour but had to be ready at any time to appear before His Majesty as matchbox, so that her and her husband's domestic tranquillity was often disturbed.

A shrewd observer, Tetens believed that the Micronesian races would die out on the approach of civilization. He was proved wrong, but it was a near thing. Tetens became supervisor of Hamburg's extensive maritime affairs in 1870, at the age of thirty-five, and he died in 1909.

Godeffroy und Sohn were so affected by the French blockade of Hamburg in the Franco-Prussian War of 1870 that they went bankrupt. In 1879, the firm was taken over by Zweignieder-lassung der Deutsche Handels-und-Plantagengesellschaft der Südsee Inseln zu Hamburg, known to the English-speaking people as the Longhandle Firm and, in the abbreviations beloved of Europeans in the South Seas, as D.H.P.G.

Theodore Weber, the German Consul in Samoa, was regarded as a master-mind in merchandise from 1861 to 1889. He helped D.H.P.G., as an imperial instrument of Bismarck, become a single, efficient organization from the Carolines in the extreme west to the Society Islands towards the extreme east.

A great deal of anti-German feeling had been engendered, no doubt through envy. Missionaries were jealous of German commercial influence, notably in Samoa. Robert Louis Stevenson depicted German company traders in uncomplimentary terms, principally because he was anxious to steer Samoa from an over-interested Germany to an under-interested Britain.

France's surprisingly quick defeat in the Franco-Prussian War left the Pacific—and the rest of the Western world—wide open to expanding German strength: this was to have repercussions from which the Western world would never recover.

Traders and missionaries did not always agree. In Tahiti, the exporting of coconut oil, sugar, pearl shell, and arrowroot and the importing of cloth and hardware had been from earliest times almost a missionary monopoly. It was big business in the 1830s both in Tahiti and in the Hawaiian group. There, the missionaries were as closely connected with commerce as they could be. If it was not competition for trade itself, there were other subjects of disagreement, such as grog and women. And when it came to traders being dominantly German and missionaries being French, British, or American, the scope for non-cooperation was far wider.

The change from trading and whaling to planting and settling is dealt with in Chapter IX. Traders and, to a smaller degree, whalers continued to be a feature of Pacific life for many years: traders never really ceased to exist, but their nature changed as they turned into settlers. Meanwhile, there can be no doubt that the phase of trading and whaling exacerbated the savage side of some Islanders.

Chapter VIII

Pagans and Missionaries

THE PIG PET.

The relative religionism of Europeans and Islanders has turned upside down. From earliest times, Europeans set out to impose their faiths on reluctant indigenous people. Nowadays Islanders in all groups adhere, often most rigidly, to Christian religions of some variety. Western missionaries to the Pacific have been ninety-nine per cent victorious—one of the more remarkable ideological triumphs in history. Even the few breakaway anti-European movements have retained Christianity in some form. On the other hand, Europeans have abandoned their ancestors' faiths in large numbers and these days they would be sceptical of the dogma with which their missionaries overwhelmed the natives.

Reading the narratives of most early missionaries of the last century, one hears the ebullient, passionate tone ringing loud and clear. Missionaries had to feel as they did in order to survive against extreme hostility, against the enervating climate, and against fearful deprivations. Courage and a wonderful vitality shine out of their writings, and they clearly helped to insulate the missionaries and their families against illness, humiliation, and massacre. There is often precious observation of previously unknown habits and customs, which were soon to disappear. Sometimes missionaries recorded them to show what they had succeeded in suppressing.

Immediately after the voyages of exploration, missionaries felt impelled to follow and convert. One such voyage was in fact also an undisguised missionary invasion. *Duff* left London in 1796 not to open up commercial activities, but to spread the faith of the London Missionary Society.

For long an unbeliever, then a passionate adherent of the faith, James Wilson was *Duff*'s captain. The youngest of nineteen children, he had gone to sea with the East India Company and had been captured in India. He made a small fortune as a trader before retiring to England. But he was unsettled there and, at the age of thirty-six, he offered his maritime ability to the London Missionary Society to take missionaries to the South Seas, the first non-Catholic proselytizing attempt by any country.

Duff's complement was chosen so that mission houses and churches could be constructed in Tahiti, Tonga, and the Marquesas, Sandwich, and Pelew Islands, which the directors of the London Missionary Society nominated for Wilson as 'the destined scene of your benevolent exertions'. Twenty-six artisans, many of them carpenters, joined the four ordained missionaries, six women, and three children. The artisans were also ordained.

This odyssey led first to Rio de Janeiro, as the intention was to go round Cape Horn, but storms caused such a huge diversion that they had to go via the opposite cape. Ninety-seven days after leaving Rio, *Duff* reached Tahiti in 1797: 13,820 miles had been covered without touching land and without seeing more than one vessel and one island.

The discovery of Tahiti thirty years earlier had been quickly followed by an unsuccessful Spanish attempt to establish Catholic missionaries. Tahiti was now to become the most important centre in the Pacific for English missionaries, although not for long.

The arrival of *Duff*'s Calvinistic missionaries at their destinations marked the greatest impact of European culture so far, and the real beginning of concerted theological effort against paganism in the South Seas. Material structures were naturally among the first things to be attacked: imposing *marae*, podia constructed from coral blocks for the worship of pagan gods, were damaged and, on Rarotonga, there was an orgy of idol burning. These were regrettably indelicate impositions of Western culture. The clash of ideologies over customs was more spectacular. The more revolting practices like cannibalism were fair targets, and missionaries set about eliminating them with ardour and bravery. Unfortunately, they were not always able to judge calmly and with detachment which of the customs, marginally less horrific, might have been restrained and discouraged rather than positively condemned.

Let us look first, however, at those practices at the top of the list for elimination. Cannibalism was the most obtrusive of the pagan customs. In the Pacific it is a large and profound subject. It has obvious justifications for survival at sea, where Europeans have also had to resort to it; the same exoneration could be extended to the adoption of it on land which lacked sources of protein. However, the excesses to which certain races, particularly Fijians, carried it could not be defended: raids on women and children could not have helped the race to increase or even to continue.

The belief that to consume one's enemy conferred psychological strength, apart from the protein boost it might provide, is understandable. William Pascoe Crook, the missionary left by *Duff* among the Marquesans, maintained that the origin of the practice was the belief that a vanquished enemy's powers and magic were acquired by eating him. Robarts, the deserter on the Marquesas (see p.72), told von Krusenstern that need of protein was the inducement. Ta'unga, a Rarotongan missionary in New Caledonia from 1842 to 1847, was certain that the two main motives for the cannibalism that he was obliged to witness were revenge and a desperate craving for human flesh. Benjamin Morrell, reporting 150 years ago, believed that, for the Maoris, revenge and the transfer of strength and courage were prime elements, the need to eat flesh being secondary, even though victims were fattened up in pens. The left eye of an enemy was regarded as the seat of the soul.

Cannibalism was at its least compromising in Melanesia, where bodies were never buried. When baked, they tasted like pork—they were regarded as long pig and were eaten for gastronomic pleasure. In Fiji where, as throughout the South Seas, eating was done by hand, human flesh was alone in never being eaten without a special wooden fork. It is believed that this fastidiousness grew out of the impression that, in the dark, human flesh gave off a phosphorescent lustre which spread to cooking utensils or hands. In Fiji, too, a special vegetable, a kind of spinach, was always reserved for eating with human flesh. Fijian women, unlike those of New Caledonia and New Ireland, did not eat people except in private.

Rev. Joseph Waterhouse was one of the missionaries trying to eliminate cannibalism, but he had to sit by and stoically watch a great deal of it:

> . . . a man's body is being cut up, and prepared for food, as is a bullock in our own country. See the commotion! The majority of the population, old and young, run to gaze upon the intended victim. He is stripped naked, struck down with his own club, his body ignominiously dashed against a stone in front of a temple, and then the body is cut up and divided amongst a chosen few, ere the vital spark is extinct. Sometimes he is dashed into an oven whilst

The port of Honolulu, painted by Louis Choris on von Kotzebue's circumnavigation of 1815–8.

yet alive, and half frizzled. The little children run off with the head, and play with it as you would with a cricket ball.

The stone referred to is now in Bau church. There was no greater humiliation for a vanquished enemy (although he was no longer in a position to acknowledge it) than to be not only killed but, then, for his opponents to refuse to eat him.

Missionaries effectively abolished cannibalism—a truly remarkable achievement. Psychologically and demographically, the demise of cannibalism was right, although Thor Heyerdahl makes a valid point when he reminds the oversanctimonious that 'We are educated to run a bayonet into a living person but not to run a fork into one who is already dead'.

Other horrendous practices were suppressed by missionaries. These were particularly evident in Fiji. When wooden posts for a chief's new house were put in their holes, live retainers were buried holding them. On the death of chiefs, their widows were strangled. Discarded wives of chiefs were killed. Under the feudal system, newly hewn canoes were launched across land over the live bodies of serfs. Infanticide was practised, notably by a Tahiti cult.

Some suppressions were more questionable, and raise the doubt as to whether missionaries thought sufficiently far ahead about the psychological effects of what they were doing. Certain prohibitions (*tabu*) of face-saving value to tribes were needlessly abolished under missionary influence, while harmless rites not totally in tune with Christian beliefs were forced out. A state of undress in torrid climates was to missionaries virtually criminal. They were unremittingly censorious: 'At these night dances, all kinds of obscenity in looks, language and gesture prevail'. Their unending denunciation of *kava*, a stupefacient, non-alcoholic drink, passes understanding. The abolition of polygamy—another remarkable missionary triumph—was not considered in relation to the effect on populations of small communities.

As a result, natives were left bewildered and devitalized, both physically and psychologically. They were given an acute sense of inferiority, against which the Christian promise of an afterlife was cold comfort. Yet, despite the destructive effects of missionaries, their sheer bravery can evoke nothing but admiration. Native priests were naturally intensely jealous when their pagan power was supplanted: it was not easy to withstand their animosity.

Impressive examples of intrepidity were frequently set by European women attached to missionary societies or living as part of missionary families. *Life in Feejee or, Five Years Among the Cannibals* by A Lady was written very early, in 1851. The Lady was a fearless American, Mary Davis Wallis, from Salem, the wife of a bêche-de-mer ship captain, Benjamin Wallis. The publication, the first by a woman on the Pacific, is full of rich descriptions of cultural contacts and accurate accounts, melodramatic and dramatic, of native customs. She knew as much about the baking of bodies and the strangling of willing women when their chiefs died as anyone before or since. She and her husband once talked to the paramount chief of Bau, and she wrote:

> He asked if I were the only wife of my husband. On being told that I was, he said 'That's bad, Mr. Wallis, you should have more'. He then became

H.M.S. *Herald* being towed into Makira (San Christobal), Solomon Islands, in 1854 to search for Benjamin Boyd. J. Glen Wilson, the talented artist on *Herald*, painted this scene.

126

animated while enunciating the advantages of polygamy, and said he had one hundred wives and ended by advising my husband to get an immediate supply. I asked him if the hundred women were not jealous and if they did not quarrel. He said that they did sometimes but when this was the case he had them clubbed and the matter was ended.

'Clubbed' meant the prevailing method of execution.

Julius Louis Brenchley, a naturalist on H.M.S. *Curaçoa* in 1865, recorded Rev. John Gibson Paton's indomitability at Tanna in the New Hebrides:

> . . . though he has had fever and ague 24 times in one year and has buried his wife there: though he has had his house and church destroyed, his own life several times attempted and only saved by interposition of a friendly chief, and though he has had to watch gun in hand by his wife's grave ten consecutive nights until her body was completely decomposed to prevent cannibals from exhuming it for food, he still wishes to return and resume his labours.

This he did and, after thirty years in this environment, died at the age of eighty-three.

Papeete Harbour, Tahiti, painted by W. Wiles at the time of incipient settling in the 1840s.

DRAWN, BY W. WILES ESQ^R

M & N. HANHART LITH.

Polynesia, the least hostile of the main regions to European influences, was the first to experience the new religious culture. As early as 1814, Rev. Samuel Marsden arrived in New Zealand and made converts with surprising speed. There were problems: Maoris, with their predilection for tribal wars, were perpetual clients for muskets. If a tribe was victorious, it would decline to follow up its advantage to the full because by doing so there could be no more fighting. Conversely, tribes running out of ammunition let their opponents know that they would be obliged to stop hostilities unless some was sent to them—requests that were invariably granted. This puzzled the missionaries, while Maoris in their turn were perplexed by missionary tactics. Mark Twain was told by a Maori that the missionary

> wants you to stop worshipping and supplicating the evil gods and go to worshipping and supplicating the Good One. There is no sense in that. A *good* God is not going to do us any harm.

There were two main features of Maori paganism besides cannibalism. One was difficult for missionaries to defeat: customs and law were enforced by a

The cession of land on Tahiti to the first missionaries. Captain James Wilson of *Duff* holds a hat. The high chief (later Pomare II, 1780–1821) and his 'queen' are borne on shoulders: otherwise, ground stepped on by nobility was theirs by custom. In the middle, dressed in Tahitian style and interpreting, is Peter Haggerstein, a Finnish beachcomber. William Wilson, the first officer, is next to his uncle: he sketched the episode in 1797. Robert A. Smirke, R.A., painted it in 1829.

rigid system of *tapu* (the Polynesian form of *tabu*), and it is questionable whether they should have disturbed this. The other, the existence of no all-powerful god but a system of polytheism, actually helped Christianity: a supreme, omnipotent God could intervene effectively when minor deities were competing with each other.

By about 1840, when the first British Governor, William Hobson, was appointed in New Zealand, there were about 2,000 *pakeha* (foreigners)—traders and missionaries; the latter had by then convinced many Maoris that they were an influence for fairness against dishonest merchants.

It took some time for missionaries to turn the corner in Tonga. Chiefs opposed them vehemently because their power was being challenged by the Church's dogma that, in the Christian God's eyes, all were equal and that there were no superiors among men. Others were won over by the European technology, riches, and influence brought by the missionaries. The latter did not make things easy for themselves by their insensitivity to Tongan customs, which had been held in great respect for centuries. Catholic missionaries

A missionary house at Matavai, Tahiti, constructed by eager ecclesiastical artisans of *Duff*. The tranquillity was short-lived. William Wilson, the captain's nephew, made this sketch.

tended to show deeper understanding and made psychological gains with their more cautious attitude towards indigenous practices: although they were severe about the dressing-up required of natives (many of whom could not take up the fashion quickly enough), they were marginally less forbidding in their attitude towards dances, sports, gambling, and smoking. Catholic leaders in the mid-nineteenth century would not have gone as far as John Wesley in fulminating against the heathen as 'the sink of all profaneness and debauchery'. Nor would they perhaps have extended the venom of their denunciation of the heathen, as the Protestants did, to snuff-taking.

What enabled missionaries to get a foot in was their medical aid. Dispensing hours were part of their timetable. The beneficial effects of medicine were there for all to see: the wonders of the performances of Christianity were a little more mysterious.

Tonga was eventually converted. However, Rev. J.B. Watkin, of the Free Church of Tonga, felt obliged to say in 1913:

> The Tongan in his undress suit, bare-legged, bare-footed, is a lordly-looking man, whose walk represents the poetry of motion. There are few Tongans who look well in European clothing. They buy boots several times too large for them.

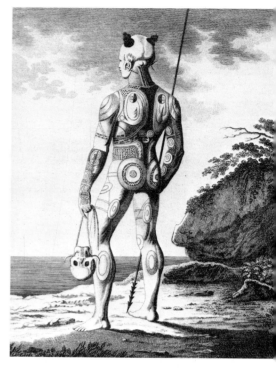

A young pagan Marquesan from Nukuhiva acquires an enemy's skull before the completion of his tattooing. He was drawn on von Krusenstern's expedition of 1803–6 (see p.72).

There are many devout worshippers of Christianity in the Pacific. Although there is no measuring stick to justify this calculation, it is the opinion of the authors that Tonga's religious zeal is excelled by that of no other Christian country. There is no lack of forms: a five minute stroll in Nuku'alofa, the capital, in 1979 included among its spectacles the Church of Tonga, the Wesleyan Church, the Free Church of Tonga, the Roman Catholic Church, the Seventh Day Adventist Church, the Church of England, and the Temple of the Mormons, each proclaiming their faith to be the right and only one.

As for Tahiti, when the captain and company of *Duff* were carried ashore on the shoulders of natives, whose delight was unbounded, everything looked rosy. James Wilson's trump card, a cuckoo-clock, was immediately produced: it terrified the natives when they heard it strike. One of them brought some breadfruit as food for the wooden bird.

Of the missionaries who disembarked, none stayed the course. Several died young, others rejected their faith and took pagan women, some involved themselves in civil wars, and the febrile enthusiasm of the remainder faded. But from 1817 to 1825 Tahiti had a rare missionary, Rev. William Ellis. Born in London of a poor family in 1794, he was more sage and tolerant than anyone could have expected a missionary aged twenty-three to be. Ellis was not repelled by tales of the country's vile manner of taking its fun. On the contrary, his unusual depth of interest in ancient customs and in the reasons for Tahiti appearing to be so carefree enabled him to discuss most subjects dispassionately with the Islanders. His *Polynesian Researches* is one of the outstanding Pacific works. It abounds with favourable accounts of the people:

> ... Among the many models of perfection in the human figure that appear in the Islands (presenting to the eye of the stranger all that is beautiful in symmetry and graceful in action) ... The countenance of the Society Islander is open and prepossessing ... They are seldom melancholy or reserved ... They do not appear to delight in provoking one another, but are far more accustomed to jesting, mirth and humour than irritation or reproachful language ...

Idols brought to John Williams, the impassioned missionary, and his wife, to be burnt on Rarotonga in the early 1830s. From a wood engraving by George Baxter.

But even Ellis could be ecstatic over the 'neat and tasteful bonnets' of the converts. A level-headed administrator, Sir Reginald St. Johnston, was prompted to judge this missionary imposition as unnecessary and unforgivable. How good a missionary Ellis was is not clear, but he was superlative as one of the earliest ambassadors of Western civilization. He would have seen this point, made penetratingly by Dillon:

> And here let me observe, that I consider it highly impolitic in the missionaries who are bachelors not to choose wives from the native females: as many advantages, both personal and as regards their conversation, would result from such marriages.

Despite the enlightenment of Ellis, his mission failed to keep Tahiti from becoming Catholic.

In the Cook Islands, the Protestant missionary establishment, directed by Rev. John Williams and Rev. Aaron Buzacott, soon became an absolute theocracy. Before the British Government annexed these islands, the missionaries' laws were downright peculiar. How else could one describe laws that imposed fines on anyone, including Europeans, who was out-of-doors after 8 p.m., and that required anyone with his arm round his betrothed's waist at dusk to carry a burning torch in his hand under penalty of a fine if he let it go out? There was also a fine for anyone found weeping over the grave of a woman not related to him.

The docile Rarotongans complied with missionaries' eccentricities, although they sometimes mistook their motives, as when they saw a European hunting butterflies with a net, and concluded that they were his favourite food. At Avarua, Rarotonga's port, missionaries had 'the best specimen of Gothic architecture in the South Seas' constructed: that is their description. The Earl of Pembroke's was 'that vile, black and white abomination paralysing one of the most beautiful bits of scenery in the world'. Rarotongans, despite the absurdities imposed on them, came off better than some of their neighbours.

The Gambier Islands were devastated for thirty-seven years by a fanatic, Père Louis Honoré Laval, who forced natives to become monks and nuns. In the end he was certified insane. By the time of his removal, it was estimated that 5,000 people had died during his dictatorship. When confronted with this, he is said to have replied: 'True, they are all dead. But they have gone to Heaven the more quickly.' Laval estimated that the population numbered 10,000 when he arrived. A century later there were only 500 people left.

As for the cannibalistic Marquesans, they were perplexed by the Communion Service's symbolic eating of the body of Christ, while they were at the same time being exhorted to steer away from associated thoughts.

Missionaries in Hawaii had an easier task than those in most other parts of the Pacific. By the 1820s, there was little strength in native religion and no powerful pagan priests. Missionaries faced, however, antagonism from foreign traders, who had found in Hawaii a land of great promise. Eventually, the traders were forced to give the Hawaiians fair payment for the profitable sandalwood. Opposition also came from whalers, mostly Americans, who had found Hawaii to be an agreeable Venusberg.

A night dance of the kind frowned upon by missionaries, drawn by John Webber on Ha'apai Island, Tonga, during Cook's last visit in 1777. Bamboos, thumped on the ground by the seated group in the centre, beat out the rhythm.

132

In 1820, a Congregationalist Calvinist from Boston, Hiram Bingham, arrived in Hawaii and remarked:

> The appearance of almost naked savages whose heads and feet and much of their sunburned swarthy skins were bare, was appalling. Some of our number, with gushing tears, turned away from the spectacle.

He saw *hula* dancers throw their *leis* (flower garlands) on to an enclosure sacred to the god of *hula hula*. In his *Journal*, Bingham reported the following discourse: 'Does the god of the hula hula know everything?' 'No'. 'Can he see?' 'No'. 'Can he hear?' 'No'. 'Can he speak?' 'No'. 'Can he do anything?' 'No'. 'What is he good for and why do you have such a god?'. 'For play'. Good

Paganism was almost completely superseded by Christianity in Polynesia by the end of the 1870s. Nothing could show more graphically the change in Pukapuka (Cook Islands) than these scenes, drawn by W. H. Sterndale, before (captioned by the missionaries as 'heathen revelling') and after the conversion. The trees alone withstand change. A trim mission lady still finds it prudent, however, to restrain a soporific pig on a leash. Incidentally, Polynesians never wore 'grass' skirts.

A VILLAGE IN PUKAPUKA, UNDER HEATHENISM

THE SAME VILLAGE, UNDER CHRISTIANITY.

manners would have prevented Hawaiians from applying an inquisition on the same lines to Bingham about his God. But it showed the chasm between the New England culture and that of Hawaii. Eventually, the missionaries won the day and, forty years later, Mark Twain reported:

> They [the Hawaiians] all belong to the Church and are fonder of theology than they are of pie: they will sweat out a sermon as long as the Declaration of Independence—the duller it is the more it infatuates them.

Micronesia, the first region known to receive Europeans, and Guam, the first island to do so, were also the first Pacific areas to have missionaries. In 1668, six Spanish Jesuits under Father Diego Luis de Sanvitores, who was to be murdered four years later, and some horses were simultaneously introduced to Guam. Because the horses had bits in their mouths, the Chamorros believed that they must be in the habit of eating iron: this accomplishment placed them above the missionaries in the estimation of natives, who made gifts of coconuts to the horses in the hope of earning their esteem.

Melanesia was the real testing-ground for missionaries, as it had been, and still was, for other types of Europeans. Discoverers, explorers, and traders had all reported how different it was from Polynesia and Micronesia. Aggressiveness, suspicion, a positive dislike of visitors: these were Melanesian characteristics, often, as we have seen, the result of inconsiderate treatment

A mass on Mangareva, one of the four Gambier Islands, at the beginning of the 1840s, drawn by Ernest-Auguste Goupil, who died on Dumont d'Urville's expedition of 1837–40 (see p.80). Polynesians are intrinsically ceremonial-minded, and Catholic ritual had an edge over Protestant austerity in supplanting pagan forms of worship. Low Church predilection for oratorical sermons, communal prayer, and vigorous hymn singing, however, helped to redress the balance and keep competition keen.

An engraving by W. Derby of the far-sighted English missionary, Rev. William Ellis (1794–1872), who took an exceptional interest in Islanders' customs.

Thanks to the missionaries' influence, a woman from Niue (Savage Island) has no doubt that she represents the height of fashion.

from Europeans. Customs here were savagely conceived and tenaciously held. The missions' successes in Melanesia, correcting the worst excesses of early whalers and traders, together with their own medical contributions, represented their greatest triumphs. But they went too far and reduced the natives to apathy.

Two invigorating missionaries, however, went to New Guinea. William George Lawes, an English representative of the London Missionary Society, moved there from Niue as early as 1874. No prig, he was curious to know first-hand about betel-nuts:

> The taste is pleasing and it is said by some authorities to be a good preventative of fever. It may be but I doubt this. It is an aromatic astringent: a sense of warmth follows the chewing but I was conscious of no other effect whatsoever ... Its constant use dyes the teeth quite black and they soon become red. Red teeth are considered handsome by the native ladies, and black teeth superlatively so.

The head of Henry Brougham Guppy, a naturalist-explorer in the Solomons contemporaneously, was weaker:

> A single nut had much the same effect on me as a glass of sherry would have had.

A comment made by Lawes in 1876 puts material products of the two cultures of which he was part in neat juxtaposition:

> One canoe, nearly finished, must have been an enormous tree: it measured 48 feet long by 10 feet round and for making it only stone hatchets had been used. My respect for the Stone Age considerably increased when I saw the stone hatchets at work. Our umbrellas were greatly admired. We walked through the village arm-in-arm with a native who shared with us the shade and the glory of the umbrella.

James Chalmers, a Scotsman, joined Lawes from Rarotonga in 1877. Both were tough yet benevolent: they were widely accepted. Lawes made many cultural contributions during the thirty-three years that he spent among the Papuans, while Chalmers (who was eaten near the Fly River in 1901) was an indefatigable explorer.

Later, Catholic missionaries in New Guinea made themselves unpopular with traders by going in for trade themselves. Wishing both to train their followers in commerce and to indulge in it themselves, they were obliged to register as companies. The Catholic Mission of the Sacred Heart of Jesus Christ Limited and the Mission of the Holy Ghost Limited have a confident ring about them.

Solomon Islanders had one of the worst reputations for inhumanity. On Malaita, offenders against their society's morals were made to eat themselves. A limb would be lopped off and cooked, and the culprit was then forced to eat it. On Santa Ysabel, in 1845, the first Catholic Bishop was murdered. Guppy was certain that:

> The great heroism of the Melanesian mission was the only redeeming feature in the intercourse of the white man with these islanders in the last 25 years.

New Hebrideans were even fiercer than Solomon Islanders. They killed more missionaries than did any other Islanders, including Rev. John Williams and a

colleague in 1839, and the first Anglican Bishop of Melanesia, John Coleridge Patteson, in 1876.

Fiji presented one of the greatest challenges to missionaries. Reports of enthusiastic cannibalism had kept visitors away, and it was not until 1835 (a peak period of pioneer evangelizing in the Pacific was 1815–25) that the first missionaries, Wesleyans, ventured from Tonga to Lau, the more Polynesian part of the Fiji group.

It is remarkable that only one missionary was eaten in Fiji. Rev. Thomas Baker, in an expedition to the interior in 1867, insulted a chief along the Rewa River by snatching back his comb after the chief had put it in his hair. To this day, Fijians crouch in front of a chief, so that they never stand higher than him; they also do not move behind his back without murmuring *'Tilou, saka'* ('Excuse me, Sir'). Chiefs prescribed this courtesy to protect their heads in the era of the rapid use of clubs. Although the Rewa River chief had been whimsical in his use of Baker's comb, the missionary, from all accounts not the most sensitive of persons, should not have touched the chief's head. As Baker left to go further up river, the offended chief sent a whale's tooth by messenger behind him with the request that Baker be killed, the reward for which would be the whale's tooth. At Navatusila, a mountain district tribe accepted the

Marae, built of coral blocks, were used for worship and sacrifices (see p.94). The Europeans depicted on the platform in Hawaii are French. Jacques Etienne Victor Arago, the artist, wears a top hat: he later went blind.

tooth, clubbed Baker, and divided his body, as they would a pig, amongst neighbours. One of these accepted a leg, on which a Wellington boot was assumed to be part of the European skin: the tribe which ate it was impressed by the toughness of the European. It was cooked and recooked in despair of ever tenderizing the joint. The more sophisticated connoisseurs of flesh did not let this tribe forget its gaffe.

To the present day, the tribe which killed Baker has hardly been forgiven by Fijians, the majority of whom were Christianized soon after his death. Philip Snow had a member of this small tribe in his police force. When drinking off duty, this policeman would forget the inferiority he felt as a result of originating from Navatusila (most of the tribe are now Seventh Day Adventists), and would claim that it was he who had killed Baker. As it was eighty years after the incident and the policeman was barely fifty years old, this statement could scarcely have been believed by his drinking companions. Nevertheless, he would be ostracized by them after each occasion: only Philip Snow seemed to be his friend. The daughter of this mixed-up policeman from the interior was Stefanie Waine's nursemaid and the first to teach her the Fijian language.

Missionaries in Fiji set about introducing literacy early: they devised an alphabet more complex than any in the Pacific. C is pronounced th, while g is ng, q is ngg, b is mb, and n is nd. The use of c for th was thought initially to be due to a shortage of letters in the mission press, but in fact it was a deliberate euphonic choice—rather on the lines of the Spanish pronunciation.

Among the greatest missionary achievements were their skilful compilations

The American evangelist, Hiram Bingham (1789–1869), preaching at Waimea, Hawaii, in 1826. The Dowager Queen, already converted, looks on in approval. Bingham himself made the sketch.

of the first dictionaries, and the introduction of literacy in most of the groups. Much of that arduous work was carried out under appalling conditions, but zeal, *naïveté*, and fanaticism carried them through—or some of them. Deaths in Melanesia were quite numerous, particularly among their wives and children; and there was a very high rate of alcoholism among missionaries. Some of their ethnographical work has still not been surpassed: the Fijian dictionary compiled by Rev. David Hazlewood in 1850 remains the best of its kind, while that for Samoa by Rev. George Pratt was the principal work from 1878 until nearly a century later.

Sir John Thurston (1836–97), the fourth governor of Fiji (1888–97) (see. p.182), photographed in 1886 with the chief whose brother killed and ate Rev. Thomas Baker in Fiji's forbidding interior.

These partners in New Guinea for the last quarter of the nineteenth century, Rev. William George Lawes (1839–1907), left, and Rev. James Chalmers (1841–1901), right, made signal contributions to European-Islander goodwill.

Most of the missionaries' books on Fiji are in a fairly excitable vein, with strongly intolerant judgements of native life until much of it was altered by the missions. There were many European critics of missionaries. This is what John d'Ewes thought:

> The missionaries, though well intentioned, seem not to be very successful with their converts. Not being very deep thinkers, or judges of human nature, except in the way of trade and looking out for their own interests (for in that they are sharp enough), they fall into great and serious mistakes. They seem to consider that the natives should have the same ideas as white men, that they should like the same things, admire the same, wish for the same luxuries, and dislike the same evils. But how different they really are! ... He likes to dine on taro and raw fish, though the missionary tells him that it is disgusting. He prefers going without more clothes than a short shirt, though his teacher tells him that it is indecent. He would rather see his chère amie with a wreath of natural flowers round her head, and her bosom bare, than up to her neck in blue baft, and a cottage straw-bonnet on her head, but the missionaries denounce all these things, and call them wicked. The poor docile native obeys him, but his life and soul are gone.

Today, native Fijians are ninety per cent Wesleyan, seven per cent Catholic, and the remainder Seventh Day Adventists and Church of England. There are no confessed agnostics or atheists. In terms of any purpose realized, Wesleyans in Fiji can hardly be transcended. There is no similar monopoly anywhere else in the Pacific. Seventh Day Adventism's one hundred per cent triumph with the handful of Pitcairn Islanders is not quite in the same dimension.

By the end of the 1870s, paganism had given way to Christianity virtually throughout the Pacific.

Chapter IX

Settlers and Planters

Discoverers had come and seen and gone away. Explorers had done much the same but, before going away, had indicated where it might be possible to open up the Islands. Castaways and beachcombers had come, sometimes inadvertently, sometimes for permanent or, more likely, semi-permanent escape from Western civilization. They had moved to a part of the world in which they might either make a mark, if they had any ambitions, or else lose themselves. Many of them had gone away. Traders and whalers were transient, the latter without exception. Profit made, they departed. Missionaries were driven by zeal and inner goading to make their impression, stay as long as they could and, while residing there, change as much around them as possible: they were the first settlers with a definite purpose.

The quintessential settlers were the planters. Theirs was a long-term purpose: they had no quick way of making profits like visiting traders, although some planters were traders who had stayed on. Land, a homestead, hands to help: these were the assets to be acquired and around which their lives would revolve from the time of settling right up to their deaths, when their children would inherit. The preparation of the land for crops, the time that it takes the crops to start to earn some money, and the increasing return on their money all depended on extending the life of crops as long as possible. Changing the bush (the Pacific word for jungle, which is in itself a Hindi word, जंगल, jngl, and would only be used in the Pacific by immigrant Indians) into cleared and cultivated plantations involved scores of years and excruciating work. In the Pacific the term 'bush' means not so much low scrub as dense forest.

In contemplating whether to settle, planters had to compare the forces of nature with other parts of the world. They also had to take into consideration the quality of the soil, the risk of being forced out by inimical people, and the chances of the development of communications.

It was not long before land became the most emotional subject in a Pacific Islander's life. At first, however, it had little value for natives: there was, at least in Melanesia, a surfeit of it, to be bought for a musket or a bottle of gin. In Polynesia, it was less easy. In Micronesia, the question hardly arose, except in the few islands with steep elevations and sizeable pockets of soil, as on Yap. Small, low coral atolls in extreme isolation were no temptation for the settler. There was little on them, except for two absolutely vital trees essential (with taro) for native life, the lean and elegant coconut palm and the squat but ornamental breadfruit tree. There also was a third tree, the pandanus or screw pine, which was not beautiful, except for the scent of its fruit, but was useful as nutrition and for making hats, fans, mats, sails, and thatch.

As settlers were the first Westerners to reside in any number in the South Sea Islands, it is as well to consider some of the local conditions that prevailed at the time. Disease was, and is, often a primary consideration when deciding about settling. From the start there has never been malaria in Polynesia and Micronesia, while for Melanesia it has been a great handicap. Only in recent years have a few Melanesian urban settlements and areas near airports begun to be able to control the anopheles mosquito. In Melanesia, too, there is the culex mosquito that proliferates in Polynesia and Micronesia. It carries not

The baptism of Hawaii's Prime Minister, Kalanimoku or Kaimoku (known initially as William Pitt and then, after his christening, as Louis) on *L'Uranie* in 1819, watched by Kamehameha II. Rose de Freycinet noted afterwards: 'In two hours these intrepid guests drank or took away enough to provide our table for more than 3 months.' The King resisted conversion, because it would have meant that he could only have one wife: Louis had given up seven. Jacques Arago and Crépin painted the occasion.

yellow fever, which is unknown in the Pacific, but elephantiasis—spectacular and incommoding. It also carries dengue, which has an eloquent alternative name: breakbone fever; there is no known cure for this, which can be fatal. By and large, however, the Pacific has very few diseases and, in that respect, compares more than favourably with most parts of the world for settlement.

With diseases had to be taken into consideration natural hazards. First of all, those likely to cause disasters: these had to be weighed heavily by settlers. There being no meteorological records, prospective settlers depended on what natives told them of the weather, and on what they could find out for themselves. Droughts could be virtually ruled out, except on atolls, and bush fires are not the menace that they are in Australia and New Zealand. But much of the Pacific has been, and is, subject to frequent hurricanes, perhaps two a year. Often they are accompanied by tidal waves, nor ordinarily a peril on a high island but alarming on an atoll or at sea. Tidal waves can also follow volcanic eruptions, and a prudent settler would have elected, if he could not

Left: In this painting by Norman H. Hardy, (d. 1914), a New Hebridean brings coconuts to a trader at the beginning of this century.

Below: A young woman of Guam, when it was under Spanish influence, painted at the beginning of the last century.

FEMME DE L'ILE GUHAM.
(Océanie.)

avoid a hurricane zone, to set up his homestead both above tidal wave limits and away from the few active volcanoes in the Pacific.

Before he contemplated the remaining physical considerations, the settler of whatever kind—commercial, administrative, educational, medical, missionary, or technical—would have had to judge whether or not he was temperamentally suited to living among indigenous Islanders, who might be his only friends. And he had to know that he could not only endure but also enjoy the tranquillity that accompanies absolute isolation. He had not to be upset by the wind whistling through casuarina trees at night (Philip Snow has known a responsible man to be driven to suicide over this). He had to find unceasing delight in the crowns of palm trees looking down at him like asterisks in serried ranks. For the settler overlooking a coast, the entire spectrum of all the greens and blues of the lagoon had to have an undying allurement. For the settler in the interior (if his island had more than a coastline), the jagged, forbidding mountains, the valleys with their wisps of rain-laden mist, and the rapids in the rivers had never to pall. He would have had to recognize that almost the greatest pleasure available to him was the indulgence of lounging back on an open veranda, watching the sun go down and the great gold moon rising and changing through lemon to silver.

The settler in Oceania would not have taken long to realize that it contains

Norman Hardy's painting of a clearing in luxuriant jungle in the Solomons at the beginning of this century. 'Though it was a brilliantly fine day, yet I remember when we were fairly into the forest depths it was just like twilight; while here and there long streaks of sunlight were streaming through the tree-tops, reminding us of the light coming through the windows of a cathedral. We all went Indian file, and in many places the bush was so thick that we lost sight of each other...' Many settlers' gardens ended in the bush.

some of the largest, most persistent insects in the world. There are more than 120,000 different species and relations. Spelt by them musquitoes, earliest explorers were unanimous in complaining about them in almost every land of the Pacific. When the long suffering Romilly was appointed the first commissioner to Rotuma Island in 1880, he could not refrain from lamenting:

The great objection to it is musquitoes. They are in millions, and although it sounds absurd to write about so small a matter, are an intense annoyance. When I shake my net in the night, it really sounds like a covey of partridges getting up.

Natives used coconut oil and turmeric as mosquito repellents and had developed some immunity to their maddening itch. Despite some physical changes in the Pacific—diseases coming in and going out, new ones replacing them, crops changing—much remains on the natural level today as it was in the seventeenth century—including those mosquitoes, the unspeakable leeches, and the flies. The last-mentioned creep along your face, alight on your eyelids, and cover the food you are taking to your mouth. With their facility for transmitting disease, flies remain the most dangerous Island creatures.

The Pacific can claim the largest flying insects in the world. Four inches long, these giant stag-beetles live in rotten logs and blunder about after nightfall. Whatever in the way of skin they hit, they cling to by piercing it with their mandibles, which are the same length as their resplendent bodies. Entangled in the hair, they are likely to stay for some time. They pierce the shirt on your back and hold on to the skin until encouraged to let go by a hot match. Less attractive are the giant flying cockroaches, which emit a stale odour and are repulsive to crush.

The stinkbugs which abound in the Pacific are small but harmless. For no apparent reason, they give off an odour which, although acrid, is nowhere near the top of our list of unpleasant smells in the Pacific. High on it would be fermenting breadfruit buried under the sand. If a stinkbug flies into your mouth its taste is sharp: whatever the company you might be in, you are obliged to spit it out.

Insects apart, settlers also had to come to terms with crabs. Those in the sea made good eating but they were not as delicious as the land species. Land crabs are perhaps the most tasteful of all Oceania's food. They penetrate homes without discrimination. Other visitors include centipedes: a foot long and venomous, they seek extra warmth in slippers or under pillows. Settlers have learnt that washing-blue is the only handy antidote to their bites. They lurk in the latrines that settlers from the beginning have had to dig in the soil, and still have to, in areas away from septic tanks or from the few sewerage systems. Other fauna over the years have included land snakes, overcome in some islands by the introduction of the mongoose. Giant toads, introduced to eat sugar pests, have grown fat on a job successfully carried out: they are so numerous that they join the land crabs, centipedes, cockroaches, gecko lizards, and bulky spiders with whom settlers' families have to share their homes.

To compensate for these unaesthetic creatures, there are the magnificent butterflies of New Guinea and the Solomons: the bird-wing species spreads 1 foot across and is one of the world's largest and most beautiful butterflies. At night the giant moths seem almost as large: they make their contribution to the nocturnal activity of the tropics.

In New Guinea and the Solomons, there are pythons the length of three men but which are not venomous, crocodiles, and monitor lizards passing for dragons, but none of the other Islands possess wild animals larger than pigs—and sows, underestimated in their ferocity. Ironically, perhaps the greatest hazard for the settler is represented by the smallest of all the organisms: the coral-building polyp. Scratches from it on reefs are hard to avoid and, even if one is in the best of health, coral poisoning is likely to follow.

The authors' former residence on the slope of an extinct volcano on Taveuni, a remote Fiji island. It is typical of an administrator's house in country districts, where copra, sugar or pineapple planters, indigenous people in their villages, and industrious Indians farming individually are often dispersed widely by geographical conditions.

If the human system is run down through dietary deficiencies, it can lead to amputations and a fearsome struggle to eradicate the germ.

Settlers mostly lived, and still do, well apart not only from the indigenous population, but also from each other, and sometimes they were separated by stretches of sea and mountains. They did not live in English- or American-style 'villages'. In their isolated positions, unconnected by roads, settlers' houses were a reflection of their influence. The wealthier resided in bungalows, raised off the ground, with large verandas: they could afford imported Western food. The most wealthy (a bare handful) lived in two-storey wooden houses. The poor were in reed huts at ground level: their diet consisted of salt-beef, taro, and biscuits, like that of the natives. Only in the incipient capitals, Levuka, Honolulu, Papeete, Apia, Nouméa, Nuku'alofa, Rabaul, and Vila, was there any early assembly of settlers composing 'townships'.

The most far-reaching consequence of the arrival of European settlers in the Pacific came from their need to find labourers. Very quickly, planters found that Islanders throughout Melanesia, Polynesia, and Micronesia had a common trait: they neither wished nor needed to be employed in a daily economic grind. Money had not yet entered their way of life, and they could afford to stay outside a European-style currency system. They had, in their own view (not shared by early visitors ignorant of social obligations), quite enough to do. Their daily programme was ordained by custom, and it was adequate for their subsistence. Demands on their labour for ceremonies, for intertribal exchange under a barter system, and for the proper marking of events provided just the right balance between a salutary activity and a sensible degree of relaxation. They could not be persuaded to work like European or Asiatic peasants.

If planters were unable to secure the necessary labour for their estates, there were two ways open to them. Blackbirding, the kidnapping of men, mostly from Melanesian Islands, is described in the next chapter. This was bound to have but short success. There was only one real answer. Demand and supply happened at this period to balance each other: many Asians needed food,

145

This photograph of Papeete, Tahiti, in 1859, by Gustave Viand, was one of the first ever to be taken of the Pacific.

money, and the chance to get away from their continent in order to survive—hence the Indians in Fiji and their significant contribution to its economy.

It was from coconut growing and the resultant copra that the Islands first made a mercantile mark beyond the bounds of the ocean. It brought international recognition of the Pacific as a rich source of a relatively cheap but important constituent of soap, nitro-glycerine, cattle food, and margarine. The smell of copra in bags awaiting shipment is one of the special impressions of the Pacific: instantly identified, absolutely individual, to some rank and rancid, to others cleanly cloying. In a period of forty years, the price of copra has fluctuated between £100 and £1 a ton, or even lower, so that at times it has not been worth selling at all.

The main street, Vila, about 1900, just before the New Hebrides Condominium was established (see p.179). Only a store and a post office show signs of settlement at this relatively late stage.

The larger Islands, with their greater space, have prudently built up other sources of income. Hawaii and Fiji developed sugar plantations. These required a greater supply of labour than the local population could ever have provided, even if it had wanted to become involved. Thus it is sugar which accounts for two major racial surprises in Oceania: the substantial numbers of Japanese in Hawaii and Indians in Fiji, in each country easily outnumbering the indigenous population. As the sugar-cane is crushed locally before being exported for refining, mills of imposing size have had to be constructed. Planters and cutters in the cane fields and mechanics in the mills are almost exclusively Japanese in Hawaii and Indian in Fiji. Indians have retained sharp Mohammedan and Hindu differences in their totally new environment.

Pineapples have been grown on a much smaller scale in the same countries. The Hawaiian variety, produced by the largest pineapple firm in the world, the Hawaiian Pineapple Company, is known as the King Pine, while the Fijian pineapple is the Queen Pine. The latter is superior but is in itself excelled by the type grown on Pitcairn which, eaten on the spot, could claim to be the world's best.

Pacific plantations of bananas and rubber have never achieved the same prominence as those in the West Indies and Malaysia. Planters have naturally in their time made many experiments, including growing cotton, but coconuts and sugar have remained unchallenged. They have also had the biggest effect on the type of settlers.

Until the last decade, Europeans were the initiating, supervising authorities and the technicians. Copra required few technicians, but more were necessary in the sugar mills. Most, however, were needed for the exploitation of minerals. In Papua New Guinea, extraction of the particularly rich gold deposits, found at Bulolo in 1925, necessitated the use of huge dredges and the employment of European engineers. Gold superseded copra as the prime export up to the

Port Moresby in 1904, scarcely a 'township'. Almost half a century was to pass before it became the capital city of Papua New Guinea.

Second World War, when the dredges were reduced to skeletons. Similarly, the discovery of gold deep down in the hills of Fiji, shortly before the Second World War, led to a number of extra European settlers in localized communities. Meanwhile, the Fijians became good miners themselves, and gold came close to sugar and copra as the country's main source of income up to the end of the 1950s.

The most spectacular mineral development has been in New Caledonia, and Nouméa has become the most intensely developed, industrial, urbanized

With settlements came courts of law, but none as heterodox as this: the Joint Court of the Condominium of the New Hebrides (see p.180). It consisted in 1912 of, from left to right (with comments by the British judge): the French judge ('the best raconteur of any nationality'), the Public Prosecutor (Count Andino from Spain, 'less of the genial man of the world'), the President (Count de Buena Esperanza, 'the best type of Spanish grandee'), the Registrar (from Holland), and the British judge.

147

centre in the Pacific. Smelting works for manganese, cobalt, nickel, and chrome now dominate the city, making it more like Cleveland, Ohio, or Corby, England, than the capital of a South Sea Island. The labour introduced was from Java and Indo-China. You can also forget that you are in the South Seas, but this time believe that you are on the surface of the moon, when looking at the phosphate diggings on Nauru, Ocean, and Makatea islands. Asians brought to these islands were Chinese and Annamese.

The Chinese have settled in many parts of the Pacific most satisfactorily. Trading, baking, vegetable growing, storekeeping, and fishing, they live contentedly in the larger towns, such as Papeete, Suva, Vila, and Honiara (a section of which is called Chinatown). In 1856, a few Chinese miners and craftsmen *en route* from Australia to California asked in Tahiti if they could stay as servants, porters, and general workmen. These 100 or so were the nucleus of the present Chinese enclave of 10,000. The Chinese also merge themselves singularly well into the bush on the outskirts of remote villages, where they keep their native neighbours well stocked with provisions and often marry indigenous women. The progeny of such a union are as aesthetically striking as those resulting from Japanese-Hawaiian marriages.

Following New Zealand, the second British settlement in the Pacific was Norfolk Island. It had been originally used to absorb convicts from Australia.

No group was without its good and bad European settlers and planters. Those living on plantations, as compared with town dwellers, had an independence that they sometimes misused. But virtues were often to be seen: in their isolated areas, they gave invaluable help to others in crises such as hurricanes and floods; they had courage and resourcefulness; and some of them even came to have a little tolerance for increasing trends of bureaucracy as Government authority expanded. Their virtues did not often include an interest in, or positive work for, the Islanders, except what the Government

Copra-loading in Fiji, while women fish with nets in a circle.

required of them under legislation for care of labour. However, generalizations about European settlers and planters can no more be made safely than about individuals of any race: Philip Snow lived among many kinds.

In New Caledonia, as in Tahiti and French Oceania generally, settlers intermingled and intermarried both with the indigenous and the introduced races to a greater extent than in the British and American colonies.

It was in Hawaii that a planter became the most powerful probably of his kind in Pacific history. Claus Spreckels virtually controlled the Government of Hawaii in the middle of King Kalakaua's reign: the entire output of sugar was in his hands. He put up on Maui Island the largest and most efficient sugar factory in the world. Hawaii's first railway, two miles in length, was built there in 1880. In eight years, from 1876 when he came from California, Spreckels became regarded as the 'ex-officio Emperor of the Hawaiian Islands'. He died in 1908 aged eighty.

One idiosyncratic settler out of many, William Richard Marsters, settled in the Cooks on Palmerston Island, a 20-foot high atoll of 1 square mile. Marsters, a well-set, short man, had left Birmingham in England for life on a whaler. He abandoned this for the Californian gold rush and reached the Pacific with a little money. He then settled in the solitude of Tongareva with three women. It was the founding of a dynasty. He always carried a loaded revolver after an

Two adjacent anomalies in Nouméa: women—regular Sunday performers—playing cricket in the French colonial capital in front of the belching chimneys of the nickel works.

attempt was made to kill him in his sleep and to drown his children in the lagoon. He lived on Palmerston from 1862 to his death in 1899. In the church and school which Marsters set up for his family, English alone was the language, with the result that Marsters' descendants (nearly 100 today on the island, most of whom are named Marsters: his sons and grandsons married women from outside the island) retain traces of a Midland accent with Victorian phraseology but have little pale skin. It has been estimated that there might be about 3,000 grandchildren of the patriarch in various islands of the Pacific.

Palmerston is the only one of ten islets on the reef to be inhabited: another islet is Leicester Island, so-named by Marsters as he had been brought up by his grandmother in Leicestershire. Joel, his eldest son and nominated his successor, was appointed in 1901 magistrate for Palmerston. In 1902, *The Cook Islands Gazette* proclaimed the following as the Palmerston Island Council: President: Joel Marsters. Members: John Marsters, Thomas Marsters, Andrew Marsters, Turn Marsters, and James Marsters. However, life on Palmerston was not diverse enough for Joel, and he moved to another Cook Island. His brother, William, succeeded him and remained in charge until his death in 1947, at the age of eighty-four. Between the First and Second World Wars he ordained that cricket should be played every evening before sundown by both men and women.

Pitcairners' way of life did not alter much after three Europeans, John Buffet, a teacher succeeding Adams, George Hunn Nobbs, who took up the priesthood, and John Evans, became the first non-*Bounty*, non-Polynesian settlers. A Pitcairn Register was kept: 'Births, Deaths, Marriages and Remarkable Family Events'. There were so many in the first category that over-population and a drought forced a total move to Tahiti in 1831. Their severe upbringing under Adams had put them out of tune with Tahitian morals, however, and they went back home. As the population swelled, the entire 193 uprooted themselves again in 1856 and went to Norfolk Island, which had recently been abandoned as a convict settlement. Nostalgic for Pitcairn, discomforted by the vastness, roads, and echoes of Norfolk, the majority returned home. One of the most weighty dates in Pitcairn's settlement was 1886, when it dawned on them that Seventh Day Adventism was exactly

Left: Surrounded by royal palms, the Honolulu mansion of the sugar tycoon, Claus Spreckels.

Below: In 1890, Nouméa was still a one-horse cowboy-type town: in the same place on the Rue de l'Alma now, there would not be room to tether a horse sideways between the cars. New Caledonia's capital has been overwhelmingly settled by Europeans, to a greater extent than that of any other Pacific group except Hawaii (Honolulu).

Opposite: Some Chinese found employment as servants to the more well-to-do European settlers. This family and its servants were photographed in Nauru in 1907, when phosphate mining started. For a century after it was discovered in 1798, Nauru was known as Pleasant Island.

151

their cup of tea. Or rather not—tea, coffee, liquor, and meat (almost) were banished for ever. They live on vegetables and fish—tinned, if possible: it is infinitely preferred that way by Islanders all over the Pacific.

For the Western planters and settlers, the South Seas environment was totally strange. They came to terms with it although, like planters and settlers elsewhere, they would not readily concede that life had more benefits than disadvantages.

The English Midlander, William Marsters, and part of the dynasty which he founded on Palmerston Island, in the Cook group.

Chapter X

Demoralization and Depopulation

By about the middle of the last century, there had been enough visits and set-tlings of Europeans for most of the Island groups, certainly the major ones, to begin to feel the effects of the foreign culture. The more tangible innovations have already been considered, but equally important were the physical and psychological effects of the meeting of such different peoples and cultures. The title of Alan Moorehead's book, *The Fatal Impact*, explicitly declared it to be the end for natives. It was not, but it was touch and go whether or not the Islanders, having had contact with the Western world, would survive.

There was nothing sudden about the clash. What was happening so dramatically was not seen with anything approaching clarity until nearly the beginning of this century. In the end, almost all the indigenous races survived, with the exception of the Moriori of the Chatham Islands and the Chamorros of the Mariana Islands. It was also a near thing for the Hawaiians and Easter Islanders. This is not a demographic survey and statistics will be kept to the minimum, but the story is told most clearly by a handful of figures.

First, the most extreme instances. The Mariana Islands were originally inhabited by the Chamorros, who were the first Islanders to have any contact with Europeans. By 1870, however, this race was extinct. In the Chatham Islands, an animated people, dressed in seal skins, were found in 1791 to number 1,200. In 1840, there were 90 Moriori. Now there are none. In Hawaii in 1836, there were thought to be nearly 100,000 natives. Now there are believed to be only a negligible number of pure stock. Statistics are no longer maintained in Hawaii to show precise racial differentations: it is too difficult to

Marquesans eating *popoi* (*taro* root pounded with water into a paste and left to ferment, as foreign to the Western palate as blue cheese is to that of the Islanders). The failure of this race and of the Hawaiians to make even moderate population growth is a Pacific tragedy.

do so when there has been so much intermingling. The total population of the territory of Hawaii is over 750,000, including more than 250,000 Japanese, about 350,000 Caucasians, 100,000 Filipinos, and 60,000 Chinese.

The Easter Islanders were roughly estimated in 1722 to number 4,000. In 1877, there were 111. Now there are about 1,500. In 1887, there were 5,000 Marquesans, but in 1924 there were only 1,000 left. Although they now number about 5,000 again, it is still a precarious few. In New Caledonia, the population nearly halved in forty years, so that in 1901 there were only 27,000 Melanesians. Since then, however, it has risen to double that number again.

In Fiji, there was one of the sharpest instances of depopulation. When the British were asked by the Fijian chiefs to take over the group in 1860, the population was estimated to be 200,000. Britain continued to decline offers of cession until 1874. In the following year, a measles epidemic eliminated a quarter of the Fijian population. At the first census in 1881, 115,000 people were counted. A decade later there was a drop of 9,000. The native population continued to drop steadily until 1921. At its lowest ebb then, Fijians numbered, in a total of 158,000 (including 60,000 Indians), only 85,000. Now the total population stands at nearly 600,000 (over 250,000 Fijians and nearly 300,000 Indians). There will be found to be a similar pattern of decline and increase in most of the other groups.

It is probable that populations were not increasing before Europeans arrived in the Islands, for three reasons. First, the great Oceanic migrations had

Opposite: A Belgian peasant, Joseph de Veuster, called Father Damien, attended lepers on Molokai Island, Hawaii, for sixteen years. This photograph was taken (by William Tufts Brigham) shortly before his death of the disease in 1889.

Below: Easter Islanders' animated entertainment for Abel Aubert du Petit-Thouars in 1838, depicted by Louis Jules Masselot (see p.170). The natives' *joie-de-vivre* was not sustained as European contact increased, and depopulation, to the point of the near-extinction of these Islanders, followed.

A Samoan-style, European-inspired lavatory, the palm-trunk access to which is tricky to negotiate. Not all coastal villages have gone in for this sanitation device, while others have enthusiastically adopted it, to the extent of having two side by side, each within a 'sentry-box'.

stopped, ambition had slackened, and mental and physical inertia had set in. There was something of a general malaise. Second, there were undoubtedly epidemics of pre-European diseases. Exploring in 1910 areas of Dutch New Guinea never penetrated by Europeans, A.F.R. Wollaston (a Cambridge don, murdered at King's College in 1930) reported the existence of venereal disease. In New Caledonia, there was a deadly form of phthisis long before French occupation. Indeed, there are no grounds for the belief that all diseases were imported by Europeans. Third, cannibalism, infant mortality, infanticide, and lack of hygiene must have acted as population checks.

Considering the contacts with the West, it is not difficult to identify the causes of the decline in the populations. The physical grounds will be taken first, although the psychological ones often ran parallel, and the two became inseparable.

Of the diseases that led to depopulation, not all, as has been said, can be attributed to the European visitations. One of the pre-European diseases was leprosy. Because of some horrific features it has received publicity out of proportion to its effect on populations: it was never a major killing disease. Normally associated with living in dirty surroundings, its prevalence in the Islands was somewhat surprising. The dozen baths that were taken by Hawaiians each day were regarded by nineteenth-century Europeans with nothing less than awe. Nowadays, Polynesians, Micronesians, and many Melanesians are still scrupulously clean, bathing in fresh water two or three times a day.

Another pre-European disease, yaws, was severe and so common that everyone could expect to contract it at an early age. In addition to leprosy, yaws, phthisis, and possibly venereal disease, there was almost certainly malaria (and its associate, blackwater fever), whooping cough, and hookworm in pre-European times. It was only as Europeans settled that positive assertions about diseases came to be made and that records began to be kept. These may colour the European physical effect too darkly. It is evident, however, that natives had no immunity to relatively minor diseases which Europeans could resist. Not unnaturally, new diseases provoked bitter hatred of Europeans, particularly after smallpox epidemics in New Guinea and the Solomons. These were on the same disastrous scale as the measles calamity in Fiji, one of the most drastic physical misfortunes of all in the Pacific. A quarter of the Fijian population died. The British Government, having just settled in, had started the concept of hospitals, which Fijians were being exhorted to put in their language as Houses of Life. Long after the catastrophe, Fijians insisted on calling them Houses of Death, largely because it was only *in extremis* that natives would consent to be taken to them, promptly to expire. The 1875 measles epidemic was held by Fijians to be the manifestation of the anger of their ancestral gods at being abandoned in favour of Christianity. Tongans and other Islanders similarly interpreted such calamities.

The overwhelming effect of measles on indigenous communities astonished Europeans. There was later to be another illness which is not fatal for Europeans (except in its pandemic form, as after the First World War), but which is lethal for Islanders: influenza, together with the common cold, has a surprisingly devastating effect on the strongest Oceanic physiques.

Every group experienced alarming health vicissitudes. It has only been since the Second World War that medicine seems to have triumphed, although early deaths from heart diseases, probably not unconnected with obesity, and cancer are now approaching Europeans' rates. Leprosy, dysentery, tuberculosis, and

blackwater fever were the last major diseases to be controlled and, before them, yaws, hookworm, measles, and smallpox were overcome. But influenza and the common cold are still proving stubbornly lethal.

A different kind of physical contribution to the weakening of the sturdiest Islanders' constitutions was the over-drinking of European liquor. Missionaries' early discouragement of *kava* drinking and betel-nut chewing left a vacuum in social intercourse that was bound to be filled by something else. Long frowned upon by various religious sects, indulgence in *kava* is one of the few pagan practices to have survived. The missionary *tabu* on *kava* was quite

Dumont d'Urville, on his 1837–40 expedition (see p.80), being offered *kava* on Bau Island, Fiji. Custom now requires the cup-bearer to use two hands. It would have been unthinkable to refuse the drink, even though the root had first been chewed by clean-gummed natives and spat into the large bowl for mixing with water. *Kava* is a most refreshing drink in a torrid climate. The high house-mound in the centre of this picture, by Louis Le Breton, is still a feature of Bau.

unnecessary: it is one of the greatest and least harmful of the world's tranquillizers.

Islanders eagerly took to the first liquor introduced by the discoverers and explorers—to spirits rather than wine. For an inordinate stretch of time they were as easily knocked out by it as adolescents. Such generally powerful people might have been expected to hold their liquor better. It has to be said, however, that some leading chiefs of modern times, accustomed to imbibing with Europeans, can comfortably out-drink them.

A quite different kind of physical cause of demoralization and depopulation was the European practice of 'blackbirding'. This amounted to the kidnapping of men for transportation to cotton and sugar plantations in Hawaii, Queensland, and Fiji, and to guano, salt, and silver mines in Peru. Once at their destinations, they were forced to work under conditions little removed from the worst kind of African, American, or Arabian slavery. Melanesian and Micronesian groups were the targets, partly because they were less well

Above right: *Kava*, peculiar to the Pacific, being mixed for a formal Fijian ceremony. Bushy hair was a common masculine feature, shared by Fijians with Ethiopians, until many Islanders abandoned the style for the first time in history in the 1960s.

organized within themselves and partly because they were mentally less nimble with Europeans. The New Hebrides, New Caledonia, the Solomons, Gilberts, and Carolines were severely depopulated. Some Polynesian groups were not exempt: the Marquesas, Tokelaus, and Easter Island never recovered their manpower.

Only a summary of the physical causes of the decline in Island populations has been possible. It is time to turn to the concomitant reasons. They were implicit in the confrontation between the missions and paganism.

As the missionaries' energies spread, so the Islanders' priests lost ground.

Their teaching suffered in contrast with the freshness and style of the new cult. It is a process that has happened throughout history, often against all the odds, in deeply traditional societies. It scarcely mattered that the Christian intention was not clear in itself. There were just enough basic similarities in what the Catholic, Wesleyan, Methodist, and other missionaries were offering to rock the pedestal of Islanders' indigenous religions.

Missionaries had an assortment of targets. First, civil wars. Fighting between tribes was a way of life in nearly every island, and certainly in every group, but few people were killed (at least, until Europeans took part, either as mercenaries with firearms, or as dispensers of these new weapons). When missionaries, with strong support from British administrations, condemned the war instinct, it was not foreseen that deprivation of this excitement would leave, as among Maoris, a vacuum of boredom and frustration. If missionaries did have doubts about the effect of this suppression, their own fervour would override them. One is very aware of the burning glow in evangelists' eyes portrayed by the artists of the period, an ardour built up from challenge and excitement in their undeviating sense of purpose.

Slowly but surely, missionaries also managed to discourage polygamy so effectively that officially the practice died out. Unofficially and discreetly, it has continued, mostly among men of rank, to the present.

While a few lives in most groups were saved by the reduction of minor intertribal conflicts, the dissuasion of polygamy meant that populations could do little more than hold their own at first. Two all-pervading features of life had been changed. After the first novelty of contact with Europeans subsided, bewilderment and monotony set in. Faces did not consciously turn to the wall, at least until later, but there was not the same will to live.

Psychologically, the Pacific Islanders had encountered problems of magnitude. This phase of contact with European settlers had a greater impact on them than had that with the earlier Europeans, the explorers and traders. Missionaries pursued their aims with a lack of empathy or foresight. Their pacification of races, and their courageous elimination of cannibalism by disapproval and often by direct intervention, are high on their list of achievements. That is on the credit side. On the debit side, one can see no justification for forcing Islanders to wear clothes in the name of 'morality'. On State or formal occasions in non-tropical areas of the world their dress, incorporating a Pacific characteristic such as knee-length skirts, is positively distinguished. But to this day, Islanders in their tropical environment seldom look right in European dress.

Many of the groups, particularly the mountainous ones, have rainfall of up to 100–200 inches a year and, in addition, a frequently near-saturation point, say ninety per cent, of humidity. In this atmosphere Islanders look, and are, overdressed in what was originally missionary-imposed apparel. Missionaries required Islanders to keep clothes on while walking for miles through torrential rain, while wading through or swimming across rivers, or while bathing in the sea or in the village pool. Dressing-up, and always remaining covered up, created extra physical menaces which had to be overcome. The health element was one of the unnecessary problems. It would not have arisen if missionaries had been more imaginative, even given the fact that, at the time of their pioneering work, Europeans in Europe were, by our present-day standards, grossly overdressed. There are few areas today in the South Seas where the state of dress or undress is what it was in pre-missionary times. Micronesians on the whole have remained more *déshabillé* than others but, if it is known that

Two missionaries, John Williams (1796–1839), above, and Aaron Buzacott (1800–64), below, their eyes burning with ardour to convert 'savages' (see p.131). Williams had to report that these converts beat their pagan enemies into pieces while they begged for mercy. Both were English ironmongers with no doubt about their utter righteousness. Williams' consuming ambition included commercial dealing. Buzacott remained in the Cook Islands for thirty years; Williams moved after twenty years from Polynesia to Melanesia, where he was immediately eaten at Erromanga in the New Hebrides in 1839.

Europeans are not about, the less sophisticated among Polynesians and Melanesians revert to the sensible requirements of the climate. Very few administrators had the foresight and resolution to oppose missionary edicts. Sir Hubert Murray specifically forbade natives to wear clothing on the upper part of the body in the Papuan climate, and Sir Harry Luke, Western Pacific High Commissioner and Fiji Governor in 1938–42, tried to turn the clock back in some areas. But it was too late: the Islanders would not entertain the idea.

Of the easily recognizable death-dealing factors of demoralization, three were controllable. Disease was subdued by medicine and European techniques: missionaries helped here, curing bodies and gaining souls. Blackbirding was squashed as officialdom strengthened. The third element, the happy-go-lucky or, rather, the unhappy-go-lucky use of firearms, was similarly confined: escaped convicts and the less respectable beachcombers who introduced weapons were deported.

Two other ingredients contributing to the native decline, European liquor and overdressing, have not been removed to this day: an unexpected resilience and power of recovery have helped their worst effects to be gradually mitigated.

'Civilization' also introduced tobacco, but until recently it has not been treated as a menace. The reeking black variety was considered by Trobriand Islanders to be the Western world's outstanding contribution to their way of life.

The interchange of food between the Western world and the Islands just about counterbalanced itself. Some native food inevitably had a peculiar effect on Europeans. As did European food on natives, but it was hardly predictable that cheese and anchovy paste would make New Guineans seriously ill.

Psychological damage went deeper. The effect of missionary ideas on indigenous customs, striking at their very roots, caused Islanders' morale to falter. Few doubted that missions were bringing anything but good, but the gap in understanding between the cultures widened rather than diminished. Thomas Nightingale, a very early Oceanic traveller, said that:

> these gentlemen [American missionaries] informed us that all their endeavours had hitherto proved futile to effect even the slightest change, either in the habits or demeanour of these barbarous and incorrigible people who, existing in the most degraded state, practise every vice of which uncivilized man is capable. Never did human nature present a more forcible picture of moral degradation than is exhibited by the Marquesan Islanders sunk in the grossest natural depravity, inaccessible to the voice of reason or religion, both the presence and the doctrine of the Missionaries are alike incapable of producing the desired reformation.

This excessive tone of denunciation in 1835 mounted with the years of contact until the missions prevailed. It was not until after the end of the nineteenth century that Christianity was identified as an unintended but potential destroyer of the Islanders' will to live. W. H. R. Rivers, in his *History of Melanesian Society*, published in 1914, attributed the New Hebrideans' decline directly to missionary influence. In all fairness, probably no missionary could see the psychological trauma for which he was responsible, but it is surprising that no-one realized the importance of making imaginative substitutions for the pagan customs that were suppressed.

The missionaries succeeded in outlawing dances and games in many parts of the Pacific. It never ceases to be astonishing, not only that the Islanders

A Papuan cannibal headman receives his first sample of Western 'civilization'—a shirt.

An unamiable-looking New Caledonian chief, equipped for most eventualities with a spear, an umbrella, and two hats, with his equally suspicious-looking attendants.

allowed themselves to be detached from the very essence of what was in their bones, but also that the early administrators were so slow to recognize the effect of this.

Frederick Walpole, on H.M.S. *Collingwood* in 1844–8, made this pertinent comment after a visit to Tahiti:

The manners and customs of the natives have now lost all their originality and nothing remains but many, alas! of the vices of civilization and most of

This Solomon Island (San Cristobal) headman has acquired quarter-deck apparel and, in the minds of himself and of his tribe, extra authority. He kept his betel nuts under his hat. He was photographed by the Austrian traveller, Comte Rodolphe Festetics de Tolna, at the turn of the century.

Tobacco was received eagerly by Islanders, not least by Maoris of both sexes and all ages. This photograph was taken in Rotorua, New Zealand, in about 1906.

the follies of the savage . . . Unfortunately, no useful employment nor occupying amusement was taught by the missionaries, all their pleasures were forbidden and nothing substituted in their place.

Haddon, in Papua and the Torres Straits in 1901, was so concerned as to say:

It is very pathetic to see the evident strivings of these people to be like the white man: to my mind they are too ready to cast away their past, for with the crudities and social unrest of savagery there are flung aside also many of the excellent moral codes and social safeguards of the old order of things.

Perhaps the most serious element of demoralization, although undetected for longer than any other, was apathy. It was not an integral part of Islanders' lives: they could be hard working to an extent that astonished Europeans. The work was mostly physical, without the mind being greatly stretched, and, governed by custom, it tended to be intermittent rather than regular. Such intense activities as constructing a native house, loading and unloading huge weights on or off boats, or clearing formidable sections of bush, all in forbidding temperatures, might be punctuated with long rests and inactivity for days afterwards. To a degree, these were to recharge the body batteries, but, in any case, there was no great urgency to carry on, until Europeans introduced the organized discipline of timekeeping. However, Pacific people had their own compulsion—to prepare mats, banquets, artefacts, and canoes for big occasions, and to build special edifices for their gods and rulers. They would adjust their tempo accordingly and produce the goods.

One can only sympathize with the Islanders when one thinks of the first major impacts of the Europeans' arrival: the native boats being dwarfed by Western vessels; the range of their weapons made to look ludicrous by those of the West; the advantage of the match over the exhausting rubbing together of two pieces of wood; and the superiority of nails, axes, and knives over wood and stone implements. The startling miracles from over the horizon, not within the natives' power to manufacture, must have tantalized, inspired a hopeless awe, and created depression, numbness, and a deep sense of inferiority.

The Islanders' own magnificent natural skills—fishing, building, climbing, hunting, and sailing—developed to conquer their ever-challenging environ-

A Fijian club dance, tolerated by missionaries and performed for Charles Wilkes' entertainment in 1840. This was drawn by the second artist on Wilkes' outstandingly equipped expedition (see p.80), Joseph Drayton, who had an eye for composition and detail (note the watch-house on a treetop).

Fijian ceremonial was, and still is, elaborate. This picture by J. B. Zwecker shows the presentation among tribes of a canoe, together with many other artefacts, the result of much laborious effort. Missionaries and other Europeans disturbed the native balance of initiative.

ment, were, in their own estimation, irredeemably put in the shade by what they suddenly saw. Many of the new wonders were coveted and could only be acquired by barter on the visitors' terms. Although some of their craft were fast and more manoeuvrable, the natives would have liked to have copied foreign ships. They could never have enough nails (not simply for use as nails but, more importantly, twisted to form fish hooks), axes, and knives, as they did not know when another ship would visit them. Weapons were seldom part of responsible barter at that time, and could therefore only be stolen. All these immediate results of contact induced despondency and an apathetic view of the usefulness of their own products. In addition, when the missionaries convinced them that their gods had nothing like the power of the Christian God, an immense slice of initiative was at once cut away. Tremendous, protracted efforts in every group throughout their history had been devoted to building and maintaining temples, as dominant in their village scene as the lofty-spired churches of Western settlements. Great ingenuity had been applied, with painfully slow and cumbersome tools, to the carving out from stone and wood of idols and platforms for the temples.

Pacific people in the nineteenth century, markedly in its last half, were deprived of incentive and filled with despair over their inferiority in intelligence (which was not true), technology, and material spheres. This could only mean a decay of customs and a dropping-off of effort, followed by cessation of it and *taedium vitae*. There was nothing to be substituted for it, except apathy, the most demoralizing of the human states. It was a short step from there to a slackening of the urge, often unconscious, to perpetuate the species. A traveller in 1875 was not far off the mark:

> We take away from converted natives their dancing, their singing and their manly sports but nothing is given to supply their place. I believe that this dancing and singing and wrestling & c. were natural and necessary habits of exercise to them and that in taking them away we ought to have sent out missionaries to teach them some useful trade such as carpentry, boat-building & c., for without such habits of industry their moral condition can never be improved. Many intelligent natives have told me that with the introduction of Christianity a kind of stupor has fallen on the people—they became idle and shiftless.

This most important cause of depopulation, apathy, came to be recognized very late for what it was. Before an official Fijian commission in 1893, a native witness lamented:

> They are great and we are insignificant. A plant cannot grow up from under a giant *ivi* [Tahitian chestnut] tree, for the great *ivi* overshadows it, and the grass or plant underneath pines away. It is thus with the chiefs of the giant lands who live amongst us. This is the reason for the decrease of the Fijians.

This was one of the most poignant statements in the clash of cultures that had been affecting the Pacific. Had there been a similar inquiry in Hawaii at about that time, or preferably earlier, perhaps the Hawaiian race could have been saved. Unfortunately, however, few administrations acted at all and, when they did, it was on the basis of too little study. And it was so late. The survival of native races has been due primarily to a residual resilience and, above all, to medical revolutions.

When Pacific administrators began to be alarmed, however, by the sharp decrease in the population, they sought every kind of panacea. To most people in the world but Anglo-Saxons, it will be incomprehensible that, in at least three widely separated groups, the most potent way of dealing with apathy among the people was to introduce them to cricket. Samoa was one territory and Fiji was another. In Papua, the Administrator, Sir Hubert Murray, organized cricket matches despite his own preference for football. Papua New Guineans play with a sometimes excessive enthusiasm. Wherever it is played, cricket has helped to stimulate a healthy, inter-village competition when there are few other expressions for it. Apathy has been dissipated, but rivalry has been known to get out of hand in New Guinea and the Trobriands. In the latter, cricket has departed far from the rules and now incorporates some baseball, much superstition and exhibitionism in fanciful costumes, and mysterious names of teams, fifty a side, in matches such as the Aeroplane v the Scarlet Reds. There are feasts, much boasting, preliminary ritual parading in imitation of, for instance, aeroplanes' manoeuvres, connections between gum (not used for chewing) and the ability to hold catches, spear-throwing motions for bowling, and no sympathy for anyone hit by the very hard home-made ball.

As indicated at the beginning of this chapter, the story of demoralization and depopulation has not been as tragic as it looked for a prolonged, dismal phase from about 1850 to the First World War. There are two dolorous exceptions: the Chamorro, and the Moriori. As for the rest, they have turned the corner safely (apart from the Hawaiians, the Easter Islanders and the Marquesans—and the Pitcairnese, whose precarious numbers are dwindling on their island). There is confidence that the sizeable revivification will continue. In Fiji, there are conceivably now too many inhabitants (not all Fijians) for the security of the country's economy. Tonga also has a problem of overpopulation, despite having been almost alone in debarring foreign immigrants. The estimated indigenous population of Papua New Guinea and adjacent islands numbers a formidable two and three-quarter million, with plenty of room for more.

The Islanders have come to terms with the Western world. It has taken some time and has caused much perturbation: there has been a great deal of sacrifice, but racial identity remains and vigour increases. That is what matters.

Chapter XI

Monarchies and Administrations

Officers from H.M.S. *Herald* watching a fortified pagan village in the interior of Vanua Levu, Fiji, under attack by Christian natives in 1856, painted by J. Glen Wilson. The hydrographic expedition in 1854–6 of Captain (later Admiral) Sir Henry Mangles Denham (1800–1897) produced valuable Pacific data and helped the Pitcairnese move to Norfolk Island.

Most Pacific monarchs naturally had a lot of contact with Europeans. Native kingship resembling a European concept of it was confined to Polynesia, with Fiji being the only exception in Melanesia, where otherwise Europeans developed administrative responsibility for natives. This synopsis is limited to only those monarchs and administrators involved in special inter-racial relationships up to the First World War. It is not a catalogue, and there are consequently gaps in chronology, rulers, and territories.

Early Europeans hoped to find 'kings' everywhere to ensure dependable communication. When Western interest turned to taking over Pacific countries, however, native sovereigns were not so desirable.

Hawaii was the first country found by Europeans to have the closest facsimile of a king as they understood it. Kamehameha I established by wars his claim to be king of all Hawaiian Islands soon after Cook's visit. He had been

Above: Agaña, now the capital of Guam, painted by Louis Choris on von Kotzebue's first circumnavigation of 1815–8. Spanish Jesuits and missionary influence suppressed Chamorro customs after 1668.

Left: Samoan girls making *kava* for an informal occasion, painted by Teuila in 1893.

substantially helped in this by two castaways, John Young and Isaac Davis, who had at first been detained for their manual skills, and were later highly rewarded. Markedly anglophile and friendly with the brilliant English explorer of North America's Pacific coastline, George Vancouver, Kamehameha ceded Hawaii to Britain in 1794. Unfortunately, however, the British cold-shouldered this magnanimous gift. Kamehameha died in 1819.

The third Kamehameha's reign, taking up a quarter of Hawaii's monarchical history of a century, saw strong, if varying, European influences trying to focus on Hawaiians. Lord George Paulet, a dashing frigate commander opposed to the missionaries' puritanism, raised the British flag, but Admiral Richard Thomas was instructed from London to lower it and restore that of Hawaii. The most powerful character then was an American, Gerrit Parmele Judd, who deserted Calvinism to become president of the kingdom's treasury. Pressing for annexation by America, he was forced to resign and, from controlling Hawaii, became an insurance salesman.

The fourth Kamehameha, a heavy drinker whose wife was granddaughter of the castaway, Young, had not long been king when, suspecting a liaison between his American personal secretary, Henry A. Neilson, and the Queen, he shot Neilson. Publicly contrite and wanting to renounce the throne, he died from melancholia.

Misfortune and ineptitude on the male side of Hawaii's royalty enabled Westerners to get closer to power. It was the females who had the talent, but both sexes tended to marry full or part Westerners.

David Kalakaua, king from 1874 for seventeen troubled years, which were particularly critical for Hawaiians' identity among Europeans, wanted to increase Hawaii's prestige in the Western world. Walter Murray Gibson, a man after the King's heart—with *folies de grandeur*, flamboyance, faith in Hawaii's Pacific destiny—and originally in Hawaii to found a Mormon colony, became instead prime minister in 1882. An envoy was sent to Samoa to put forward the idea of a Polynesian confederation, with Kalakaua as king of Polynesia and perhaps Oceania, or even emperor of the Pacific. When Bismarck, the German Chancellor, expressed disapproval, the project was abandoned. Gibson was deported when he antagonized a local movement which was trying to set up a republic. This partnership of a Western adventurer and a native monarch was disastrous. Kalakaua died of liver cirrhosis in 1891. His sister Liliuokalani, who was married to an American, became the last monarch. Missions, planters, and mercantile elements, all European, were now omnipotent. Lacking no resoluteness, the Queen tried to confine the franchise to Hawaiian subjects. The Westerners successfully resisted: Hawaiians now formed only a third of the population. Liliuokalani desperately asked America to annex Hawaii, but it refused and she was deposed by Sanford Ballard Dole, a local lawyer and the son of a missionary, who became president of the republic set up in 1894. One hundred and ninety Hawaiians and sympathetic Westerners were put on trial for treason, including the Queen, who was sentenced to five years' hard labour and fined 5,000 dollars. Her imprisonment was commuted and she abdicated. It was the end of the line for Hawaiian monarchs: nearly all lacked the ability to deal with Western opportunists, but they did fit the part in appearance. After the Spanish-American war of 1898, America wanted a Pacific base: Hawaii was accordingly annexed.

Tahiti shared Hawaii's traumatic relationship between monarchs and Europeans. The first discoverers (including Cook, always sovereign-minded)

King Kamehameha II (1797–1824) and his suite in 1824 at the Theatre Royal, Drury Lane, London, depicted by J. W. Gear. Kamehameha, the son of King Kamehameha I by the highest ranking of his wives, went to England to ask George IV how best to deal with the growing numbers of Europeans in Hawaii (see p.78).

thought that Tu (otherwise known as Pomare I) and his descendants were the undisputed royal dynasty. By undervaluing equally powerful chiefs, they were a cause of Tahiti's instability for seventy-five years.

Queen Pomare IV, granddaughter of Pomare I, came under the influence of Rev. George Pritchard of the London Missionary Society. This was to have a momentous effect on Tahiti and to go as far as to rock the Government of France, bringing that country and Britain close to war. Like Queen Victoria at about the same period, Queen Pomare, aged fourteen on her accession in 1827, needed an adviser. In 1832 she unsuccessfully tried to have Pritchard made British consul. But a Belgian pearl merchant, Jacques-Antoine Moerenhout, a Catholic and as ambitious as Pritchard, competed as first American, then French, consul for manipulation of the native sovereign.

From the Gambiers, Père Laval and another missionary tried to enter Tahiti, but they were expelled from the Protestant stronghold in the Queen's name. This provoked King Louis Philippe to instruct Captain Abel Aubert du Petit-Thouars in 1838 to obtain Tahiti's submission. Although Pritchard encouraged the Queen to resist, she was obliged to acknowledge that Louis Philippe was virtually king and that she was queen only in name. Pritchard was

Sanford Ballard Dole (1844–1926), Hawaii's first president, with Lorrin Andrews Thurston (1858–1931), the grandson of a pioneer missionary. The radical Thurston was the prime mover in ousting Liliuokalani. Diplomatic and dignified, Dole was Hawaii's only president (1894–8).

Liliuokalani (1838–1917), Hawaii's last monarch. Her niece, Princess Kaiulani, the heir-apparent, who had a European father, died at the peak of her outstanding looks, aged twenty-four, in the last year of the nineteenth century, after the American flag had been raised over Iolani Palace.

Rear-Admiral Abel Aubert du Petit-Thouars (1793–1864) obtained in 1838 an apology from Queen Pomare IV of Tahiti for, under the influence of the Protestant Pritchard, deporting the first Catholic missionaries. She left Pritchard to pay the demanded fine himself. In 1842, du Petit-Thouars took over the Marquesas: 'Following one of the oldest customs of Polynesia, I exchanged names with the King: he became Du Petit-Thouars, I became Youtati.' This lithograph of du Petit-Thouars' commanding, somewhat saturnine head is by A. Charpentier.

deported in 1844, which made it an affair between England and France, with prime ministers involved. The French Government apologized to Britain but it did not rest there. The French nation disapproved of the capitulation to Britain, adding this to its reasons for overthrowing both the Government and Louis Philippe's own monarchy. It was the first instance of a leading European power being seriously affected by events in a Pacific country. Moerenhout found no zest in staying after Pritchard's departure and also left. When Queen Pomare died in 1877, she had been a monarch for half a century, made over-eventful by Europeans.

In anticipation of the opening of the Panama Canal (survey work began in 1877), the French, wanting undisputed authority over Tahiti, pensioned off the next and last monarch, Pomare V, in 1880. His tomb is surmounted by a funeral urn resembling a massive bottle of Benedictine, a drink to which he was partial. Had the males of the Tahitian and Hawaiian royal lines been less prone to liquor, they might have retained their status somewhat longer than they did.

Just as Nauru is the smallest republic in the world, so Tonga is the smallest kingdom. Its monarchical history was at first in the pattern of Hawaii and Tahiti. Taufa'ahau emerged from among rivals to become King George Tupou I in 1845. He was as much responsible as anyone for Tonga both staying unfragmented and remaining strong enough to be the sole independent native monarchy at the end of the century. He had become a Christian by 1831, and he was thus strenuously supported by Wesleyan missionaries. George had disposed of any internal rival by encouraging his cousin, Enele Ma'afu'otu'itoga (with dangerously close rights to the succession), to campaign in Fiji, where George had possible ulterior imperialistic claims, and to worry Cakobau's aim for supremacy there.

When the King wanted European advice for a constitution, Rev. Shirley Waldemar Baker insinuated himself as premier in 1880. As will be shown in the next chapter, this meant a far from serene phase towards the close of the King's half-century reign, until the hypocritical Baker suffered the same fate as the corrupt Gibson and the scheming Pritchard and was deported.

Take-overs by Germany and France were narrowly averted. It must have mildly surprised France and Prussia to be told by Tonga in authoritative terms that it intended to be absolutely neutral in the Franco-Prussian War. Tonga's salvation was a treaty of friendship with Britain in 1900. A protectorate, negotiated by Sir Basil Thomson, hived off only a minimum of power to Britain, which exercised the barest European influence up to Tonga's complete independence in 1970.

Perhaps King Kalakaua of Hawaii should have devoted his early energies towards a similar treaty of friendship with America. Queen Pomare might have been advised to have tried the same tactic with France. It was possibly the only hope of some continued autonomy in each case.

Sir Basil Thomson, seconded to Tonga by the Western Pacific High Commissioner as assistant prime minister in 1890 after the Baker débâcle, was warned that he would need to be an elder brother to George I. Thomson commented: 'At twenty-nine to be elder brother to a monarch of ninety-two is an unusual experience.' He found that Baker had promulgated everything in English to make government so complicated that Tongans would believe that it was an art beyond any powers but his.

Thomson's career was remarkable. The son of an Archbishop of York, he followed Sir William MacGregor from Fiji to British New Guinea in 1888 as his private secretary, which involved chasing malefactors in that untamed area. He returned to Fiji as an administrator and, following his secondment to Tonga, became the governor of Northampton, Dartmoor, and Wormwood Scrubbs prisons. He was then commanded in 1900 to arrange for Britain the treaty of friendship with Tonga. At the same time, by request of the King of Niue, he annexed that country to Britain. During the First World War, he became a principal interrogator of spies at Scotland Yard, Britain's crime detection centre. A prolific, scholarly, and elegant writer, Thomson was one of the few Pacific names to be also known for different achievements in Britain.

King George I of Tonga had died of a chill, after one of his daily early morning bathes in the sea, in 1893 at the age of ninety-seven. Thomson therefore had to negotiate the 1900 treaty with his great-grandson, George Tupou II, and he found it hard-going. The placidity of George II's reign was due principally to the treaty, under which Britain's protection discouraged the kind of activity exerted by Germany in Samoa and New Guinea, and to his fondness for ladies. He finally selected his queen from two Tongan princesses the night before the wedding. When he died in 1918, his eighteen-year-old daughter, Salote Tupou III, succeeded him.

Of the three major monarchical dynasties in Polynesia, the Tongan royal family alone, perhaps out of an instinct for self-preservation, was disinclined to marry into European or part-European stock, despite close working associations.

Samoa's administrative history was different. Throughout the nineteenth century, there was acute rivalry between chiefly factions of comparable strength, with Europeans in the wings waiting to capitalize. Jostling for power, the British and Americans favoured High Chief Malietoa, while the Germans were for High Chief Tamesese. Neither high chief won: the Western countries did. Samoa was a monumental example of combined parochial and international loggerheads. In an 1899 agreement, Germany annexed Samoa and surrendered a substantial sphere of influence in the Solomons to Britain. In return for recognition of nine islands of Western Samoa as a German colony, America was allowed to have the much smaller, Eastern part of Samoa (six islands) as a colony.

Dr. Wilhelm Heinrich Solf, governor to 1910, brought prosperity to Samoa before being promoted to head the German Imperial Colonial Service until the end of the First World War. Assessed from his subsequent career, he was Germany's most celebrated proconsul in the Pacific. Without practising indirect rule, his policy was that Samoans could be guided but not forced.

This outline can do no more than make a passing reference to the considerable history of New Zealand, so significant in the cordiality of its later European-Maori relationship. Like Samoa, there was no paramount ruler: the tribes were too diverse and equally balanced. But in 1858, some Maoris did elect a king for the area known as King Country.

Relations were delicate long before the British-Maori wars of 1860–72. Sir George Grey, governor from 1845 to 1853 and from 1861 to 1867, helped to consolidate British settlement by getting on at first equally well with settlers and Maoris. Later, he tried to reduce the chiefs' authority and circumscribe native customs. When he was replaced, it appeared to be the end of his career, but he then became prime minister from 1877 to 1879.

Richard John Seddon was a liberal prime minister of New Zealand from 1893 to 1906. His aim for a confederation with Fiji, the Cook Islands, Niue, and Tonga was suppressed by the Colonial Secretary in London (Joseph Cham-

Rev. George Pritchard (1796–1885) in consular uniform, painted by George Baxter in 1845. Originally a Birmingham brassfounder, Pritchard arrived in Tahiti in 1824 and, after being involved in intrigue and counter-intrigue for the control of Queen Pomare IV (1813–77), was deported twenty years later. He was so detested by the French settlers that the greatest contempt for a person would be expressed by the phrase: 'Pritchard that you are'.

Opposite: George Baxter painted in 1845 Queen Pomare IV's bewildered features and her husband's despairing gestures on the veranda of the British Consulate, where they had taken refuge when the French, from four warships under du Petit-Thouars, had landed in Tahiti in 1843 to haul down the royal flag.

The coral tomb of Tahiti's last monarch, Pomare V (1839–91). It is surmounted by a corrugated-iron roof with ambivalent ornamentation.

berlain) and by Australia. Seddon recognized the marked intelligence of the Maoris, of whom native leaders in the Maori-Western coalescence were Sir Apirana Ngata, a lawyer, Sir Maui Pomare, a doctor appointed minister for the Cook Islands, and Sir James Carroll, acting prime minister. European-Maori relationships became a model for the Pacific.

Earlier, a dominant personality in Gilbertese history, Tem Baiteke, High Chief of Abemama, had a European problem. He dealt with the increasing number of traders and settlers who affected the native way of life by having all nine killed in 1851. His son, Tem Binoka, varied this terminal policy for Europeans by capturing their products. His collection became an obsession. Blue spectacles, musical boxes, knitted waistcoats—the list of his possessions was too long to memorize: 'I think I no got him' he would say, and the European artefact would be obtained. Stevenson recorded that Binoka also acquired European-style etiquette, law, and police. He ordered missionaries to leave, arranging for them to go to islands of his enemies. His business capabilities were unusual among natives, his bargaining razor-sharp. Binoka died in 1891, just before the Gilberts came under the British High Commissioner for the Western Pacific.

In the Marshalls, Carolines, and Marianas, Spanish religious fervour inhibited native self-reliance. In 1885, Germany seized the Marshalls and, in 1899, bought the other archipelagoes from Spain. Any potential native incentive was suppressed by a third change of foreign occupancy when the Japanese dispossessed the Germans in 1914. There could hardly have been more different types of influence, Spanish, German, and Japanese, to which Micronesians would have to adapt. Guam had been ceded by Spain to America in 1898.

Away from Polynesia, monarchies or paramount chiefs diminish in importance. For this reason, Western administrators were often the main source of stimulus, the initiators, in Melanesia, in contrast with those in Polynesia (and, sometimes, in Micronesia). It was vital that they should be there for more than career-making: they had to guide Melanesians but, above all, to like them and be liked.

Although the Dutch acquired Dutch New Guinea in 1828, virulent malaria caused the country to be administered from the Moluccas up to the 1930s, with consequently little European-native contact. The other part of New Guinea was itself split into halves: in both, Islanders and Westerners started to look long and hard at each other.

In 1884 Germany annexed northeast New Guinea. An imperial colony by 1899, it was named Kaiser Wilhelm's Land. Dr. Albert Hahl, governor to 1914, tried to resist copra planters' demands for native labour, including women. Thinking of depopulation, he wanted to introduce Chinese, Filipinos, and Indians, but had to give way to local German insistence that there were plenty of natives in the interior. When the First World War started, Australia took over.

In neighbouring southeast New Guinea, a British protectorate was declared in 1884. In danger of German colonial intentions, it was annexed in 1888 as the Crown Colony of British New Guinea. Hugh Hastings Romilly, once the private secretary of Fiji's first governor, Sir Arthur Gordon, was temporarily the Administrator before annexation. He died of malaria after leaving the

R. J. Seddon (1845–1906), Prime Minister of New Zealand, and his wife with the King and Queen of Niue (formerly Savage Island) in 1900. The King was over seventy years old, whilst the Queen was under twenty-three. Niue had unfortunate reputations, quite unmerited, for its ferocious natives, hence the original name of Savage Island, and for the preponderance of flies there. Store-owners were reputed to call out to natives as they entered, 'Brush off your flies'; but Niue had, if anything, fewer of the pests than most Pacific countries.

country at the age of thirty-six. Romilly was so spirited and sagacious that he must surely have attained real fame if he had lived. His technique for getting on with the natives was always studied, as in wild New Ireland:

> I had taken care, according to my invariable custom, to make a small present to every old woman I saw. There is no better general rule to observe among savages than this, and many a life has been saved by the intercession of old women.

Samuel H. Romilly recorded that 'infliction of punishment on savage tribes for outrages committed on white men' was most distasteful to his brother, knowing that in nine cases out of ten it was the Europeans' fault.

The colony's first governor in 1888 was a formidable personality. The son of a Scottish crofter and formerly Fiji's chief medical officer, Sir William MacGregor never compromised and was critical of all his assistants, including Basil Thomson, whom he thought a malingerer. From Thomson's diary for New Guinea in 1888, it is clear how domineering MacGregor could be:

> Dr. MacGregor here indulged in betel-nut and insisted on my doing the same. I was handed half a nut bearing unmistakeable teeth marks on it, a lime calabash and a half-chewed stick of pepper. Being an adaptable person

In 1900, Queen Makea Takau Ariki ceded the Southern Cook Islands to Queen Victoria via the Earl of Ranfurly, the Governor of New Zealand. For the ceremony, she wore a Mother Hubbard and a boater, and carried an umbrella. In 1901, the rest of the Cooks followed, together with Niue which, like Fiji and Hawaii, had in their history each asked to become a British possession three times.

Charles Morris Woodford (1853–1927) was distinctive among British resident commissioners in the Pacific. Primarily a naturalist who became an administrator, he virtually ruled the Solomons from 1886 to 1914, at the same time collecting specimens for the British Museum. This photograph was taken on Guadalcanal Island in 1886.

by nature and used to the ways of savages I did chew the nut and suck the lime spoon but when it came to that chewed stick of pepper I "passed". On which Dr. MacGregor gravely said he didn't see the use of a private secretary who wouldn't eat and drink anything that was offered to the Governor and I retorted that I preferred being called arrogant to being poisoned.

Like one of his successors, Sir Hubert Murray, MacGregor could not tolerate frailty and, by some, his administration was judged to be too ready to use force. His successor was Sir George le Hunte. Both set a high standard of care for Papuans, following their training in Fiji under Gordon in the system of indirect rule. Neither was able to practise it in Papua's 'untamed' conditions, although they would have liked to do so.

In 1906, British New Guinea became the Australian Territory of Papua. Its capital, Port Moresby, is the only one in the Pacific bearing a European name. During the change, Sir Hubert Murray assumed authority in the MacGregor and le Hunte mould, though his native policy could afford to be closer to 'peaceful penetration'. He was an Irish Catholic lawyer of insatiable ambition and inordinate stamina. As the first lieutenant-governor of Papua, his policy was fundamentally that of Gordon in Fiji and Lugard in Africa. These three were the pioneers of indirect rule in the British Empire. Murray believed in district officials keeping their ears close to the native ground. He required strenuous patrols, with the double object of getting Papuans to co-operate with the Government and of protecting them. Murray described the difficulty of getting through to his Melanesians:

> Very often they will not actually show fight, but will simply remain in the village, of course fully armed, and consumed with curiosity to know why these strange ghost-like creatures have come to them—who they are and what they are seeking. Then if you have some common language you can probably give a more or less satisfactory explanation of the objects of your

The proclamation of the British protectorate over southeast New Guinea in 1884 at Port Moresby by Commodore (later Admiral of the Fleet Sir) James E. Erskine.

visit, but, if you can not talk at all, you may be in a difficult position. In that case the only thing to do is to "hang on" and to look as friendly and as amiable as you can, and to take the chance of an odd arrow that may be let fly by some suspicious person of conservative views who does not like the look of you.

He followed Haddon's axiom: 'It is a common experience among travellers that many, if not all, savages are gentlemen'. Bearing in mind what Sir William des Voeux, a governor of Fiji, had written: '. . . in some of the Crown Colonies where there are different races with sharply opposed interests the unpopularity of a Governor may be in direct proportion to his performance of his duty', Murray was convinced that an administrator could only gain popularity by neglecting his duty towards natives. Which he did not propose to do. His faith in Papua was great. His policy for rapport with primitive Papuans included this approach:

> Of course there are some things that must be suppressed, whatever the result may be—as, for instance, head-hunting. This is a custom which the most sympathetic administrator could not be expected to preserve, however great his devotion to the science of anthropology, though in its suppression he will probably influence all sorts of other things of which he knows nothing. In such a case as this, he must take the risk, and perhaps the best thing he can do is to induce the head-hunters to make use of a pig's head, or to persuade them, as I think has been done in Borneo, to put up with old heads and to make-believe that they are new. So with cannibalism. You can get them to give up the practice without so much difficulty as one might imagine. Savages are snobs like the rest of us, and if you appeal to their snobbery, you can get them to do a great deal. So, if you can get it into their heads that cannibalism is not good form, and is rather looked down upon by the 'nicest' people of Papua, and that a cannibal can hardly be received in the best villages, they will give it up quickly enough.

One of the many Murray legends was that he was totally devoted to Papua. In fact, ambition made him apply for Colonial Service judgeships and Australian State governorships. In the event, he was to live wholly and exclusively in, and for, Papua, protecting Papuans' land, labour, and customs. He died in Port Moresby in 1940, aged eighty, still in office as lieutenant-governor. The length of time—thirty-three years—that he was proconsul in one territory is without equal in British imperial history and perhaps has not been exceeded in the history of any empire.

New Caledonia became a French territory in 1853. However, Napoleon III selected it as an ideal place for keeping prisoners and, after the revolution of 1870, 7,000 Communards were sent there. This penitentiary function dominated it to the end of the century. A French-native relationship was very retarded, in particular because the Government allowed the alienation of much native land.

To obviate German designs on the New Hebrides which, as late as 1906, did not have a European government, the Anglo-French Condominium was set up. At worst described as, and for long stuck with the *bon mot*, 'the Anglo-French Pandemonium', at best it has been a commendable example of three cultures coexisting amicably in a confined space. But many of its facets have bewildered natives—not least the separate administrators and police, French and British, operating with three official languages, British, French, and Pidgin. Each

Sir Hubert Murray (1861–1940), the first lieutenant-governor of Papua, on the veranda of Government House, Port Moresby, 1907. A lawyer up to the age of forty-two, he was lieutenant-governor for the next thirty-three years.

Resident Commissioner has been answerable to French and British High Commissioners. There are also separate sets of laws and separate administration of the Joint Condominium itself. To provide strictest impartiality, the Joint Court consists of a French and British judge, its president an appointee of the King of Spain—even now. The first president was Count de Buena Esperanza: he knew little French and English and no Pidgin, but this did not matter as he was deaf.

There has been a deliquescent effect on both native and nationalistic character. Like New Guineans and New Caledonians, New Hebrideans were not sufficiently advanced or cohesive to produce national leaders when it was traditional to have chiefs of nothing but small clans. The ambivalence of the

European set-up might have encouraged a native opportunist for power but, up to very recently, it did not.

The Solomon Islands also lacked any but very localized leaders. Its British protectorate came under the Western Pacific High Commissioner in Fiji.

Associated with Fiji were many Europeans renowned throughout the Pacific for their relationship with Islanders. Native society had chiefs of great power with whom Europeans worked closely under the indirect rule policy: this brought out the best qualities of the Europeans. Furthermore, Fiji is the largest group in the Pacific, except for New Guinea, and was for long the pivot of the British Western and Central Pacific.

Paramount Chief of Bau, Ratu Cakobau was suzerain over parts of the group from the mid-1850s. His most formidable competitor was Ma'afu, whom George I had transplanted from Tonga. Ratu (an honorific meaning high chief, which is unique in the Pacific; it is never neglected among Fijians, who expect it to be used by Europeans) Epenisa Seru Cakobau was as voracious a cannibal as has ever been known and, after conversion, a vigorous Wesleyan.

The inability to pay a debt to America led to the chiefs asking Britain to take over the islands in 1860. Britain refused. It may come as a surprise to find an observation on the way remote Islanders should not be treated coming from Count Leo Tolstoy. When he published a soul-searching *What Then Must We Do* in 1866, he wanted to hand over his estates to his peasants and become a manual labourer. In his view, Fiji was a classic example of where the world had gone wrong:

> If I wanted to invent a most striking illustration of the way in which the demand for money has become in our days the chief instrument by which some men enslave others, I could not invent anything more glaring and convincing than this true story, which is based on documentary evidence and occurred the other day . . . The Fijians and their King Thakombau needed money. They needed 45,000 dollars for contributions or indemnities demanded by the United States of America for violence said to have been inflicted by Fijians on some citizens of the American Republic.

How the 'semi-savage monarch' and his subjects extricated themselves from this dilemma is not too inaccurately described by Tolstoy. His conclusion is emotive:

> This tragic episode in the life of the Fijians is the clearest and best indication of what money is and of its significance. Here all is expressed: the first basis of slavery—common threats, murder, the seizure of land, and also the chief instrument—money, which replaces all other means.

Meanwhile, Ma'afu, with local Germans' support, was coming close to supremacy, but Britain and America, anxious to forestall him, proclaimed Ratu Cakobau king in 1871. It seems amazing that, at the peak of his power, Ma'afu should have accepted Cakobau as king, but he did.

Like George of Tonga, Cakobau needed European advisers. Initially, he was no better at selection: the first two premiers were Sydney Charles Burt, an absconding bankrupt Australian auctioneer, and Lieutenant George Austin Woods, a marine surveyor. As a result of their inadequacy, Fiji again had to ask Queen Victoria to accept the group. Cakobau reasoned:

> If matters remain as they are, Fiji will become like a piece of driftwood on the sea and be picked up by the first passer-by. Of one thing I am assured, that if

Left: The customary form of transport for the Administrator's wife in the Fiji interior: Lady Berkeley and members of the Armed Native Constabulary, 1897.

Opposite: Commodore James Graham Goodenough (1830–75), commanding the Australian Station, was invited to scrutinize Fiji's offer of its islands to Britain, and was present at the cession ceremony on 10 October 1874. In mid-1875, he went to examine labour traffic and kidnapping in New Hebrides. His last journal entry at Santa Cruz, near where Patteson, the Bishop of Melanesia, had been murdered in 1871 in revenge for Islanders killed by blackbirders (see p.145), stated: 'I saw a man with a gleaming pair of black eyes putting an arrow to a string and . . . *thud* came the arrow into my left side . . . I felt astonished . . . pulled the arrow out . . . another arrow hit my head a good sharp rap, leaving an inch and a half of its bone head sticking in my hat . . . Having been picked out at once, no poison (supposing them to have poison in them) could have been dissolved in the time.' Goodenough died of tetanus eight days later.

we do not cede Fiji, the white stalkers on the beach, the cormorants, will open their maws and swallow us.

It is not clear how he knew of cormorants—they have never been Fijian birds. In 1874, Britain accepted.

Cakobau's greatest backer was an Englishman, Sir John Bates Thurston. Possibly once a ship's boatswain, he decided to live in Fiji when he was shipwrecked off Rotuma. He became the mate on a mission schooner, a planter, the chief secretary in the Cakobau Government, and an authority on the land. He aspired to be the first governor, but Sir Arthur Gordon was appointed.

The younger son of a prime minister, the Earl of Aberdeen, Gordon came from three gubernatorial posts. He was the first high commissioner for the Western Pacific in 1877. He tried repeatedly to be viceroy of India, but, in the introduction to his *Records of Private and Public Life*, the opening words are:

> The Governorship of Fiji was certainly the most interesting of all my Colonial experiences. I had very nearly a clear field to work in.

Under his rule, Fijian customs were respected, and Fijian chiefs retained power over their own people. Gordon was ahead of Lugard (the Africa proconsul, often accredited with pioneering this policy) in softening the impacts of Western power over existing chiefly institutions. It was the pattern in Fiji from 1874 to independence in 1970. Gordon's was, for its time, a daring experiment

which history, as judged by mutual Fijian-British affection for more than a century, has ratified. As determined a man as he was liberal, he never sought popularity. Made Lord Stanmore, he died in 1912.

Polynesia had a few kings and queens of stature. Micronesia's rulers were in a minor key. King Cakobau was the first and last monarch in Melanesia. Happy with his elevation as king, he readily acknowledged European statecraft, and recognized that he nearly lost everything to Ma'afu. After a life involved in more deaths than the majority of his contemporaries, he died peacefully in 1883, aged sixty-five. As for Ma'afu, the irrevocability of cession was slow to dawn on so intelligent a man. When he realized that he had lost all when he had been within an inch of total power, he resided moodily in Lomaloma, spending £2,000 a year, mostly on drink.

When Gordon became governor-general of New Zealand in 1880, he could not have had a better successor in Fiji than Sir George William des Voeux. Native policies were maintained; the country settled down. In 1888, Thurston finally got the job that he had first wanted in 1874. He was the governor of Fiji and the Western Pacific high commissioner almost to the end of the century.

Fijians were fortunate in their first European administrators. They had not been let down by their decision to invite Europeans to show them ways of running the country in which they could participate as much as they wished. Their indigenous leaders after 1874 were not in the class of Cakobau or Ma'afu: conspicuous chiefs were thin on the ground for a long time. But less so than in most of the Pacific: by 1914 Europeans had taken over nearly all of it.

Chapter XII

Knaves and Larrikins

With distances at their longest, the arm of the law was just about at its shortest in the Pacific. In addition to having remoteness on their side, rogues of both unmistakable and plausible varieties saw other advantages in Oceania. The great back-of-beyond in the world was almost a vacuum. Such governments as there were formed but slowly, and then were so fragmented as to delight the fugitive.

Up to the end of the nineteenth century, when governments of archipelagoes became identifiable, there was a wonderfully large area for hide-and-seek, for knaving and larriking. This last word is one of those Australian expressions that have a true ring of atmosphere. A larrikin is close to a scoundrel but rather less sinister than that term implies. It is perhaps closer to a rascal or a bounder: but those words are regarded as high English and are seldom heard among the European population of the Islands. A larrikin has the additional implication of being a layabout who is a trouble-maker, perhaps only in spasms, of a not altogether very serious or subtle species.

The Island life, with its lack of complexity, its absence of co-ordination between archipelagos and within archipelagos themselves, was ideal for a man with an occasional surge of misdirected energy, from which he could relapse into undisturbed, total apathy when he wished. Of course there were, and are, knaves and larrikins among the indigenous peoples of the Islands, but they had fewer opportunities. In all the groups the structure of society, whether comprising chiefs, as in Polynesia, or less obvious leaders as in Melanesia and Micronesia, was such as to make it difficult for individuals to go on the rampage. Native society has always tended to go in for concerted, communal action and to look sideways at individual enterprise.

But there were no such inhibitions for the interloping Europeans. Unlike so many deliberate beachcombers, rogues and swindlers were mostly on a short-term jaunt for a quick haul: they would then disappear and re-emerge in quite another area. Their skill was in deceiving others. That nearly always, anywhere, requires a presence and a personality. The larger the man, the more likely his success.

Most of the shady characters had bulk as well as cunning. The less famous were those who vanished at night to another part: they thrived on remaining relatively obscure and untraceable. But there were characters who are still remembered after a century. They came to have territorial appellations. To this day one discusses Steinberger of Samoa, de Reys of New Ireland, Baker of Tonga, Hill of Pitcairn, O'Keefe of Yap, Gibson of Hawaii, and Banks of the Cooks as though they were heraldic titles.

There was one, however, who cannot be given a specific territorial tag. An omnifarious knave and larrikin, his playground was the entire Pacific. He ranged far and wide for a long period, from 1857 to 1877. His celebrity was probably assured by the sheer impact of his picaresque personality; but it was guaranteed by his having a tame writer to record his exploits, thinly disguised in fiction and sometimes not concealed at all. Indeed, legend and fact about Bully Hayes are inextricably intertwined. His invaluable friend was the Australian, George Lewis Becke who, under the name of Louis Becke, wrote

Louis Becke (1855–1913), Boswell to Hayes' Johnson. Becke and Loti gave radically different interpretations of European-Islander feelings (see p.208).

184

prolifically on the Pacific near the turn of the last century (see p.208). Hayes expanded into twice the man he really was as a result of Becke's Boswellian underpinning.

William Henry Hayes, a Mississippi pilot, became a skilled exponent of lifting natives from their islands against their wills. From Cleveland, Ohio, where he was born in 1829, he deserted a wife and, after involving himself in horse-stealing, fled to Singapore. On a visit to Australia in 1857 he married a widow, whom he claimed to be his first wife, but it is generally thought (although, as in so much about Hayes, never known for certain) that she was his third. No sooner had Hayes married than he was declared bankrupt. He promptly absconded, leaving that quandary to settle itself. Hayes found it preferable not to pay any of his debts in his lifetime. He deserted his wife and turned up in the deep south of New Zealand as a member of a travelling entertaining troupe, the Buckinghams. There, he bigamously married Roma Buckingham, another widow, who had five children. While sailing in a yacht, Roma, their daughter and two others were drowned: Hayes was the only survivor. Such was his reputation that some believed the drownings were not accidental. He then married Emily Mary Butler, again bigamously.

During the Maori War it was believed that he supplied Maoris with ammunition in secluded coastal coves. After his death, Emily Mary Hayes became a respected citizen of Levuka in Fiji, where she died. The twin daughters of this marriage, Leonora Harriet Mary and Laurina Helen Jessie, were exceptionally beautiful. Laurina married the Collector of Customs in Levuka: a son became a close friend of Philip Snow when he first went to Fiji and, through him, Philip Snow met this daughter of Bully Hayes.

Bully Hayes' appearances on Island beaches were in a white shirt and trousers, with a red sash round the waist—a fashion that he had acquired while gold prospecting in California. His beard covered his chest. Long curls concealed the absence of one ear (thought to have been cut off when he was caught cheating at cards in California) and of part of the other. Weighing all of 15 stone and measuring 6 feet tall, Hayes was described by Constance Gordon Cumming as:

> a very erratic comet, coming, and especially vanishing, when least expected, each time in a different ship, of which by *some* means he had contrived to get possession; ever bland and winning in manner, dressed like a gentleman, decidedly handsome, with long silky brown beard; with a temper rarely ruffled, but with an iron will, for a more thoroughgoing scoundrel never sailed the seas.

As an American citizen, he avoided British justice, which might otherwise have caught up with him. To Sir Arthur Gordon he was 'Captain Hayes of infamous piratical notoriety'. He was variously charged in different groups with defrauding natives, blackbirding, gun-running, bigamy, swindling, piracy, barratry, theft of other traders' produce, and murder. At Apia, he was given a gaol sentence for kidnapping natives, but he escaped—not for the first or for the last time.

He had one trait that was somewhat unusual for the period: his attitude towards Islanders, apart from kidnapping them, was humane. He avoided bullying them and treated them with civility. At one and the same time, he would switch from blackbirding in aid of Fiji sugar planters, and from nefarious undertakings in Niue and Rarotonga, to taking the side of natives in Micronesia (his centre in the early 1870s) against overbearing traders. This,

The only known picture of Bully Hayes (1829–77). He did not like to be too well recorded.

despite the likelihood that he had kidnapped the natives in the first place. He acquired ships in the same high-handed manner as he helped himself to labour, sometimes by means of handing over stolen goods to purchase them.

In 1874, a sloop was sent out from Sydney to watch the labour trade in the Pacific, and in particular to enquire about Hayes. When it arrived at Strong's Island (Kusaie), where Hayes had taken refuge after a shipwreck, an American missionary sent a note to the captain:

> You would be doing a most praiseworthy act of taking him [Hayes] on board the Rosario and on to Sydney where he may be brought under the cognisance and jurisdiction of Civil Law . . .

Hayes was taken on board, where he lost no time in knocking several marines down; he then sprang into the sea, swam to the mangroves, and escaped.

Time was running out for Hayes. In 1877, on a new ship in the Marshalls, he criticized his cook, a Norwegian, Peter Radeck, known as Dutch Pete, for his steering of the vessel. Dutch Pete had previously been punished by Hayes for attempting to desert. Hayes went to fetch his revolver to shoot the cook. Romilly reported:

> The cook, however, objected, and snatching up the first piece of wood he saw gave him a blow which killed him on the spot. The cook seems to have been doubtful whether Hayes was even now dead, so he fetched the largest anchor the cutter possessed and bound the body to it after which he hove the anchor and body overboard, remarking 'For sure Missa Hayes dead this time'.

Another scoundrel of some significance was David Dean O'Keefe, a larger-than-life-size figure with red hair. Soon after arriving in Yap from America, he achieved for his new country an industrial revolution virtually overnight. By the simple use of modern tools, he speeded up and cheapened the process of quarrying the Palauan stone, which was used as currency. He then introduced a fleet of small vessels superior to the Yapese rafts and canoes, and was thus able to ensure quicker and safer transport of larger quantities of stone from Palau. In a European society, this would have been regarded as enterprise to be rewarded. He unbalanced the Carolines' way of life, however, with his monopoly of the gigantic stone *fei*, and was able to corner virtually all the sea-slugs, copra, and trochas shell, out of which he secured a wealth of real estate in Hong Kong. O'Keefe fortified his station, repelling an attack on Yap by Bully Hayes' pirates, and deported any opponent. He lived on Yap for thirty years with a Nauru wife: their daughters were renowned for their looks. Traders knew him as 'His Majesty O'Keefe'. In 1901 he was drowned in a hurricane at sea. From about 1870, he had preserved his supreme position and Yap from the effect of any change other than that which he had personally achieved. Prestige and prosperity are still associated with the great stones, although they are not now the conventional currency.

Micronesia, with its generally milder indigenous inhabitants, was a congenial area for the uncongenial, while Melanesia, its ferocity well-known, was less encouraging to the knavish and villainous. If they found themselves in that region, their wits were more often than not fully exercised in self-preservation against inhabitants with sometimes stronger inborn toughness, able to match themselves against all-comers. It was the ambiance for one of the most bizarre confidence tricks. The presiding genius was the Vicomte de Reys, the island New Ireland, the period the early 1880s. After a mention of lesser rogues, he will have the honour of concluding this gallery.

BACHELORS' CLUB-HOUSE AT LAI, SOUTH YAP

The gargantuan stone coinage of Yap, capitalized upon by 'His Majesty' O'Keefe (1830?–1901).

Polynesia was a softer option for a larger number of shady characters, and advantage was taken of its genial and indiscriminating hospitality. Sometimes, however, the knaves were not complete blackguards but eccentrics with an edge of crookedness. Melanesia's noble scoundrel, the Vicomte de Reys, was almost balanced in social eminence by that of Polynesia, Baron Charles de Thierry. But de Thierry's charlatanry never came to much. A genuine French aristocrat, he settled in Nukuhiva in the Marquesas and aspired in 1835 to have himself known as 'Charles I, King of Nuku Hiva'. Not content with this, and having bought a large tract of land from a Maori chief, he laid claim to being king of New Zealand. This was stretching his luck: he ended his days in New Zealand, but as a music teacher in Auckland.

A different technique of aspiration was exemplified by Charles William Banks. His chosen territory was the Cook Islands. As the cashier of Wells, Fargo & Co., the firm of fast mail carriers and bankers, in their San Francisco branch, he robbed it of 20,000 dollars. He had gone there from England—he had been born in Birmingham in 1839—and, evading the 1,000 dollars reward in 1886, sloped off successfully to Rarotonga. There he married a Cook Islander. A handsome man, he was well liked, except by those whom he defrauded, wherever he settled. With his business acumen, twisted or not, he had little difficulty in acquiring two of the most reputable of offices, those of government auditor and registrar of deeds. As 1900 approached, an inquiry into the administration of the Cook Islands made it desirable for him to give up these appointments. It was not that it would have been difficult for him to leave the Cook Islands: he never wanted to and never did. He died in Rarotonga in 1914.

Samoa also had its knave. He was so successful that he headed the Government of Western Samoa for almost a year. Colonel Albert Barnes Steinberger, a San Francisco clerk with a self-conferred rank, arrived in the Islands claiming to have the American Government behind him. Samoa was disorientated in 1873 by opposing chiefly factions, backed by rival Europeans, supporting one or other of two indigenous claimants for the kingship. Steinberger, ostensibly an American Government agent, simply installed himself as the hereditary premier in 1875, with power claimed to be unlimited. It was based on the much flaunted commission from Washington: this was later found to be two old passports pasted together.

Steinberger was not wholly bad. Two laws which he instituted were the prohibition of the sale of liquor and of land, both areas in which Samoans were particularly vulnerable. He had an affair with the half-Samoan Emma Coe (later known as 'Queen' Emma from her demeanour after making a fortune as a copra planter in New Britain), and as a result of this she gave America land beyond value at Pago Pago to mark her attachment to Steinberger. When he returned from Germany after commercial negotiations with Godeffroy und Sohn, the American and British consuls had him arrested. This was not legal: nor were the 'trial' on H.M.S. *Barracouta* and his deportation to Fiji. Both consuls were immediately dismissed, as was the captain of the British warship. But Steinberger's government had collapsed and he never returned.

Another Westerner insinuated himself with the same opportunistic guile into a similar position of influence, this time in Tonga. Shirley Waldemar Baker was in no way an attractive character, and it is difficult to understand how the Tongans, who are particular about the Europeans whom they encourage, allowed themselves to be led by anyone so unprepossessing. Little is known about Baker until he arrived in Australia from England. He then joined the Wesleyan Mission in Tonga in 1860. European nations were beginning to show interest in this group and political judgement was needed. Baker induced the King in 1880 to make him prime minister, a post he was to occupy for a decade. He was quick to have cards printed 'Hon. Rev. Shirley W. Baker, Premier of Tonga', which were handed out to all visitors. An astute, if dissembling, missionary, he was an inept politician, with a singular capacity for making himself disliked.

Baker's personality was wholly alien to the lovely group in which he had settled. As prime minister, he regulated the Islanders' lives with a ferocious puritanism, ultimately exposed as hypocritical. His own life was filled with financial dishonesty and manifold scandals and, after several shows of blustering, he was forced to resign. The force against him was a British Government in Fiji anxious to ensure that Tonga remained friendly with Britain and would not be seduced by Germany, with whom Baker was courting favour. Firmness shown by the Fiji Governor, as High Commissioner for the Western Pacific, and the core of toughness of his envoy, Basil Thomson, resulted in Baker's deportation in 1889. In his phase of power, Baker had helped to draw up a constitution, provided a national anthem, a flag, crown, and coat-of-arms for the King, and assisted in establishing an independent church. In 1888, he had narrowly escaped assassination, for which he blamed the Wesleyans and the British Vice-Consul, and six men were shot. Baker came back later to Tonga and died obscurely in 1903: all the churches, Wesleyan, Church of England, Free Church, and Catholic, declined to bury him.

We travel to the furthest corner of Polynesia for an arch-example of sheer blague. It takes us back to a slightly earlier period than in most of the other cases. This hardly matters, however, for on Pitcairn, more so than in the rest of Polynesia, time had scarcely begun to exist at all. Only a handful of ships had

Opposite: King George I of Tonga (1797–1893), left, and his dubious adviser, Rev. Shirley Baker (1836–1903), right.

Opposite, bottom: An accomplished opportunist, Colonel Steinberger obtained supreme power in Samoa. Like others of his kind, he did not escape deportation.

Below: Emma Coe with her last husband, Paul Kolbe: they died on successive days in strange circumstances at Monte Carlo in 1913. 'Queen' Emma lived in high and ruthless style on New Britain from 1879. The botanical brilliance of her brother-in-law, Richard Heinrich Robert Parkinson, helped her to establish a copra empire.

called at Pitcairn after the first one to do so had discovered the only surviving *Bounty* mutineer. In 1832, one of the ships brought a man who declared himself to be Captain Lord Joshua Hill.

Hill asserted that he had authority from Britain to be governor of Pitcairn. He also stated that he was a very near relative of the Duke of Bedford. Already on the island were three Europeans. Nobbs, the missionary, gave Hill board and lodging in his house, but he was very soon turned out by his guest. Hill prohibited liquor-making and established as puritanical a regime as that of Baker in Tonga. He made a quick reputation for sadistic treatment and for excessively hard judgement of the misdemeanors that were almost impossible to avoid. He altered his title to 'President of the Commonwealth of Pitcairn'. His megalomania was absolute. He declared his credentials publicly in a self-testimonial, unique by any standard in the world, here abbreviated:

... I have visited the four quarters of the globe, and it has ever been my desire to maintain, as far as lay in my power, the standing of an English gentleman. I have lived a considerable while in a palace, and had my dinner parties with a princess on my right, and a General's lady upon my left. I have had a French cook, a box at the opera, I have drove my dress carriage (thought the neatest then in Paris, where I spent five or six years; . . .) and the handsomest lady, Madame R———, to grace my carriage ... I have (at her request) visited Madame Bonaparte, at the Tuileries, St. Cloud, and Malmaison ... I have had the honour of being in company; i.e. at the same parties, with both his late Majesty George IV then Prince Regent, and his present Majesty William IV then H.R.H. Duke of Clarence, as well as with their royal brothers . . . And I have given the arm to Lady Hamilton (of Naples renown), whom the hero of the Nile has given his (one) to more than once. I have dined with a Viceroy Governor (who was a General and a Count), and with Admirals, both on board their ships and on shore. I have entertained Governors, Captains (R.N.), on board my ship, more than once . . . I have visited and breakfasted with the late Warren Hastings, Esq., at his seat in Gloucestershire . . . Entertained etc., two or three days at the sporting lodge of an Earl, now a Marquis . . . I have danced with the Countess Bertand; i.e., Mademoiselle Fanny Dillon, before she married the Marshall. I was at Napoleon's coronation . . . I am decidedly against the use of ardent spirit (malt liquor may do for those who like it), tobacco, etc. And as for wine, that only at dinner; it even then ought to be good, if not the very best, as the Gourmet would have it, when speaking of Clas-Vangeat, and Romance, etc. I have had a fine band of music on board my ship, and my four kinds of wine on my table. (I am not sleeping on a 'bed of roses' now, but in a humble hut or cabin). After all, what does the foregoing amount to?—vanity of vanities. I will merely add, that I have had a year in the Church of Christ, and that I am a life member of the Bible Society. That I am looking with the blessed Lord's help to something of far more intrinsic worth and consideration—'the price of our high calling'—the life to come. I am now in my sixty-second year of age, and of course it is high time that I should look upon this world as nearly to close on me. I might perhaps say much more, but must stop. I am now an humble teacher upon Pitcairn's Isle for the time being.

June, 1834.
(signed) J. HILL.

The Islanders suffered in silence. Ships called and had no reason to doubt the credentials displayed by the ruler until, in 1837, the impossible happened: H.M.S. *Actaeon* called. Its commander was Lord Edward Russell, son of the Duke of Bedford. Declaring his credentials with customary *élan*, Hill failed to ascertain in advance the captain's identity. Russell recognized him as an impostor, but could not depose him without first travelling 4,000 miles to Valparaiso to report. It was a year before a ship could come to remove the despot. Nobbs and his colleagues then returned; while Hill went first to Valparaiso and then back to England. There he had the gall to ask the British Government to pay for the time he had spent on the Pitcairn Islands.

It was a genuine aristocrat who was the supreme knave of all known in the Pacific. For him we have to revert finally to Melanesia. Charles-Marie-Bonaventure du Breil, Vicomte de Reys, of ancient Breton lineage, had a noble appearance and a style to the manner born. His family castle had been destroyed not long after the 1789 revolution. Before inheriting his title (which he always claimed as a marquisate), du Breil, who was born in 1832, found the new family abode not sufficiently imposing and turned to a number of occupations. These included ranching in America's Far West, peanut-broking in Senegal, and undistinguished jobs in Madagascar and Indo-China. He was forty-five years old when he had his great vision. It flowed from a favourable report by Captain Louis Isidore Duperrey on a part of New Ireland which the latter had visited in 1823.

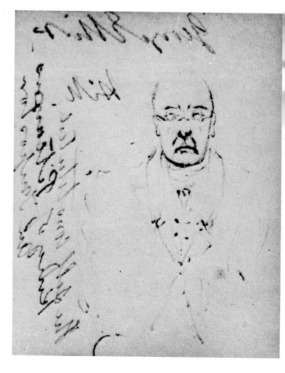

The only known representation of Captain 'Lord' Joshua Hill (1773–?) is this sketch, ascribed: 'The self constituted King at Pitcairns. An Impostor.'

The island of Borabora, Tahiti, painted by Lejeune and T. A. de Chazal on Louis Isidore Duperrey's expedition of 1822–5. It was the report of Duperrey (1786–1865) on a different part of the Pacific, New Ireland, that supplied the inspiration for a rogue *distingué*—the Vicomte de Reys.

Fifty-four years after this report, the Vicomte de Reys advertised land in the 'Free Colony of Port Breton' (de Reys' name for the territory) at two francs an acre, assuring buyers that they would make a rapid fortune without leaving France. De Reys had never been to New Ireland, but he would be 'King Charles I of La Nouvelle France'. There were bonuses besides land: purchasers of 12 square miles would become aristocrats of the first class—dukes or marquises; 6 square miles on the coast secured an earldom, viscounty, or barony; and 6 square miles inland merited a baronetcy or knighthood. The land would be worked by Chinese and Malayans: their labour would be the source of profits for the absentee landlords.

A prospectus by a Dr. de Groote handsomely conceded:

Possessed of ample means, there is nothing to prevent the Marquis [de Reys] enjoying peace and prosperity in his beautiful Château of Quimerc'h near Bannalec but he prefers to use his money and his administrative talents to found a free and independent colony in Polynesia ...

This was supplemented by a new Marseilles journal, *La Nouvelle France*, stating:

Port Breton is not a pleasure resort. Ballet dancers are lacking, also nightclubs. But in compensation heavenly tropical nights replace theatrical decoration. No frivolous pictures (or pictures worse than frivolous) are there to distract one's thoughts from the dignity of labour or the simple pleasures of home; it is the land where peace and virtue flourish.

191

The journal reported that treaties had been made with great powers and nations, among them le Roi de Lamboumboum who, to show his friendly disposition, was reported to have kissed the images of the Virgin Mary and de Reys, which had been erected side by side on the landing in the colony.

Romilly, who knew the area well, considered that the 'selection of such a spot for the colony was a very remarkable choice to make'. The Vicomte de Reys acquired a fortune. He convinced those who wanted to leave France that they were transporting themselves to a veritable paradise, with copra, the sea-slug, timber, and all kinds of food in abundance. He purchased a ship for prospective settlers with the assistance of another crook, Paul Titeu de la Croix, created Baron de Villeblanche, the new Governor of the King's land.

The voyage out was adventurous and dismal. When, in 1880, the 150 settlers reached the bay, it was as far from paradise as could be imagined. Rank jungle, swamps, venomous insects, torrential and unending rain, malaria, rocks and no soil, and cannibalistic natives. The colonists asked to be taken back but were marooned.

Cannibals, disease, and insects started to make their inroads. Part of the trouble was in Duperrey's inaccurate location (much of the rest of the island was distinctly hospitable, with fresh water and rich soil), but de Reys had envisaged and carried through his fraud with criminal disregard of what he was organizing. The Baron de Villeblanche, who had ventured out as far as Australia, reported back to de Reys on the landing in such a way as to encourage a wider prospectus and the despatch of a second vessel under Captain Gustave Rabardy. In the stamp of Bully Hayes, Rabardy was an arch-

Above: Theodor Kleinschmidt (?–1881) had a crystal-like clarity of artistic touch (see p.201): this drawing is of the Hot Springs, now in the centre of the township of Nasavusavu, Fiji. Kleinschmidt was also a pioneer among scientific investigators in the field, until he was eaten in 1881. His death was avenged by Captain Gustave Rabardy, one of the reprobates associated with the Vicomte de Reys.

Opposite: Ratu Epenisa Seru Cakobau (1817–83), supreme cannibal and energetic churchgoer, painted by P. Spence in 1885. As King Cakobau of Fiji, he was Melanesia's only monarch.

villain most of the time: he did, however, carry out a punitive expedition in 1881 to avenge the death of the German naturalist, Theodor Kleinschmidt (see p.201).

A third ship was chartered, the life savings of the bulk of the emigrants, Italian peasants, taken without remorse, and all ordered to disembark on the Island of Inhospitability. But at last the truth was beginning to percolate back to Europe. Not, however, until a fourth ship had set out. Meanwhile, the erratic and violent Rabardy kept the handful of survivors tied to their miserable conditions.

Port Breton is to this day little improved, while the rest of New Ireland could be considered to have paradisial aspects. The few settlers who managed to survive did not abandon French political ideology: they converted the Kingdom of La Nouvelle France to the Republic of Port Breton. Rabardy died, presumably from poison, and was buried next to Kleinschmidt on Duke of York Island. The Vicomte in France had made a million pounds by then and had parted with only a fraction of it in his scheme. Of the 600 colonists who set out, about half survived by escaping and were utterly impoverished: the other half could not be traced.

In 1884, de Reys was sentenced to imprisonment for six years. The daughter of one of those taken in by him described the knave as looking handsome and self-reliant at the trial. When released, the resilient Vicomte promptly organized a world cruise on a luxury ship limited to titled passengers—with no call at Port Breton.

Above: H.M.S. *Herald* in 1855 off Levuka, the original capital of Fiji. J. Glen Wilson's painting shows the double canoes of King George I of Tonga and of Ratu Cakobau, Fiji's paramount chief, together with Islanders anxious to satisfy their curiosity. In nearly half a decade as monarch, the main threats to King George's independence were actions taken by his *éminence grise*, Rev. Shirley Baker.

Below: The Vicomte de Reys (1832–93).

Chapter XIII
Artists and Writers

Of the major Pacific areas, Polynesia most inspired artists and writers. Reports brought back by explorers, accompanied by captivating drawings and paintings by ships' artists, many of them of high quality, tantalized the imaginative and accentuated their desire to eat the lotus in the Polynesian Islands. Few pure writers and artists bothered, or even wanted, to question the accuracy of the words and pictures of the early visitors. Indeed, the mood of the nineteenth century was ripe for a belief in an innocent idyll, where individuality could be expressed and eccentricity would be tolerated.

Some, disillusioned at discovering that their nirvana had inevitably long since disappeared (and had perhaps never existed in the first place), nevertheless perpetuated the myth. So more and more followed—either as a means of escape from a life of constraint and boredom in their own lands or simply out of curiosity.

The name associated outstandingly in an artistic sense with Polynesia in general and with Tahiti in particular is of course that of Paul Gauguin. Born in

Notebooks and sketchbooks were never far away when Europeans made their first contacts with Islanders during and following the Cook era. De Sainson drew this scene of early recording in the field with Maoris at Houahoua, on Dumont d'Urville's expedition of 1826–9 (see p.80).

Paris in 1848, Gauguin joined a stockbroking firm after serving in the navy. He had a passion for art from an early age and, according to his son, Emile, abandoned business for it at the age of thirty-four. Nine years later, in 1891, he left for Tahiti, attracted by Pierre Loti's book, *Le Mariage de Loti*, which had suddenly made an impact on the world (see p.203).

During his early days in Tahiti, Gauguin produced about fifty paintings, considered by many to be his best, and began writing *Noa Noa*. He was soon to become bitterly disillusioned by the effects of a rapidly advancing civilization:

> It was the Europe which I had thought to shake off, and that under the aggravating circumstances of colonial snobbism. There was the imitation of our customs, fashions, vices and absurdities of civilization. Was I to have made this far journey only to find the very thing from which I have fled?.

He called one governor of Tahiti, Etienne Lacascade, who had a totally European appearance, a negro, while another governor, Gustave Gallet, was 'a corpulent robot with a stupid countenance'.

Gauguin, like Loti, had more than his fair share of *naïveté*. What could they have expected when a century and a quarter had passed since de Bougainville was first enraptured? Gauguin's ideal shattered, it was some time before he realized, as Loti had done before him and countless others after him, that the real Tahiti was not to be found in Papeete. Gauguin retreated from the capital in his search for untouched natives to paint, but found even the remoter parts 'too civilized'. There were still many South Sea Islands which were comparatively unspoilt by civilization, but Gauguin happened to have picked out the one with the heaviest European influence.

In 1898, burdened by financial problems and ill health (absinthe and morphine injections were taken to anaesthetize pain from an intestinal disorder that was probably cancer), Gauguin made an abortive attempt at suicide. Three years later he fled to an 'even more barbarous' region: Hivaoa Island, in the Marquesas archipelago. There, he found a sort of peace and was inspired once more to paint and even to write again. *Intimate Journals*, completed just before he died in 1903, is a long essay containing random reflections and observations about the Marquesas, and about art, literature, and episodes in his life. He felt that the extinction of the Marquesan race was imminent through tuberculosis—and because of wearing shoes.

Gauguin's paintings have always been controversial. They have been described as angular and gauche, pagan and luxuriant. Gauguin himself maintained that he did not try to portray his people in anything other than an abstract fashion. His faces can still be seen anywhere in Tahiti. They haunt you: the timeless Polynesian soul stares out of the canvases, as memorable, if not as quizzical, as the *Mona Lisa*. Gauguin is without doubt the best-known European artist to have adopted a part of the Pacific, perhaps because he represents to so many the romantic conception of the artist.

Gauguin's son by a Tahitian woman, Emile, born in 1899, could neither read nor write. In 1961, he was described by Père O'Reilly as *'sans doute le seul mendiant et le seul clochard de Tahiti'* ('without doubt the only beggar and the only tramp of Tahiti'). Because he was Gauguin's son, tourists would take photographs of him, for which he would accept payment. The French wife of an American resident in Tahiti, however, took him in hand and gave him paint and a brush. In 1963, he had his first exhibition in London, followed by others in Paris and New York. Belatedly, he became more than just Gauguin's son.

The list of artists of quality in Polynesia is not, however, long. Men like

Louis (or Ludovik) Choris (1795–1828), a Russian, above, and Jacques Etienne Victor Arago (1790–1855), a Frenchman, below, were two of the finest half-dozen artists in the golden age of Pacific illustration—the century from the 1770s to the 1870s, when cameras were over the horizon.

Paul Gauguin (1848–1903).

Angas, Earle, Martens, Chevalier, and Robley had the representational skill to add something to ethnography. One or two, such as La Farge and Gibbings, were also accomplished writers. Henri Matisse (1869–1954) made a point of visiting the Tuamotu group and Tahiti in 1930 but declared that, despite his expectations, he found no inspiration there.

Melanesia has, however, attracted a number of talented, if sometimes odd, artists. Outstanding among them was Constance Frederika Gordon Cumming. An undaunted Englishwoman, she accompanied Fiji's Governor, Gordon, nominally as the family governess, on visits to various parts of the group in 1875–80. She was described rather unflatteringly by Maudslay, in *Life in the Pacific Fifty Years Ago*, as being:

House of Tanoa. 'Tui Fiti'. Mbau.

Above: *The House of Tanoa, 'Tui Fiti', on Bau Island, Fiji*, by Conway Shipley of H.M.S. *Calypso*, 1849. Tanoa was King Cakobau's father. The artist's Polynesian paintings were in unusual dark shades.

Opposite: Arago had difficulty in drawing a tattooed Maori chief, the epitome of menace. He was obliged to hold a pistol in his illustrating hand and also, in the other, a second pistol pointed permanently at the chief who, brandishing a hatchet and club, was of unpredictable temper and did not know what to make of Arago's drawing of him.

a very tall, plain woman ... no tact, very pushing when she wants anything done ... She is sufficiently clothed in suits of brown holland or blue serge and wears an enormous pith hat.

Her paintings are pleasing in their composition, in their meticulous attention to detail, and in the extreme fineness of touch and nuances of colour. Maudslay fails to give them proper credit:

She sketches in her outline with the most wonderful rapidity and accuracy, and when her pictures are about three parts done they are often most admirable but she persists in taking them home to finish them, and that takes away much of their merit ... She travels about the country a good deal with the Missionaries, and is given to looking at things not only from their point of view, but from the ideas they have crammed her with. I think she is absolutely frightened to write a book on Fiji, which is a great relief.

Left: Hon. Sir Arthur Gordon (1829–1912), Fiji's first resident governor and, later, the governor of New Zealand (see p.182), had an eye for talent. A markedly introspective writer, he encouraged his protégés in artistic and literary pursuits. He is shown here with Captain Louis Knollys, his A.D.C., in 1876. Barefooted, they had been 'persuading' tribes in the interior to accept the group's cession to Queen Victoria by leading maritime chiefs.

Below: Constance Gordon Cumming, photographed at the age of fifty, in 1887. Her touch with pencil and brush—and with pen—was sensitive and adventurous. Typical of her indomitability was this pronouncement: '. . . I have never once experienced the great heat which many find so trying, and have always found a dress of navy serge and pilot-cloth jacket the most comfortable clothing.'

One deduces that he was not greatly taken with Miss Gordon Cumming and must have been somewhat put out when she published her excellent *At Home in Fiji* in 1881, as well as *A Lady's Cruise in a French Man-of-War* and *Fire Fountains of Hawaii*. (She was an exuberant writer not only on the Pacific: China and the Himalayas were also among her subjects.)

Another Englishman who transports you right into the essential character of the Melanesian landscape and peoples was Norman H. Hardy. He went to Australia to be a reporter and illustrator on the *Sydney Morning Herald* in 1891, and was soon travelling extensively in the Pacific. His paintings of the New Hebrides are delightful in their soft-hued precision work.

One of the most pleasing artists, with a delicate clarity of touch, was also a pioneer among scientific investigators in the field. Theodor Kleinschmidt collected flora for the Royal Academy and Museum of Berlin and completed sepia drawings of scenes and natives in Fiji. In 1881, he suffered the ultimate Pacific fate: he was killed and eaten on New Ireland.

Perhaps the most unexpected artist to have emerged from the Antipodes in recent years is a Fijian, Semisi Maya. A native of Bau, he lived on the leper island of Makogai for fourteen years from 1938 and then moved to the rehabilitation home for lepers. The more remarkable for the fact that he is barely able to hold a brush, his work has a bold, lush style reminiscent of the work of Henri Rousseau, which he could never have seen. Apart from the work of Semisi Maya, very little painting or drawing has been forthcoming from the Islanders.

In the last few years, however, indigenous writers have begun to emerge. They have had to lose their inhibitions which originated in societies dominated by chiefs, where, unless one were of rank, it was presumptuous to air one's views. A periodical from the University of the South Pacific, *Pacific Perspective*, is rather unusual. As yet, it is full of zeal, with much political orientation, perhaps a natural result of some new freedoms. There are tilts at 'colonialism', which put one in mind of African student writing, although Pacific writers are more relaxed. Soon they may be completely liberated from their own liberalism. We can look forward to a literature which should reflect the deep joyousness of the Pacific character, the innate sharp wit, the percipience of man's foibles, the interest in and general friendliness towards fellow human beings, and the fascination that the spoken story has held for centuries.

There may have been no indigenous writers until recently, but there have been plenty of outsiders. The first to find his way to the Pacific and to achieve international distinction was a young man full of 'visions of outlandish things'. Herman Melville was born in New York in 1819, of upper-class Scottish and Dutch parentage. His father, a merchant, went bankrupt when his son was eleven. Fascinated by the sea, Melville, in a reckless escape from the tedium of life as a country schoolmaster, joined a whaling expedition to the Pacific: this was reckless because whalers were known to be favourite retreats for blackguards, and he was signing away a portion of his life.

What actually happened to Melville became for a long time the subject of a weighty literary controversy. In 1842, *Acushnet* made a landfall in the Marquesas. Melville had been on this whaler for some months but, repelled by the crew's brutishness, he and Richard Tobias Greene ('Toby' of *Typee*) decided to jump ship. They were captured by the Typee valley tribe—notorious for its penchant for human flesh. After a month, in which Melville and Toby were not only spared the cooking-pot but were inexplicably given four-star treatment, they managed to elude their hosts and be picked up by an Australian whaler. The crew of this were mutinous: Melville was held to be involved and spent a term in the farcical Calabooza Beretanee in Tahiti.

In 1844, Melville returned to America, after having been a beachcomber in Tahiti, a harpooner on another whaling voyage, and a clerk in Hawaii. These occupations prompted Edward Lucett, in *Rovings in the Pacific* (written under the pseudonym 'A Merchant Long Resident at Tahiti'), to describe him as a 'most reckless loafer' and bearing 'as much relation to the truth as a farthing does in value to a sovereign'. Melville then wrote what he strenuously purported to be a faithful account of his experiences 'among the natives of a valley of the Marquesas Islands'.

With its descriptions of cannibal feasts and pagan rituals, *Typee*, rejected by Harper of New York and accepted by John Murray of London in 1846, was an outstanding success—despite a degree of scepticism over its authenticity, not least on the part of the publisher. Melville undoubtedly included distilled essences of the accounts of the earliest explorers and embellished them. He was attacked for what many maintained was unadulterated fiction claimed as fact, but his story was later backed up by the unexpected appearance of his fellow deserter. As a straightforward tale, *Typee* is first rate. From an anthropological viewpoint, although veering to the romantic, it is significant for its presentation of a remote society not yet turned upside down by an alien culture. The book has also one particular quality that is patently lacking in so many of its successors—a trenchant sense of fun:

The entourage of Fiji's governor, Sir Arthur Gordon, included, besides Constance Gordon Cumming, another gifted artist: his cousin, Arthur John Lewis Gordon, whose post as private secretary extended to suppressing any remaining cannibals. This drawing by him shows *Tiqa*, a reed-throwing competition between villages, which sometimes led to fighting.

His countenance, thus triply hooped, as it were, with tattooing, always reminded me of those unhappy wretches whom I have sometimes observed gazing out sentimentally from behind the grated bars of a prison window; whilst the entire body of my savage valet, covered all over with representations of birds and fishes, and a variety of most unaccountable-looking creatures, suggested to me the idea of a pictorial museum of natural history, or an illustrated copy of Goldsmith's *'Animated Nature'*.

The sequel to *Typee*, *Omoo* (1847), was based on the author's experiences in Tahiti. It was the first time that the South Seas had been written about in such a way. His third book, a rather enigmatic one, *Mardi* (1849), has Pacific undertones. It was intended to be the last of the trilogy, exhausting his South Seas material, but this became intermingled with a host of allegorical references. The 'man who lived among cannibals', as he came to be called, married the daughter of a Supreme Court judge, wrote *Moby Dick*, and ended up as an officer in the New York Customs for twenty years: a curiously sedate end to a far from sedentary beginning. He died in 1891 in some obscurity, from which his reputation revived in the 1920s and has ridden high ever since.

Perhaps no one did as much to create the mythology of a South Sea idyll inhabited by bewitching ingénues as a young French naval officer, Louis-Marie-Julien Viaud, writing under the pseudonym of Pierre Loti. Born in 1850, the son of the Town Clerk of Rochefort, Loti was, like Melville, obsessed by the sea from an early age. His elder brother had visited Tahiti while in the navy and Loti was determined to follow him. Tahiti was for Loti 'the scene of my childish dreams'. For a fanciful young man from a straightlaced, bourgeois milieu, this distant land was the realizable *Nouvelle Cythère* of the de Bougainville concept. Loti fulfilled the first part of his ambition by joining the navy, embarking (literally) on what was to be a lifelong career, to which he adhered with a tenacity unshaken by his literary fame. In 1872, after visiting Easter Island, he reached his beloved Tahiti. It was as a gifted draughtsman that Loti was first of all to depict the South Seas. His initial reaction to Tahiti was—inevitably after such a build-up—one of disillusionment: 'I have found nothing but melancholy and bitter disappointment', he was to write in *Le Mariage de Loti*.

But a romantic youth of twenty-two was not to be put off by the Westernized decadence of Papeete. Like Gauguin, he sought the beguilement of less sophisticated parts of the group. His pseudonym suggested itself from the nickname given to him by young Polynesian women. More than Melville's *Typee*, Loti's was a highly sentimentalized description of a way of life rapidly being submerged by another culture. Although nowadays his work is generally dismissed as being naïve, unastringent, and hopelessly histrionic, his story is nonetheless written with more than a touch of poetry and humanity, even if it is of a self-indulgent kind.

Photographs of him give an impression of a rather effete young man, hardly that of a great romantic. But on the strength of *Le Mariage de Loti*, males from all over Europe descended on the Tahitian idyll in shiploads. Some managed to make a living in the islands, often forming liaisons with *vahines*, for whom they had given up everything. It is ironic that Loti had, through his book, encouraged the very thing that he was deploring—a European take-over. He died at Hendaye, on the Franco-Spanish border, in 1923.

The only writer to go out to the Pacific with an international reputation already made was Robert Louis Stevenson. Born in Edinburgh in 1850, he was puny and soon suffered from the tuberculosis which was to be with him in varying degrees for most of his life. A friend gave this graphic, unflattering description of him:

> To begin with, he was badly put together, a slithering loose flail of a fellow, all joints, elbows, and exposed spindle-shanks . . . He was so like a scarecrow that one almost expected him to creak in the wind.

At the age of thirty-seven, Stevenson went to America. Here, for the first time, he received something like a reasonable income by writing articles for the *New York Sun*: incredibly, up to then, he had had to be supported by his father. He never returned to Europe.

When there was a rapid decline in his already fragile state of health, an American newspaper syndicate hired a millionaire's luxury yacht for a cruise among the Islands in return for a series of fifty South Sea letters and a fee of 10,000 dollars. For a while it saved him.

Stevenson and his party landed at Nukuhiva in the Marquesas in 1888. They were not welcomed by the natives. One of his biographers, Richard Aldington, plausibly put this down to the fact that Marquesans had never seen a pleasure yacht before and felt insulted that presents fitting such grandeur were not forthcoming: it was a slight to one of their most rigorous traditions. Stevenson, however, managed to win their confidence. Intrigued by their customs, in a short space of time he was able to gain some knowledge of their way of life. By reciting Scottish folklore, including a yarn about the Loch Ness monster, he encouraged natives to forget their reserve and relate stories from their own history and mythology. Aldington's comment must be right: 'Hearers have testified that Stevenson's telling of a story was even more fascinating than his writing of it.'

The following year the Stevenson entourage called, this time in a trading schooner, at Butaritari in the Gilberts, to be greeted by stone-throwing. The 'king' had, together with most of his subjects, been in an alcoholic stupor for over a week, although liquor had been banned by the American missionaries. After the 'king' had been informed that, in the event of Queen Victoria's son, Mr. Stevenson, being harmed, his island would be invaded by one of Her Majesty's warships, lapidation ceased, respectability reigned, and alcohol could no longer be bought.

Stevenson's decision—on his first sight of it in 1889—to settle in Samoa was influenced almost solely by his health. The group's climate seemed to be the only one likely to allow him to lead something like a normal life, free from the severe haemorrhages which had plagued him for so long. At the house which he had built on a forested hill called Vailima, he provided regal-style feasts for chiefs and their retinues, served by natives dressed in Royal Stewart tartan *lavalava* (the Samoan answer to the kilt). Stevenson regarded himself as the chief of the Vailima clan. He maintained a strong affection for the Polynesians and called them 'God's best, at least God's sweetest work'.

However, life for the writer was not all bountiful entertainment, as B.F.S. Baden-Powell discovered to his cost:

> At first—I hope he will excuse me if he ever sees these lines—I mistook him for a postman, and a very peculiar-looking one, too; but directly he opened his mouth and began talking (and it was some time before it closed again) one could not fail to realize that he was no ordinary mortal: the Doctor Jekyll then appeared . . . He asked me if I came up to lunch to bring my own provi-

The ultra-sensitive Pierre Loti (1850–1923). Nothing could diminish the warmth of his affection for Tahiti, even when a chieftainess confided in him that, as a former cannibal, she considered that European flesh tasted like ripe bananas.

Opposite: Robert Louis Stevenson (1850–94) and King Kalakaua (1836–91) at the King's beach-house at Waikiki. Stevenson, who would have stayed in Hawaii if its climate had been hotter, noted that, in four hours, the King drank five bottles of champagne and two bottles of brandy—'a bottle of fizz is like a glass of sherry to him'. Stevenson would have liked to support Kalakaua's collapsing monarchy.

sions, and indeed hinted that I might bring two portions! Such is living in the exalted sylvan retreats of glorious Samoa!

Basil Thomson, meeting him in Tonga, described him:

In his Vailima days he looked more exotic than he ever did in Europe. His skin was tanned a deep brown, his thin black moustache and his black eyes gave him a very Egyptian aspect, and his scarlet tie and cummerbund seemed quite in keeping with the Romany folk at Seville.

Stevenson's literary output, always prolific, was still impressive, despite the fact that precious energy was used to take sides in bitter conflicts between the

The 'Vailima clan' in 1892, two years before Stevenson died. His American stepson and literary collaborator, Lloyd Osbourne (1868–1947), is on his right: next to Osbourne is Stevenson's mother. On Stevenson's left is Fanny, his wife. In front of her is Belle, the stepdaughter of Stevenson and the wife of Joe Strong, the inebriated 'painter' supporting a parrot and himself on a veranda post.

Sir Basil Thomson (1861–1939) (see p.171), receiving a letter in Tonga from King George II in 1900. Thomson was a versatile figure, not least as a writer.

high chiefs. Three non-Pacific works were written at Vailima. Of a local story, 'The Beach at Falesa' in *Island Nights' Entertainment* (1893), he said that it was:

> The first realist South Sea story . . . Now I have got the smell and the look of the thing a good deal. You will know more about the South Seas after you have read my little tale than if you had read a library.

This is not an opinion that we would endorse: nearly all Stevenson's writings of the Pacific are characterized by an untypical greyness, relieved by only a modicum of humour, as in *In the South Seas* (1888). In our view, the best of Stevenson's Pacific stories is *The Bottle Imp*, in his own estimation 'one of my best works'. The story was unprecedented in that it was printed in the Samoan language before it was available in English. Curiously, it is markedly similar to stories written by native South Sea writers in their own languages: apart from its extreme inventiveness and refinements, it could have been an Oceanic rather than a European concept. Samoans, finding it difficult to differentiate between fact and fantasy, were disappointed that their Tusitala did not keep a demon captive in a bottle.

Michener and Day are dismissive generally about Stevenson's writings on the South Seas: 'To most old Pacific hands, it is positively impossible to get a single breath of ocean air from R.L.S.'

Stevenson's stepson, Lloyd Osbourne, who was later American vice-consul in Samoa, regarded a writing partnership with his stepfather as 'a mistake for me, nearly as much as for him'. Their joint stories did little to achieve fame for Osbourne: he remained a minor writer, although his *Wild Justice* has some first-class passages.

Stevenson died on his veranda in 1894 of an apoplectic stroke. Samoans made a road in his honour from the capital to his house four miles out of Apia. Stevenson might have felt that it was fitting that Vailima was to become Government House.

Twenty years before Stevenson settled in Samoa, an Australian was acquiring a first-hand knowledge of the rougher side of Pacific life, not surpassed in the nineteenth century. Born in Port Macquarie, New South Wales, in 1855, George Lewis Becke—who wrote as Louis Becke—set out aged twelve with his brother for Pacific Island adventure. Five years later, he was a stowaway on a boat bound for Samoa and then roamed among the Islands as a trader on a cutter. An uncultivated man, Becke tried many occupations in the Pacific: shark-catching, blackbirding, whaling, beachcombing, gun-running, pearl-shell fishing—anything carrying a degree of risk. They brought excitement but no fortune. Almost destitute, Becke was persuaded to write down the stories that he excelled in telling, and he was surprised to find that they flowed from him as effortlessly on paper.

By Reef and Palm, a collection of short stories, was published in 1894. At the age of forty he had found his *métier* and, to his death in 1913, he was able to exist entirely by his writing, which was copious. Becke was the first to depict the Pacific in the raw. Rousseau and de Bougainville would have frowned: here was no 'noble savage' but the scoundrel, 'Bully' Hayes (see pp.184–6), the boorish trader, the native-girl-and-the-European. His tales are bloody and powerful—'decivilized', as one gracious lady called them. They work better than Stevenson's for no other reason than that Becke had for so long been a part of the unrefined society that he described: Stevenson had remained the refined observer. The gauche style and the unconventional grammar do not matter to Becke *aficionados*: for them, they enhance the coarseness of the scene. He unfailingly puts over the type of dialogue or conversation that must have been heard among the Islands in those times. The trouble is that it is remarkably unsubtle.

Another writer whose genre was the short story and who enjoyed popularity in a short, adventurous life was the American, Jack London. In style and content, his writing was not too dissimilar from that of Becke. Reputed to have been born, in 1876, the illegitimate child of a San Francisco astrologer, a wild, rumbustious life does not seem a surprising consequence. Raiding oyster beds along the Californian coast near the slums where he was brought up was his main pastime, until he joined a sealing expedition to Japan at the age of seventeen. Later, he was in the Klondike gold rush. Like Melville, Loti, and Stevenson, London had from boyhood an insatiable craving for the sea. He

Jack London (1876–1916) and his wife, Charmian, in Honolulu the year before he committed suicide.

decided to build his own craft and circumnavigate the globe. *Snark* left San Francisco in 1907 but, due to a skin allergy caused by the sun, London sailed no further than the Solomons. *The Cruise of the Snark* (1908) is obsessed with navigational details. *South Sea Tales*, published in 1909, is a collection of short stories in the pattern of Becke's 'yarns'—violent, even savage. His heroes are primitive and brutish. His work, like that of a number of Pacific writers, is dominated by gusty dialogue of a kind that might have formed conversation in the wilder parts nearly a century ago. London's output of fifty books in the space of sixteen years was formidable by any standards. He became unable to produce anything without the stimulus of alcohol. For a time, London was one of the most overrated of literary names, and he has been published in larger editions in Russian than any other writer in our language. His admirers included Lenin and Anatole France.

In the year of Jack London's death (1916), a withdrawn English writer with a stammer was travelling leisurely around Polynesia. William Somerset Maugham, born in 1874, had, like Henry de Vere Stackpoole, author of *The Blue Lagoon*, qualified as a doctor. He gave up medicine for a literary career. Having been admitted to a clique of painters in Paris, Maugham was fascinated by the life of Gauguin. Determined to see for himself the 'paradise' to which the artist had escaped, he arrived in Tahiti in 1916 and returned triumphantly with one of the artist's compositions. Maugham had visited a bungalow, where friends of Gauguin had lived, to see a door with a painted glass panel bearing the inimitable evidence of Gauguin's brush. Believing the present owner to be ignorant of its value, Maugham gave him 200 francs for a new door, dismantled the old one, and carried it off. The Tahitian, however, had not been entirely fooled: he was aware of the painting, but to him a new door was infinitely more useful. As for Maugham, he sold the old door in 1962 for £17,000.

Another result of Maugham's Pacific peregrination was the publication in 1919 of *The Moon and Sixpence*, written while convalescing from tuberculosis. Coming as it did after the grimness of the First World War, it was the first of Maugham's novels to achieve an immediate success. It was based only loosely on Gauguin's life. First and foremost a work of fiction, it is largely responsible for the erroneous belief that Gauguin died of leprosy.

Maugham's only other book on the Pacific was a collection of short stories, a form in which, for sheer narrative expertise, he has perhaps never been surpassed. *The Trembling of a Leaf*, published in 1921, includes probably his most famous short story, *Rain*, set in American Samoa. Sadie Thompson was based on a figure familiar to anyone frequenting Pago Pago at the time. All the stories have ingenious dénouements, and Maugham himself described them as being 'studies of the effect of the climate of the Pacific Islands on White People'.

Until independence shifted some of the scenery, caricatures of Maugham's 'colonials' could be encountered all over the Pacific. At the Grand Pacific Hotel in Suva, a few denizens seemed to be waiting in the bamboo chairs for the curtain to go up on them in a dramatization of a Maugham story.

In the same year that Maugham produced *The Trembling of a Leaf*, the first of many South Sea romances produced by a highly profitable collaboration of two American authors was published. Some of their work, if not all, had quality. James Norman Hall and Charles Bernard Nordhoff went to Tahiti to try and escape from the trauma of having fought as airmen in the French Foreign Legion in the First World War. Each wrote novels individually, but they are best known for an unusual partnership producing, among others, three books

Charles Bernard Nordhoff (1887–1947), left, and James Norman Hall (1887–1951), right, in the latter's library in Tahiti. Both married Tahitians.

about *Bounty* and its sequel (1932–5), and *The Hurricane* (1936). Successful films were made out of them. The uncompromising portrayal of Bligh in the *Bounty* books and in the film discredited completely the character of a man already maligned by so much that had been written with too little knowledge. The literary double act covered a span of almost twenty years. Hall went on to produce books alone until 1945. Nordhoff died in 1947. A solitary character, Hall died in 1951 in Tahiti, aged sixty-two.

The 1920s were marked in Pacific literary history by a heightened romanticism, the reaction to the cynicism engendered by the First World War which had just ended. Disillusionment over man and his motives led to a yearning for the exotic. From the maleficent realism of Becke and London there was a turn full circle to Rousseau's 'Noble Savage' and Loti. The extreme of frothiness was probably reached by a wandering violinist, Arnold Safroni-Middleton, in the 1920s. Two titles, *Wine Dark Sea and Tropic Skies* and *South Sea Foam: The Romantic Adventures of a Modern Don Quixote in the Southern Seas*, are sufficient with which to leave that name.

Georges Simenon has set some novels in the Pacific, with his incomparable sense of place. Other accomplished writers, such as J.B. Priestley and Alec Waugh, have had a shot; but it has usually been enough to have a look and then go away. Sometimes a longed-for haven, even when reached, did nothing to alleviate the melancholia inherent in a man like Robert Dean Frisbie. Like Bully Hayes, Frisbie came from Cleveland, Ohio. Born in 1896, he was pensioned out of the army in 1918 with tuberculosis. He bought a very small plantation outside Papeete and then managed a store for fourteen years. He found the existence untramelled by convention, for which he had left America, but he did not find the peace that he had imagined would go with it. He married a Pukapukan: she died young of tuberculosis in 1939 and he himself contracted filariasis. His six books were published during the course of twenty years, starting in 1929 with *The Book of Pukapuka*. Frisbie was a sick man. In an attempt to relieve the misery into which he had sunk, he took to alcohol and drugs. His *Dawn Sails North* was published in 1949, the year after he had died of tetanus in Rarotonga in poverty and wretchedness. He had acquired a rare insight into his adopted islands. James Ramsay Ullman analysed him in *Where the Bong Tree Grows*:

> He had brought to Paradise his talent, his hopes, his dreams—and his human weakness. And Paradise found his weakness and had no mercy.

Micronesia has been, in more ways than one, less subject to attention, although it was the first of the areas to have received it and, in the Second World War, possibly the most deeply affected by it. Polynesia, perhaps unfairly, has received most of the eulogies, with Melanesia holding the balance somewhere

Sir Arthur Grimble (1888–1956) in the Gilbert Islands, where he was the resident commissioner from 1926 to 1933.

in between. All the same, one man cornered an obvious market in writing about part of Micronesia.

Born in 1888, Arthur Francis Grimble, regarded as a dilettante at Cambridge, was posted to the Gilbert and Ellice Islands in 1914 as a cadet in the Colonial Service. He became a Gilbertese scholar, publishing several ethnological papers about this area, which had hitherto hardly been touched upon, and reached gubernatorial status with its concomitant knighthood. From that height he was able to indulge in attractive self-denigration, uncommon in the British Colonial Service. It was as an engaging raconteur of his own experiences, although on minute specks of coral 12,000 miles away and forty years earlier, that Sir Arthur Grimble became a familiar name in Britain after his retirement. He had submitted random stories to the B.B.C. and, in his unassuming way, was taken aback by the fact that not only were they accepted, but that he was also asked to relate them himself. He achieved enormous popularity. In 1952, he published the tales in a collection entitled *A Pattern of Islands*. The stories are rich in comedy: *joie de vivre* abounds. The book was a bestseller. It is not difficult to understand why: war-weary readers were thankful for something that represented the ultimate in escapism.

An Englishman who belongs with Loti to the romantic, poetic category of Pacific writers, as opposed to the aggressive school of Becke and London—with Melville and Stevenson in a third, or rather first, class of their own—and who did much to perpetuate the myth of a South Seas paradise, was Rupert Brooke. As in his ecstatic war poems, Brooke paints only one side of the picture. 'The most beautiful young man in England', as W.B. Yeats called him, sailed for the Pacific in late 1913, mainly to try and recover his emotional equilibrium after an *affaire* at Cambridge. Financed largely by the *Westminster Gazette*, for which he was to send back a number of letters about his travels, Brooke spent some months in Fiji, Hawaii, Samoa, New Zealand, and Tahiti. In Fiji, he wrote,

> I got some beastly coral-poisoning into my legs, & a local microbe on the top of that, & made the places bad by neglecting them and sea-bathing all day (which turns out to be the worst possible thing).

From there, he wrote to Edmund Gosse:

> At home everything is so simple, and choice is swift, for the sensible man. There is only the choice between writing a good sonnet and making a million pounds. Who could hesitate? But *here* the choice is between writing a sonnet and climbing a straight hundred-foot coco-nut palm, or diving forty feet from a rock into pellucid blue-green water. Which is the better, there? One's European literary soul begins to be haunted by strange doubts and shaken with fundamental fantastic misgivings.

In Samoa he had wandered,

> seeking peace ... Several times I've nearly found it: once, lately, in a Samoan village. But I had to come away from there in a hurry, to catch a boat: and forgot to pack it.

It was in Tahiti, in the dark years of 1914, that Brooke wrote some of his most poignant poems—*Tiare Tahiti*, *The Great Lover*, and *Retrospect*—inspired largely, like Loti before him, by a carefree liaison with an Island girl.

The simplicity of existence in the other hemisphere moved him to write from there in his euphoric, breathless fashion to the actress, Cathleen Nesbitt:

> Will it come to your having to fetch me? The boat's ready to start; the brown lovely people in their bright clothes are gathered on the old wharf to wave

her away. Everyone has a white flower behind their ear. Mamua has given me one. Do you know the significance of a white flower worn over the ear? A white flower over the right ear means 'I am looking for a sweetheart'. And a white flower over the left ear means 'I have found a sweetheart'. And a white flower over each ear means 'I have one sweetheart, and am looking for another'. A white flower over each ear, my dear, is dreadfully the most fashionable way of adorning yourself in Tahiti.

Brooke had gone to 'hunt for lost Gauguins' (he had just been beaten in the chase by someone) but was somewhat unfairly harsh on the artist, considering his own tendency to dramatize:

> Gauguin grossly maligned the ladies. Oh, I know all about expressing their primitive souls by making their bodies square and flat. But it's blasphemy. They're goddesses. He'd have done a Venus de Milo thus ...

On the way to the Dardanelles in 1915, at the age of twenty-seven, Rupert Brooke died from blood-poisoning after a mosquito bite on the lip. He had never seen a battlefield. It is our theory that, as mosquito bites do not kill, there was still in Brooke's blood-stream coral-poisoning from the year before. Coral infection is most serious and long-lasting. Philip Snow asked Sir Geoffrey Keynes, Brooke's literary executor, famous bibliographer, brother of Maynard Keynes, and eminent surgeon, if this could account for the tragic death. Geoffrey Keynes agreed that it could well have done so, although the connection between the two had not occurred to him before.

From one war to the next: to James A. Michener, the American, whose *Tales of the South Pacific*, set in New Caledonia and the Solomons (and therefore an exception to the Polynesian literary monopoly), was one of the bestsellers of the post-1945 years. It was awarded the Pulitzer Prize as the best novel in 1947, and made into one of the most successful films of all time: *South Pacific*. Michener, born in 1907, served in the New Hebrides, New Caledonia, and Norfolk Island in the American Navy. He has collaborated in some works with Arthur Grove Day, retired Professor of English at Hawaii University, who has written a number of Pacific works, including a biography of Louis Becke. Day's *Pacific Islands Literature* is a valuable guide to reading from a knowledgeable adviser.

Another able American writer, who died early, was John W. Vandercook. His *Dark Islands* (1938), about Melanesia, as the title implies, was written with verve and a bright eye for the unusual; and his detective story, *Murder in Fiji*, is not without merit.

Now, at the end of this chapter, it may have been wondered why Daniel Defoe has not been included. This is partly because he has already been referred to in the adventures of Alexander Selkirk (see p. 41), but also because, although his material was plainly Pacific, his setting was the Caribbean. The scene for Jonathan Swift's *Gulliver's Travels* has to be imagined as being in the unknown Pacific.

In the category of artists and writers it is legitimate to include Robert John Flaherty, the brilliant American film director (1884–1951), whose *Moana of the South Seas*, made in 1923, was a superb ethnological study. Flaherty also filmed *White Shadows in the South Seas* (1927) and *Tabu* (1931), which had two Boraborans as the principal actors.

So far as writers were concerned, the Pacific was unlikely to attract many of established distinction. It was, and is, a part of the world too strong in the facts

Rupert Brooke (1887–1915), the second from the right, dressed in Samoan costume, in front of Robert Louis Stevenson's house at Vailima. In letters to Cathleen Nesbitt of 1913–14, he wrote: (of Samoans) 'The loveliest people in coloured loin cloths ... I've been living in Samoan villages and losing my heart to brown maidens'; (of Fijians) 'What fragment of heart the Samoans had left me (which wasn't much) I left with the Fijians ... They are such a fine and delightful people ...'; (of Tahitians) 'I've found the most ideal place in the world, to live and work in ... lovely people ... surely nothing else like them in this world, and very possibly nothing in the next ...'

surrounding it to need creative fiction. Fact represented too much competition for fiction: few creative writers could have faced it or wanted it. Further, the sage creative writer would instinctively have judged the great isolation and space as being too unstimulating, for such a writer, to be in the first class, needs to have his eye, ear, nose, and instinct close to the bustling world. That sort of writer has no need of the exotic, and must perhaps avoid it (at least professionally).

It is less clear why distinguished artists have kept away from the South Seas. One can scarcely think of a more picturesque scene. It can only be suggested that the reason must be the same as for creative fiction writers: the exoticism is too rich and too real, leaving no scope for inventiveness and interpretation.

Chapter XIV

The Two World Wars and the Interim

When the First World War began, there was in the Pacific a confrontation of almost all the principal European powers. Germany had been overtly imperial. Supported by a powerful navy, from the last decade of the nineteenth century it had made colonies of parts of New Guinea and the Solomons, of Samoa, Nauru, the Marshalls, the Carolines, and the Marianas. A quarter of a century up to 1914 was not long enough in which to assess its effect in the Pacific. Administratively, Germans were authoritarian and direct: not for them the indirect, over gentle paternalism of British Pacific policy. By 1914, France had occupied its acquisitions much longer: New Caledonia, the Society Islands, Marquesas, Tuamotus, Wallis, and Futuna. By varying processes, Britain at the outbreak of war found itself with colonies in the Gilbert and Ellice Islands, Fiji, Rotuma, and Pitcairn, and a protectorate in the major part of the Solomons. Australia was responsible for Papua and Norfolk Island, New Zealand for the Cook Islands and Niue. Taking advantage of Germany's pre-occupation with other parts of the world, Japan entered the war to dispossess Germany of the Carolines, Marianas, and Marshalls, and to become a Pacific power in 1914. America owned Hawaii, Guam, and American Samoa. By 1914, it had made a naval base at Pearl Harbour, its part in history to be reserved for a quarter of a century. The only other non-native governing countries were neutral: Holland in Dutch New Guinea, Ecuador in the Galapagos, and Chile in Easter Island and Juan Fernandez. Tonga was unique in being independent under British protection. This time it did not inform the opening antagonists, Germany and France, that it intended to remain neutral.

The Grand Pacific Hotel, constructed just before the First World War.

The presence in the ocean at the outbreak of war of a German fleet, led by two powerful ships, *Gneisenau* and *Scharnhorst*, under Admiral Count von Spee, caused anxiety. It was short lived. When war was declared on 4 August 1914, von Spee had assembled his ships for coaling at Eniwetok in the Marshalls. Learning that a New Zealand force had instantly attacked the German settlement in Apia, von Spee steamed there at full speed. Arriving three days too late, to find that the 200 German residents had been shipped to New Zealand, von Spee decided not to bombard Apia. At this stage, the British thought that the squadron's next move would be to shell Suva. Von Spee took a different course: on 22 September, *Gneisenau* and *Scharnhorst* bombarded Papeete. The town was severely damaged, but the inhabitants were saved by taking refuge in the hills. Von Spee's intention to seize 2,000 tons of coal on the wharf was thwarted by a French gunboat commander, Maxime Destreneau, setting fire to it. He was to have a Papeete street named after him. Von Spee, cautious about being further involved, turned away to the Eastern Pacific. Calling at Easter Island, he was entertained (and returned the courtesy) by the formidable, pioneering English archaeologist, Katherine Routledge. Neither she nor Percy Edmunds, the English manager of 40,000 sheep, who sold the fleet fresh meat, knew of the state of war.

At Easter Island, von Spee learnt that a British squadron under Rear-Admiral Sir Christopher Cradock had come round Cape Horn: he annihilated it at Coronel off Chile on 1 November. He then went round Cape Horn himself, but was attacked and defeated by Sir Doveton Sturdee off the Falklands, while the Governor, Sir William Allardyce, a distinguished Western Pacific administrator for a quarter of a century, watched apprehensively through binoculars.

This left, in practical terms, only the likelihood of an isolated raider disturbing the Pacific peace. With no supporting fleet, all the German Government's colonies were safely taken over.

The Australians, who in their Pacific campaign lost only six men, were about to take over the Carolines, the Marshalls, and the Marianas when the Japanese forestalled them in October and then proceeded to consolidate their hold with ominous determination.

An isolated raider materialized in 1917 in the quixotic person of Count Felix von Lückner who, attacking and sinking vessels without the loss of even the ships' cats, was wrecked in the Society Islands. He then travelled in a veritable floating arsenal of a lifeboat to the Fiji group, where he was bluffed into surrendering to half a dozen firearms of the police. His gallantry and manners were legendary. Before his capture, he had stocked up with fresh food on a Fiji island, showing courtesy to the native caretaker, and leaving twelve shillings with a note in colloquial English for the absent owner over the signature 'M. Pemberton', the popular English writer.

Native troops took only a limited part in this war. A leading Fijian chief, Ratu Josefa Lalabalavu Vanaaliali Sukuna, who was taking a degree at Wadham, Oxford, asked to join the British Army. Under the rules of the time, this was not permissible: the only non-Europeans permitted to be associated with the British Army were those in the Indian Army. Sukuna joined the French Foreign Legion. Involved in fierce action on the Western Front, he was severely wounded at Compiègne. From intimate knowledge of him over many years, one would never have heard a hint from him that he had been awarded the highest French decoration for bravery, the Médaille Militaire. He returned to Fiji wearing a turban in the style of chiefs not seen for half a century (he had

Count Felix von Lückner (1881–1966).

Opposite: *Ea Haere Ia Oe Go!*, 1893. Gauguin's painting of a Tahitian girl holding a breadfruit captures a scene still common today in the outer villages.

Palace Yard Bau Fiji.
Houses of Cacombau Vunivalu and Lateilevu
and of Ada Litia and Puki Loralevu
C. F. Gordon Cumming
May 1877

Levuka Ovalau Fiji
19th Sept 1875
C. F. Gordon Cumming

This regal corner (the palace yard) of the 20-acre island of Bau, Fiji, was painted by Constance Gordon Cumming a century ago. Bau's power was considerable in the first half of the nineteenth century. It was, and still is, the home of the Cakobau dynasty.

found it warm in the trenches but it was not approved of by his father). After his convalescence, he went back again to France with a Fijian labour contingent. Sukuna's French, despite little practice, remained excellent to the end of his life. An historian was to describe him as more completely the man of two cultures than any other Islander of his time, except for one or two Maoris.

Hermann Detzner, of the German Defence Brigade in New Guinea, had an unusual war career. On the outbreak of war, he went alone on a tour of exploration into the interior, and he did not emerge until a month after the end of the war in 1918. He kept notes of his explorations for the whole period.

An immediate sequel of the First World War was that the Pacific did not escape the influenza pandemic of 1918. It found so little immunity among the Tahitians that a third of the native population died: Western Samoa lost a fifth. Other archipelagoes experienced a singular rate of demographic disaster, just when the depopulation problems of the last part of the nineteenth century had been for the most part overcome. American Samoa, through the very quick imposition of rigid quarantine, escaped.

The tempo of change in the two decades between 1919 and 1939 generally in the Pacific was not as great as in previous or subsequent periods. Occupying countries stayed where they were. It was not known until later (after the Second World War) how much the Japanese had entrenched themselves in the Carolines, Marshalls, and Marianas. These islands, for which they were given a mandate to administer by the League of Nations, were sealed off to all other countries. This enabled them to build a large naval base at Truk in preparation for their imperial expansion. They imposed a regimental existence on the Islanders, who saw no attraction in it and were to welcome the reprieve that was to come—but not for another thirty years.

New Guinea, administered by Australia under mandate, was not merged with adjacent Papua until the Second World War. Between the two wars, administrative officers in Papua, under the inestimable Murray, were active and courageous. Their patrols into mountains and valleys separating Papua from New Guinea produced revelations, such as the discovery of large populations in areas considered void. In about 1927 the Tasmanian, Errol Flynn, was a cadet patrol officer. He resigned from the administration, was unsuccessful in recruiting native labour and in gold mining and, turning to adventures on film, left behind a mass of debts.

A district commissioner, James Patrick Sinclair, recently reminisced of this exploring phase only forty years ago:

> No experience I can imagine can equal that of leading a patrol into new country: of contacting primitive bush people seeing their first white man, their first Government patrol. To stand on a mountain-top and see below populated villages not marked on any map! Where else in the world could this have happened? Even the nerve-tingling business of attack and ambush was, in retrospect, an experience to be cherished now.

Constance Gordon Cumming's delicate view of a tough settlement, Levuka, the capital of Fiji when it became a British colony in 1874. It was sketched on the day of her arrival on *Egmont*, 19 September 1875, after a passage during which 'The Pacific proved false to its name', and found favour with no one 'except the beautiful albatross who evidently gloried in the gale': even the captain was sick. But, once in the lagoon, the artist exulted in 'the little town, with its background of richly wooded hills, and dark craggy pinnacles far overhead appearing above the white wreaths of floating mist.' Levuka was too hill-bound for development (the capital soon moved to Suva), and it has remained a *fin-de-siècle* town.

It was in 1933 that the central highlands were first properly penetrated and the myth of inner New Guinea being simply a mass of uninhabited mountains exploded. There is now a township of 10,000 people close to Mount Hagen (13,000 feet).

In this most heavily populated area of infinitely the largest island in the Pacific, the Chimbu, who have been living in the highlands for possibly thousands of years, are among the more remarkable of tribes. They were only discovered by Europeans in the early 1930s but, because they have always been virile, unselfconscious, and competitive people, they have been able to come to terms with some of the most complicated technology of the twentieth century in, for example, transistor radios, bulldozers, and helicopters. The men retain the most unusual of global greetings. In villages, on jetties, at bus stops, and on airstrips, what is widely known as the Chimbu handshake can be seen: it is a solemn, polite exchange of a touch of genitals. It is something of a tourist attraction but otherwise draws no public comment. Clothed in next to nothing to service helicopters, the Chimbu people have managed to merge a neolithic culture with instruments that will still be here in the year 2000.

Fiji, like French Oceania and the Gilberts, progressed calmly between the two world wars, except for a serious strike in 1926, when Fijians took the opportunity to show an inherent disapproval of the Indians who, as the main workers, were the strikers. Native leadership was gently nurtured: Gordon's precepts and the basic Fijian-European joint running of indigenous life were honoured.

As for Polynesia, Tonga, under the gracious and wise Queen Salote Tupou III, was serenity itself. Samoa was in sad contrast. Mandated by the League of Nations to New Zealand, it was from 1920 under military rulers who did not appreciate Samoan capabilities. A prominent part-European, Olaf Frederick Nelson, was exiled twice between 1926 and 1936: this Swedish trading family had intermarried with high-ranking indigenous families. Friction between the administration and a nationalistic movement, the Mau (meaning the Opposition), went as far as bloodshed. In 1935, however, a new government was formed in New Zealand by the Labour party. This, together with gentle guidance by Sir Alfred Turnbull, the Administrator for a decade, who was given wider responsibility for Samoans, radically improved the whole relationship.

Soon after the First World War, America developed Pago Pago (arguably the most beautiful harbour in the Pacific) and Guam as naval bases. They also built up Pearl Harbour to be the most powerful Pacific stronghold.

In 1929, Hawaii suffered perhaps more than any other Pacific Island from the Depression. Ten thousand Filipino labourers were sent back home and the pineapple business was seriously affected. By the mid-1930s, however, there were signs of a financial revival. Hawaii steadily progressed towards being an American State in character, if not in actuality, before the Second World War.

In the 1930s, America, foreseeing the needs of aviation, asserted claims to small and very isolated but now strategic atolls in the mid-Pacific (Palmyra in the Line Islands, and Wake and Midway Islands had been acquired before the First World War). The shape of things to come had been in the first flight to Hawaii from America a month after Lindbergh's crossing of the Atlantic in 1927. But the epoch-making event was that of two Australians in 1927: they made the first transpacific flight from California to Hawaii (1,000 miles), then from Hawaii to Fiji (3,000 miles), and finally flew the 2,000 miles to Australia. Sir Charles Kingsford-Smith as pilot and Charles T.P. Ulm as navigator had accomplished a most perilous air journey over 6,000 miles of ocean, using two specks of land *en route*.

Distances and time were dramatically curtailed four years later, when Wiley Post and his Tasmanian navigator, Harold Gatty, flew round the world in eight days. The first commercial air route followed quickly afterwards in 1935, going from America via Honolulu, Midway, Wake, and Guam to the Philippines.

With its promise of benefits, the use of the air also brought unwelcome influences. The Second World War started on 3 September 1939 in rather the

The foremost Fijian leader, Ratu Sir Lala Sukuna (1888–1958), at the first meeting of the United Nations in 1946. His attributes included speaking and writing impeccable English. Through his influence, more natives of Fiji took part in the Second World War in the Pacific than did those of any other Islands.

Government House, Suva, one of the best examples of European architecture in the South Seas.

same way, so far as the Pacific was concerned, as the First World War. The Pacific archipelagoes were just as vulnerable in 1939 as they had been a quarter of a century earlier. As in 1914, there were immediate reports of isolated German warships in the ocean. Most of them emanated from a prudent wariness that sometimes verged on panic, although Philip Snow, whose first duty in the war was to decipher communications, cannot imagine why there were so many false alarms in the 1939–40 period. Ironically, there seemed to be less edginess (to, of course, a quite unjustified extent) when the Japanese were preparing in earnest to enter the war in 1941.

Almost the only untoward evidence of the existence of the Second World War in its first two years were shortages of some food and essential supplies and French bewilderment in the New Hebrides and New Caledonia when Germany defeated France. This was really the only effect that Germany had on the Pacific in the Second World War. There was little to guide the residents of New Caledonia and the New Hebrides as to whether they should support the unknown de Gaulle or accept Pétain and an apparently hopelessly ruined France. With a little pressure from Fiji, the Condominium of the New Hebrides decided to follow the Free French Movement, as, with less conviction, did New Caledonia and the rest of French Oceania.

The hero was the short-bearded, stocky, and courageous French Resident Commissioner in the New Hebrides since 1933, Henri Camille Sautot. In June 1940, he became the first leader of any French overseas territory to opt for de Gaulle. He did so by telling 400 Frenchmen at Vila that he was personally con-

223

Left: The largest of the world's sovereigns ruled the smallest of its monarchies. Queen Salote III of Tonga (1900–1965) beamed the broadest of Polynesian smiles, mopping the rain off her oil-anointed skin, at Queen Elizabeth II's coronation in London in 1953. The least substantially built representative, Malaya's Head of State, was selected to share her carriage, the only one in the procession with the hood down. Queen Salote explained later that it would have been impolite to Britain's Queen to have covered the carriage. The Malayan demurred repeatedly, but Queen Salote pretended not to understand him. She was probably the most anglophile of monarchs. Her reign spanned the period from the First World War to twenty years after the end of the Second World War.

Left: Edward VIII, as Prince of Wales, watching dances at Apia with Samoan chiefs and administrators in 1920. He was the most senior member of the British royal family to visit the Pacific since his father had journeyed there (as a midshipman and the Duke of York) nearly half a century earlier. No British sovereign went there until 1953.

tinuing the fight against Germany and that, if the community would not follow him, he would offer himself to the English.

The confusion into which France was plunged in 1940 extended to French Polynesia. The Governor in Papeete from 1937, Chastenet de Gery, decided for Pétain against de Gaulle. In August 1940, the vote in Tahiti was 5,564 for de Gaulle, 18 for Pétain. The Government was taken over by four leading residents. Dr. Emile de Curton, administrator of the Marquesas in 1939 and of the Iles-Sous-le-Vent in 1940, was made governor, and this appointment was ratified by de Gaulle. However, de Gaulle then sent to Papeete an envoy, Commandant Richard Brunot, who promptly deposed de Curton and proclaimed himself governor.

An odd character next appeared on the scene. Rear-Admiral Georges Thièry d'Argenlieu, a Carmelite monk between the wars and then a naval commander when Germany invaded France in 1939, escaped to England from a German prison in Cherbourg after France's defeat. De Gaulle sent him to Papeete in 1941 as high commissioner for Free France in the Pacific. After appointing Georges Orselle governor of French Oceania, d'Argenlieu went to New Caledonia not only to depose Sautot from the governorship but also to exile him. It required the intervention of the American military commander, General Patch, to prevent a civil war. D'Argenlieu was recalled by de Gaulle to London, but his official career advanced when he was appointed high com-

The principal store (Burns Philp), the post office, and the Bank of Western Samoa line The Beach, Apia's main street. It has changed little in the last four decades, and still retains the character of the period between the two world wars.

missioner in Indo-China in 1945 and promoted to admiral before he retired to his religious order. Orselle remained governor of French Oceania for the rest of the war. Sautot became governor of Oubangui-Chari from 1942 to 1946 and then retired to Nouméa, where he was mayor from 1947 to 1952.

As long before the actual event as April 1940, the American Senate had been told by Rear-Admiral Joseph Taussig that war with Japan was inevitable. On 30 November 1941, the *Honolulu Advertiser*'s headline was 'Japanese may strike this weekend'. On 5 December, the regular liner left Hawaii for America crammed with passengers: the Honolulu press had been full of news about Japanese troop movements near Thailand. The public were partially prepared: the base at Pearl Harbour was less so. On 7 December only two men were watching the radar. Seeing on the screen a large number of aeroplanes, the lieutenant on duty assumed that they were American. The American Board of Inquiry was to report that, in the next two hours, casualties numbered 3,435 members of the armed forces and 57 civilians; 18 warships were destroyed or heavily damaged, and 188 aeroplanes were obliterated on the ground. As for the Japanese, their losses were 29 aeroplanes, 1 large and 5

The new mode of travel in the Pacific. In 1936, the aeroplane, *Hawaii Clipper*, was first used to carry passengers from San Francisco to Hawaii. Connoisseurs of both travel and the Pacific, however, generally agree that the Islands are best approached from the horizon on a slow boat.

small submarines, and less than 100 men. Later that day, four American aeroplanes from an aircraft carrier, which were returning to Pearl Harbour, were shot down by the island's anti-aircraft guns. The Board of Inquiry concluded its report: 'The outstandingly disproportionate extent of losses marks the greatest military and naval disaster in our Nation's history.'

Japan's devastating action, without a declaration of war and in a *coup d'oeil*, had a most traumatic effect on the Pacific Islands. Feelings were highly confused. It was not known until years later how much damage had been done at Pearl Harbour, but the Japanese swept down the ocean from the Carolines, Marshalls, Marianas, and Japan to the Gilberts, Solomons, and New Guinea. Guam, where it had been popularly believed that America had for years been building up vast naval strength, was the first American territory to fall to the Japanese—almost without resistance. It was to be under Japanese control for two years.

Rabaul, New Guinea's capital, was captured on 27 January 1942. Finschhafen, Lae, and Salamaua quickly followed. The Gilberts were captured. In March Tulagi, the Solomons' capital, was bombed. It was captured in May, but the Resident Commissioner, William Sydney Marchant, appointed in 1939, who had decided not to evacuate himself to Australia, retired into the bush of Malaita Island with a transmitter. The Japanese were unable to discover the isolated European administrators, traders, missionaries, and settlers in the mountainous jungle overlooking the coasts of the Solomons and New Guinea. Armed only with transmitters and supported by loyal natives, they sent out vital information to the American Forces. The Solomons, from being the absolute backwater in Whitehall's official judgement, became a crucially important area, not only to Britain but to the rest of the world.

After the fall on 15 February 1942 of Singapore, supposed to be Britain's protection for the Pacific as well as for the Far East, morale among Europeans was at its lowest. New Zealand took the audacious tactic of deploying several of its meagre forces away from New Zealand itself to form a semicircle round it. Its first-line strength on the outbreak of war was thirty-six bombers. Six were sent to Fiji. America, with astonishing resilience, began to pour men and machines into South Pacific Islands about three months after the Pearl Harbour catastrophe. In a number of groups, Australian and New Zealand Forces were alongside them. They differed enough from Americans for natives (who absorbed this, their first impact of Westerners in a mass, with sang-froid) to notice distinctions between the nationalities in behaviour, economic backgrounds, and political standpoints. It looked, however, as though New Guinea, the Solomons, and the Gilberts were under permanent Japanese occupation.

Internal security in the unsettled French Oceanic possessions and in Fiji and Hawaii, with their mixed populations, which included so many of Asiatic origin, was an additional complication. The Japanese spread anti-European, 'Co-Asian' propaganda: it carried no weight at all with indigenous Islanders, but made an impression among a few Indians in Fiji.

In Hawaii, the question was of a different dimension. For many of Japanese descent, there were severe restrictions, internment, and constant surveillance. Only in the last year of the war did Americans allow Japanese-descended citizens of Hawaii to enter the forces.

The first major Pacific sea confrontation, the Battle of the Coral Sea on 7 May, between the fleets of Vice-Admiral Inouye and Rear-Admiral Frank J. Fletcher, was indecisive, except that it prevented a building-up of Japanese strength in New Guinea. The large Japanese fleet had gone from Truk to

Rabaul and was making for Port Moresby when American and Australian Forces dispersed it south of the Solomons. All the action was from the air, the warships never being closer than 200 miles. The Coral Sea battle may have been indecisive, but it was also an indication, the first to most people in the Pacific, that the whole American fleet had not been wiped out at Pearl Harbour.

It was evident that the Japanese strategic aim was to cut the lifeline between America and the Antipodes. That lifeline was New Caledonia, New Hebrides, Fiji, and Tonga. The second major sea battle, known as Midway, was the consequence of this aim. It proved to be as much a turning-point in the Second World War as Hitler's invasion of Russia.

In April 1942, when General Douglas MacArthur became Supreme Allied Commander of the South West Pacific, Admiral Chester William Nimitz was made Commander-in-Chief of the whole Pacific from the Aleutians to New Zealand. Admiral Ernest Joseph King, Commander-in-Chief of the American

The U.S.S. *Arizona* sank in Pearl Harbour, Honolulu, with the loss of 1,177 lives. The site of the wreck is now marked by a stark white concrete monument, which was designed by an Austrian interned in Hawaii during the Second World War.

Admiral Chester Nimitz (1885–1966), the American Naval Commander-in-Chief of the whole of the Pacific during the Second World War. No individual had exercised supreme control over the ocean before (or since) then. He was arguably, with Marshal Zhukov, the outstanding strategist of the war.

Navy, and MacArthur asked repeatedly for maximum priority to be given to first containing, and then pushing back, the Japanese. Had Churchill had his way, the Pacific would not have been given a priority in the Second World War. King's was the strongest influence against Churchill: he insisted that the New Guinea-Fiji-Samoa-Hawaii line be protected on the level of the highest priority. It was King's decision that the Japanese were to be defeated in the Solomons. As he made his plans, the Japanese were organizing the great move down to the South Pacific.

The Japanese code was cracked at Pearl Harbour in time to discover that they were about to take their huge step south. Different views were held by the Americans as to the interpretation of the first target, but Nimitz decided that it must be Midway Island. Calling to the area every available ship, he was told that the aircraft carrier, *Yorktown*, damaged in the Coral Sea battle, would take three months to repair. Nimitz ordered the work to be completed in three days: it was.

Between 4 and 8 June, 200 miles north of Midway Island, the great fleets, loaded with aircraft, had the momentous show-down. The fighting was carried out by aircraft against each other from ships which were hardly in range—in range of their respective aircraft, that is. Among all the confused entanglements in the world's long history of epic battles, none reached this height of chaos. So frantic was the confusion that American and Japanese planes, needing to come down to refuel, found themselves on the decks of their enemies' aircraft carriers. They often managed to take off rapidly enough to outwit their surprised hosts. Although American losses were heavy, those of the Japanese were much greater. The intention of the Commander-in-Chief of the Japanese Navy, Isoroku Yamamoto, a sailor in Nimitz's class, which is putting him very high, was for the fleet, under Vice-Admiral Nagumo, to take Midway Island and go on to New Caledonia, Fiji, Samoa, and then ultimately to New Zealand and Australia. That was stopped for good. The Midway battle was effectively won by eighty American naval airmen. It proved that aeroplanes from aircraft carriers were decisive. Japan lost the Pacific War because it had not found any American aircraft carriers tied up inside Pearl Harbour, and because of the ability of the American commanders at sea—Fletcher and the most competent tactician of all, Vice-Admiral Raymond A. Spruance, under the sharp attention of the widely disliked King and the likeable Nimitz. From June 1942, the Americans had naval superiority in the Pacific: Japanese domination on the sea had lasted barely six months. However, the Japanese had landed on many Islands and had to be forced out.

That the Solomons were very likely to be the location of a key struggle in any Pacific War had been prophesied by Admiral Earl Jellicoe when, as Governor-General of New Zealand, he had visited the group after the First World War. It was a remarkable prognostication. The battle for Guadalcanal in the Solomons was a turning-point, equivalent to the Midway battle on the ocean. Generals Alexander Vandegrift and Alexander Patch won the field after many reversals.

The American and New Zealand Forces in the Solomons had valuable support from Fijians, who provided the first example of superiority over the Japanese in warfare within the bush. A Fijian was awarded posthumously the only Victoria Cross given to a non-European colonial. Admiral William Frederick Halsey, the American Allied Naval Commander in the South Pacific, said after the war:

I thought the Japanese were good jungle fighters. But after one of the Fijian battalions had spent nearly two months behind their lines we found that the enemy was an amateur compared with the Fijians.

As the Americans cleared Guadalcanal, Australians under General Thomas Blamey, in another major Pacific turning-point, pushed the Japanese out of Papua.

The invasion of Fiji seemed as inevitable as anything could be in the war. However, confidence was restored around the middle of 1942, when American aeroplanes poured into the hastily constructed Nadi airfield, which is now the largest international airport in the Pacific. The American Navy could also occasionally be seen in strength as it awaited the chance to catch the Japanese.

In the Gilberts, there was nothing but tragedy. Three days after the bombing of Pearl Harbour, the Japanese landed on Tarawa. They destroyed as much as possible and, before departing, informed the people that they were now under

Above: 'Red Beach' at Guadalcanal in the Solomons, where the American marines landed on 7 August 1942. Initially, to their surprise, there was no opposition, but critical Japanese resistance was soon encountered inland.

Opposite: John Frum cargo cult adherents on Tanna, New Hebrides, practise discipline in anticipation of the advent of power when American goods return (see p.234). Red paint has been used for the letters 'U.S.A.' on their chests, and for the ends of 'rifles' to represent bayonets. Broadly similar cults, which principally originated during and immediately after the Second World War, were those of 'Marching Rule' in the Solomons and 'The New Men' in Papua.

Right: Ratu Sir Edward Cakobau (1908–73) was the son of Tonga's King George II and of the granddaughter of Fiji's King Cakobau (see p.181). Highly respected in Tonga and in Fiji (of which he was deputy prime minister), he commanded battalions in the Solomons during the Second World War and in the Malayan emergency of 1952–56 as to the manner born. The resemblance to his half-sister, Queen Salote, was marked. Shown here with Philip Snow in 1971, he was a raconteur *par excellence*.

RATU SIR EDWARD CAKOBAU K.B.E., M.C.,
(Deputy Prime Minister of Fiji) and
PHILIP A. SNOW M.A., F.R.A.I, J.P.

Christmas Day, 1942, at Buna, New Guinea. The Australian soldier being led by a villager to an aid station later died.

Japanese directions, one of which was that none must leave the islands. Most Europeans promptly fled to Fiji, but a handful elected to stay to watch the coast. The Japanese publicly beheaded them before lines of Gilbertese, who were ordered to watch.

Micronesia, the first jumping-off point for the Japanese, was appropriately the scene of the Japanese death-throes. At Saipan, thousands of Japanese and Saipanese civilians leapt to their death after the American invasion. It came to be called Suicide Cliff. For the Japanese (if not for the impressionable Saipan natives), it was a totally fitting last act. In the effort of taking back Saipan, 3,000 Americans (as many as in the recapture of Tarawa) were killed and 13,000 were wounded.

It was from Micronesia—from Tinian in the Marianas—that the aircraft

BETIO BEACH, TARAWA ATOLL,
AFTER THE ASSAULT

Betio Beach on Tarawa atoll in the Gilbert Islands, after the American assault on the Japanese occupiers in 1943: a demolition heap of palm trees, machines, and bodies. The lagoon is still strewn with wrecks, but palm trees cover the land again. Women's favourite hair adornments are glinting slivers of aluminium from the crashed aeroplanes, and salvaged American helmets have made splendid cooking pots.

took off with the atom bomb for Hiroshima, the eighth largest city in Japan. Four days later (a day after the second bomb had been dropped on Nagasaki), the Japanese stopped all fighting.

The saving of the Pacific was preponderantly an American triumph—a magnificent one. It had been a desperately close-run affair. An ineradicable effect was on the subsequent postwar influence of Europeans in the Pacific.

233

Chapter XV

Peace, Restlessness and Moralization

Japan's surrender on 14 August 1945 left a great deal of the Pacific, in terms of territorial occupation, where it had been before the start of the war. Central and Eastern Polynesia had been very little affected, except as regards shortage of supplies. Western Polynesia had been nearer events but was only indirectly involved. Northern Polynesia—Hawaii and Midway—saw violent action but, with the exception of Wake Island, escaped occupation. Micronesia and Melanesia, however, had been occupied by the Japanese (the former wholly so), and were battlegrounds, emergency areas likely to become them, or bases almost to the war's end.

As for Melanesia, New Caledonia, Fiji, and the New Hebrides recovered some serenity after the mass of forces, predominantly American, left to push the Japanese back towards Japan: but marks remained.

All through the Islands there were physical problems after the peace; but there were also worrying ones that were in the main psychological—it would have been astonishing if there had not been any. The huge successes of the Japanese gave the Islanders cause for real doubts about Europeans. The grave loss of European face, however, did not help the handful of anti-Western movements that had existed before the war. These were barely revived as such.

It was in the less sophisticated parts of Melanesia that disturbances manifested themselves immediately after the war. The restlessness was caused by what came to be called cargo cults. Intrinsically, they represented the hopes of Islanders who had seen unprecedented wealth pass over their land whenever Americans had appeared. There were stories of shiploads of refrigerators, jeeps, cranes, bulldozers, lamps, electricity plants, wiring, and tinned food, never unpacked from crates, being pitched overboard at sea. These were true enough. American businessmen did not want the postwar market embarrassed by the surfeit of cheap goods. This could not be understood by the Islanders, who became sure that the day would return when *mana* would again descend from the clouds in aeroplanes, or from over the horizon in ships. Crude jetties and airstrips were built by the Islanders for their reception. Once this frenzy of preparation was complete, natives saw no purpose in doing anything but wait for the millennium.

Taxes were not paid. No work was done. There was resistance, sometimes in para-military form, to any direction, and an absolute reluctance to believe those who told them that they were living in their dreams. The cargo cults sprang up quite independently in group after group. In the New Hebrides, it was John Frum who would bring the goods. Who he was supposed to be has never been established. Some have thought that the name was derived from that of a profusely generous American Army quartermaster, who handed out material treasures—tobacco, tinned fish and meat, and kerosene (paraffin for their lamps)—and promised much more to come. In 1942, when Americans exhibited goods on a scale that the parsimonious French and British never seemed to possess, the prophecies were coming true.

The cargo cults, symptomatic of doubts as to the ability or intention of Western governments to alter materially the Islanders' economic or political

A traumatic start to Micronesia's new Japanese-free status after the Second World War was the first nuclear bomb explosion at Bikini atoll in the Marshalls in 1946. Empty battleships were material guinea-pigs. The Bikinians have still not been able to return home, over thirty years later.

status, continued into the 1960s: there were hopes that there would be another cataclysm involving the Western countries.

Native morale had dropped in parts of the Pacific. So had non-native morale. Fortunately, the demoralization was different from that which had caused depopulation in the last half of the previous century. The causes were clearer, as were the symptoms. Natives had not this time lost faith in themselves, but in their rulers. It was more a case of bewilderment than despair, and was consequently without the same serious psychological depths. The frenetic changes in the Islands—the war that was waged over them and the Americans' material wealth (which also astounded Europe and Asia)—supplied the *raison d'être* for the strength and number of immediate postwar cults.

Increases in the tempo of transfer of political and material power in Papua New Guinea and the Solomons to the stage of independence knocked the bottom clean out of the cults. Only in the New Hebrides, where to the natives there seemed to be little change affecting them or likely to do so, did cults continue to simmer. There were amusing sides to the cargo cults. In different parts of the Pacific, single Japanese had hidden themselves in the bush as the war went against them. They emerged several years after the end of the war in full expectation of being liquidated. A pale one, who decided that he could stand the situation no longer, appeared tremulously in a New Guinea village. There, to his astonishment, his lighter-than-brown features were interpreted as those of the returning spirit of an ancestor. He was made the centre of a cult that happened to be in existence and only needed a manifestation like him to prove how right it was.

In 1964, a cargo cult on New Hanover, off New Guinea, insisted on voting for President Lyndon B. Johnson in the first elections ever held for their New Guinea Parliament: the New Hanoverians had been given the idea, tongue-in-cheek, by an American geodetic survey team making maps on the island. Johnson, it was suggested, could certainly deliver the goods. Officially informed that the American President was not a candidate, the Islanders told the electoral officer that, even if Johnson was not in the ballot, they would still vote for him. Money was collected with which to buy him as their representative. Johnson had to convey a message that he was too busy to go to New Hanover but that he would gladly send Barry Goldwater.

One of the greatest contributions to the moralization—if we may use this word in contrast with its opposite—that is now so striking a characteristic of many of the Pacific groups has been the medical benefits conferred by Europeans. At the very least, the detrimental aspects that they introduced have been neutralized; at best, a great deal more has been accomplished. Influenza, venereal disease, and tuberculosis have been held in check. Yaws and leprosy, which were indigenous, have been almost extinguished. There have been many doctors and nurses who have worked under repellent conditions. The devoted Catholic Fathers and Sisters who went to the leper island of Makogai, mostly from France, were often young; they sometimes contracted the disease and never left.

It has been due partly to this sometimes spectacular medical advance, partly to a prosperity that their fathers or grandfathers, the original immigrants, did not know, and partly to congenial conditions in almost every sense that Asiatic elements in Pacific populations have increased dramatically since the war. The Chinese in Tahiti, Japanese in Hawaii, Indians in Fiji, Indo-Chinese in New Caledonia—they have all virtually doubled in number. The same medical improvements, and a coming-to-terms with new economic forces and with

Change in Micronesia is dividing its society into two more obviously than in Polynesia and Melanesia. A Micronesian observed: 'The young would rather have a Coca-Cola than a coconut. The aged would rather have a coconut than a Coca-Cola.' This gratuitous advertising was photographed in the Palau group of the Caroline Islands.

themselves psychologically have also enabled the indigenous populations in all groups not only to hold steady but to increase—with the exception of the Marquesans and Pitcairnese. There is no obvious explanation for the Marquesas' failure to follow the general population pattern. In the case of the Pitcairnese, it is simply that the bright lights of Auckland have been seen from far away. It has proved impossible for enough interest to be kindled in life on Pitcairn for the young to be dissuaded from drifting away. Pure Hawaiians, no longer counted separately, are believed not to have increased in number, but Easter Islanders have increased by fifty per cent.

In a number of groups, young indigenous people have moved to the cities and towns. Villages, successfully maintained by old and middle-aged men in the war, have declined in standards. It was expected that when the young men returned after the war to New Guinea, Fiji, and Tonga, village life would revive. Instead, to young men's taste, it was moribund.

In the last decade a growth of confidence among almost all the indigenous people of the Pacific has been very marked. There have been few setbacks: indeed, as the Western world has seemed to lose face and pursue new insanities, the Pacific has become an oasis of common sense and dignified performance in the public eye. The world outside has noticed this tranquillity with some wonderment and much envy.

There has never been in the Pacific an apartheid policy such as there is in Africa—or signs like 'whites only'. The term 'whites', in itself emotive, is not in the vocabulary of indigenous people: instead, they use words akin to 'people from the horizon'. Racial distinctions would have been unthinkable at any time in modern Pacific history. This is not to say that discrimination has not been part of its history: it has, but little of it has been publicly flaunted. Not that, in the present postwar conscience, this excuses the past for some leaders of the time.

Philip Snow was surprised to find much discouragement, before the Second World War and for a while after it, of his fraternizing with anyone regardless of their nationality. Attracting some unpopularity among his European friends, he either founded personally some multinational organizations and clubs or joined a tiny handful of Europeans doing the same. He was on the founding committee of the first inter-racial social club in Fiji. What disappointed him was not so much the attitudes of Europeans in commerce, industry, or other competitive lines, as the disapproval and non-cooperation of some senior officials and colleagues. Not until the 1960s, two decades after those efforts, did multiracialism become recognized policy.

The Second World War had other effects. The initial Japanese threat was directed at most of the Pacific. It gave rise to co-operation between the Islands following the Australian and New Zealand lead. Distances shortened: a quite new sense, that of propinquity, came in. The South Pacific Commission in Nouméa, a university of the South Pacific in Suva (in itself developed from the nucleus of the Central Medical School for the Pacific in Suva, set up in 1888), and the South Pacific Games were established. In addition, of course, there has been the spread of independent governments, which look to each other for moral buoyancy.

To a large extent, the obvious has happened nearly everywhere. With United Nations' pressures for overseas possessions to cease to exist, there is little doubt that changes will occur affecting the American Trust Territory of Micronesia, the New Hebrides Condominium, American Samoa, Guam, and Pitcairn's Island. It would be ironical, considering its manner of establishment, if the last of all the colonies in Britain's empire was Pitcairn. The United Nations make little progress with French Oceania. In the Pacific one hears it said that the only imperialists now in the area are the Americans and the French—and the Indonesians. If the Americans are clinging on as a protective measure against any rush of blood to Japanese heads on the lines of their 1941 military mania, from which America rescued the Pacific, there is ample justification. If the French are doing so for the same reason, that is also obviously an unassailable motive. Their claim is principally that New Caledonia and French Polynesia are part of France, that they are culturally inseparable. It is a reflection of the

different policies that the British and French have applied to their possessions. From the start, the British showed the greatest anxiety to keep and strengthen native cultures so that they could leave the Islanders to look after themselves. The French have tended to regard their colonies as French *préfectures* and, with the exception of a few savants like Père Patrick O'Reilly (despite his name, wholly French), the greatest Pacific bibliographer and historian of French Oceania, lay less emphasis on indigenous systems and land tenure. The United Nations are quiet about Irian Jaya, which has been unethnically absorbed into Indonesia.

The Pacific territories are now a very heterogenous assembly. There are thirteen in Polynesia (not including New Zealand) at present, six in Micronesia and seven in Melanesia. They include a republic, a monarchy, a trust territory, two crown colonies, two unincorporated territories, two provinces, two condominia (the second is the American-British one of Canton and Enderbury Islands), an associated state, a dominion, two associated territories, two dependencies, and five independent countries.

Unforeseen things have happened, such as the explosion of American and French nuclear bombs, which is not popular among the Islanders. There has also been Nauru. Independence was given without acrimony by Australia in 1968 to President Hammer de Roburt. The smallest member of the United Nations, it is, however, the richest republic in the world *per capita*. Its 8 square miles contain 7,000 people: 4,000 are Nauruans, and the rest are Chinese, Gilbertese, and some indispensable Europeans. After the wartime exile of the whole native community to Truk by the Japanese, the population is increasing on an island which will be too small to accommodate everyone in the not very distant future. A fund levied from each ton of calcium phosphate dug up has

Left: Former colleagues: the 6-foot-7-inches-tall Prime Minister of Fiji, Ratu Sir Kamisese Mara, and Philip Snow in 1970..

Right: The Government buildings, Suva, in 1949. They look massive for a South Seas archipelago, but they were found to be not large enough when they were built in 1939. Extensions added over the last fifteen years, in the foreground, have not enhanced the original architectural style: the administrative headquarters are still overcrowded.

been established to provide for the time when the phosphates have been worked out—by the year 2000 perhaps, at the latest.

Not unpredictably, one of the three main Pacific regions has tried to think in terms of practical cohesion. But no sooner had the Congress of Micronesia, aiming at a government free from Westerners for the Carolines, Marshalls, and Marianas, been formed in 1965 than there was fissure. Indeed, the unification of these quite diverse people seems a long way off. The North Marianas would prefer a kind of Commonwealth union with America, which is anxious to retain military bases in Micronesia.

The British have mainly taken the initiative for autonomy in their possessions. Native pressures have been mild where economic dependence has to continue. The Gilberts expect independence imminently (in 1979): they already have a chief minister. As these 50,000 Micronesians had little in common, except shared administration, with the 8,000 Polynesians of the Ellice Islands, the break-up of the jejune Gilbert and Ellice combination was not unexpected. Fearing domination by an independent Gilbert group, in 1976 the Ellice Islands took the almost old-fashioned step of becoming a British dependency with the name of Tuvalu, its own currency, and with Funafuti as its capital. Full independence within the Commonwealth came in 1978. The economic viability of these atolls is precarious. As in the Gilberts, subsistence is on seafood and coconuts.

Overcrowding in 1947 caused a radical migration from a sea-level coralline atoll, Vaitupu, to Kioa, a craggy, volcanic Fijian island. Since then, the Ellice Islanders have successfully settled among Fijians, close to Europeans, and adjoining the ethnically different Banabans on Rabe Island.

In the New Hebrides Condominium, the French and British adhere to their own sports: *pétanque* and cricket. The indigenous people play the latter.

Ocean Island, which is seeking independence from the Gilberts, has a viability problem associated with Europeans. While the land was being dug away for its phosphates, in 1942 its inhabitants, the Banabans, had to find somewhere else to live. They bought Rabe, a rugged island in Fiji, and moved after the Second World War. It was the largest native transplantation in the Pacific in European times. Legal action taken in 1976 in London by the Banabans against the British Government and the Phosphate Commission for rehabilitation and higher royalties constituted the longest (225 days) and most expensive (an estimated £750,000) law suit in British judicial history.

Since 1945, Melanesia has put the clock forward to a greater extent than Micronesia or Polynesia. Fiji has doubled its population. Not all the increase has been of the Indians who, just before the Second World War, were estimated to be double the number of Fijians within two decades. This has not proved to be so, and the number of Fijians has kept closer to that of Indians.

Leading Fijian chiefs negotiating the independence in 1970 were Ratu Sir Kamisese Mara, a Catholic who became prime minister and an internationally recognized statesman, and Ratu Sir Edward Cakobau, later deputy prime minister. The governing party is largely Fijian, the Opposition almost totally Indian. In taking the rare status of a dominion, the Fijian administration has kept a close friendship with Britain.

Suva, with a population of 65,000, is the third largest city in the Pacific after Honolulu (400,000) and Port Moresby (76,000). Like Tonga and the French colonies, Fiji has adopted standard forms of Western jollification. Western gloom has not altogether been avoided: inflation has been one of the principal problems. Class distinction in indigenous societies has evaded the raised eyebrow given it in Western countries, although a Bauan chief, who is also a minister, did suggest that 'Ratu' might be a title for life only, on the lines of a British life peerage. This idea was not accepted. With independence following British administration, Fiji continues to set a shining example to many countries of cool level-headedness holding together a heterogeneous community.

The old unabashedly mixes with the new in Nouméa: the Hotel New Orleans and the Super Foch.

Although short of leaders, the Solomons are now independent. The New Hebrides have not attained that status. The British would consider delegation to competent indigenous leaders like George Kalkoa, but the French own much of the land and are reluctant to part with it. As for New Caledonia, where the 50,000 Melanesians are balanced by as many Europeans, the fact that it is the world's third largest producer (after Russia and Canada) of nickel, and that it has much assorted mineral wealth, makes it too important for France to withdraw.

One of the most fundamental changes in the Pacific has been in Dutch New Guinea. Very soon after the Second World War, Indonesians, with virtually no support from the ethnically quite different natives, dispossessed the Dutch, who in the 1950s were preparing New Guinea for independence. When the Indonesians decided to forestall this change in 1962, the Dutch left in the largest evacuation known in Pacific history. First named West Irian and now

Papua New Guinea has adopted some new customs and retained some of the old ones—with an effect only considered odd by Westerners.

In Papua New Guinea's irreverently abbreviated House of Ass., Sir John Guise in 1968 took the Speaker's chair in a wig, a white bow tie, and resplendent shoes. He added a *tapa* robe, a *kina* shell, and went without socks.

Irian Jaya, the status of the territory of a million New Guineans is only that of the seventeenth province of Indonesia. The Dutch *en bloc* were not the only Western disappearance. It was in this territory that Michael Rockefeller, son of the former American Vice-President, while collecting carvings for a New York museum, was last seen in 1961. There has never been proof that he was perhaps the last Western victim of Pacific cannibalism, but tribes in that area do retain the custom.

After Irian Jaya, Papua New Guinea has seen perhaps the most striking examples of change anywhere in the Pacific since the Second World War. Arthur Grenfell Price has pondered: 'how quickly head-hunters could become vote-hunters; cannibals conservatives and sorcerers statesmen.'

The war between Occidentals and Orientals had not involved many natives, except that it was fought over their settlements and gardens and that when it was over they were left hungry, impoverished, and baffled. For four years after the Second World War, New Guinea and Papua had separate Australian

Queen Elizabeth II and Prince Philip with Papua New Guinea's Prime Minister, Michael Somare, in 1977.

administrations. Fusion into a single unit took place in 1949; it was governed from Port Moresby which, as the only large settlement not damaged in the war, became the capital. To Papua's economy, in which copra and rubber are the main commodities, New Guinea has contributed coffee, cocoa, and more copra. Gold has shrunk to a low place among exports.

Between the two world wars, one of the most violent natural happenings in the Pacific was when New Guinea's Mount Vulcan literally blew its top off near Rabaul in 1937, killing 300 natives. After the Second World War, it was Papua which provided the Pacific's most dramatic physical event: Mount Lamington near Kokoda split open its side in 1951. This time, as many as 4,000 were killed.

In 1962, a United Nations mission criticized Australia, the trustees, for being slow to develop New Guinea (as distinct from Papua, with which the mission was not concerned: it was not a trust territory). Universal suffrage and a parliament for New Guinea were recommended. The elections held in 1964 had comic features, in addition to New Hanover's forlorn pursuit of Lyndon B. Johnson. European candidates thought that they would improve their chances by changing their names to native ones: John Pasquarelli turned into Master February and Peter Murray became Petamari. Two native candidates showed originality in their canvassing: one promised, if elected, to arrange for doctors to give natives injections to turn their skin white; while one of the credentials of the other was the fact that he had killed nine men. A man wanted for murder was so keen to vote that he did so and was promptly arrested. A member elected by a remote tribe knew only one of the 700 dialects that complicate Papua New Guinea: his dialect was not used in the parliamentary proceedings and for four years he sat through them with a broad smile, happily not understanding a word.

The first Speaker of the House of Assembly for New Guinea and Papua was John Guise, who had an English grandparent. He had started work as a messenger for the firm of Burns Philp and, after being a police sergeant-major and an accomplished cricketer, became a picturesque politician in 1961, when he was elected to the Legislative Council. He showed flair in the post and became, as Sir John Guise, the first governor-general when independence was gained for Papua New Guinea in 1975.

The Chief Minister, Michael Somare, became prime minister on independence. There is no more formidable governmental task in the Pacific than the administration of nearly three million diverse people in this country, which has come from the Stone Age to the Nuclear Age in three decades—perhaps the sharpest transition experienced anywhere in the world.

A note about colour comes from a letter written by a native of Bougainville Island, which seceded from Papua New Guinea:

A modern store near Port Moresby. Generally, Papuan girls prefer to wear grass skirts and show their tattooes. The tendencies towards the sack and the mini-skirt in the 1960s, however, reflected Western fickleness of fashion: the changes are slow, yet just as inevitable.

We feel too that it is bad for Europeans to marry native girls because we natives are black and we don't want to lose our black skins. We want to remain as black as we are. Europeans may be right to marry Red Skin girls [i.e., from New Guinea] to make them white. But not in Buka and Bougainville—because our skin is nice black shining like a shoe polished . . .

In Polynesia, the years 1945–79 have been more serene than in Micronesia and Melanesia. There has been nowhere more quiescent than Tonga—as befits the country which has the longest unchanged form of government. Queen Salote Tupou III was herself the embodiment of genial composure. She died in 1967, aged sixty-seven. Her elder son became king. As crown prince he was prime minister and minister of foreign affairs and agriculture. With his brother now holding these posts, Tonga is as close to an enlightened oligarchy as any existing, and closest of all to the epitome of traditional Polynesian civilization. It has developed a hard shell against some of the world's less desirable habits. A reverent Parliament consists of seven nobles elected from the thirty-three hereditary titles, seven commoners elected by adult franchise, the Cabinet, and two governors. There are no parties and one House of Parliament. The country is uniracial. However, elements of restlessness among young Tongans can now be discerned.

In 1970 Tonga, which was widely thought to be already independent and to have been so for at least half a century, acquired full independence. In practice, this meant that it no longer had to consult Britain in foreign affairs. Little else changed. Of all the Pacific countries, by preserving its independence, Tonga had not acquired a complex about Europeans, apart from discouraging them (and any other non-Tongans) from living there.

Samoa was the first Pacific group to approach Tonga's status of independence. Given a large measure of self-government by New Zealand in 1948, independence was amicably achieved in 1962, but it was bedevilled by the nineteenth-century embarrassment of there being no dominant ruling family. Eventually a compromise was reached, whereby the ruling families took it in turn to provide the Head of State.

Apia has not altered as much as Honolulu, Nouméa, or Suva. There is still something of the nineteenth century about it, as there is about Papeete. Weather-board houses and streets with potholes are still common sights. The waterfront contains as many churches (of different denominations) as the Levuka beach in the 1870s used to contain hotels.

Eastern Samoa has remained virtually unchanged since the war. Its administration, naval for half a century, became a civil one in 1951. Pago Pago is still a lovely harbour; the town itself retains its quota of corrugated-iron shanties. The United Nations do not seem to have pressed for East Samoan independence. It is paradoxical that America, which disapproves of colonies, is one of the last colonial powers in the Pacific.

Hawaii took some time to recover from the disaster at Pearl Harbour. In the event, this proved to have longer psychological effects than physical ones. Honolulu became a Pacific Miami and, in 1959, Hawaii became the fiftieth state of America. Unfortunately, the puny number of pure Hawaiians—estimated at 10,000—is not increasing.

In 1965, the Cook Islands gained an independence which has to be regarded as elemosynary, as they are still virtually financed by New Zealand. After independence, Sir Albert Henry held not only the premiership, but a dozen other portfolios. In 1978, after being leader of the Opposition for thirteen years,

The pig has long been, and still is, the bastion of socio-economic life in the remote jungle villages of Papua New Guinea. A Huli woman from the southern highlands nurses an orphan piglet.

Dr. Thomas Davis, a physician, at last became premier. Niue continues to be a New Zealand territory: the Premier, Robert R. Rex, has one less extra portfolio than had Henry.

Politically, Tahiti has had more disquiet than any other area of Oceania, except for parts of Melanesia affected by cargo cults. In 1958, a left-wing party under a part-Dane, Marcel Pouvanna a Oopa, made nationalistic noises which were loud enough to result in the leader's long banishment. The current autonomist leader is Francis Ariioehau Sanford, a former administrator who brought the Gambiers and Tuamotus on to Free France's side in 1940.

French Polynesia is no more likely than French Melanesia to have independent status. Continued nuclear tests in French Polynesia upset the rest of the Pacific, solely but exasperatedly on environmental grounds. Installations connected with them, together with parking meters and decibel-drunk motor-scooters, have detracted from Papeete's Gallic-Oceanic charms, enough of which remain, however, to enthral the Western visitor.

Waikiki beach, Honolulu. It is so small that its sand has to be replenished from other Hawaiian beaches.

Meanwhile, the ocean's horizons are more full of Japanese vessels than those of any other nationality. Since the Second World War, they have phlegmatically built up the fishing monopoly from the far west to the furthest east, with canning bases in numerous groups: their clients are the natives, for whom tinned fish remains the supreme culinary delicacy. So far, however, Occidentals rather than Orientals monopolize the air routes.

In the Pacific of today, tourists have taken the place of beachcombers. In the souls of many tourists there is a beachcombing instinct. When they disgorge from the ever multiplying number of aircraft and from the shrinking number of ships on to the Pacific Islands, they are escaping from the Western world. They know what they are escaping from but they are not quite sure what they are escaping to. Many spend their time simply looking in shop windows for duty-free items: these are not in the potential beachcomber category. Those who opt for sojourns in opulent hotels come near to combing the beaches. The luxury of their accommodation aside, they are putting themselves as close to nature as they can manage. They live for a month like natives (as they think) near the sea, stretched on the sand under the sun, away from the telephone and television, out of sight, sound, and smell of traffic. A few would wish to stay forever.

They may be akin in spirit to the old beachcombers but their effect on the Island economy has been rather different. For many groups, tourism has

Pomare V of Tahiti was the last royal occupant of the Pomare Palace in Papeete (left): it was demolished in 1966. The present supreme residence is the Governor's Mansion (right).

248

become nearly the most profitable of all sources of income—a far cry from the effect of the odd denizen of a beachcomber. In Hawaii, which was the first country in the Pacific to experience it in depth, tourists each year outnumber permanent residents.

There are differing views in Polynesia, Melanesia, and Micronesia, as in other parts of the world, as to the influence of tourists on custom and of custom on tourists. The impact of tourists on native ceremonial, which has been debased to fall in with the requirements of tour organizers, has worried conscientious Island administrators. But a distinctly good result has been the revival of native cultures: dances have been resuscitated and crafts resurrected.

There are still areas which are not on the regular tourist routes: the dazzling Gilberts, Tuvalu, and the Tuamotus for anyone searching for atolls; the haunting Marquesas; the nigrescent Solomons; Papua New Guinea's offshore islands, such as the enticing Trobriands; the versatile Carolines (surprisingly, Truk has three hotels); and dignified Norfolk Island. On Easter Island each Saturday, a Chilean aeroplane regularly calls *en route* from Tahiti to Santiago, depositing tourists to goggle wide-eyed at the statues. These are, and must be for some time, the places to be visited if one wants to see what the Pacific looked like in its most picturesque days. It is comforting for those who worry about tourism that many islands out of sight and reach of the capitals of the groups

Suva wharves filled with tourist liners looming over the inter-island copra vessels in the late 1960s.

are visited only by the occasional administrator or other official, trader, missionary, or anthropologist.

'There is always pain in the contemplation of perfect beauty', Maugham has said, and there will be plenty of it for the sightseer in the Pacific as he is aware, when looking over the green-blue sea to the jagged peaks of Moorea, of the ineluctable fact that beauty fades.

In concluding a personal synopsis of what the Pacific and the Western worlds have meant to each other, a brief summary can only start with what the Pacific has contributed to the European world: four Oceanic words to the English language; artefacts, carvings, and pottery, notably from Melanesia; melodious music, principally from Polynesia (solo singing is not traditional, but that of the Maoris, Inia te Wiata and Kiri te Kanawa, has reached international heights); ancient, but not modern, sculptures from both Polynesia and Melanesia; no painting, nor any memorable indigenous literature as yet, but a mass of mythology and native poetry; much variety of dancing; and, less tangibly, a general reputation for *bien-être*. Perhaps most important, and still as a generalization over so vast an area, the Pacific has offered to the Western world a model of amicable coexistence of different racial types, and a refreshing absence of resentment and complexes marring so much of the world.

We have seen many records—in different styles—of what Westerners thought of Pacific Islanders. It required literacy to arrive among the Islanders for them to put anything on paper, and this has come too late. They were, however, as able as Westerners—more so, in the absence of the medium of writing—to commit to memory what they observed or were told, but very few indigenous accounts have been written. In most areas, writing has been

A view from Government House of Agaña, the capital of Guam. In the centre is the Catholic Cathedral, and the skyscraper houses *The Daily News*. Although technically part of the Marianas group, Guam is still American territory. Tourist handbooks in English and Japanese invite visitors to 'Come to Guam, U.S.A, where America's Day Begins'.

developed for over a century, but, in New Guinea, the period has been much shorter. Islanders throughout the Pacific are now beginning to write a little, but the past has yet to be examined, except by a few indigenous scholars.

It is therefore difficult to form an assured concept of what Islanders thought of the Western appearance in the Pacific. People came from the horizon, and changed their lives. In the Fijian language, a word similar to the horizon is *wailagilala*—sea, sky, void. There is an island bearing this name. Occupied by only a lighthouse to warn ships off its low reef, it is surrounded by desolate ocean.

Westerners, in giving their own impressions of their meetings with the Islanders, have often consciously surmised and unconsciously revealed native reactions. This has made the vacuum of written accounts by the indigenous people themselves less serious. The Islanders have experienced discovery and exploration, followed by demoralization and depopulation, then by recoveries, set-backs and, to date, by a moralization and a re-acquisition of confidence. At the beginning, there was not much to choose between the Western and the Island civilizations. Both were capable of ingenuity, waywardness, generosity, prejudice, hospitality, treachery, exhibitionism, audacity, magnanimity, callousness, intimidation, misconception, and selfishness. Polynesians were undoubtedly nearer in spirit to Europeans, with Micronesians not too far removed. Melanesians were different again. It is regrettable that early Europeans did not use greater perspicacity to distinguish between the various areas and make more allowances for the peoples whose lands they were visiting or, as occurred so often, were invading. It is equally regrettable that the Islanders, despite their much slighter knowledge of the world and its ways, overreacted. Helping oneself to irresistible, new objects on the one hand, and having salt in one's eyes on the other, were not sufficient causes for mutual massacre.

It is no use, though, trying to alter the past. It is to be hoped that, in this last quarter of the twentieth century, something of what the Western world introduced to the Islands will prove to have been of value.

The last thirty years in Oceania have been a time of continual change. Moralization has totally replaced the demoralization that started with the first contact with Europeans and reached its nadir a century ago. The indigenous people of the Pacific have now virtually come into their own, with and without the Europeans.

The Guam Hilton Hotel. The first Pacific island to be visited by Europeans, over 450 years ago, has changed more than most in the last forty years. As in other Pacific capitals, Agaña's recently built façades give little joy to the eye.

Enigma

The Islanders are now more familiar to us than when we referred at the outset to mysteries forming part of the Pacific's charm, and to the occupation of the Islands before the arrival of Europeans. We can thus close by speculating more knowledgeably on the questions that Europeans faced when they came from the horizon.

It was in the period covered by the last chapter, 1945 to the present, that the most important practical test of a theory affecting the Islands took place. In 1947, the spectacular *Kon-Tiki* voyage brought Pacific mysteries and con-

Within New Guinea, the Solomons, and New Hebrides there are pygmies—possibly Oceania's first inhabitants — whose history is still mysterious. A 1910 expedition, which discovered some in Dutch New Guinea, described them as 'merry little people but exceedingly shy'. Two are illustrated here with Lord Moyne, one of the last patron-travellers, on his expedition in 1935 into wild parts of New Guinea. He became British minister of state in Egypt, but was assassinated there in 1944.

The island of Rotuma is a mystery in itself. Although attached to Fiji for administrative purposes, its people are not Melanesian. They look like a mixture of Polynesian and Micronesian, while their language is an oddity. This picture of Rotumans signalling a ship in 1824 was drawn either by de Sainson or by Danvin.

troversies, always in the background and sometimes near to the foreground among scientists, right into the public eye. From then on, controversies have raged fast and furious.

Before then, however, from the time of the first European explorers, the mysteries have been pondered over, and the question asked: what was the pre-European history of the Islanders? Because no Oceanic people (except possibly the Easter Islanders) had a written language, although this has been partly compensated for by their remarkable memories, much of the thinking has been done in the dark. There are, however, some material relics. It is in those parts of the Marianas (documented as the first group seen by Europeans) and the Carolines which are volcanic and rugged, with solidified lava and limestone, that some of the main Pacific puzzles exist. Frederick William Christian wrote about Yap in 1899:

The island is full of relics of a vanished civilization—embankments and terraces, sites of ancient cultivation and solid roads neatly paved with regular stone blocks, ancient stone platforms and graves, and enormous council lodges of quaint design, with high gables and lofty carved pillars. . . Yap has beautiful scenery: the groves of bamboo, croton, coconut and areca palms are magnificent. Huge green and yellow tree lizards, called

Left: Rotuman girls of the 1970s fanning flies off the cooked breadfruit vegetable with banana leaves at a feast.

Below: Admiral Lord Anson's *Centurion* in 1742 off Tinian in the Marianas, drawn by Lieutenant (later Admiral Sir) Piercy Brett. Micronesia's unexplained relics include flat-topped pyramids and lofty pillars. On top of each pillar 'there is a semi-globe, with the flat part upwards'. Fifty years earlier, the Spanish had transferred the Chamorros from Tinian to a military garrison on Guam, so that they could be more easily subdued by missionaries. However, deserted as Tinian was, except by wild cattle and pigs, Anson's men were impressed by 'the neatness of the lawns, the stateliness, freshness and fragrance of its woods'.

A View of the Watering Place at TENIAN.

Galuf, are found in the bush and the nights are brilliant with fireflies, glittering in and out of the woods like showers of golden sparks.

In the subsequent three-quarters of a century less enduring features have eroded, but the more ancient traces have remained. In addition to paved streets, there were on Yap in earlier times paved squares for meetings and stone ceremonial houses. Stone was also used for money.

More impressive creations are on Ponape. In the swamps between the 100 islets in this lagoon of over 9 square miles, there are waterways that were probably deepened and widened, and 80 islets that were moulded, by earlier inhabitants than the ancestors of the present people. They were possibly the work of a different race altogether. Irrefutably man-made slabs of basalt hold up the banks. Truncated pyramids, platforms, vaults, terraces, steps, pillars, cornices, walls of crysaltic prisms laid alternately crosswise, courtyards on land—all were made from massive basalt and limestone blocks at Nan Madol, a town built on water and therefore often described as the Venice of the Pacific. Skulls found in the vaults were dolichocephalous, not the shape of the present

Walled ruins at Nan Madol, Ponape, in the Carolines.

inhabitants' heads. Latest research gives a date of AD 1100–1200 for the Caroline group structures. The present natives do not claim that their ancestors were the builders: there is no inheritance of masonic interest or skill. In that case, who were they? The nearest sizeable lands to Micronesia are Japan and China. The possibility that the original inhabitants of the Carolines might have come from those countries cannot be dismissed. The next question is, why did the builders leave? And where did they go?

It is unlikely that they were driven out by the present race of Caroline Islanders. An alternative theory is that they returned to previous homes, either voluntarily or under duress, perhaps because of volcanic upheaval, over-population, or starvation. If they moved elsewhere in the Pacific, on voyages made at the whim of wind and current, they might be supposed to have left examples of their stonework in their new islands. A similar style of architecture can be seen in Polynesian Islands, the inhabitants of which cannot be ruled out as being responsible for the Micronesian structures. However, because Micronesians have no known history of a migration to Polynesia, it does not seem feasible that the earliest Caroline Island occupants went there ahead of the present Polynesian settlers.

There are no comparable relics of stone engineering in any known Melanesian areas. At the present time of writing, Melanesia, making up the largest of all the Pacific land segments, does not have diminutive Micronesia's archaeological riches. All that it has are some coral limestone platforms and stone terraces in New Guinea and its archipelagoes, in New Caledonia, and in the New Hebrides. They hold no meaning for the present inhabitants. In Fiji, there are some individual stone structures connected, as far as can be established, with ancestral pagan rites of up to a century ago.

What Melanesia lacks in stone megaliths it makes up for in petroglyphs. Some exist in Micronesia, but far more are to be found in New Caledonia, the Solomons, the New Hebrides, and Fiji. Usually found on boulders, the marks

Petroglyphs on Vanua Levu, Fiji.

Tonga is the only Pacific country where the palace remains a monarch's residence and has not been converted into use as a European institution.

are roughly similar. Some important Fijian ones are incisions, 2 inches deep, on tough, fresh basalt surfaces, which are so smooth that they might have been selected for display. These petroglyphs are spread across a cluster of a dozen boulders, each around 6 feet square, in the thickest bush. A British Museum authority considered that, if the almost geometrical lines formed a script, they would be nearest in style to the characters of the Kharosthi language of North-west India, in which are written the first legible inscriptions in India's history. The Fijian inscriptions have so far proved indecipherable.

Archaeologically, Polynesia is the wealthiest of the three parts of the Pacific. First, it has its share of indecipherable petroglyphs, as widely distributed as on Pitcairn's Island rocks, in Tonga, Samoa, the Society Islands, Hawaii, the Marquesas, and Easter Island, where they are in shapes of the sun, moon, stars, circles, fishes, birds, animals, and human figures. It is in the larger works, however, that Polynesia is pre-eminent. In the Society Islands, Rarotonga, the Australs, Marquesas, Hawaii, the Cooks, and Chatham Islands, there are stone forts and basalt terraces and, in particular, pillars and platforms (*marae*) of coral cubes, crudely like those on Ponape and used as ceremonial places for worship or for conferences. In Tonga, there are pyramidal tombs of chiefs, recalling monuments in Mexico and Egypt: the stepped pyramids exist too in Samoa, Hawaii, and even on tiny Fanning Island at the top of the Line Islands. In addition, Tonga possesses something unique in the Pacific: a trilithon. It looks as though it came from Stonehenge and has baffled all but the present King of Tonga, who judges it to have been used for measuring the solstice. Foljambe recorded, in 1865, that the crossbar had a large bowl of the same stone on top of it, occupying about a third of the whole of the horizontal block. It seems to have disappeared, but one theory is that it was used for containing blood in human sacrifices.

Sir Peter Buck, the anthropologist, referred to mysteries on Pitcairn's Island and, even with the benefit of his half-Polynesian origin (his Irish father married a Maori chieftainess), confessed himself perplexed:

> On a peak near the edge of the cliff facing Bounty Bay they [the mutineers on Pitcairn] saw an arresting sight. Rocks had been carefully placed together to form a quadrangular platform, and on each corner a stone image with its back to the sea gazed disapprovingly at intruders on their sacred domain. But the temple and the gods were mute, for the people who had created them

Above: Ratu Sir George Kadavulevu Cakobau at Government House, Suva. The great-grandson of King Cakobau, he became the first Fijian governor-general in 1973: nominal power has come round full circle within a century.

Left: The Tongan royal family after the coronation of King Taufa'ahau Tupou IV in 1967. The Crown Prince, on the extreme right, resembles his great-grandfather, King George II. From a cosmopolitan upbringing, he has gained notable wit and the acumen which the future ruler of Tonga will need.

Opposite: Fish has always been a choice part of the diet throughout the Pacific, but ways of carrying it home have changed. This method was photographed in Papeete.

Above: The Tongan trilithon is a pockmarked arch of three elephantine blocks of coral limestone. The bowl on the top has been missing for close on a century. This drawing was made by Hon. Cecil Foljambe of H.M.S. *Curaçoa* in 1865.

Opposite: Tourists now visiting the Papua New Guinea highlands, opened up by European explorer-administrators only three decades ago, can see as primitively dressed a woman (in red paint and pig-grease) as any-where in the world.

had mysteriously disappeared. The mutineers or their offspring dismantled the temple ... The helpless stone gods were rolled over the nearby cliff. In destroying the Bounty Bay temple, a human skeleton was found interred in the structure with its head pillowed on a large pearl-shell. The pearl-shell gave some evidence of contact with Mangareva or some atoll in the Tuamotu archipelago. In digging the foundations of houses and preparing cultivations, the mutineers found human bones interred below the surface.

Stone figures of antiquity have been found in sporadic parts of Polynesia, markedly in the Marquesas, Hawaii, Cook and Tahiti archipelagoes. They are almost as large as those on Easter Island and, like them and the Tongan trilithon, were assumedly erected by sloping elevations of soil and rock with some fibre, probably liana creeper, used as a rope. Heyerdahl states that figures of this kind were only built on Islands directly facing South America, but he overlooked their incidence on Tahiti, a vast distance from South America, and on Hawaii, which 'faces' on to North America.

Many figures are just huge faces. They are ugly, resembling those that Maoris pulled (and still pull) in their ceremonies both to frighten off enemies

and to welcome strangers. Because of their basic resemblance, the images could reasonably have been made by a generic type, such as Polynesians. It is generally thought that they are not portraits but caricatures of their creators.

There is nothing whatever like the lonely carvings on Easter Island, 2,300 miles from the nearest part of America. Heyerdahl has called them

> ... some of the strangest and most impressive mausolea human hands have ever created: monuments raised in a fanatical effort to commemorate what are now long-forgotten men.

Easter Island is near nowhere else—its neighbour is the Pitcairn group, a mere 1,200 miles away to the west. It is bleak and desolate, quite un-Polynesian in appearance. There are no reefs to break the seas, no forests, few birds, a couple of beaches, one grove of coconut palms and a few straggly ones, and a great deal of stunted, dusty grass. But the island contains the Pacific's *pièce-de-résistance*: the aquiline-nosed, pendant-eared, top-hatted heads on narrow shoulders. So prominent a feature of the carvings, the long ear-lobes are still marked in some modern Easter Islanders, who also have the narrowest heads in Polynesia. Stone noses protruding like prows of canoes remind one of a Samoan conviction, expressed with typical candour: 'You Europeans would be handsome if it were not for your canoe noses'.

Present Easter Islanders know virtually nothing reliable about the past,

Sardonic statues dominating Easter Island's inhospitable landscape. They are still, perhaps, the most enigmatic of all the Pacific mysteries.

262

except that the statues were there when their ancestors arrived. They might be the descendants of the sculptors, but they simply believe the work to be the creation of the gods. Radiocarbon dating gives AD 386 as the earliest year for signs of habitation, but it may have been as much as 500 years later when the construction of the statues began. The process possibly continued until near the end of the seventeenth century. Some of the figures were surmounted on platforms, under which bones have been found, but it is not certain whether the platforms were primarily for burial purposes. The statues are in all sorts of positions and sizes: one is 66 feet long but was never moved from the quarry, while many of them average a height of 15 feet above ground level and around 10 tons in weight. A hundred and fifty were left recumbent and half-complete in the quarries (possibly because of flaws in the stone), while 200 (Admiral Roggeveen counted 276 when he discovered them two and a half centuries ago) lie sprawled between the quarries and on the slopes, stand upright on platforms, or lean at angles. Some of the torsoes, with their haughty, eyeless faces, are slender, others are corpulent.

Thor Heyerdahl, who had permission from the Chilean Government to

With a stone image from Ra'ivavae (the Australs) is Sir Peter Buck (1880–1951). He was first a medical expert and then, while director of the Bishop Museum, Honolulu, attained international recognition as an anthropologist. Being half-Irish and half-Maori, he was very much a man of two worlds.

excavate so long as the monuments were not damaged, confirmed that statues embedded in the soil were carved down to the hips with arms ending in long, curved fingernails or hands folded across the stomach. Legless but long torsoed, they were half-bodies, perhaps either to fix them better upright in the ground or to minimize the task of transporting them. They had been dragged 10 miles from the quarry. The 6-feet-high topknots, weighing as much as two elephants and coming from a red stone quarry 7 miles away on the opposite side of the island, had to be elevated above the heads to the level of a four-storey house. In the case of statues measuring, say, 15 feet, erected on 15-feet-high platforms, their crowning with the topknots represented a sizeable operation. Using increasing inclinations of stones, a dozen of Heyerdahl's men with poles were able to erect one in eighteen days. The carving with stone adzes and the dragging from the quarries consumed more time, a factor that may never have come into their creators' world. Even so, the carvings may not have been too formidable a task: the material worked was soft volcanic tufa from the extinct crater.

That the work stopped suddenly is an inescapable conclusion. Thousands of discarded basalt adzes have been found near the quarries containing unfinished statues. One theory is that two tribes, the Long Eared and the Short Eared (alternatively, the Thick-Set and the Lissom), respectively the overlords and the slaves, with different cultures and languages, confronted each other. The enslaved triumphed and the image-making ceased.

As intriguing as the stone structures and rarer, wooden tablets with inscriptions have been found on Easter Island—and on that island alone—which represent the best chance of a script from the pre-European Pacific. As Oceania is equatorial, tropical, or subtropical, few wooden relics have survived. There has been no discovery of indigenous metallic objects: stone and pottery are therefore almost alone in withstanding a climate in which rot sets in extraordinarily quickly and thoroughly. Because the inscriptions on the small tablets (each measuring 20 × 12 inches) fit exactly the size of driftwood used for the purpose, it is thought that a language is not being conveyed so much as a picture framed by its size. Only twenty tablets escaped destruction by Christianized Easter Islanders. They were inscribed with obsidian tools over their whole surfaces and edges in a boustrephedon arrangement, alternate rows being put upside down, so that the tablets had to be held the other way up at the end of each line in order to read the next one. As yet, however, they have not been interpreted.

In addition to the stone structures dispersed throughout the three Pacific regions and the single source of wooden relics, pottery has also been found. Excavations have recently been intensified where remnants of an individual style known as Lapita have been located. Archaeologists are attempting to establish whether the broken shards that have turned up in scattered parts of the Pacific are of the same design, and therefore might have been manufactured by the same race. The answer may not be too far away. Pottery has also helped to date the earliest human habitation. Of the areas so far researched, Micronesia is believed to have been inhabited from 2000 BC, Fiji and New Caledonia 1,000 years later, with Samoa, Tonga, the Society, and Cook Islands following in possibly that order.

These are some of the mysteries that exist in material form all over the Pacific. As few of the present Islanders or their ancestors who were met by the early Europeans know, or knew, anything about them, questions abound as to the origin of the inhabitants themselves. Are they of the same race as those

Monuments on Easter Island in 1786. Natives are mischievously stealing sailors' hats while women distract the Frenchmen. This penchant for hats continues to the present. The first European to live there, Father Eugène Eyraud, noted hats made of the following: half a melon, the carcass of a bird, a calabash, two buckets—one inside the other—and a shoe. This drawing by Duché de Vancy survived the loss of de Lapérouse's ships (see p.66), because some records had been taken earlier across Siberia by Vicomte Jean de Lesseps.

responsible for the megalithic remains? If they are, how long have they lived in the Islands? If not, where did they come from, when, how and why? There are few more fascinating problems than these.

It has been roughly estimated that, before Europeans discovered the Pacific, there might have been as many as two million inhabitants in New Guinea, 300,000 in the rest of Melanesia, 500,000 in Polynesia, and rather less than 100,000 in Micronesia.

Taking the question of where the Islanders might have come from, and looking first at Micronesians (who are generally believed to have been the first settlers of any of the three great regions), there is more general agreement over how their area might have been inhabited than there is over Polynesia. Micronesians, more conventionally Oriental-looking than other indigenous Pacific Islanders, are considered to have come by an easy island-chain route from the Chinese mainland or from the close off-shore archipelagoes of Asia.

Because of their proximity to Southeast Asia, Melanesians are also confidently thought to have come from there (but from how far, Indonesia, India, Ceylon, or further, can only be guessed) along the East Indian and Melanesian chains of islands to as far east as Fiji. (As previously mentioned, the Fiji group is the cultural 'frontier' between Melanesian expansion from the westward direction and Polynesian settlement from other approaches.)

It is Polynesia which represents the greatest problem. Did its inhabitants come from Asia or America? Or have the Polynesians always been in Polynesia? These are the ruling questions. As suggested later, there are good reasons for thinking that there could have been migrations from both Asia and America. If so, which came first? Or were the movements nearly simultaneous? Depending on how one regards the megalithic remains in Polynesian countries, it does seem that Polynesia was the last part of the Pacific to be inhabited. The Micronesian stone structures could be older than those in Polynesia, while on a different plane the petroglyphs of Melanesia point to real antiquity.

The origin of the Polynesians is a major mystery, providing one of the most fertile fields for imagination, argument, theory, and counter-theory. A belief more strongly held some years ago than now is that most Polynesians spread from Hawaiki, a supposedly no longer extant group in the huge space south of Hawaii and north of the Polynesian clusters. Hawaiki has sometimes been closely associated with Samoa or with the Society Islands. It has been suggested that Polynesians spread out as Hawaiki subsided progressively into the ocean. This theory is now no longer credited. Then there are those who contend that Polynesians originated in Asia generally, or in Southeast Asia or Indonesia more particularly, to make their way eastwards either through Micronesia and/or Melanesia, or bypassing them to the present Polynesian groups. Sir Peter Buck, classifying Polynesians as Europoid, insisted dogmatically that they had travelled via Micronesia.

Leading Pacific ethnologists, archaeologists, linguists, historians, anthropologists (physical, cultural, and social), botanists, geneticists, maritime authorities, geologists, and synthesizers of all those fields have given Polynesians alone a dazzling range of other places of origin. The following list is not exhaustive but shows how varied the theories were until the disconcerting Heyerdahl voyage: Iceland (audaciously), Mesopotamia, Arabia, Egypt, Madagascar, India, Assam, China, Indo-China, Malaya, Indonesia, Philippines, Papua, Micronesia, and Central America. One or two people suggested that Polynesia was autochtonous.

An Easter Island woman with dilated earlobes, photographed in 1914.

The brilliant 4,000 miles' voyage of the raft, *Kon-Tiki*, undertaken by five Norwegians (including the hydrophobic Heyerdahl) and a Swede, began at the end of April 1947 from Callao on the Peru coast, and ended on Raroia atoll in the Tuamotu archipelago of Eastern Polynesia in early August 1947. It rightly proved the practicality of a strong alternative possibility that had long been in the minds of some of the more imaginative thinkers. It showed that South American Indians on balsa-tree rafts could have made use of currents and winds to find Polynesian Islands. This was a more dramatic theory than the Hawaiki one, which it did not necessarily contradict. It could be complementary to it, but the *Kon-Tiki* theory had the added force of an actual successful experiment, followed by some persistent scientific support for associating Polynesia with the American continent. Claimants for this theory are divided as to whether the Islanders originated in Central or South America (never North America), before reaching their destinations in Polynesia after dispersal by the trade winds. A physical observation that influenced Heyerdahl was one made by an American anthropologist before the Second World War. Louis Robert Sullivan was sure that Marquesans were somatically much closer to American Indians than to Malaysians or Mongols, races which had been conventionally related to theories of Polynesian migration.

Other theories include a claim that the Polynesians came from Asia, crossed the Pacific and inhabited it, and then went on to the American continent, either to stay or to return to the Islands with material American acquisitions.

Although so much more academic probing and practical experimenting is now being applied to the migration possibilities than at any previous time, no definite assertions can yet be made.

In our view, it is likely that Polynesia, perhaps to a lesser extent Melanesia, and, to a far less degree, Micronesia, were peopled by a combination of circumstances. With so much sea about them, coastal Islanders showed, not surprisingly, skills in moving about on it. An exception was the Samoan archipelago—ironically, since de Bougainville named it Navigators' group.

The indecipherable hieroglyphics on an Easter Island tablet.

Samoans have relatively little fame for voyaging: they rarely venture out of sight of land.

Blessed by an almost complete absence of atmospheric haziness and fog and with quite lengthy periods of tranquil ocean, Pacific Islanders memorized the paths of stars, of which they knew about 200 by name. They made sailing charts of interlaced reeds showing currents and winds, small shells indicating on the pattern the sites of islands. They observed the currents. Winds were studied as if they were human beings with traits to be recognized. Natives scanned the clouds for reflections of green lagoons many miles distant beyond the horizon. They watched the birds. Indeed, frigate birds might have been taken on voyages: when released, they soar into the sky and make for the nearest land. This bird aspect is especially controversial and is in need of a great deal more research. Harold Gatty, who lived in the Pacific after having been the fastest to fly round the world in 1931, was asked in the Second World War to write *The Raft Book*. It was obligatory to carry this in every American aircraft in the Pacific War so that, if forced to come down on the ocean, crews without instruments would stand a chance of survival. His assurance that, if you saw a frigate bird, you were no further than 100 miles from land has not yet been proved. He told Philip Snow that he had developed doubts about this bird's behaviour.

Natives were well provisioned when they set out on deliberate voyages that might last a year or two. Food was stored on shelves, and liquid was kept in calabashes clear of bilge water in the hold. The voyagers would travel up to 1,000 miles on flat craft, 3 feet above sea-level. These were most likely to be double-hulled canoes, which were broad, with primitive sails and paddles for modest auxiliary power (not feasible on tall European ships). Although shelter was provided on deck, difficulty was experienced in heating stones for baking yams wet from the sea. It would have been nothing for the ocean-going canoes, which could carry up to 200 people, to sail 200 or 300 miles. Tasman and Cook were among the early visitors who were astonished by their manoeuvrability, sea-worthiness, and speed. Anson, on his circumnavigation in 1742, found that canoes in the Marianas were three times faster than his warships.

The people were sea-orientated. What surrounded them was all-important, a perpetual challenge. The constant boom of the ocean crashing on the coral barrier reef was like a repeated knocking on the door that must be heeded. The sea had to be used, lived on, and subjugated. A vast amount of physical effort and mental concentration went towards these objects.

It is generally believed that Polynesians were superior to Micronesians and Melanesians both in the craft they built and in navigational skill. There were grades, too, within Polynesia. The double canoes of the Society Islands were more imposing than the single canoes in Hawaii or New Zealand. Tongan double-hulled craft excelled all others.

When Europeans first saw Polynesian Islands close on 500 years ago, they acknowledged the superiority of Polynesian seafaring. The chances were, therefore, that on courses taken to the east or west, the more intrepid Island voyagers were bound to make landfalls among the many clusters of islands that extended across the ocean. Those found uninhabited by the first Europeans had almost certainly been visited beforehand by Islanders. Not all the native discoveries could have been intentional: accidental voyages would have happened; mistakes would have been made, and there would have been surprising successes. Both accidental and deliberate voyages resulted in discoveries centuries before the heavy, high European ships arrived.

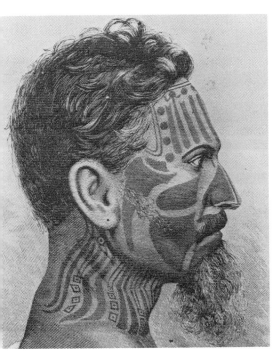

A tattooed Easter Islander. The custom of tattooing was common throughout Polynesia.

Why did the Islanders set out on deliberate voyages? There were multiple reasons for families, tribes, and individuals setting out voluntarily for other lands. They included famine, drought, oppressive social obligations, inquisitiveness, ambition to increase power with extra territory and subservient people, feuds, volcanic eruptions and subsidences, escape from disputes, overbearing neighbours, and wars. After battles, the weakest went to the wall: in this area it had to be over the waves.

Legend (unfortunately) has to be leant upon in meditating these overlapping questions. How long have present races been in their Islands? Did they find on arrival earlier inhabitants of different races? As to how long, this naturally varies from group to group: what is gathered from myth has, as usual, to be treated carefully. Typical of the difficulties in trying to find answers is that there are three contrary traditions among Marquesans as to where they might have come from. The Vava'u group in Tonga is pinpointed by some legends to be the original home of the first settlers in the Marquesas. Such a movement would have meant a voyage of 2,000 miles against prevailing winds and currents. On the other hand, Heyerdahl states that, during his stay in the Marquesas before the Second World War, the natives alluded to an ancestral fatherland on the American mainland—in quite the opposite direction. In addition, there is a Marquesan belief that their ancestors did not migrate to their present location at all, but that they were always there.

There are plenty of legends in the Marquesas about emigrations from there to other parts of Polynesia. War, famine, restlessness, and prophesies by seers led Marquesans to depart in organized expeditions. Where did they go? A piece of the jigsaw seems to fit in as a result of radiocarbon dating of charred wood found on Hawaii camp sites. This indicates that the Hawaiian Islands were populated by about the year 1000, probably from the Marquesas by accidental or predetermined voyaging, likely to have been helped by currents, 2,000 miles northwards. Plants and the bones of pigs, chickens, dogs, and rats which have been found could point to a calculated settlement.

The individual characters of the Samoans and of Sir Peter Buck are revealed in this story told by Buck:

Influenced by mythology and local legends, the Samoan regards himself as truly autochthonous. At a kava ceremony in Ta'u, I was welcomed by a talking chief in the stilted phrases of his office. In my reply, I alluded to the common origin of the Polynesians somewhere in Asia and the wonderful voyages our ancestors had made in peopling Polynesia. The talking chief replied: 'We thank you for your interesting speech. The Polynesians may have come from Asia, but the Samoans, no. We originated in Samoa'. He looked around with an air of infallibility, and his fellow scholars grunted their approval. In self defence, I became a fundamentalist. I said: 'The good book that I have seen you carry to church on Sundays says that the first parents of mankind were Adam and Eve, who were created in the Garden of Eden'. In no way disturbed, the oracle replied: 'That may be but the Samoans were created here in Manu'a'. A trifle exasperated, I said: 'Ah, I must be in the Garden of Eden'. I took the silence which followed to be a sign of affirmation.

Like Samoans, Tongans consider that they too have been in their islands from time immemorial. They maintained to early visitors that their ancestors had been accustomed to visit Fiji (which contains much Tongan influence) before

present Fijians arrived. It seems reasonably certain that, compared with Samoans, Tongans, and Marquesans, Fijians are relative newcomers.

In recent years, arguments about the populating of the Pacific have tended to polarize between two uncompromising views. One has been Heyerdahl's—the Drift Theory: settlement by design after following winds and currents. The other is the Accidental Voyaging Theory: settlement by chance and whim after having been blown away. Each is tenable on its own but unlikely. Careful reasoning points to a combination of both as being more plausible. What does happen to craft drifting in the Pacific largely depends on the area: prevailing winds or the doldrums, currents, and the barrier of reefs. Much of the extreme Eastern Pacific is free of coral: the Juan Fernandez, Galapagos, and Pitcairn groups and Easter Island are not encircled by reefs, which are such a striking feature of the Central and Western Pacific. This obstacle out of the way, there needed to be proof as to how currents and winds would carry a craft having no power except sails.

Thor Heyerdahl, zoologist, archaeologist, and Norwegian Resistance parachutist, set out in 1947 to show that a belief which he had held for a decade might be feasible. The feat of half a dozen Scandinavians on a balsa raft merely drifting on clockwise currents of sea and air was a physical demonstration of a theory that stands on its own for courage, obstinacy if you like, and for proving

Polynesians made incredible voyages on rafts, like this one from the Gambier Islands, as well as in canoes. William Smyth drew this example on Beechey's voyage of 1825–8 (see p.65).

a point or, at best, for offering an alternative possibility in the most realistic terms. This was what Heyerdahl limited his claim to: in the introduction to his *American Indians in the Pacific*, he thanks his colleagues whose 'participation in the *Kon-Tiki* expedition made it possible to settle a disputed link'.

Reaction to the enterprise still remains extraordinarily mixed. The opposition was led by Buck. There are those who concede no merit in it, not even courage, which is patently ridiculous. Others grudgingly admit that it *might* prove that there were handfuls of American-Indian navigators who settled in Polynesian pockets. Some think that such migrations were few, late, and relatively insignificant. Others admit the proof of Heyerdahl's experiment, but dispute any consequential ethnological effects. Some go the whole way and maintain that this was how Polynesia was inhabited in advance of the present Islanders.

No one can yet be positive—or perhaps ever will be. Attitudes are now perhaps a little less entrenched. A reasonable stance to take is surely that some South American influence drifted on rafts, canoes, logs, or merely floated on the sea to parts of Polynesia. This has at least been shown physically to be feasible, or more than feasible, but certainly not less.

Kon-Tiki's voyage was one of the most extraordinary on record. The leader of the expedition, Thor Heyerdahl, justly attained international eminence. The only Swede on board, Bengt Danielsson, became a scholarly and entertaining Pacific writer, settling in the remote French Polynesian group where *Kon-Tiki* was wrecked.

The artist (Piron) let his imagination run away with him in this representation of a Tongan double canoe, drawn in 1791. Tongans nevertheless produced the finest craft of their kind in the Pacific. Note the dalliance and absorption in the mirror on the lower deck.

Heyerdahl, in his theory about the peopling of Polynesia, has placed much reliance on the movement west on rafts or currents of plants of American origin—the coconut, tomato, sweet potato, gourds and cotton—from Peru or Mexico to Polynesia and even Indonesia. The sweet potato and the tomato probably did not migrate on currents: they are not good travellers in the sea. The coconut is non-porous. Buck maintained that Polynesians sailed east to South America, a great land mass that simply could not be missed, and brought back the sweet potato. Botanical migrations tend to favour theories of movements west to east rather than the Heyerdahl supposition.

Even more remarkable feats than *Kon-Tiki*'s were to follow, instances of imitators surpassing the model once the way had been shown. Seven years after *Kon-Tiki*, an American in his sixties, William Willis, underlined Heyerdahl's accomplishment by floating in a balsa raft from Peru to American Samoa in four months—further and faster than *Kon-Tiki*. With the difference, too, that, apart from the inevitable parrot and cat, he made it alone.

In 1957, Eric de Bisschop, a sixty-eight-year-old Frenchman, sailed in the opposite direction, from east to west. His raft, *Tahiti Nui*, constructed of 800 bamboos, travelled 5,000 miles from Papeete to within 500 miles of Chile, where it sank. Enfeebled by double pneumonia, he set off to return on another raft, *Tahiti Nui II*, made from cypress wood: this disintegrated and a substitute had to be fabricated in mid-ocean. De Bisschop died from a broken neck when this craft capsized on a reef in the Cook Islands, the return almost

The size of the old Polynesian canoes can be assessed from this drawing, made by Louis Le Breton in the Vava'u group of Tonga, on Dumont d'Urville's expedition of 1837–40 (see p.80).

accomplished. The way out against currents and prevailing winds and the return made it doubly as courageous as *Kon-Tiki*'s voyage.

In 1970, a cosmopolitan quartet led by a Spaniard, Vital Alsar, with three parrots and two cats, floated on a raft, *La Balsa*, from Ecuador 8,600 miles across the Pacific to Australia in six months. This was the longest drift in history.

Most adventitious voyages in the last 100 years—made by canoes with Islanders drifting before storms and eventually landing on other groups after weeks of near-death—have shown a broadly east to west, or northeast to southwest, course within Polynesia, Micronesia, and Melanesia. This has been in line with the prevailing southeast trade winds in that part of the Pacific which has the most Islands. The east to west drifts have been quite contrary to general theories of races peopling the Islands from west to east.

Great though one's admiration for Heyerdahl must be, he is of course not infallible. In *Fatu Hiva*, he blames Europeans for the mosquito's introduction to the Pacific Islands. It was the 'only devil in his paradise', but surely it has cursed the Pacific Islands for as long as man has inhabited them. Why not also blame on the European that other devil, the fly?

More important, his general theory falters on a major ground left to the end of this sketch of pre-European origins. Languages being of the greatest significance for racial origins, it is unfortunate that they are left in the rear by Heyerdahl amongst his exhaustive production of evidence of almost every other kind. The fact that there is no language homogeneity between South America and anywhere in the Pacific (not merely Polynesia) is a basic weakness in the idea of American Indians having peopled any parts of Oceania.

Polynesia is less complex than Melanesia and Micronesia when it comes to languages. In essence, no area in the world covering as vast a distance as Polynesia contains so much linguistic affinity. Basically, there are related languages right through the huge triangle which has Easter Island, Hawaii, and New Zealand as its apices. They uniformly have little over a dozen letters in their alphabets, all words end in a vowel and, depending on the group, are full of the letters f, k, l, p, and v—with a pleasing euphonic result. The Tongan language abounds in the letter h: Cockneys would find themselves quite misunderstood. Syntax and the general form of expressions are common throughout Polynesia. There is a fundamental similarity between the languages of the Marquesans and Maoris, and of the Samoans and Tuvaluans, enabling them to communicate to about the same extent as can the Portuguese with the Spanish. Understanding between Maoris, Tahitians, and Cook Islanders is easier still. But all the Polynesian languages nevertheless require separate translations, grammars, and dictionaries. Samoa is generally considered to have the most ancient language, and this fact might still give credence to its being, if not Hawaiki, the historic fulcrum of Polynesian dispersal. Tonga and Samoa, unlike other major groups in Polynesia, have the advantage today of using only one working language.

Despite the linguistic affinity in Polynesia, the Pacific contains about a quarter of the world's languages. This large number (1,200) is largely due to Melanesia, where lack of uniformity constitutes the most intricate philological complexity in the world, though (or perhaps because) it is the most compressed ethnic area of the three main divisions of the Pacific. There are 700 separate languages (not dialects: they may be structurally similar but their vocabulary is totally different) in Papua New Guinea, 100 in the New Hebrides, 80 in the Solomons, 36 in New Caledonia (among only 50,000 inhabitants), and others in remaining parts of Melanesia. Because superstition prevented tribes from crossing a mountain or descending a valley to others' territories, contacts in New Guinea have been minimal. There, and in the New Hebrides, New Caledonia, and the Solomons, many neighbouring villages cannot communicate with each other except in 'Pidgin'. Built up from the talk of whalers and traders, and with its rules of order of words, special grammar, and vocabulary derived from English, German, Portuguese, and Malay, it has to be learnt. Usually circumambulatory, it can be succinct, as in this simple excerpt quoted in a report by Sir Hubert Murray, describing the event of 1936:

> King George, he dead. Number one son Edward, he no want him clothes. Number two son he like. Bishop he make plenty talk along new King. He say: 'You look out good along all the people'. King he talk: 'Yes'. Then Bishop and plenty Government official and storekeeper and soldier and bank manager and policeman, all he stand up and sing and blow him trumpet. Finish.

Only in this style can much of Melanesia begin to understand itself.

Micronesia, with its diversifications in other ways, is more homogeneous linguistically than might be expected, although there are considerable variations of dialects and accent.

A mere glance at the language composition of these three great partitions of the ocean cannot be expected to lead far.

With such divergent data it would be rash to attempt much by way of conclusion on the pre-European Pacific. The fascination which the origins of the Pacific people hold can be estimated from the heat of the enveloping controversy. It must be said here, however, that Islanders have not—yet—been anything like as excited about their antecedents as have Europeans.

Whatever the numerous differences, there is a large measure of agreement that many of the Islands' first inhabitants were migrants. That is, they were not autochtonous in the strict sense of that word, 'sprung from the particular island'. For our part, the great question of pre-European migrations is given an open verdict: they were neither all deliberate nor all accidental. We believe that there must have been voyages of both kinds, over considerable distances and from all directions (except from the south), in greater or lesser degree for a thousand or more years, and that there must consequently be cultural overlaps and underlaps.

Quite how long ago it was before the numerous voyages of Polynesians, Micronesians, and Melanesians lost their impetus, and why, is not known. It has been estimated that the sweeping, restless movements ceased at least 200 years before the arrival of the first Europeans.

It can only be hoped that it is not now too remote in time for solutions to appear. If we knew the answers to the questions about the order and manner of settlement, then other jigsaw pieces like the stone structures and the petroglyphs might fall into place. There has been constant research into these enigmas. For about 200 years, ever since the earliest Western explorers saw most of them for the first time, the relics have intrigued many types of scientists.

It might be thought that an examination of the blood groups of the various Islanders would throw some light on their origins. It is known that Central and Eastern Polynesians have a high percentage of type O blood, as do South American Indians: both have no type A and AB and little type B. But what little research has been carried out has been in small quantities in isolated groups. Another physical differentiation is provided by cerumen, the wax secreted in ear canals, which, falling into but two categories, wet or dry, may provide clues to Island and continental connections.

Surely these lines of research will produce strong evidence to support one of the competing theories before the end of this century? It will be surprising if the physical grouping, perhaps even more than the archaeological fieldwork, does not come up with important answers or pointers.

There remains the greatest mystery of all, cosmic in both its dimension and nature. Only the briefest mention can be given in this summary to literal questions of oceanic and celestial space. The furthest speculation backwards that can be made is on the origin of the massive hole filled by Pacific water. The deepest parts of any ocean in the world are in the Pacific, most profound of all in the Marianas group, where peaks rise 6 miles from the ocean floor and are still amply covered by fathoms of sea. Basically, the bottom of the ocean is basalt. Long before the first visits to the moon, it was confidently diagnosed that the lunar surface was also basalt. No doubt the fact that the moon was originally a third of the earth's size, and that the Pacific Ocean occupied a third of this globe, contributed to the belief that the basalt moon had formed itself in space (and expanded, as it is now thirty times larger than the Pacific) after spinning out of the earth and was then replaced on its basalt bed by sea water. When the first astronauts splashed down into the Pacific with samples of lunar rock which were principally basaltic, the theory of the origin of the Pacific appeared to have as much proof as is likely to be forthcoming.

Bibliography

This has to be a strictly selective bibliography. We have consulted literally thousands of sources over the years, but have had to compress into a manageable list those most frequently used by us. It has not been possible, regrettably, to include valuable articles, except for one or two used in the text. For detailed research, the newspapers of the countries are, of course, essential reading, and an invaluable source is the news magazine, *Pacific Islands Monthly*, published since 1930 by Pacific Publications, Sydney. The *South Pacific Bulletin* (or the *Bullétin du Pacifique Sud*), issued quarterly since 1961 in both English and French by the South Pacific Commission, Nouméa, also provides useful information.

In addition to general sources of material, some works have been consulted for specific chapters of this book. In those cases, the relevant chapter numbers are given at the end of the entries.

Abercromby, Hon. Ralph. *Seas and Skies in Many Latitudes* ... London: Edward Stanford, 1888.

Abbott, J.H.M. *The South Seas (Melanesia).* London: Adam & Charles Black, 1910. (IV; IX)

Adams, Ben. *Hawaii* ... New York: Hill & Wang, 1959. (XI)

Adams, Emma H. *Jottings from the Pacific* ... Oakland, Calif.: Pacific Press, 1890.

Adler, Jacob. *Claus Spreckels, the Sugar King in Hawaii.* Honolulu: University of Hawaii Press, 1966. (IX)

Ainsworth, William Francis, ed. *All Round the World* ... London: William Collins, 1871–2. (VI; IX)

Albert Victor Christian Edward, Prince (later Duke of Clarence), and Wales, Prince George Frederick Edward Albert of (later King George V of England). *The Cruise of* ... *'Bacchante' 1879–1882.* 2 vols. London: Macmillan, 1886.

Aldington, Richard. *Portrait of a Rebel. The Life and Work of Robert Louis Stevenson.* London: Evans, 1957. (XIII)

Alexander, Gilchrist Gibb. *From the Middle Temple to the South Seas.* London: John Murray, 1927.

Alexander, Michael. *Omai, 'Noble Savage'.* London: Collins, 1977. (IV)

Allardyce, Sir William Lamond. *The Western Pacific.* MS., n.d.

Allen, Percy S. *The Cyclopaedia of Fiji.* Sydney: McCarron & Stewart, 1907. (XI)

—— comp. *Stewart's Handbook of the Pacific Islands* ... Sydney: McCarron & Stewart, 1918. (VIII; IX; XI; P)

Alpers, Antony. *Legends of the South Sea.* London: John Murray, 1970.

Alsar, Vital, and Lopez, Enrique Hank. *La Balsa to Australia.* London: Hodder & Stoughton, 1973. (P)

Amherst of Hackney, 1st Lord (Amhérst, William Amhurst Tyssen), and Thomson, Basil, eds. *The Discovery of the Solomon Islands by Alvaro de Mendaña in 1568.* 2 vols. London: Hakluyt Society, 1901. (II)

Anderson, Charles Roberts. *Melville in the South Seas.* New York: Columbia University Press, 1939. (XIII)

Anderson, George William. *A New ... Collection of Voyages Round the World* ... London: Alexander Hogg, 1784. (IV)

Andreyev, A.I., ed. *Russian Discoveries in the Pacific* ... Ann Arbor, Mich.: J.W. Edwards, 1952. (V)

Angas, George French. *Polynesia* ... London: S.P.C.K., n.d. [1866?] (I; II; III; IV; V; XIII)

Ansdell, Gerrard. *A Trip to the Highlands of Viti Levu.* London: H. Blair Ansdell, 1882. (IX)

Arago, Jacques Étienne Victor. *Promenade autour du monde ... 1817, 1818, 1819 et 1820, ... L'Uranie et La Physicienne, commandées par M. Freycinet ...* 2 vols. and atlas. Paris: Leblanc, 1822. (V)

—— *Souvenirs d'un Aveugle.* 4 vols. Paris: Hortet et Ozanne, 1839. (V)

Archaeology of Easter Island. Reports of the Norwegian Archaeological Expeditions ... Vol. I. London: George Allen & Unwin, 1961. (P)

Armstrong, Richard. *The Discoverers.* London: Ernest Benn, 1968. (II; III)

Aylmer, Capt. Fenton A., ed. *Cruise in the Pacific* ... 2 vols. London: Hurst & Blackett, 1860. (V)

Baarslag, Karl. *Islands of Adventure.* London: Travel Book Club, 1944. (III; V; VIII; XIII; P)

Baden-Powell, Baden Fletcher Smyth. *In Savage Isles and Settled Lands.* London: Richard Bentley, 1892. (I; XI; XII; XIII)

Baessler, Arthur. *Südsee-Bilder.* Berlin: A. Ascher, 1895.

Bain, Kenneth Ross. *The Friendly Islanders.* London: Hodder & Stoughton, 1967.

Balfour, Graham. *The Life of Robert Louis Stevenson.* 2 vols. London: Methuen, 1901. (XIII)

Ball, Ian M. *Pitcairn.* London: Victor Gollancz, 1973. (V; XII)

Ballantyne, Robert Michael. *The Coral Island.* London: S.W. Partridge, n.d. (XIII)

—— *Gascoyne, the Sandal-Wood Trader* ... London: James Nisbet, n.d. (XIII)

Barjot, Amiral Pierre, and Savant, Jean. *History of the World's Shipping.* Shepperton: Ian Allen, 1961. (IV; V)

Barradale, Victor Arnold. *Pearls of the Pacific.* London: Missionary Society, 1907. (VIII)

Barrett, Charles Leslie, ed. *The Pacific.* Melbourne: N.H. Seward, n.d. (I; II; III; XIII; P)

Barrow, Sir John, Bt., ed. *Cook's Voyages of Discovery.* Edinburgh: Adam & Charles Black, 1874. (IV)

—— *The Eventful History of the Mutiny and Piratical Seizure of HMS Bounty, its Causes and Consequences.* London: John Murray, 1831. (V)

Barrow, Terence Tui. *Art and Life in Polynesia.* London: Pall Mall Press, 1972.

Bassett, Lady Marnie. *Realms and Islands. The World Voyage of Rose de Freycinet ... Uranie 1817–1820.* London: Oxford University Press, 1962. (V)

—— *Behind the Picture. H.M.S. Rattlesnake's Australia New Guinea Cruise 1846 to 1850.* Melbourne: Oxford University Press, 1966. (V)

Bayly, Capt. George. *Sea Life Sixty Years Ago* ... London: Kegan Paul & Trench, 1885. (I; VII)

Beaglehole, John Cawte. *The Exploration of the Pacific.* London: Adam and Charles Black, 1947. (I; II; III; IV; V)

—— ed. *The Journals of Captain Cook.* 3 vols. Cambridge, 1955–1967. (IV)

—— ed. *The Endeavour Journal of Joseph Banks 1768–1771.* 2 vols. Sydney: Angus & Robertson, 1962. (IV)

—— *The Life of Captain James Cook.* London: Adam and Charles Black, 1974. (IV)

Becke, George Louis. *Pacific Tales.* London: T. Fisher Unwin, 1897. (XIII)

—— *By Reef and Palm* and *The Ebbing of the Tide.* London: T. Fisher Unwin, 1914. (XIII)

—— *Edward Barry (South Sea Pearler).* London: T. Nelson, n.d. (XIII)

—— *Notes from My South Sea Log.* London: Collins, n.d. (XIII)

Beechey, Capt. Frederick William. *Narrative of a Voyage to the Pacific ... in ... Blossom ... 1825, 26, 27, 28.* 2 vols. London: Henry Colburn & Richard Bentley, 1831. (V)

Behrens, Carl Friedrich. *Carl Friedrich Behrens Reise durch die Süd-Lander und um die Welt.* Frankfurt und Leipzig, 1737. (IV)

Belcher, Lady Diana. *The Mutineers of the Bounty and their Descendants in Pitcairn and Norfolk Islands.* London: John Murray, 1870.

276

(V; P)

Belcher, Capt. Sir Edward. *Narrative of a Voyage round the World . . . in . . . Sulphur 1836–1842.* 2 vols. London: Henry Colburn, 1843. (V)

Bellingshausen, Capt. Baron Thaddeus Fabian Gottlieb von. See Debenham, Frank.

Bentley, Sqn. Ldr. Geoffrey. *R.N.Z.A.F.* Wellington: A.H. & A.W. Reed, 1967. (XIV)

Beriot, Agnès. *Grands Voiliers du Monde.* Paris: Éditions du Pont Royal, 1962. (IV; V)

Best, Elsdon. *The Maori Canoes . . .* Wellington: Government Printer, 1925. (P)

Bettex, Albert W. *The Discovery of the World.* London: Thames & Hudson, 1960. (II; IV)

Bingham, Rev. Hiram. *A Residence of Twenty-one Years in the Sandwich Islands . . .* Hartford: Hezekiah Huntington, 1842. (VIII; XI)

Bisschop, Eric de. *Tahiti Nui.* New York: McDowell; and London: Collins, 1959. (P)

Bjerre, Jens. *Savage New Guinea.* London: Michael Joseph, 1964. (XV)

Bligh, Capt. William. *A Voyage to the South Sea . . .* London: Nicol, 1792. (V)

Boddam-Whetham, John W. *Pearls of the Pacific.* London: Hurst & Blackett, 1876. (IV; XI)

Borden, Charles A. *South Sea Islands.* London: Robert Hale, 1961. (I; II; VIII; XI; XII; XIV)

Bougainville, Vice-Adm. Comte Louis Antoine de. *Voyage autour du Monde, par . . . La Boudeuse, et . . . L'Etoile; . . . 1766, 1767, 1768 & 1769.* Paris: Saillant et Nyon, 1771. (IV)

Brassey, Annie Allnutt. *A Voyage in the "Sunbeam".* London: Longmans, Green, 1878.

Brenchley, Julius Louis. *Jottings During the Cruise of HMS Curaçoa Among the South Sea Islands in 1865.* London: Longmans, Green, 1873. (V; VIII; P)

Brendon, J.A. *Great Navigators and Discoverers.* London: George G. Harrap, 1929. (II; III; IV)

Brewster, Adolph Brewster. *The Hill Tribes of Fiji.* London: Seeley, Service, 1922. (VIII; IX; X; XI)

—— *King of the Cannibal Isles.* London: Robert Hale, 1937. (XI)

Brigham, William Tufts. *An Index to the Islands of the Pacific Ocean . . .* Honolulu: Bishop Museum Press, 1900. (I; II; III; IV; V; P)

Brodie, Walter. *Pitcairn's Island and the Islanders in 1850.* London: Whitaker, 1851. (V)

Brooke, Rupert Chawner. See Keynes, Sir Geoffrey.

Brosses, Charles de. *Histoire des Navigations aux Terres Australes.* 2 vols. Paris: Durand, 1756. (I)

Brown, Rev. George. *George Brown, D.D., Pioneer Missionary and Explorer: an Autobiography.* London: Hodder & Stoughton, 1908.

Brown, John Macmillan. *Maori and Polynesian.* London: Hutchinson, 1907. (P)

—— *The Riddle of the Pacific.* London: T. Fisher Unwin, 1925. (P)

—— *Peoples and Problems of the Pacific.* 2 vols. London: T. Fisher Unwin, 1927. (I; P)

Brown, Paula. *The Chimbu.* London: Routledge, 1973. (XIV)

Bryan, Edwin Horace, jun. *American Polynesia and the Hawaiian Chain.* Honolulu: Tongg, 1942.

Buck, Sir Peter Henry (Te Rangi Hiroa). *Vikings of the Sunrise.* Philadelphia: J. B. Lippincott, 1938. (P)

—— *Explorers of the Pacific.* Honolulu: Bernice P. Bishop Museum, 1953. (II; III; IV; V)

Bulu, Rev. Joel. *Autobiography of a Native Minister in the South Seas.* London: Wesleyan Mission House, 1871. (VIII; X)

Burnett, Frank. *Through Tropic Seas.* London: Francis Griffiths, 1910.

—— *Through Polynesia and Papua.* London: G. Bell, 1911.

—— *Summer Isles of Eden.* London: Sifton Praed, 1923.

Burney, Rear-Adm. James. *A Chronological History of the Voyages and Discoveries in the South Sea or Pacific Ocean.* 5 vols. London: G. & W. Nicol, 1803–17. (II; III; IV)

—— See Hooper, Beverley.

Burns, Sir Alan Cuthbert Maxwell. *Fiji.* London: H.M.S.O., 1963.

Burton, Rev. John Wear. *The Fiji of Today.* London: Charles H. Kelly, 1910.

Caillot, Auguste Charles Eugène. *Les Polynésiens Orientaux au contact de la Civilization.* Paris: Ernest Leroux, 1909.

—— *Histoire de la Polynésie Orientale.* Paris: Ernest Leroux, 1910.

Callahan, James Morton. *American Relations in the Pacific . . . 1784–1900.* Baltimore: Johns Hopkins Press, 1901. (V)

Calvert, Rev. James. See Rowe, Rev. George Stringer.

Cameron, Ian. *Magellan and the First Circumnavigation of the World.* London: Weidenfeld & Nicolson, 1974. (II)

Cameron, Roderick. *The Golden Haze with Captain Cook in the South Pacific.* London: Weidenfeld & Nicolson, 1965. (IV; VIII)

Campbell, Archibald. *A Voyage Round the World, from 1806 to 1812 . . .* Edinburgh: Archibald Constable, 1816. (VI)

Campbell, Lord George Granville. *Log-Letters from "The Challenger".* London: Macmillan, 1876. (V)

Campbell, Vice-Adm. Gordon. *Captain James Cook, R.N., F.R.S.* London: Hodder & Stoughton, 1936. (IV)

Campbell, Ramon. *El Misterioso Mundo de Rapanui.* Buenos Aires: Francisco de Aguirre, 1973. (P)

Carano, Paul, and Sanchez, Pedro C. *A Complete History of Guam.* Vermont: Rutland; and Tokyo: Charles E. Tuttle, 1964.

Cargill, Rev. David. See Schütz, Albert James.

Carmichael, Peter, and Knox-Mawer, June. *A World of Islands.* London: Collins, 1968.

Carrington, Major Arthur Hugh, ed. *The Discovery of Tahiti. A Journal of the Second Voyage of H.M.S. Dolphin Round the World, under the command of Captain Wallis, R.N., . . . 1776, 1777 and 1778, written by her master, George Robertson.* London: Hakluyt Society, 1948. (IV; VII)

Carteret, Capt. Philip. See Wallis, Helen M.

Castex, Louis. *Los Secretos de la Isla de Pascua.* Santiago: Joaquin Almendros, 1968. (P)

Central Office of Information. *Colonial Empire. Introducing the Pacific Islands.* London: H.M.S.O., n.d. [1950?].

Chapman, James Keith. *The Career of Arthur Hamilton Gordon, First Lord Stanmore 1829–1912.* Toronto: University of Toronto Press, 1964. (XI)

Cheever, Rev. Henry Theodore. *The Island World of the Pacific . . .* New York: Harper, 1851.

Cheyne, Andrew. *A Description of Islands in the Western Pacific Ocean . . .* London: J.D. Potter, 1852. (V; VII)

—— See Shineberg, Dorothy.

Choris, Louis. *Voyage Pittoresque Autour du Monde . . .* Paris: Firmin Didot, 1822. (V; XIII)

—— *Vues et Paysages . . .* Paris: Paul Renouard, 1826. (V; XIII)

Christian, Frederick William. *The Caroline Islands, Travel in the Sea of the Little Lands.* London: Methuen, 1899. (II; VII; P)

—— *Eastern Pacific Lands.* London: Robert Scott, 1920. (II; IV; V; P)

Christmann, Fr., and Oberländer, Richard. *Ozeanien, die Inseln der Südsee . . .* Leipzig: Otto Spamer, 1873. (IV; V)

Churchill, Llewella Pierce. *Samoa 'Uma.* London: Sampson Low, Marston; and New York: Forrest and Stream, 1902.

Coates, Austin. *Western Pacific Islands.* London: H.M.S.O., 1970. (I; II; IX; X; XIV)

—— *Islands of the South.* London: Heinemann, 1974. (P)

Cockroft, John. *Isles of the South Pacific, Papua and New Guinea, New Britain, New Ireland, Bougainville.* Sydney: Angus & Robertson, 1968. (XV)

—— *Polynesian Isles of the South Pacific.* Sydney: Angus & Robertson, 1968. (XV)

Codrington, Robert Henry. *The Melanesians . . .* Oxford: Clarendon Press, 1891.

Condliffe, J.R. *Te Rangi Hiroa. The Life of Sir Peter Buck.* Christchurch: Whitcombe & Tombs, 1971. (XIV; P)

Cook, Capt. James, and King, Capt. James. *A Voyage to the Pacific Ocean . . . under . . . Captains Cook, Clarke and Gore, In . . . Resolution and Discovery . . . 1776, 1777, 1778, 1779, and 1780.* 3 vols. London: W. & A. Strahan, 1784. (IV)

Cooper, H. Stonehewer. *Coral Lands.* 2 vols. London: Richard Bentley, 1880. (IX; XI; XII)

Coote, Walter. *Wanderings South and East.* London: Sampson Low, Marston, Searle and Rivington, 1882.

Coppinger, Richard William. *"Cruise of the Alert".* London: Swan Sonnenschein, 1885. (V)

Corney, Bolton Glanvill, ed. *The Voyage of Captain Don Felipe Gonzalez ... to Easter Island in 1770–1 ...* Cambridge: Hakluyt Society, 1908. (IV; P)

—— comp. *The Quest and Occupation of Tahiti by Emissaries of Spain ... 1772–1776 ...* 3 vols. London: Hakluyt Society, 1913–9. (IV)

Cousins, Rev. George. *The Story of the South Seas.* London: John Snow, 1894. (VIII)

Cowan, James. *Samoa and Its Story.* Christchurch: Whitcombe & Tombs, 1914.

Cranstone, Bryan Allan Lefevre. *Melanesia ...* London: Trustees of the British Museum, 1961.

Crocombe, Ronald George. *The New South Pacific.* Canberra: Australian National University Press, 1973. (IX; XV; P)

Crocombe, Ronald George, and Crocombe, Marjorie Tuainekore, eds. *The Works of Ta'unga ...* Canberra: National University Press, 1968. (VIII)

Cumming, Constance Frederika Gordon. *At Home in Fiji.* 2 vols. Edinburgh: William Blackwood, 1881. (XI; XIII)

—— *A Lady's Cruise in a French Man-of-War.* Edinburgh: William Blackwood, 1882. (XII; XIII)

—— *Fire Fountains.* 2 vols. Edinburgh: William Blackwood, 1883. (XIII)

—— *Memories.* Edinburgh & London: William Blackwood, 1904. (XIII).

D'Albertis, Luigi Maria. *New Guinea: What I Did and What I Saw.* 2 vols. London: Sampson Low, Marston, Searle and Rivington, 1880. (V)

Dalrymple, Alexander. *An Historical Collection of the Several Voyages and Discoveries in the South Pacifick Ocean.* 2 vols. London: J. Nourse, T. Payne, P. Elmsley, 1770–1. (II; III; IV)

Dampier, Robert. See Joerger, Pauline King.

Dampier, William. *A New Voyage round the World.* London: James Knapton, 1698. (II; III)

Daniel, Hawthorne. *Islands of the Pacific.* New York: G.P. Putnam's, 1943.

Danielsson, Bengt Ellerik. *The Happy Island.* London: George Allen & Unwin, 1952.

—— *Love in the South Seas.* London: George Allen & Unwin, 1956. (VIII; X)

—— *Forgotten Islands of the South Seas.* London: George Allen & Unwin, 1957. (X)

—— *From Raft to Raft.* London: George Allen & Unwin, 1960. (P)

—— *Gauguin in the South Seas.* London: George Allen & Unwin, 1965. (XIII)

D'Auvergne, Edmund B. *Pierre Loti.* London: T. Werner Laurie, 1926. (XIII)

David, Edgeworth. *Funafuti.* London: John Murray, 1899. (P)

D'Avigdor, E.H. See 'Wanderer'.

Daws, Gavan. *Shoal of Time. A History of the Hawaiian Islands.* Honolulu: University of Hawaii Press, 1968. (IV; V; VI; XI; XIV)

Day, Arthur Grove, ed. *Louis Becke, South Sea Supercargo.* Honolulu: University of Hawaii Press, 1967. (XIII)

—— *Pacific Islands Literature.* Honolulu: University of Hawaii Press, 1971. (III; XIII)

Day, Arthur Grove, and Stroven, Carl, eds. *True Tales of the South Seas.* London: Souvenir Press, 1967.

Deane, Wallace. *Fijian Society.* London: Macmillan, 1921.

Debenham, Frank, ed. *The Voyage of Captain Bellingshausen ... 1819–1821.* 2 vols. London: Hakluyt Society, 1944. (V)

Decrease of the Native Population. Suva: Government Printer, 1892. (X)

Defoe, Daniel. *The Life and Strange Surprizing Adventures of Robinson Crusoe of Yorks, Mariner.* London: W. Taylor, 1719. (III)

Degener, Otto. *Naturalist's South Pacific Expedition ...* Honolulu: Paradise of the Pacific, 1949.

Delano, Capt. Amasa. *In the Northern and Southern Hemispheres.* Boston: E.G. House, 1807. Reprint, Upper Saddle River, N.J.: The Gregg Press, 1970. (III; V; VII)

Deniker, Joseph. *The Races of Man.* London & New York: Walter Scott Publishing Co., n.d. (I; P)

Dening, Gregory M., ed. *The Marquesan Journal of Edward Robarts, 1797–1824.* Canberra: Australian National University Press, 1974. (II; V; VI)

Déribéré, Maurice. 'A Tahiti avec Pierre Loti'. *Courrier des Messageries Maritimes.* No. 127. Paris, March-April, 1972. (XIII)

Derrick, Ronald Albert. *A History of Fiji.* Suva: Printing and Stationery Department, 1946. (VIII; XI)

Des Voeux, Sir George William. *My Colonial Service ...* 2 vols. London: John Murray, 1903. (XI)

Detzner, Hermann. *Vier Jahre Unter Kannibalen von 1914 bis zum Waffenstill-stand ...* Berlin: A. Scherl, 1921. (XIV)

D'Ewes, John. *China, Australia and the Pacific Islands ... 1855–56.* London: Richard Bentley, 1857. (P)

Diapea, William. *Cannibal Jack.* London: Faber Gwyer, 1928. (VI; P)

Dictionary Catalog of the Library Bernice P. Bishop Museum, Honolulu, Hawaii. Supplements 1 and 2. Boston, Mass.: G.K. Hall, 1967 and 1969.

Dillon, The Chevalier Capt. Peter. *Narrative and Successful Result of a Voyage in the South Seas ...* 2 vols. London: Hurst, Chance, 1829. (V; VII; VIII)

Dix, William Giles, and Oliver, James. *Wreck of the "Glide" ...* Boston: William D. Ticknor, 1846. (VI)

Dodd, Edward. *Polynesian Seafaring.* New York: Dodd, Mead, 1972. (P)

Dodge, Ernest Stanley. *New England and the South Seas.* Cambridge, Mass.: Harvard University Press, 1965. (II; V; VI; VII)

—— *Beyond the Capes.* London: Victor Gollancz, 1971.

Domville-Fife, Charles William, ed. *The Encyclopaedia of the British Empire ...* 5 vols. London: Virtue, 1924.

Dumont d'Urville, Jules Sébastien César. *Voyage de ... L'Astrolabe ... 1826, 1827, 1828 et 1829.* 5 vols. and 3 vols. of atlas. Paris: J. Tastu, 1830–3. (V)

—— *Voyage pittoresque autour du Monde.* 2 vols. Paris: L. Tenre, 1834–5. (IV; V)

—— *Voyage au Pole Sud et dans l'Océanie sur l'Astrolabe et La Zélée; 1837–1838–1839–1840 ...* 23 vols. and 2 vols. of atlas. Paris: Gide, 1841–6. (V)

Dunbabin, Thomas. *Sailing the World's Edge.* London: Newnes, n.d. [1931?]. (V)

Dunmore, John. *French Explorers in the Pacific.* 2 vols. Oxford: Clarendon Press, 1965 and 1969. (IV; V)

Duperrey, Louis Isidore. *Voyage Autour du Monde ... sur ... La Coquille ... 1822, 1823, 1824 et 1825.* Atlas vol. Paris: Arthus Bertrand, 1826–34. (V)

Du Petit-Thouars, Abel Aubert. *Voyage Autour du Monde sur ... La Vénus ... 1836–1839.* 4 vols. and atlas. Paris: Gide, 1840–3. (V; XI)

Du Rietz, Rolf Einar. *Bibliotheca Polynesiana ...* Oslo: privately published, 1969.

Earl, The (Herbert, George Robert Charles, 13th Earl of Pembroke and Montgomery), and Doctor, The (Kingsley, George Henry). *South Sea Bubbles.* London: Richard Bentley, 1872. (VIII; X)

Eason, William John Eric. *A Short History of Rotuma.* Suva: Government Printer, 1951.

Edge–Partington, James. *Random Rot.* Altrincham: Guardian Office, 1883. (IX)

Edwards, Capt. Edward, and Hamilton, George. *Voyage of H.M.S. Pandora ... with an introduction by Sir Basil Thomson.* London: Francis Edwards, 1915. (V)

Eggleston, George T. *Tahiti.* New York: Devin, Adan, 1953.

Elkington, Ernest Way, and Hardy, Norman H. *The Savage South Seas.* London: A & C Black, 1907. (IX; XIII)

Ellis, Sir Albert Fuller. *Ocean Island and Nauru ...* Sydney: Angus & Robertson, 1935. (XIV)

Ellis, Rev. William. *Polynesian Researches, during a residence of nearly six years in the South Sea Islands.* 4 vols. London: Fisher Son & Jackson, 1839. (I; II; IV; VIII; X; P)

Elwes, Robert. *A Sketcher's Tour Round the World.* London: Hurst & Blackett, 1854. (XIII)

Emory, Kenneth Pike. *Archaeology of the Pacific Equatorial Islands.* Honolulu: Bernice P. Bishop Museum, 1934. (P)

Encyclopaedia of Papua and New Guinea. 3 vols. Carlton, Victoria: Melbourne University Press, 1972.

Englert, Père Sebastián. *La Tierra de Hotu*

Motu'a. Santiago: Universidad de Chile, 1974. (P)

Erskine, Capt. John Elphinstone. *Journal of a Cruise Among the Islands of the Western Pacific . . . In . . . Havannah*. London: John Murray, 1853. (V)

Ethnographic Bibliography of New Guinea, An. Canberra: Australian National University Press, 1968.

Eykyn, Rev. Thomas (A Peripatetic Parson). *Parts of the Pacific*. London: Swan, Sonnenschein, 1896.

Faivre, Jean-Paul. *L'expansion française dans le Pacifique 1800–1842*. Paris: Nouvelles éditions latines, 1953. (XI)

Fanning, Capt. Edmund. *Voyages Round the World*. London: O. Rich, 1834. (V; VII)

Far East and Australasia 1978–79, The. London: Europa Publications, 1978.

Farmer, Sarah Stock. *Tonga . . .* London: Hamilton Adams, 1855. (VIII; X)

Farwell, George Michell. *Last Days in Paradise*. London: Victor Gollancz, 1964. (V; XIII)

Feher, Joseph, comp. *Hawaii: A Pictorial History*. Honolulu: Bishop Museum Press, 1969. (IV; V; VI; IX; X; XIV; XV)

Finsch, F.H. Otto. *Samoafahrten: Reisen in Kaiserwilhelmsland und Englisch-Neu Guinea . . . 1884 und 1885 . . .* Leipzig: Ferdinand Hirt, 1888. (V)

Fisher, John. *The Midmost Waters*. London: The Naldrett Press, 1952. (VIII; XI; XII)

Fisk, E.K., ed. *New Guinea on the Threshold . . .* Canberra: Australian National University Press, 1966. (XV)

Fison, Lorimer. *Tales from Old Fiji*. London: Alexander Moring, 1904.

Fleurieu, Comte Charles Pierre Claret de, ed. *Voyage autour du Monde . . . 1790, 1791 et 1792 par Etienne Marchand*. 4 vols. Paris: Imprimerie de la République, n.d. [1798–1800]. (V)

Foljambe, Hon. Cecil George Savile. *Three Years on the Australian Station*. London: Hatchard, 1868. (VII; P)

Forbes, Litton. *Two Years in Fiji*. London: Longmans Green, 1875.

Forman, Werner, and Syme, Neville Ronald. *The Travels of Captain Cook*. London: Michael Joseph, 1971. (IV)

Fornander, Abraham. *Account of the Polynesian Race . . .* 3 vols. London: Trubner, 1878–85. (P)

Forster, Johann Georg Adam. *A Voyage Round the World in . . . Resolution . . . 1772, 3, 4, & 5.* 2 vols. London: B. White, J. Robson, P. Elmsly & G. Robinson, 1777. (IV)

Fox, Frank. *Oceania*. London: Adam & Charles Black, 1911.

Francis, B. *The Isles of the Pacific; or Sketches from the South Seas*. London: Cassell, Petter, Galpin, 1882.

Fraser, John A. *Gold Dish and Kava Bowl*. London: J.M. Dent, 1954. (XIV)

Friis, Herman R., ed. *The Pacific Basin*. New York: American Geographical Society, 1967. (II; III; IV; V)

Frisbie, Johnny (Hebenstrait, Johnny). *The Frisbies of the South Seas*. London: Travel Book Club, 1961. (XIII)

Fuchida, Mitsuo, and Okumiya, Masataki. *Midway. The Battle that doomed Japan*. London: Hutchinson, 1957. (XIV)

Further Correspondence respecting the Affairs of Fiji on the Native Population. In continuation of C.5039, April 1887. London: H.M.S.O., 1895. (X)

Gardner, Robert, and Heider, Karl G. *Gardens of War*. London: Andre Deutsch, 1969.

Garran, Andrew, ed. *Picturesque Atlas of Australasia*. 3 vols. Sydney and Springfield, Mass.: The Picturesque Atlas Publishing Co., 1886.

Gatty, Harold Charles. *Nature is Your Guide*. London: Collins, 1958. (P)

Gauguin, Eugène Henri Paul. *Noa Noa*. Paris: Editions de la Plume, n.d. [1901]. (XIII)

—— *Intimate Journals*. London: William Heinemann, 1923. (XIII)

Geil, William Edgar. *Ocean and Isle*. Melbourne: William T. Pater, 1902. (V)

Gerbault, Alain. *In Quest of the Sun*. London: Hodder & Stoughton, n.d. [1929].

—— *The Gospel of the Sun*. London: Hodder & Stoughton, 1933.

Gerstle, Donna. *Gentle People. Into the Heart of Vava'u, Kingdom of Tonga 1781–1973*. San Diego: Tofua Press, 1973. (V)

Gerstle, Donna, and Raitt, Helen. *Tonga Pictorial*. San Diego: Tofua Press, n.d.

Gibbings, Robert. *Over the Reefs*. London: J.M. Dent, 1949. (V; XIII)

Giglioli, Enrico Hillyer. *Viaggio Intorno al Globo Della R. Pirocorvetta Italiana Magenta . . . 1865–66–67–68*. Milan: V. Maisnere, 1874. (V)

Gill, Rev. William Wyatt. *Gems from the Coral Islands . . .* London: Ward, 1856.

—— *Life in the Southern Isles; or Scenes and Incidents in the South Pacific and New Guinea*. London: The Religious Tract Society, n.d. [1876]. (I; IX; P)

—— *Jottings from the Pacific*. London: The Religious Tract Society, 1885. (VIII; IX)

Glover, Lady Elizabeth Rosetta. *Great Queens*. London: Hutchinson, 1928. (XI)

Goepp, Edouard, and Cordier, Emile L. *Les Grands Hommes de la France*. 3 vols. Paris: P. Ducroq, 1872–4. (IV; V)

Golson, Jack, ed. *Polynesian Navigation. A Symposium on Andrew Sharp's theory of accidental voyages*. Wellington: Memoirs of Polynesian Society, 1963. (P)

Gonzalez, Capt. Don Felipe. See Corney, Bolton Glanvill.

Goodenough, Victoria Henrietta, ed. *Journal of Commodore Goodenough*. London: Henry S. King, 1876. (XI)

Gordon, Hon. Sir Arthur Charles Hamilton. See Stanmore, 1st. Lord.

Gorsky, Bernard. *Island at the End of the World*. London: Rupert Hart-Davis, 1966.

Gough, Barry M., ed. *To the Pacific . . . with Beechey. The Journal of Lieutenant George Peard of H.M.S. Blossom 1825–1828.* London: Hakluyt Society, 1973. (V)

Grattan, Clinton Hartley. *The Southwest Pacific to 1900*. Ann Arbor: University of Michigan Press, 1963. (II; VII; XI)

—— *The Southwest Pacific since 1900*. Ann Arbor: University of Michigan Press, 1963. (XIV; XV)

Gray, Capt. John Alexander Clinton. *Amerika Samoa*. Annapolis, Md.: United States Naval Institute, 1960. (XI; XII; XIV; XV)

Grayland, Eugene. *Coasts of Treachery*. Wellington: A.H. & A.W. Reed, 1963. (III; IV; V; XII; XIV)

Grimble, Sir Arthur Francis. *A Pattern of Islands*. London: John Murray, 1952. (XIII)

Grimble, Rosemary. *Migrations, Myth and Magic from the Gilbert Islands*. London: Routledge & Kegan Paul, 1972. (P)

Grimshaw, Beatrice. *From Fiji to the Cannibal Islands*. London: Eveleigh Nash, 1907.

—— *In the Strange South Seas*. London: Hutchinson, 1907. (VIII; XI)

Guiart, Jean Charles Robert. *The arts of the South Pacific*. London: Thames & Hudson, 1963. (P)

Guillemard, Francis Henry Hill. *The Life of Ferdinand Magellan and the First Circumnavigation of the Globe 1480–1521*. London: George Philip, 1890. (II)

Gunson, Walter Niel. 'On the Incidence of Alcoholism and Intemperance in Early Pacific Missions'. *Journal of Pacific History*. Vol. I. Canberra, 1966. (VIII)

Gunther, John. *Inside Australia and New Zealand*. Edited by William H. Forbis. London: Hamish Hamilton, 1972. (XI; XIV; XV; P)

Guppy, Henry Brougham. *The Solomon Islands and their Natives*. London: Swan, Sonnenschein, Lowrey, 1887. (I; II; P)

Gutch, John. *Martyr of the Islands. The Life and Death of John Coleridge Patteson*. London: Hodder & Stoughton, 1971. (VIII; X)

—— *Beyond the Reefs. The Life of John Williams, Missionary*. London: Macdonald, 1974. (VIII; X)

Haddon, Alfred Cort. *Head Hunters*. London: Methuen, 1901. (I; X)

Haldane, Charlotte. *Tempest Over Tahiti*. London: Constable, 1963. (IV; XI)

Hale, Horatio. *United States Exploring Expedition . . . 1838, 1839, 1840, 1841, 1842 under . . . Charles Wilkes, U.S.N.* Vol. VI. Philadelphia: C. Sherman, 1846. (P)

Hale, John R. *Age of Exploration*. Amsterdam: Time-Life International, 1966. (III; IV)

Hall, James Norman. *Mid-Pacific*. Boston and New York: Houghton Mifflin, 1928. (XIII)

—— *The Far Lands*. London: Faber & Faber, 1951. (XIII)

—— *My Island Home*. Boston: Little, Brown,

1952. (XIII)

Handy, Edward Smith Craighill. *The Native Culture of the Marquesas*. Honolulu: Bernice P. Bishop Museum, 1923. (P)

—— *History and Culture of the Society Islands*. Honolulu: Bernice P. Bishop Museum, 1930. (P)

Harlow, Vincent Todd, ed. *Voyages of Great Pioneers*. London: Oxford University Press, 1929. (III)

Harrer, Heinrich. *Ich Komme aus der Steinzeit*. West Berlin: Ullstein Gmbh, 1963. (XV)

Harrisson, Tom. *Savage Civilization*. London: Victor Gollancz, 1937. (I; IV; VII; X; XI)

Hassell, Christopher. *Rupert Brooke*. London: Faber & Faber, 1964. (XIII)

Hastings, Michael. *The Handsomest Young Man in England. Rupert Brooke*. London: Michael Joseph, 1967. (XIII)

Hastings, Peter, ed. *Papua-New Guinea*. Sydney: Angus & Robertson, 1971.

Hawaii. Register of Historical Places. Bibliography of Hawaiiana. Honolulu: Department of Land and Resources, n.d.

Hawkesworth, John, ed. *An Account of the Voyages ... by Commodore Byron, Captain Wallis, Captain Carteret and Captain Cook ...* 3 vols. London: W. Strahan & T. Cadell, 1773. (IV)

Heaps, Leo, ed. *The Log of the Centurion*. London: Hart-Davis, MacGibbon, 1973. (IV)

Heawood, Edward. *A History of Geographical Discovery in the Seventeenth and Eighteenth Centuries*. London: Cambridge University Press, 1912. (II; III; IV)

Heine, Carl. *Micronesia at the Crossroads*. Honolulu: University Press of Hawaii, 1974. (I; XIV; XV)

Henderson, Daniel MacIntyre. *The Hidden Coasts*. New York: William Sloane, 1953. (V)

Henderson, George Cockburn. *The Journal of Thomas Williams, Missionary ...* 2 vols. London: Angus & Robertson, 1931. (VIII; X)

—— *The Discoverers of the Fiji Islands*. London: John Murray, 1933. (III; IV)

Henley, Sir Thomas. *A Pacific Cruise*. Sydney: John Sands, 1930.

Henry, Teuira. *Ancient Tahiti*. Honolulu: Bernice P. Bishop Museum Press, 1928. (IV; V)

Herrman, Paul. *Conquest by Man*. London: Hamish Hamilton, 1954. (I; P)

Heyerdahl, Thor. *The Kon-Tiki Expedition*. London: George Allen & Unwin, 1950. (P)

—— *American Indians in the Pacific*. London: George Allen & Unwin, 1952. (P)

—— *Aku Aku*. London: George Allen & Unwin, 1958. (P)

—— *Sea Routes to Polynesia*. London: George Allen & Unwin, 1968. (P)

—— *Fatu Hiva*. London: George Allen & Unwin, 1974. (VIII; P)

—— *Early Man and the Ocean*. London: George Allen & Unwin, 1978. (VIII; P)

Hilder, Brett. *Navigator in the South Seas*. London: Percival Marshall, 1961. (VIII)

Hocart, Arthur Maurice. *Lau Islands, Fiji*. Honolulu: Bernice P. Bishop Museum, 1929.

Holden, Horace. *A Narrative of the Shipwreck, Captivity and Sufferings of Horace Holden and Benj. H. Nute, who were cast away in the American ship Mentor, on the Pelew Islands, in the year 1832; ...* Boston: Russell, Shattuck, 1836. (VI)

Hood, Thomas H. *Notes of a Cruise in H.M.S. "Fawn" in the Western Pacific in the year 1862*. Edinburgh: Edmonston & Douglas, 1863. (V)

Hooper, Beverley, ed. *With Captain James Cook in the ... Pacific. The private journal of James Burney ... 1772–1773*. Canberra: National Library of Australia, 1975. (IV)

Horton, Dick Crofton. *The Happy Isles*. London: Heinemann, 1965. (XIV; XV)

—— *Fire over the Islands. The Coast Watchers of the Solomons*. Wellington: A.H. & A.W. Reed, 1970. (XIV)

Hough, Richard. *Captain Bligh and Mr. Christian*. London: Hutchinson, 1972. (V)

Howells, William White. *The Pacific Islanders*. London: Weidenfeld & Nicolson, 1973. (I; P)

Humphreys, A.R. *Melville*. Edinburgh: Oliver & Boyd, 1962. (XIII)

Huxley, Thomas Henry. *Diary of the Voyage of H.M.S. Rattlesnake, July 1847 to October 1850*. London: Chatto & Windus, 1935. (V)

Im Thurn, Sir Everard Ferdinand. *Thoughts, Talks and Tramps*. Edited by R.R. Marrett. London: Oxford University Press, 1934.

Im Thurn, Sir Everard Ferdinand, and Wharton, Leonard C., eds. *The Journal of William Lockerby, Sandalwood Trader ...* London: Hakluyt Society, 1925. (VI)

Introducing the British Pacific Islands. London: H.M.S.O., 1951.

Irwin, George. *Samoa: a Teacher's Tale*. London: Cassell, 1965.

Jack-Hinton, Colin. *The Search for the Islands of Solomon 1567–1838*. Oxford: Clarendon Press, 1969. (II; III)

Jacoby, Arnold. *Senor Kon-Tiki*. London: George Allen & Unwin, 1968. (P)

Jenkins, John Stilwell. *Recent Exploring Expeditions to the Pacific and the South Seas, under the American, English and French Governments*. London: T. Nelson, 1853. (IV; V; VIII)

Joerger, Pauline King, ed. *To the Sandwich Islands on H.M.S. Blonde*. Honolulu: University Press of Hawaii, 1971. (V)

Joesting, Edward. *Hawaii: An Uncommon History*. New York: W.W. Norton, 1972. (IV; V; VI; VII; XIV)

Jouan, Henri. *Les Iles du Pacifique*. Paris: Librairie Germer Baillière, n.d.

Joyce, Roger B. *Sir William MacGregor*. Melbourne: Oxford University Press, 1971. (XI)

Jukes, Joseph Beete. *Narrative of the Surveying Voyage of H.M.S. Fly, commanded by Captain F.P. Blackwood, R.N. in Torres Strait, New Guinea ... 1842–46*. 2 vols. London: T. & W. Boone, 1847. (V)

Jung, Karl Emil. *Der Weltteil Australien*. Leipzig: H. Freutag, 1882.

Kamakau, Samuel M. *Ruling Chiefs of Hawaii*. Honolulu: Kamehameha School Press, 1961.

Karig, Walter, and Kelley, Welbourn. *Battle Report: Pearl Harbour and Coral Sea*. New York: Farrar & Rinehart, 1944. (XIV)

Keable, Robert. *Numerous Treasure*. London: Hurst & Blackett, n.d. (XIII)

—— *Tahiti: Isles of Dreams*. London: Hutchinson, n.d. (XIII)

Keane, Augustus Henry. *The World's Peoples*. London: Hutchinson, 1908. (P)

Keate, George. *An Account of the Pelew Islands ...* London: G. Nicol, 1788. (V; VI)

Keesing, Felix Maxwell. *Modern Samoa*. London: George Allen & Unwin, 1934.

—— *Native Peoples of the Pacific World*. New York: Macmillan, 1945. (I; P)

Kelly, Fr. Celsus, ed. *La Austrialia del Espiritu Santo ... Voyage of Pedro Fernañdez de Quirós (1605–1606)*. 2 vols. Cambridge: Hakluyt Society, 1966. (II)

Kent, Janet. *The Solomon Islands*. Harrisburg: Stackpole Books, 1973. (II; VII; VIII; XIV; XV)

Keynes, Sir Geoffrey, ed. *The Letters of Rupert Brooke*. London: Faber & Faber, 1968. (XIII)

King, Agnes Gardner. *Islands Far Away*. London: Sifton Praed, 1921.

King, Joseph. *W.G. Lawes of Savage Island and New Guinea*. London: The Religious Tract Society, 1909. (VIII; X; XI)

Kingsford-Smith, Sir Charles Edward, and Ulm, Charles T.P. *The Great Trans-Pacific Flight*. London: Hutchinson, 1929. (XIV)

Kippis, Andrew. *A Narrative of the Voyages Round the World Performed by Captain James Cook with an Account of his Life ...* 2 vols. Chiswick: C. Whittingham, 1826. (IV)

Kirker, James. *Adventures to China. Americans in the Southern Oceans 1792–1812*. New York: Oxford University Press, 1970. (VI; VII)

Klein, Ir. Willem C. *Nieuw Guinea; Ontwikkelingen op economisch, sociaal, en cultureel gebied in Nederlands en Australisch Nieuw Guinea*. 3 vols. The Hague: Staatsdrukkerij, 1953. (XIV; XV)

Kleinschmidt, Theodor. 'Reisen auf den Viti-Inseln.' *Journal Museum Godeffroy*. Vol. XIV. Hamburg, 1876–9. (XIII)

Knibbs, Stanley George Curthoys. *The Savage Solomons As they Were and Are ...* London: Seeley, Service, 1929.

Knox-Mawer, June. *A Gift of Islands*. London: John Murray, 1965.

Koskinen, Aarne A. *Missionary Influence as a Political Factor in the Pacific Islands*. Helsinki: Finnish Academy of Science and Letters, 1953. (VIII; X; XI)

Kotzebue, Otto von. *A Voyage of Discovery into the South Sea ... 1815, 16, 17 and 18*. 3 vols. London: Longman, Hurst, Rees, Orme & Brown, 1821. (V)

—— *A New Voyage round the World ... 1823, 24, 25 and 26*. 2 vols. London: Henry Colburn & Richard Bentley, 1830. (V)

Kraemer, Stabsartz Augustin. *Die Samoa Inseln ...* 2 vols. Stuttgart: E. Naegele, 1902.

Krusenstern, Adm. Adam Johann Crusius (Ivan Fedorovitch) von. *Voyage Round the World 1803–6 ... Nadezhda and Neva*. London: John Murray, 1813. (V)

—— See Ross, Rear-Adm. Sir John.

Kuykendall, Ralph Simpson. *The Hawaiian Kingdom 1778–1854*. Honolulu: University of Hawaii Press, 1938. (IV; V; VI; VIII; XI)

—— *The Hawaiian Kingdom 1854–1874*. Honolulu: University of Hawaii Press, 1966. (XI)

—— *The Hawaiian Kingdom 1874–1893*. Honolulu: University of Hawaii Press, 1967. (XI)

La Billardière, Jacques Julien Houton de. *Rélation du Voyage à la Recherche de La Pérouse ... 1791, 1792, 1793*. 2 vols. and atlas. Paris: H.J. Jansen, 1800. (V)

La Borde, Jean Benjamin de. *Histoire abrégée de la Mer du Sud*. 3 vols. Paris: P. Didot L'aîné, 1791. (II; III; IV)

Lady, A (Wallis, Mary Davis Cook). *Life in Feejee, or, Five Years Among the Cannibals*. Boston: William Heath, 1851. (VIII)

La Farge, John. *Reminiscences of the South Seas*. London: Grant Richards, 1914. (XIII)

Lambert, Charles J., and Lambert, S. See Young, Gerald.

Lambert, John C. *Missionary Heroes in Oceania*. London: Seeley, Service, n.d. (VIII; X)

Lamont, E.H. *Wild Life Among the Pacific Islanders*. London: Hurst & Blac. (VI; VIII)

Langdon, Robert Adrian. *Island of Love*. London: Cassell, 1959. (IV; V; XIII)

—— *The Lost Caravel*. Sydney: Pacific Publications, 1975. (II; III; IV; P)

Langridge, Albert Kent. *The Conquest of Cannibal Tanna*. London: Hodder & Stoughton, 1934. (VII; VIII; X)

Langsdorff, Georg Heinrich von. *Voyages and Travels ... 1803, 1804, 1805, 1806 and 1807*. London: Henry Colburn, 1813. (V)

Lapérouse, Comte Jean François Galaup de. See Milet-Mureau, Baron Général Marie Louis Antoine Destouff de.

Laplace, Cyrille Pierre Théodore. *Campagne de circumnavigation de ... L'Artémise ... 1837, 1838, 1839 et 1840 ...* 6 vols. Paris: A. Bertrand, 1841–54. (V)

Larsen, May, and Larsen, Henry. *The Golden Cowrie*. Edinburgh: Oliver & Boyd, 1961.

Latukefu, Sione. *Church and State in Tonga*. Canberra: Australian National University Press, 1974. (VII; X; XI)

Lawry, Rev. Walter. *Friendly and Feejee Islands*. Edited by Rev. Elijah Hoole. London: Charles Gilpin, 1850. (VIII; X)

—— *A Second Missionary Visit to the Friendly and Feejee Islands in the year MDCCCL*. Edited by Rev. Elijah Hoole. London: John Mason, 1851. (VIII; X)

Ledyard, Patricia. *Tonga ...* New York: Appleton-Century-Crofts, 1956.

Lee, Ida. *Captain Bligh's Second Voyage to the South Sea*. London: Longmans, Green, 1920. (V)

Legge, Christopher Connlagh. 'William Diaper'. *Journal of Pacific History*. Vol. I. Canberra, 1966. (VI)

Legge, Christopher Connlagh, and Terrell, Jennifer. 'James Toutant Proctor'. *Journal of Pacific History*. Vol. V. Canberra, 1970. (VII)

Legge, John David. *Britain in Fiji 1858–1880*. London: Macmillan, 1958. (VII; VIII; X; XI)

Le Guillou, Elié Jean François, and Arago, Jacques Étienne Victor. *Voyage autour du Monde de l'Astrolabe et de La Zélée ... 1837, 38, 39, et 40*. 2 vols. Paris: Berquet et Pétion, 1842. (V; XIII)

Le Maire, Jacob. *Spieghel der Australische Navigatie ...* Amsterdam: Michiel Colijn, 1622. (III)

Lennox, Cuthbert. *James Chalmers of New Guinea*. London: Andrew Melrose, 1902. (VIII; XI)

Le Roux, C.C.F.M. *De Bergpapoea's van Nieuw-Guinea ...* 2 vols. Leiden: E.J. Brill, 1948–50.

Lesson, Pierre Adolphe. *Les Polynésiens, Leur Origine, Leurs Migrations ...* 4 vols. Paris: Ernest Leroux, 1880–4. (P)

Lesson, René Primavère. *Voyage autour du Monde ... sur ... La Coquille*. 4 vols. Paris: P. Pourrat Frères, 1838–9. (V)

Leutemann, H. *Graphic Pictures of Native Life in Distant Lands*. London: George Philip, 1888.

Lewis, Aletta. *They Call Them Savages*. London: Methuen, 1938.

Lewis, David. *We, the Navigators: the ancient art of landfinding in the Pacific*. Canberra: Australian National University Press, 1972. (P)

Liliuokalani (Hawaii's Queen). *Hawaii's Story*. Boston: Lothrop, Lee & Shepard, 1898. (XI)

Lindsay, Lionel. *Conrad Martens: The Man and His Art*. London: Angus & Robertson, 1920. (XIII)

Linklater, Eric. *The Voyage of the Challenger*. London: John Murray, 1972. (V)

Linton, Ralph. *Archaeology of the Marquesas Islands*. Honolulu: Bernice P. Bishop Museum, 1925. (P)

Lisiansky, Urey Fedorovich. *A Voyage Round the World in the Years 1803, 4, 5 & 6; ...* London:

John Booth, Longman, Hurst, 1814. (V)

Lockerby, William. See Im Thurn, Sir Everard F., and Wharton, Leonard C.

Lohse, Bernd. *Australia and the South Seas*. Edinburgh: Oliver and Boyd, 1959.

London, Jack (John Griffith). *The Cruise of the Snark*. London: Mills & Boon, 1908. (XIII)

—— *South Sea Tales*. New York: World Publishing Co., n.d. [1909]. (XIII)

Loon, Hendrik Willem van. *The Story of the Pacific*. London: George G. Harrap, 1940. (II; III; X; P)

Loti, Pierre (Viaud, Louis Marie Julien). *Le Mariage de Loti (Rarahu)*. Paris: Calmann Lévy, 1898. First published as *Rarahu, Idylle Polynésienne par l'auteur d'Aziyadé*. 1879. (XIII)

Lowndes, A.G., ed. *South Pacific Enterprise: The Colonial Sugar Refining Company Ltd*. Sydney: Angus & Robertson, 1956. (IX)

Lubbock, Basil. *Bully Hayes*. London: Martin Hopkinson, 1931. (XII)

Lucett, Edward. See Merchant Long Resident in Tahiti, A.

Luke, Sir Harry Charles. *Britain and the South Seas*. London and New York: Longmans, Green, 1945.

—— *From a South Sea Diary 1938–1942*. London: Nicolson and Watson, 1945. (XIV)

—— *Queen Salote and Her Kingdom*. London: Putnam, 1954. (XIV)

Lütke, Frédéric (Fyodor) Petrovitch. *Voyage autour du monde ... sur ... Le Séniavine ... 1826, 1827, 1828 et 1829*. 3 vols. and atlas. Paris: Firmin Didot, 1835–6. (V)

Lynch, Bohun, ed. *Isles of Illusion*. London: Constable, 1923.

Macdonald, Sir John Denis. 'Proceedings of the Expedition for the Exploration of the Rewa River and its Tributaries ... ' *Geographical Journal*. Vol. XXVII. London, 1857. (V)

MacGillivray, John. *Narrative of the Voyage of H.M.S. Rattlesnake ...* 2 vols. London: T. & W. Boone, 1852. (V)

MacGregor, Anne. *Papua New Guinea Independence 1975*. Port Moresby: Papua New Guinea Government Printer, 1975. (II; XI; XIV; XV)

Mackaness, George. *The Life of Vice-Admiral William Bligh*. 2 vols. Australia: Angus & Robertson, 1931. (V)

MacQuarrie, Hector. *Friendly Queen*. London: William Heinemann, 1955. (XIV; XV)

McArthur, Norma Ruth. *Island Populations of the Pacific*. Canberra: Australian National University Press, 1968. (X)

McCarthy, John Keith. *Patrol into Yesterday*. London: Angus & Robertson, 1964. (XV)

McClure, Herbert Reginald. *Land-Travel and Seafaring*. London: Hutchinson, n.d. [1924].

McKern, Will Carleton. *Archaeology of Tonga*. Honolulu: Bernice P. Bishop Museum, 1929. (P)

McNally, Ward. *New Zealand*. London: Robert

Hale, 1966. (XII)

Malaspina, D. Alejandro. See Novo y Colson, Don Pedro de.

Mangin, Arthur. *Voyages et Découvertes Outre-Mer au XIXe Siècle*. Tours: Ad. Meme, 1863. (V)

March y Labores, Don José. *Historia de la marina . . .* 1854. (II; III; IV)

Marchand, Étienne. See Fleurieu, Comte Charles Pierre Claret de.

Markham, Sir Clements Robert. *The Sea-Fathers: a Series of Lives of Great Navigators of Former Times*. London: Cassell, 1884. (II; III)

—— ed. *The Voyages of Pedro Fernández de Quirós, 1595 to 1606*. 2 vols. London: Hakluyt Society, 1904. (II)

Marshall, Donald Stanley. *Island of Passion*. London: George Allen & Unwin, 1962.

Martin, John. *An Account of the Natives of the Tonga Islands . . .* 2 vols. London: John Murray, 1818. (VI)

Martin-Allanic, Jean-Etienne. *Bougainville navigateur et des découvertes de son temps*. 2 vols. Paris: Presses Universitaires de France, 1964. (IV; V)

Masterman, Sylvia. *The Origins of International Rivalry in Samoa 1845–1884*. London: George Allen & Unwin, 1934. (XI)

Maude, Henry Evans. *Of Islands and Men*. Melbourne: Oxford University Press, 1968. (II; V; VI; VII; VIII)

Maudslay, Alfred Percival. *Life in the Pacific Fifty Years Ago*. London: George Routledge, 1930. (XI; XII; XIII)

Maugham, William Somerset. *The Moon and Sixpence*. London: William Heinemann, 1919. (XIII)

—— *The Trembling of a Leaf*. London: William Heinemann, 1925. (XIII)

Mavor, Rev. William Fordyce. *Historical Account of the Most Celebrated Voyages, Travels and Discoveries . . .* London: E. Newbery, 1796–97. (II; III; IV)

Mazière, Francis. *Archipel du Tiki*. Paris: Robert Laffont, 1962.

Meade, Lieut. Hon. Herbert. *A Ride through the Disturbed Districts of New Zealand, together with some account of the South Sea Islands*. London: John Murray, 1870. (V)

Medina, José Toribio. *El Descubrimientó del Océano Pacífico . . .* 2 vols. Santiago de Chile: Imprenta Universitaria, 1913–14. (II)

Melville, Herman. *Typee*. London: John Murray; and New York: Wiley and Putnam, 1846. (XIII)

—— *Omoo: a Narrative of Adventures in the South Seas*. New York: Harper; and London: John Murray, 1847. (XIII)

Merchant Long Resident in Tahiti, A (Lucett, Edward). *Rovings in the Pacific from 1837 to 1849 . . .* 2 vols. London: Longmans, Brown, Green and Longmans, 1851. (VI; VII; XIII)

Métraux, Alfred. *Ethnology of Easter Island*. Honolulu: Bernice P. Bishop Museum,

1940. (P)

Michael, Charles D. *John Gibson Paton, D.D.* London: S.W. Partridge, n.d. (VIII; X)

Michener, James Albert. *Tales of the South Pacific*. New York: Macmillan, 1947; and London: Collins, 1951. (XIII)

—— *Hawaii*. New York: Random House, 1959; and London: Secker & Warburg, 1960.

Michener, James Albert, and Day, Arthur Grove. *Rascals in Paradise*. London: Secker & Warburg, 1957. (XII)

Milet-Mureau, Baron Général Marie Louis Antoine Destouff de, ed. *Voyage de La Pérouse . . . 1785–1788 . . .* 4 vols. and atlas. Paris: l'Imprimerie de la République, 1797. (V)

Mitchell, Mairin. *El Cano, the First Circumnavigator*. London: Harden, 1958. (II)

Moerenhout, Jacques Antoine. *Voyage aux Iles du Grand Océan . . .* 2 vols. Paris: Arthus Bertrand, 1837. (V)

Monckton, Charles Arthur Whitmore. *Some Experiences of a New Guinea Resident Magistrate. Second Series*. London: John Lane, The Bodley Head, 1920.

—— *Last Days in New Guinea*. London: John Lane, The Bodley Head, 1922.

Monfat, Antoine. *Les Samoa ou Archipel des Navigateurs*. Lyon: Librairie Général Catholique et Classique, 1890. (VIII; X)

—— *Les Tonga ou Archipel des Amis . . .* Lyon: Emmanuel Vitte, 1893. (VIII; X)

Moorehead, Alan McCrae. *The Fatal Impact*. London: Hamish Hamilton, 1966. (X)

—— *Darwin and The Beagle*. London: Hamish Hamilton, 1969. (V)

Moors, Harry J. *With Stevenson in Samoa*. London: Collins, n.d. (XIII)

Mordaunt, Elinor. *The Venture Book*. London: John Lane, The Bodley Head, 1926. (VIII)

Moresby, Adm. John. *New Guinea and Polynesia*. London: John Murray, 1876. (V)

—— *Two Admirals*. London: Methuen, 1913. (V)

Morison, Rear-Adm. Samuel Eliot. *The Two-Ocean War . . .* Boston: Little, Brown, 1963. (XIV)

Morrell, Capt. Benjamin, jun. *A Narrative of Four Voyages, to the South Sea, North and South Pacific Ocean . . . 1822 to 1831 . . .* New York: J. & J. Harper, 1832. (V)

Morrell, William Parker. *Britain in the Pacific Islands*. Oxford: Clarendon Press, 1960. (II; III; IV; VII; VIII; X; XI; XIV; P)

Morrison, James. *Journal*. Paris: Musée de l'Homme, 1966. (V)

Mortimer, Faver Lee. *The Night of Toil; or, a Familiar Account of the Labours of the First Missionaries in the South Seas*. London: J. Hatchard, 1838. (VIII)

Mortimer, Lieut. George. *Observations and Remarks made during the Voyage to . . . Owhyee . . . Mercury*. Dublin: P. Byrne, 1791. (V)

Moseley, Henry Nottidge. *Notes by a Naturalist on the "Challenger" . . .* London: Macmillan,

1879. (V)

Moss, Frederick Joseph. *Through Atolls and Islands in the Great South Sea*. London: Sampson Low, Marston, Searle & Rivington, 1889.

Mourant, A.E., Kopic, Ada C., and Domanicwska-Sobczak, Kazimiera. *The ABO Blood Groups . . .* Oxford: Blackwell Scientific Publications, 1958. (P)

Moyne, 1st. Lord of Bury St. Edmunds (Guinness, Walter Edward). *Walkabout*. London: William Heinemann, 1936. (XIV)

Muir, Surg. Rear-Adm. John Reid. *The Life and Achievements of Captain James Cook, R.N., F.R.S., Explorer, Navigator, Surveyor and Physician*. London: Blackie, 1939. (IV)

Murray, Hugh, ed. *Adventures of British Seamen in the Southern Ocean*. London: Constable's Miscellany, 1826. (III; IV)

Murray, Sir John Hubert Plunket. *Papua or British New Guinea*. London: T. Fisher Unwin, 1912.

—— *Papua of Today, or An Australian Colony in the Making*. London: P.S. King, 1925. (II; XI)

Murray, Rev. Thomas Boyles. *Pitcairn: The Island, the People and the Pastor*. London: SPCK; and New York: Pott, Young, 1857. (XII)

Murray-Oliver, Anthony Aubrey St. Clair Murray. *Augustus Earle in New Zealand*. Christchurch: Whitcombe & Tombs, 1968. (XIII)

—— Comp. *Captain Cook's Artists in the Pacific 1769–1779*. Christchurch: Avon Fine Prints, 1969. (IV)

Nairne, W.P. *Greatheart of Papua (James Chalmers)*. London: Oxford University Press, 1913. (VIII; XI)

Nan Kivell, Sir Rex de Charembac, and Spence, Sydney Alfred. *Portraits of the Famous and Infamous. Australia, New Zealand and the Pacific 1492–1970*. London, n.d. (II; III; IV; V; VI; VII; VIII; XI; XII; XIII)

Navarette, Martin Fernandez de. *Collecion de los viajes y descubrimientos . . .* 4 vols. Madrid, 1829. (II)

Neale, Tom. *An Island to Oneself*. London: Collins, 1966. (IX)

Neill, James Scott. *Ten Years in Tonga*. London: Hutchinson, 1955. (XIV)

Newbury, Colin William. *The History of the Tahitian Mission 1799–1830*. Cambridge: Hakluyt Society, 1941. (VIII)

New Zealand 1826–1827 . . . Voyage de l'Astrolabe . . . With an introductory essay by Olive Wright. [New Zealand:] Wingfield Press, n.d. [1950]. (V)

Niau, Josephine Hyacinthe. *The Phantom Paradise. The Story of the Expedition of Marquis de Reys*. Sydney: Angus & Robertson, 1936. (XII)

Nicolson, Robert B. The *Pitcairners*. Sydney: Angus & Robertson, 1965. (V; IX; XII)

Nightingale, Thomas. *Oceanic Sketches*. London: J. Cochrane, 1835. (VIII)

Noort, Olivier van. *Beschryvinghe vande Voyagie ... 1598 ... 1601 ...* Rotterdam: Jan van Waesberghen, [1602]. (III)

Nordhoff, Charles Bernard, and Hall, James Norman. *Mutiny on the Bounty.* Boston: Little, Brown, 1932. (XIII)

—— *Pitcairn's Island.* Boston: Little, Brown, 1934. (XIII)

—— *The Hurricane.* Boston: Little, Brown, 1936. (XIII)

Novo y Colson, Don Pedro de. *Viaje Político-científico Alrededor del Mundo por ... Descubierta y Atrevida al mando de los capitanes de navío D. Alejandro Malaspina y Don José de Bustamente y Guerra ... 1789 á 1794.* Madrid: Imprinta de la viudá é Hijos de Abienzo, 1885. (V)

O'Brien, Frederick. *Mystic Isles of the South Seas.* London: Hodder & Stoughton, 1921.

—— *White Shadows in the South Seas.* New York: The Century Co., 1921.

O'Connell, James F. *A Residence of Eleven Years in New Holland and the Caroline Islands.* Edited by Saul H. Riesenberg. Boston: B.B. Mussey, 1836. Reprint, Canberra: Australian National University Press, 1972. (VI)

Oliver, Douglas Llewelyn. *The Pacific Islands.* Cambridge, Mass.: Harvard University Press; and London: Oxford University Press, 1951. (VII; XIV; P)

—— *Ancient Tahitian Society.* 3 vols. Honolulu: University of Hawaii Press, 1974. (V)

Orange, James, ed. *Narrative of the Late George Vason, of Nottingham.* Derby: Henry Mozley, 1840. (VI)

O'Reilly, Père Patrick Georges Farell. *Calédoniens.* Paris: Musée de l'Homme, 1953. (VII; VIII; IX; XIII; XIV; XV)

—— *Bibliographie ... de la Nouvelle-Calédonie.* Paris: Musée de l'Homme, 1955.

—— *Bibliographie ... des Nouvelles-Hébrides.* Paris: Musée de l'Homme, 1958.

—— 'Bibliographie des îles Wallis et Futuna'. *Journal de la Société des Océanistes.* Paris, 1963. (V; VIII; XIV)

—— *Tahitiens.* Paris: Musée de l'Homme, 1966. (XIII; XIV; XV)

O'Reilly, Père Patrick Georges Farell, and Reitman, Edouard. *Bibliographie de Tahiti et de la Polynésie française ...* 2 vols. Paris: Musée de l'Homme, 1967. (IV; V; VII; VIII; IX; XIII; XIV; XV)

O'Reilly, Père Patrick Georges Farell, and Teissier, Raoul. *Tahitiens ...* Paris: Musée de l'Homme, 1962. (IV; V; VII; VIII; XIII; XIV; XV)

Osborn, Fairfield, ed. *The Pacific World.* London: George Allen & Unwin, 1945. (I; II)

Osbourne, Lloyd. *Wild Justice.* London: William Heinemann, 1922. (XIII)

Pacific Islands. BR 519 (Restricted). Geographical Handbook Series for Official Use Only. 4 vols. Naval Intelligence Division, n.d. [1945].

Pacific Saga. The Personal Chronicle of the 37th Battalion ... Wellington: A.H. & A. W. Reed, n.d. [1945?]. (XIV)

Palmer, Bruce, and Clunie, Fergus. *Rock Paintings and Engravings in Fiji ...* Suva: Fiji Museum, 1970. (P)

Palmer, Rear-Adm. George. *Kidnapping in the South Seas.* With a new introduction by Philip Snow. London: Dawsons of Pall Mall, 1971. (IX; X)

Parkinson, Richard Heinrich Robert. *Dreissig Jahre in der Südsee.* Stuttgart: Strecker und Schroder, 1907. (IX; XI)

Parkinson, Stanfield, ed. *A Journal of a Voyage to the South Seas in ... Endeavour ...* London: Stanfield Parkinson, 1773. (IV)

Parnaby, Owen W. *Britain and the labour trade in the Southwest Pacific.* Durham, N.C.: Duke University Press, 1964. (IX)

Paton, James. *The Story of John G. Paton.* London: Hodder & Stoughton, 1892. (VII; VIII)

Patterson, Samuel. *Narrative of the Adventures and Sufferings ...* Mass.: Press in Palmer, 1817. (VI)

Paulding, Lieut. Hiram. *Journal of a Cruise of ... Dolphin ...* With a new introduction by A. Grove Day. Honolulu: University of Hawaii Press, 1970. (V; VI)

Pearce, G.L. *The Story of the Maori People.* Auckland: Collins, 1968. (VIII; XI)

Peard, Lt. George. See Gough, Barry M.

Peebles, James Martin. *Around the World, or Travels in Polynesia or other "heathen countries".* Boston: Colby & Rich, 1876. (VIII; X)

Perkins, Edward T. *Na Motu: or, Reef-rovings in the South Seas ...* New York: Pudney and Russell, 1854.

Péron, Capt. Pierre. *Mémoires du Capitaine Péron ...* 2 vols. Paris: Brissot-Thivers, 1824. (V)

Perruchot, Henri. *Gauguin.* London: Methuen, 1958. (XIII)

'Petrel' (pseud). *Southern Seas.* Edinburgh: R. Grant, 1888. (VIII; X)

Phelps, Steven. *Art and artefacts of the Pacific ...* London: Hutchinson, 1976.

Phillips, Charles. *Samoa: Past and Present.* London: John Snow, n.d.

Pickering, Charles. *United States Exploring Expedition ... 1838, 1841, 1842.* Vol. IX. Boston: Charles C. Little & James Brown, 1848. (I; V)

Pierson, Delavan L., ed. *The Pacific Islanders.* New York and London: Funk & Wagnalls, 1906. (VIII; X)

Pigafetta, Antonio Francisco. See Skelton, Raleigh A.

Pitman, Emma Raymond. *Central Africa, Japan and Fiji: a Story of Missionary Enterprise, Trials and Triumphs.* London: Hodder & Stoughton, 1882. (VIII; X)

Pochhammer, Hans. *La Dernière Croisière de l'Amiral von Spee.* Paris, 1929. (XIV)

Porter, Capt. David. *Journal of a Cruise made to the Pacific Ocean ... in ... Essex ... 1812, 1813,* and 1814. 2 vols. Philadelphia: Bradford & Inskeep, 1815. (V)

Price, Sir Archibald Grenfell. *The Western Invasions of the Pacific and its Continents.* Oxford: Clarendon Press, 1963. (X; P)

—— *The Challenge of New Guinea.* Sydney: Angus & Robertson, 1965. (XV)

Price, Willard. *Adventures in Paradise.* London: William Heinemann, 1956.

Priestley, John Boynton. *Faraway.* New York: Harper, 1932. (XIII)

Pritchard, William Thomas. *Polynesian Reminiscences; or, Life in the South Pacific Islands.* Edited by Berthold Seeman. London: Chapman & Hall, 1866. (XI)

Pritchett, Robert Taylor. *Pen and Pencil Sketches.* London: Edward Arnold, 1899. (XIII; P)

Prout, Ebenezer. *Memoirs of the Life of the Rev. John Williams ...* London: John Snow, 1843. (VIII; X)

Purves, David Laing, ed. *Voyages round the World by Captain James Cook.* London and Edinburgh: William P. Nimmo, 1878. (IV)

Quirós, Pedro Fernández de. See Kelly, Fr. Celsus, and also Markham, Sir Clements Robert.

Rabling, Harold. *Pioneers of the Pacific.* London: Angus & Robertson, 1967.

Radiguet, Maximilien René. *Les derniers sauvages.* Paris: Calmann Lévy, 1882. (V)

Raitt, Helen. *Exploring the Deep Pacific.* London: Staples Press, 1956. (P)

Randier, Jean. *Hommes et Navires au Cap Horn 1616–1939.* Paris: Librairie Hachette, 1966. (II; III; IV)

Rannie, Douglas. *My Adventures among South Sea Cannibals.* London: Seeley, Service, 1912. (V; IX)

Ratzel, Friedrich. *The History of Man.* 2 vols. London and New York: Macmillan, 1896.

Read, Kenneth E. *The High Valley.* London: George Allen & Unwin, 1966. (XV)

Reclus, Jean Jacques Elisée. *Australasia.* London: Virtue, n.d.

—— *Nouvelle Géographie Universelle.* Vol. XIV. Paris: Librairie Hachette, 1889.

Redwood, Rosaline. *On Copra Ships and Coral Isles.* New York: A.S. Barnes, 1966.

Reeves, Edward. *Brown Men and Women, or The South Sea Islands in 1895 and 1896.* London: Swan Sonnenschein, 1898.

Rienits, Rex, and Rienits, Thea. *The Voyages of Captain Cook.* London and New York: Paul Hamlyn, 1968. (IV)

Rienzi, Grégoire Louis Domény de. *Océanie, ou La Cinquième Partie du Monde ...* 3 vols. Paris: Firmin Didot. 1836–7.

Riesenberg, Felix. *The Pacific Ocean.* London: Museum Press, 1947. (II; III; V)

Riethmaier, Gregory, and Goodman, Richard A. *Samoa ma le Fa'asamoa.* Auckland and London: Collins, 1973.

Riverain, Jean. *Concise Encyclopaedia of Explorations.* London: Collins; and Chicago: Fallett, 1969. (II; III; IV; V)

Rivers, William Halse Rivers. *The History of Melanesian Society*. 2 vols. London: Cambridge University Press, 1914.

—— ed. *Essays on the Depopulation of Melanesia*. London: Cambridge University Press, 1922. (X)

Robarts, Edward. See Dening, Gregory M.

Roberts, Sir Stephen Henry. *Population Problems of the Pacific*. London: George Routledge, 1927. (II; III; VII; VIII; IX)

Robertson, George. See Carrington, Major Arthur Hugh.

Robinson, William Albert. *Return to the Sea*. London: Peter Davies, 1973.

Robson, Robert William. *Queen Emma ...* Sydney: Pacific Publications, 1965. (IX; XII)

Rogers, Timothy. *Rupert Brooke*. London: Routledge & Kegan Paul, 1971. (XIII)

Roggeveen, Jacob. *Tweejaarige reyze rondom de Wereld ...* Dordrecht: Joannes van Braam, 1728. (IV)

Rollin, Louis. *Les Iles Marquises*. Paris: Société d'Editions Géographiques, Maritimes et Coloniales, 1929. (II; V; X; P)

Romilly, Hugh Hastings. *A True Story of the Western Pacific in 1879–80*. London: Longmans, Green, 1882.

—— *The Western Pacific and New Guinea*. London: John Murray, 1886. (VII; X; XII)

—— *From My Verandah in New Guinea*. London: David Nutt, 1889. (XI)

—— *Letters from the Western Pacific ... 1878–1891*. Edited by Samuel H. Romilly. London: David Nutt, 1893. (IX; X; XI; XII)

Rose, John Holland. *Man and the Sea*. Cambridge: W. Heffer, 1935. (II; III; IV)

Rose, Lyndon. *People in the Sun*. Sydney: Angus & Robertson, 1961.

Roskill, Stephen Wentworth. *The War at Sea 1939–1945*. Vol. II. London: H.M.S.O., 1956. (XIV)

Ross, Angus, ed. *New Zealand's record in the Pacific Islands in the twentieth century*. Auckland: New Zealand Institute of International Affairs, 1964. (XIV; XV)

Ross, C. Stewart. *Fiji and the Western Pacific*. Geelong: H. Thacker, 1909. (X; XI)

Ross, Rear-Adm. Sir John, ed. *Memoir of the celebrated Admiral Adam John de Krusenstern, the First Russian Circumnavigator*. London: Longmans, Green, Brown & Longmans, 1856. (V)

Rossel, Rear-Adm. Elizabeth-Paul-Edouarde de. *Voyage de D'Entrecasteaux, envoyé à la recherche de La Pérouse*. 2 vols. Paris: L'Imprimerie Royale, 1808. (V)

Roth, George Kingsley. *Native administration in Fiji ...* London: Royal Anthropological Institute, 1951. (XI)

—— *Fijian Way of Life*. 2nd ed. With a new introduction by George Bertram Milner. Melbourne: Oxford University Press, 1973.

Routledge, Katherine Scoresby. *The Mystery of Easter Island*. London: Sifton Praed, n.d.

[1919]. (XIV; P)

Rowe, Rev. George Stringer, ed. *Fiji and the Fijians*. Vol I: 'The Islands and their inhabitants', by Rev. Thomas Williams. Vol. II: 'Mission History', by Rev. James Calvert. London: Alexander Heylin, 1858. (VIII; X)

—— *The Life of John Hunt ...* London: Hamilton, Adams, 1859. (VIII)

—— *James Calvert of Fiji*. London: Charles H. Kelly, 1893. (VIII)

Rowe, Newton Allan. *Samoa under the Sailing Gods*. New York: Putnam, 1930.

—— *Voyage to the Amorous Islands*. London: André Deutsch, 1955. (IV)

Ruhen, Olaf. *Mountains in the Clouds*. London: Angus & Robertson, 1964. (V; VI; XIV)

Russell, Alexander. *Aristocrats of the South Seas*. London: Robert Hale, 1961. (I; P)

Russell, Rt. Rev. Michael. *Polynesia: Or An Historical Account of the Principal Islands in the South Sea including New Zealand*. Edinburgh: Oliver & Boyd, 1842.

Rutherford, Noel. *Shirley Baker and the King of Tonga*. Melbourne: London: Oxford University Press, 1971. (XI; XII)

Rutter, Owen, ed. *The Court-Martial of the "Bounty" Mutineers*. Edinburgh: William Hodge, 1931. (V)

—— *Turbulent Journey. A Life of William Bligh ...* London: Ivor Nicholson & Watson, 1936. (V)

Ryan, John. *The Hot Land. Focus on New Guinea*. Melbourne: Macmillan; and New York: St. Martin's Press, 1969. (XV)

Sabatier, Ernest. *Sous l'Equateur du Pacifique*. Issoudun: Archiconfrérie de N-D du Sacré-Coeur, 1939.

Sager, Gordon. *Hawaii*. London: Ward, Lock, 1969. (VIII; XI; XIV)

Sahlins, Marshall David. *Moala: Culture and Nature on a Fijian Island*. Ann Arbor: University of Michigan Press, 1962.

St. Johnston, Alfred. *Camping among Cannibals*. London: Macmillan, 1883.

St. Johnston, Sir Thomas Reginald. *The Lau Islands*. London: The Times Book Club, 1918.

—— *The Islanders of the Pacific or, The Children of the Sun*. London: T. Fisher Unwin, 1921. (VIII; P)

—— *South Sea Reminiscences*. London: T. Fisher Unwin, 1922.

—— *Strange Places and Strange Peoples, or Life in the Colonial Service*. London: Hutchinson, 1936.

Sanderlin, George. *First Around the World*. London: Hamish Hamilton, 1966. (II)

Saulnier, Tony, and Bisieux, Marcel. *Head Hunters of Papua*. London: Paul Hamlyn, 1963. (XV)

Saville, Gordon, and Austin, John. *King of Kiriwina*. London: Leo Cooper, 1974. (X; XIV)

Scherzer, Karl von. *Narrative of the Circum-*

navigation of the Globe by ... Novara (Commodore B. von Wullerstorf-Urbain) ... 1857, 1858 and 1859. 3 vols. London: Saunders, Otley, 1862. (V; VII)

Scholes, S.E. *Fiji and the Friendly Isles ...* London: T. Woolmer, n.d.

Schouten, Willem Cornelisz. *Journal ou déscription du merveilleux voyage de Guillaume Schouten ...* Amsterdam: Guillaume Janson, 1618. (III)

Schütz, Albert James, ed. *The Diaries ... of David Cargill 1832–1843*. Canberra: Australian National University Press, 1977. (VIII)

The Right Hon. R.J. Seddon's Visit to the South Sea Islands. Wellington: Government Printer, 1900. (XI)

Seeman, Berthold Carl. *Viti: an account of a Government Mission to the Vitian or Fijian Islands 1860–1861*. With a new introduction by Philip Snow. London: Dawsons of Pall Mall, 1973. (VI; IX)

Shadbolt, Maurice, and Ruhen, Olaf. *Isles of the South Pacific*. Washington: National Geographic Society, 1968. (X)

Shapiro, Harry Lionel. *The Heritage of the Bounty*. London: Victor Gollancz, 1936. (IX; XII)

Sharp, Andrew. *The Discovery of the Pacific Islands*. Oxford: Clarendon Press, 1960. (II; III; IV)

—— *Adventurous Armada*. Christchurch: Whitcombe & Tombs, 1961. (II)

—— *Ancient Voyagers in Polynesia*. London: Angus & Robertson, 1964. (P)

—— *The Voyages of Abel Janszoon Tasman*. Oxford: Clarendon Press, 1968. (III)

—— ed. *The Journal of Jacob Roggeveen*. Oxford: Clarendon Press, 1970. (IV; P)

Shillibeer, Lieut. John. *A Narrative of the Briton's Voyage to Pitcairn's Island*. London: Law and Whitaker, 1817. (IX)

Shineberg, Dorothy. *They Came for Sandalwood*. Carlton: Melbourne University Press, 1967. (VII)

—— ed. *The Trading Voyages of Andrew Cheyne, 1841–1844*. Canberra: Australian National University Press, 1971. (VII)

Shipley, Lieut. Conway. *Sketches in the Pacific: the South Sea Islands ...* London: E. McLean, 1851. (XIII)

Shrimpton, A.W., and Mulgan, Alan E. *Maori and Pakeha*. Auckland: Whitcombe & Tombs, 1930.

Siers, James. *Polynesia in Colour*. Wellington: A.H. & A.W. Reed, 1968.

—— *Fiji in Colour*. Wellington: A.H. & A. W. Reed, 1969.

—— *Samoa in Colour*. Wellington: A.H. & A.W. Reed, 1970.

Sievers, Wilhelm. *Australien und Ozeanien*. Leipzig and Vienna: Bibliographisches Institut, 1895. (IX; X; XI)

Silverman, David. *Pitcairn Island*. Cleveland, N.Y.: The World Publishing Co., 1967.

Simenon, Georges. *Touriste de bananes ou les Dimanches de Tahiti*. Paris: Gallimard, 1938. (XIII)

Sinclair, James Patrick. *Behind the Ranges. Patrolling New Guinea*. London and New York: Melbourne University Press, 1966. (XIV; XV)

Skelton, Raleigh Ashlin. *Explorers' Maps ...* London and New York: Spring Books, 1958. (II; III; IV)

—— trans. and ed. *Antonio Pigafetta: Magellan's Voyage. A Narrative Account of the First Circumnavigation*. New Haven, Conn.: Yale University Press, 1969. (II)

Skinner, Henry Devenish. *The Morioris of Chatham Islands*. Honolulu: Bernice P. Bishop Museum, 1923. (X)

Skogman, Carl Johann Alfred. *Fregatten Eugenies Resa Omkring Jorden Åren 1851–1853, under befäl af C.A. Virgin*. 2 vols. Stockholm: A. Bonnier, 1854–5. (V)

Smith, Bernard. *European Vision and the South Pacific 1768–1850*. Oxford: Clarendon Press, 1960. (IV; V)

Smith, Stephenson Percy. *Hawaiki: The Original Home of the Maori; with a Sketch of Polynesian History*. Auckland: Whitcombe & Tombs, 1921. (P)

Smythe, Sarah Maria. *Ten Months in the Fiji Islands*. Oxford and London: John Henry & James Parker, 1864. (XI)

Snow, Philip. 'Rock Carvings in Fiji'. *Transactions for 1950*. Vol. IV. Suva: Fiji Society, 1953. (P)

—— ed. *Best Stories of the South Seas*. London: Faber & Faber, 1967. (VI; XII)

—— *Bibliography of Fiji, Tonga and Rotuma*. Canberra: Australian National University Press; and Coral Gables, Fla.: University of Miami Press, 1969.

Somerville, Vice-Adm. Boyle Townshend. *Will Mariner ...* London: Faber & Faber, 1936. (VI)

Souter, Gavin. *New Guinea: The Last Unknown*. London: Angus & Robertson, 1964. (IX; XI)

Sparrman, Anders. *A Voyage round the World with Captain James Cook in H.M.S. Resolution*. London: Robert Hale, 1953. (IV)

Spilbergen, Joris van. *Speculum orientalis occidentalisque Indiae navigationum; quarum una Georgii à Spilbergen ... 1614 ... 18 ...* Geelkercken: Lugduni Batavorum apud Nicolaum, 1619. (III)

Spry, William James Joseph. *The Cruise of ... 'Challenger'*. London: Sampson Low, Marston, Searle & Rivington, 1875. (V)

Stackpole, Edouard A. *The Sea-Hunters*. Philadelphia: J.B. Lippincott, 1953. (V; VII)

Stanley of Alderley, 3rd. Lord (Stanley, Henry Edward John). *The First Voyage round the World by Magellan ...* London: The Hakluyt Society, 1874. (II)

Stanmore, 1st. Lord (Gordon, Hon. Sir Arthur Charles Hamilton). *Letters and Notes ...* 2 vols. Cambridge: R. and R. Clark, 1879. (XI)

—— *Fiji. Records of Private and Public Life, 1875–1880*. 4 vols. Edinburgh: R. & R. Clark, 1897–1912. (XI)

Stanton, William. *The Great United States Exploring Expedition of 1838–1842*. Berkeley: University of California Press, 1975. (V)

Stead, E. Herbert. *Captain James Wilson*. London: Missionary Society, n.d. (VIII)

Steuart, J.A. *Robert Louis Stevenson ...* 2 vols. London, 1924. (XIII)

Stevenson, Robert Louis, *Island Nights' Entertainments*. London: Cassell, 1893. (XIII)

Stevenson, Robert Louis, and Osbourne, Lloyd. *The Wrecker*. London: Cassell, 1892. (XIII)

—— *The Ebb Tide*. London: William Heinemann, 1922. (XIII)

Stoddard, Charles Warren. *Summer Cruising in the South Seas*. London: Chatto & Windus, n.d. [1873?].

Strong, Isobel, and Osbourne, Lloyd. *Memories of Vailima*. Westminster: Archibald Constable, 1903. (XIII)

Suggs, Robert Carl. *The Island Civilizations of Polynesia*. New York: The New American Library, 1960. (P)

Sukuna, Ratu Sir Josefa Lalabalavu Vanaaliali. *The Fijian's View of the European*. Suva: Defence Club, Cyclostyled, 1939.

Sullivan, Louis Robert. *Marquesan Somatology ...* Honolulu: Bernice P. Bishop Museum, 1923.

Sunderland, Rev. James Povey, and Buzacott, Rev. Aaron, eds. *Mission life in the Islands of the Pacific ...* London: John Snow, 1866. (VIII; X)

Sundowner (Tichborne, Herbert). *Noqu Talanoa*. London: European Mail, 1896.

—— *Rambles in Polynesia*. London: European Mail, 1897.

Sutherland, James. *Defoe*. London: Longmans, Green, 1956. (III)

Swire, Navigating Sub-Lt. Herbert. *The Voyage of H.M.S. Challenger ... 1872–1876*. England: the Golden Cockerel Press, 1938. (V; P)

Sydow, Eckart von. *Die Kunst der Naturvölker und der Vorzeit*. Berlin: Im Propyläen-Verlag, 1923.

Tahiti and its Islands. Papeete: Les Editions du Pacifique, 1972.

Tahiti and the French Islands of the Pacific. London: The Oak Tree Press, 1967.

Tasman, Abel Janszoon. ... *Journal of his Discovery of ... New Zealand in 1642 ... to which are added Life and Labours of Abel Janszoon Tasman by J.E. Heeres ...* Amsterdam: Frederik Muller, 1898. (III)

Ta'unga. See Crocombe, Ronald George, and Crocombe, Marjorie Tuainekore.

Tavernier, Bruno. *Les Grandes Routes Maritimes*. Paris: Robert Laffont, 1970. (IV)

Tetens, Capt. Alfred Friedrich. *Among the Savages of the South Seas*. Stanford, Calif.: Stanford University Press, 1958. (VII)

Thiéry, Maurice. *Bougainville*. London: Grayson and Grayson, 1932. (IV)

Thomas, Julian (Vagabond, The). *Cannibals and Convicts*. London and New York: Cassell, 1886. (XI; XII)

Thomas, Lowell. *The Sea Devil. The Story of Count Felix von Lückner, the German War Raider*. London: William Heinemann, 1929. (XIV)

Thompson, Laura Maud. *Archaeology of the Mariana Islands*. Honolulu: Bernice P. Bishop Museum, 1932. (P)

—— *Fijian Frontier*. San Francisco: American Council Institute of Pacific Relations, 1940.

—— *Guam and Its People*. Princeton, N.J.: Princeton University Press, 1947. (II; XIV; P)

Thomson, Sir Basil Home. *New Guinea 1888*. MS., owned by Philip Snow. (XI)

—— *South Sea Yarns*. London: William Blackwood, 1894.

—— *The Diversions of a Prime Minister*. London: William Blackwood, 1894. (XI; XII)

—— *Journal* (Tonga and Niue) 1900. MS., owned by Philip Snow. (XI)

—— *Savage Island*. London: John Murray, 1902. (XI; P)

—— *The Fijians*. London: William Heinemann, 1908. (X; XI)

—— *The Scene Changes*. London: Collins, 1939. (X; XI)

Thomson, J.P. *British New Guinea*. London: G. Philip, 1892.

Thurston, Lorrin Andrews. *Memoirs of the Hawaiian Revolution*. Honolulu, 1936. (XI)

Tihoti (Calderon, George). *Tahiti*. London: Grant Richards, 1921.

Todd, Ian. *Island Realm*. Sydney: Angus & Robertson, 1974.

Tokarev, Sergei Aleksandrovich, and Tolstov, Sergei Pavlovich. *Narody Avstralii i Okeanii*. Moscow: Academy of Sciences of U.S.S.R., 1956. (IV; V; VII; VIII; IX; XI; XV)

Tolna, Comte Rodolphe Festetics de. *Chez les Cannibales*. Paris: Librairie Plon, 1903. (IX; X)

Tolstoy, Count Leo. *What Then Must We Do?* Translated by L. & A. Maude. London: Oxford University Press, 1935. (XI)

Trusler, John. *A Descriptive Account of the Islands Lately Discovered in the South-Seas ...* London: R. Baldwin, 1778. (II; III; IV)

T'Serstevens, Albert. *Taïa*. Paris: Albin Michel, 1930. (XIII)

—— *L'Or du "Cristobal"*. Paris: Albin Michel, 1936. (XIII)

—— *Tahiti et sa Couronne*. 3 vols. Paris: Albin Michel, 1950–1.

—— *La Grande Plantation*. Paris: Albin Michel, 1952. (XIII)

Tudor, Judy Ethel Ellen. *Pacific Islands Year Book and Who's Who*. Sydney: Pacific Publications, 1968.

Turnbull, John. *A Voyage Round the World in the Years 1800, 1801, 1802, 1803 and 1804 in which the author visited the principal islands of the Pacific Ocean*. London: A. Maxwell, 1805. (V)

Turner, Rev. George. *Nineteen Years in Polynesia: Missionary Life, Travels and Researches in the Islands of the Pacific*. London: John Snow, 1861. (VIII; X)

—— *Samoa A Hundred Years Ago and long before*. London: Macmillan, 1884. (I; P)

Twain, Mark. *More Tramps Abroad*. London: Chatto & Windus, 1907. (VIII; XI)

Twyning, John Poyer. *Shipwreck and Adventures ... among the South Sea Islanders ...* 2nd ed., enlarged. London: Dean, n.d. [1850]. (VI)

Ullman, James Ramsay. *Where the Bong Tree Grows. The Log of One Man's Journey in the South Pacific*. London: Collins, 1964. (VIII; IX; X: XIII; XIV)

Vancouver, Capt. George. *A Voyage of Discovery to the North Pacific Ocean ...* 3 vols. London: G.G. and J. Robinson & J. Edwards, 1798. (V)

Vandercook, John Womack. *Dark Islands*. London: William Heinemann, 1938.

—— *King Cane: The Story of Sugar in Hawaii*. New York: Harper, 1939. (IX)

Varigny, Crosnier de. *L'Océan Pacifique*. Paris: Hachette, 1888. (X)

Vason, George. See Orange, James.

Verschuur, G. *Aux Antipodes ...* Paris: Hachette, 1891. (V; P)

Villiers, Alan John. *Oceans of the World*. London: Museum Press, 1963. (P)

—— *Captain Cook, the Seamen's Seaman*. London: Hodder & Stoughton, 1967. (IV)

Vincendon-Dumoulin, Clément-Adrien, and Desgraz, César Louis François. *Îles Tahiti*. 2 vols. Paris: Arthus Bertrand, 1844.

Viviani, Nancy. *Nauru: phosphate and political progress*. Canberra: Australian National University Press, 1970. (XI; XIV; XV)

Vojnich, Oscar. *The Island World of the Pacific*. Budapest: Pallas Literary Publishing Co., 1909.

Waern, Cecilia. *John La Farge*. London: Shelley, 1896. (XIII)

Wahlen, Auguste. *Moeurs, Usages et Costumes de tous les Peuples du Monde*. 4 vols. Brussels: Librairie Historique-Artistique, 1843–4.

Walker, H. Wilfrid. *Wanderings Among South Sea Savages ...* London: Witherby, 1910.

Wallace, Alfred Russel. *Australasia*. London: Edward Stanford, 1883. (V)

Wallis, Helen M., ed. *Carteret's Voyage Round the World 1766–1769*. 2 vols. London: Hakluyt Society, 1965. (IV)

Walpole, Hon. Fred. *Four Years in the Pacific in ... 'Collingwood' from 1844–1848*. 2 vols. London: Richard Bentley, 1850. (V;X; XI)

Walter, Richard. *A Voyage round the World in the Years MDCCXL, I, II, III, IV by George Anson ...* 2 vols. London: John & Paul Knapton, 1748. (IV)

'Wanderer' (D'Avigdor, E.H.). *Antipodean*

Notes. London: Sampson Low, Marston, Searle & Rivington, 1888.

Ward, Alan D. *A Show of Justice*. Toronto: University of Toronto Press, 1974. (VIII; XI)

Ward, John Manning. *British Policy in the South Pacific 1786–1893 ...* Sydney: Australian Publishing Co., 1948. (IX; XI)

Ward, Ralph Gerard, ed. *Man in the Pacific Islands*. Oxford: Clarendon Press, 1972. (II; VI; VII; IX; P)

Waterhouse, Rev. Joseph. *The King and the People of Fiji*. London: Wesleyan Conference Office, 1866. (VIII; X; XI)

Watson, R.M. *History of Samoa*. Wellington: Whitcombe & Tombs, 1918.

Waugh, Alexander (Alec) Raban. *Hot Countries*. New York: Farrar and Rinehart, 1930. (XIII)

Wawn, William T. *The South Sea Islanders and the Queensland Labour Trade*. London: Swan, Sonnenschein, 1893. (IX; X)

Webber, John. *Views in the South Seas*. London: Boydell, 1808. (IV)

Wenkam, Robert. *Maui: The Last Hawaiian Place*. New York: McCall Publishing Co., n.d. [1972].

Wenkam, Robert, and Baker, Byron. *Micronesia*. Honolulu: University Press of Hawaii, 1971. (I; II; VII; IX; P)

West, Francis James. *Hubert Murray*. Melbourne and New York: Oxford University Press, 1968. (XI)

West, Rev. Thomas. *Ten Years in South-Central Polynesia ...* London: James Nisbet, 1865. (VIII; X)

Westgarth, William. *Half-a-Century of Australasian Progress ...* London: Sampson Low, Marston, Searle & Rivington, 1889.

Wharton, Rear-Adm. Sir William James Lloyd, ed. *Captain Cook's Journal ...* London: Elliot Stock, 1893. (IV)

Whipple, A.B.C. *Yankee Whalers in the South Seas*. London: Victor Gollancz, 1954. (V; VII)

White, Gail Milton. *Kioa: An Ellice Community in Fiji*. Eugene: University of Oregon (Department of Anthropology), 1965. (XV)

White, Osmar. *Parliament of a Thousand Tribes*. London: Heinemann, 1965. (XV)

Whitney, Henry M. *The Hawaiian Guidebook ...* Honolulu: Henry M. Whitney, 1875.

Wild, John James. *At Anchor. A Narrative of Experiences Afloat and Ashore During the Voyage of H.M.S. "Challenger" from 1872 to 1876*. London: Marcus Ward, 1878. (V; P)

Wilkes, Rear-Adm. Charles. *Narrative of the United States Exploring Expedition ... 1838, 1839, 1840, 1841, 1842*. 5 vols. Philadelphia: Lea and Blanchard, 1845. (V)

Wilkins, William. *Australasia ...* London: Blackie, 1888.

Wilkinson, Cuthbert Selby. *The Wake of the Bounty*. London: Cassell, 1953. (V)

Willey, Keith. *Assignment New Guinea*. London:

Angus & Robertson, 1966. (XV)

Williams, Rev. John. *A Narrative of Missionary Enterprises in the South Sea Islands ...* London: John Snow, 1837. (VIII; X)

Williams, Maslyn. *Stone Age Island*. London: Collins, 1964.

Williams, Rev. Thomas. See Henderson, George Cockburn, and also Rowe, Rev. George Stringer.

Williamson, James Alexander. *Cook and the Opening of the Pacific*. London: Hodder & Stoughton, 1946. (II; III; IV)

Williamson, Robert Wood. *The Mafulu Mountain People of British New Guinea*. London: Macmillan, 1912. (I)

—— *The Social and Political Systems of Central Polynesia*. 3 vols. London: Cambridge University Press, 1924.

Willis, William. *The Epic Voyage of The Seven Little Sisters*. London: Hutchinson, 1955. (P)

Wilson, Capt. James. *A Missionary Voyage to the Southern Pacific Ocean ... 1796, 1797, 1798 in the ship Duff ...* London: T. Chapman, 1799. (II; IV; VI; VIII; P)

Wollaston, Alexander Frederick Richmond. 'An Expedition to Dutch New Guinea'. *Geographical Journal*. Vol. 43. London, 1914. (X)

Wood, Alfred Harold. *A History and Geography of Tonga*. Nuku'alofa: Government Printer, 1932. (XI)

Wood, C.F. *A Yachting Cruise in the South Seas*. London: Henry S. King, 1875. (X)

Wood, Rev. John George. *The Natural History of Man; Being an Account of the Manners and Customs of the Uncivilized Races of Men*. London: George Routledge, 1880.

Woodcock, George. *South Sea Journey*. London: Faber & Faber, 1975. (IV; P)

Woodford, Charles Morris. *A Naturalist among the Head Hunters ...* Melbourne: E.A. Petherick, 1890. (XI)

Worsley, Peter. *The Trumpet Shall Sound. A Study of Cargo Cults in Melanesia*. London: McGibbon & Kee, 1957. (XV)

Wright, Olive. *The Voyage of the Astrolabe—1840*. Wellington: A.H. & A.W. Reed, 1955. (V)

Wycherley, George. *Buccaneers of the Pacific ...* London: John Long, n.d. (II; III; IV)

Young, Gerald, ed. *The Voyage of the "Wanderer". Journals and Letters of C. and S. Lambert*. London: Macmillan, 1883. (V)

Young, Rosalind Amelia. *Mutiny of the 'Bounty' and Story of Pitcairn Island 1790–1894*. Oakland, Calif.: Pacific Press Publishing Co., 1894. (V; IX)

Zaragoza, Don Justo de. *Historia del Descubrimiento de las Regiones Australes hecho por el General Pedro Fernandez de Quirós*. 3 vols. Madrid, 1876. (II)

Zimmerman, Heinrich. *Reise um die Welt mit Capitain Cook*. Mannheim: C.F. Schwan, 1781. (IV)

Zweig, Stefan. *Magellan*. London: Cassell, 1947. (II)

List of Illustrations and their sources

Index